Digital Hinduism

Digital religion does not simply refer to religion as it is carried out online, but more broadly studies how digital media interrelate with religious practice and belief. This collection explores digital Hinduism and consequentially studies how Hinduism is expressed in the digital sphere and how Hindus utilize digital media.

Highlighting digital Hinduism and including case studies with foci on India, Asia and the global Hindu diaspora, this book features contributions from an interdisciplinary and international panel of academics. The chapters focus on specific case studies, which, in summary, exemplify the wide variety and diversity of what constitutes digital Hinduism today.

Applying methods and research questions from various disciplinary backgrounds appropriate to the study of religion and digital culture, such as Religious Studies, South Asian Studies, Anthropology and Media and Communication Studies, this book is vital reading for any scholar interested in the relationship between religion and the digital world.

Xenia Zeiler is Associate Professor of South Asian Studies at the University of Helsinki, Finland. Her research is situated at the intersection of digital media, religion and culture in India and the worldwide Indian community. Other foci are Digital Humanities (with a focus on video games) and Tantric traditions. She is author of numerous articles and book chapters on digital and mediatized Hinduism and co-edited several volumes and special journal issues, including *Mediatized Religion in Asia* (Routledge 2019) and *Methods for Researching Video Games and Religion* (Routledge 2018).

Routledge Studies in Religion and Digital Culture

Series editors: Heidi Campbell, Mia Lövheim, and Gregory Price Grieve

Buddhism, the Internet, and Digital Media
The Pixel in the Lotus
Edited by Gregory Price Grieve and Daniel Veidlinger

Digital Judaism
Jewish Negotiations with Digital Media and Culture
Edited by Heidi A. Campbell

Methods for Studying Video Games and Religion
Edited by Vít Šisler, Kerstin Radde-Antweiler and Xenia Zeiler

Online Catholic communities
Community, Authority, and Religious Individualisation
Marta Kołodziejska

Digital Existence
Ontology, Ethics and Transcendence in Digital Culture
Edited by Amanda Lagerkvist

Blogging My Religion
Secular, Muslim, and Catholic Media Spaces in Europe
Giulia Evolvi

Digital Hinduism
Edited by Xenia Zeiler

Digital Hinduism

Edited by Xenia Zeiler

Routledge
Taylor & Francis Group
LONDON AND NEW YORK

First published 2020
by Routledge
2 Park Square, Milton Park, Abingdon, Oxon OX14 4RN

and by Routledge
605 Third Avenue, New York, NY 10017

First issued in paperback 2021

Routledge is an imprint of the Taylor & Francis Group, an informa business

British Library Cataloguing-in-Publication Data
A catalogue record for this book is available from the British Library

Library of Congress Cataloging-in-Publication Data
Names: Zeiler, Xenia, editor.
Title: Digital Hinduism / edited by Xenia Zeiler.
Description: Abingdon, Oxon ; New York, NY : Routledge, 2020. |
Series: Routledge studies in religion and digital culture |
Includes bibliographical references and index.
Identifiers: LCCN 2019034215 (print) | LCCN 2019034216 (ebook) |
ISBN 9781138092358 (hbk) | ISBN 9781315107523 (ebk)
Subjects: LCSH: Hinduism—Computer network resources. |
Digital media—Religious aspects—Hinduism.
Classification: LCC BL1111.5 .D54 2020 (print) |
LCC BL1111.5 (ebook) | DDC 294.50285—dc23
LC record available at https://lccn.loc.gov/2019034215
LC ebook record available at https://lccn.loc.gov/2019034216

Typeset in Sabon
by codeMantra

ISBN 13: 978-1-03-208648-4 (pbk)
ISBN 13: 978-1-138-09235-8 (hbk)

Contents

Figures

Tables

Contributors

Sravana Borkataky-Varma teaches at the University of North Carolina-Wilmington and the University of Houston. She received her PhD in Religion from Rice University and MA in Buddhist Studies from Delhi University. She specializes in Hindu Śakta Tantra, rituals and gender. Her publications include the articles *The Dead Speak: A Case Study from the Tiwa Tribe Highlighting the Hybrid World of Śākta Tantra in Assam* (2017) and *Red: An Ethnographic Study of Cross-Pollination between the Vedic and the Tantric* (2019).

Aparajita De is Assistant Professor at the Department of Geography, Delhi School of Economics, University of Delhi. She largely works and publishes on popular imaginations and identity formations in everyday lives and on digital spatiality and transnational feminism. Her current project examines the mapping and reimagining of colonial Calcutta in new media.

Knut A. Jacobsen is Professor in the Study of Religions at the University of Bergen, Norway. His latest book is *Yoga in Modern Hinduism: Hariharānanda Āraṇya and Sāṃkhyayoga* (Routledge 2018). He is the founding Editor-in-Chief of the six volumes *Brill's Encyclopedia of Hinduism* (Brill 2009–2015) and the *Brill's Encyclopedia of Hinduism Online.*

Jesna Jayachandran is Assistant Professor at the Department of Sociology, Guru Nanak Dev University, Punjab, India. Her research interests are in media sociology, new media, news and politics and pedagogy. Her recently published work focuses on Media in Indian Sociology and online news and reader comments.

Juli Gittinger is Lecturer of South Asian religions at Georgia College. She received her PhD from McGill University in Montreal, with emphasis on contemporary issues in Hinduism. Her areas of research interest include Hindu nationalism and religion in media/popular culture. Her book, *Hinduism and Hindu Nationalism Online* (Routledge), was published in 2018.

Nicole Karapanagiotis is Assistant Professor of Religion at Rutgers University, Camden, and an Affiliated Faculty Member at University of Pennsylvania's South Asia Center. A specialist in Hindu Vaishnavisms, digital Hinduism and theoretical approaches to religion and marketing, she has published articles in a number of journals – including the *International Journal of Hindu Studies* and *Nova Religio* – and has a book manuscript awaiting publication.

Yael Lazar has a PhD in Religious Studies from Duke University. Specializing in digital Hinduism, Lazar's current work examines Hindu adoption of digital media and its various networks. Lazar follows the actors who weave the digital Hindu web, addresses digital media's public as networked, considers religions – specifically, Hinduism – as networks themselves, and tracks the global and local along these webs.

Hanna Mannila currently finalizes her PhD at the University of Helsinki, South Asian Studies. Her PhD project investigates the changes and continuities in the guru tradition and the perceptions of the guru's authority in Indian classical *kathak* dance. Based upon ethnographic data gathered in India in 2015–2017, the research focuses on the contemporary, mediatized *kathak* gurus, with reference to textual sources on gurus from the classical period onwards.

Rajib Nandi is Research Fellow at the Institute of Social Studies Trust, India. He is a social anthropologist by training, having worked and published on ethnic identities and social movements, information and communication technologies, women's contribution in informal economy and development evaluation. He is currently working for his book project on new media and popular culture.

Pramod K. Nayar teaches at the Department of English, The University of Hyderabad, India. Among his newest work is a chapter on Bollywood victim celebrity film in *The Routledge Handbook of Celebrity Studies* and a forthcoming one in *The Routledge Companion to Charisma*, besides the books *Brand Postcolonial* (2019), *Bhopal's Ecological Gothic* (2017), *The Extreme in Contemporary Culture* (2017), *Human Rights and Literature* (2016) and others.

Heinz Scheifinger is Assistant Professor in the College of Humanities and Social Sciences, Zayed University, United Arab Emirates. Prior to this he has held academic positions in Scotland, Singapore, Brunei Darussalam, Saudi Arabia, South Korea and Bangladesh. Recent publications include the book chapters *The Significance of Non-Participatory Digital Religion: The* Saiva Siddhanta Church *and the Development of a Global Hinduism* (2018) and *Online Hinduism* (2019).

Vineeta Sinha is Professor and Head, Department of Sociology, at the National University of Singapore. Her research interests include Hindu religiosity in the diaspora, intersections of religion, commodification and consumption processes, interface of religion and materiality and Eurocentric and Androcentric critique of classical sociological theory. Her select publications include *A New God in the Diaspora? Muneeswaran Worship in Contemporary Singapore* (NUS Press and Nordic Institute of Asian Studies Singapore, 2005) and *Religion and Commodification: Merchandising Diasporic Hinduism* (Routledge, 2010). She is Associate Editor of *The Sociological Quarterly* and Co-Editor of the *Routledge International Library of Sociology.*

Dheepa Sundaram is Assistant Professor of Hinduism and Hindu Studies at the University of Denver, holding a PhD in Comparative Literature from the University of Illinois (2014). Her research interests include South Asian performance, rituals and traditions in virtual and material spaces. Her current monograph project explores the lucrative business of online Hinduism and its impact on the growth of ethno-nationalist ideologies within Indian socio-political arenas.

Fritzi-Marie Titzmann is Lecturer in Modern South Asian Studies at Leipzig University since 2014 and is a Visiting Professor at Humboldt University Berlin in 2019. Her research focuses on gender, media and social change in contemporary India. She has published on the Indian online matrimonial market, including a monograph (2014, in German), social activism and media representations of gender and social change.

Xenia Zeiler is Associate Professor of South Asian Studies at the University of Helsinki, Finland. Her research is situated at the intersection of digital media, religion and culture in India and the worldwide Indian community. Other foci are Digital Humanities (with a focus on video games) and Tantric traditions. She is author of numerous articles and book chapters on digital and mediatized Hinduism, and co-edited several volumes and special journal issues, including *Mediatized Religion in Asia* (Routledge 2019) and *Methods for Researching Video Games and Religion* (Routledge 2018).

Introduction

Digital Hinduism: Studying Hinduism at the intersections of digital media and culture

Xenia Zeiler

The study of religion and digital media has been moving forward ever since the pioneering days some two decades ago and has produced a wide range of publications. Today, the field is established, and keeps expanding continuously. The so-far highlighted approaches and themes within the research on digital religion are numerous and diverse, a fact which reflects the understanding that "'Digital religion' does not simply refer to religion as it is performed and articulated online, but points to how digital media and media spaces are shaping and being shaped by religious practice" (Campbell 2013, 1). The range of topics, themes, methods and approaches in research on digital religion is remarkable. Nevertheless, within this range, it is noticeable that existing studies have largely centered on particular religious traditions (Christian and partly Islamic traditions). It is now time to include so far under-researched religious traditions in the study of digital religion. This need has already started to be addressed in a number of new and groundbreaking volumes, for example, on digital Buddhism (Grieve 2016; Grieve and Veidlinger 2015) and digital Judaism (Campbell 2015).

To date, research on digital culture and religious traditions has only tangentially touched on Hinduism. This is true in spite of the fact that Hindu institutions, groups and individual actors today increasingly use various genres of digital media and take part in dynamic debates and, accordingly, in diverse construction processes related to Hindu practices and beliefs. In fact, Hinduism was a feature on the Internet rather early, as one of the first studies on Hinduism and cyberspace has shown (Scheifinger 2008). Online practices such as online pilgrimages or online rituals, especially online *pūjā* and online *darśan*, have become increasingly popular with Hindu actors in both India and the Hindu diaspora since about 2005 (and partly even earlier). Not surprisingly, these practices have been an object of study in some articles and book chapters. However, studies beyond online practices and on media genres beyond the Internet, for example on video games which increasingly are an important genre for negotiating religion, have remained at the margins for some years. Only rather recently studies have emerged that focus more intensively on the intersection of digital media and Hinduism beyond online practices and on other genres than the Internet; by now they include studies on social media (e.g., Facebook, Instagram and Twitter), chat and messenger applications (e.g., WhatsApp), and video games. To expand the scholarship of digital Hinduism thus – to what Campbell and Lövheim (2011) defined as a need for a more nuanced understanding and more careful consideration of what digital religion encompasses – is one of the declared rationales of this volume *Digital Hinduism*. Specifically, the volume acknowledges the agency of religious actors in the shaping of the many facets of digital religion (Lövheim 2011) and emphasizes actor-centered research.

This volume is intended to contribute to our understanding of what constitutes the varied spectrum of digital Hinduism and to offer exemplary approaches and perspectives on how to study the increasingly important intersection of Hinduism and digital media in a nuanced way. Overall, *Digital Hinduism* presents and discusses a broad range of influential, and often brand new, developments that illuminate how and why Hindu actors (individuals, groups or institutions) interact with digital spaces and, as a consequence, shape the constructions of contemporary Hindu beliefs and practices. The discussions on what shapes, configures and constitutes digital Hinduism today will additionally support reflections on various existing approaches and theoretical and methodical frameworks, which have been applied in digital religion overall, as well as the advance of promising new perspectives.

Contextualizing digital Hinduism: The study of digital media and Hindu traditions

It is not surprising that the existing studies on the interrelations of digital media and Hinduism are based in various disciplinary backgrounds, with South Asian Studies and Religious Studies heading the list. Much of the existing research is interdisciplinary and has been published as case studies in book chapters in edited volumes and journal articles. We find studies focusing on specific digital media genres as well as studies applying cross-media perspectives. In short, studies on intersections of media, especially but not exclusively digital media, and Hinduism so far have been published in a wide variety of venues with different scopes, even though their focus generally lies on singular case studies. More structured and systematized overview publications are almost absent.

When looking at the broader scope of media and Hinduism research, not touching yet on digital media, the pioneering edited volume *Media and the Transformation of Religion in South Asia* (Babb and Wadley 1995) deserves special mention. As the first comprehensive work of this kind, it now belongs to the classics in the field. It is also notable that we find work on Indian film (especially but not exclusively Bollywood) and Hinduism. Most of these studies are book chapters and journal articles, with Dwyer's (2006) monograph *Filming the Gods: Religion and Indian Cinema* as an exception. Less prevalent are studies on TV and Hinduism (e.g., Zeiler 2018c). Additionally and somewhat related to the intersection of media and Hinduism, we find scholarship on religion and technology in India: for example, *Religion and Technology in India: Spaces, Practices and Authorities* (Jacobsen and Myrvold 2018) presents discussions of various religious traditions and technology in India, including chapters on religion and media.

While Hinduism has traditionally embraced new technology (e.g., Helland 2010, 148; Scheifinger 2008), research on the intersection of particularly digital media and Hinduism started only in the late 2000s. The first publication exclusively on this topic (Scheifinger 2008) focuses on Hinduism and its relationship to cyberspace and the Internet. Most of the early studies discuss online Hindu rituals, both in India and in Hindu diaspora settings. Online *darśan* belonged then, and still belongs, to the most studied practices in the writings (e.g., Herman 2010; Karapanagiotis 2013; Mallapragada 2012), and attention has also been given to online *pūjā* (e.g., Karapanagiotis 2010; Scheifinger 2010). Since 2014, some studies have also clearly emphasized developments at the intersection of digital media and Hinduism beyond the mentioned online practices. For example, Lal (2014) published on the globalization of Hinduism as related to the cyberspace. Bachrach (2014), Scheifinger (2014) and Warrier (2014) focused on the employment of the Internet by Hindu gurus, that is, on online advice forums, online *yātrā* and online *bhakti* in contemporary guru traditions, respectively. Several authors, including but not limited to Udupa (e.g., 2015) and Gittinger (e.g., 2018), have published on political and ideological dimensions of digital Hinduism, in Indian as well as in diaspora communities.

Since about 2015, research on the interrelations of digital media and Hinduism has continuously, and not surprisingly, included new digital media genres. While by far the largest number of publications still study Hinduism on, and as related to, the Internet (websites in particular), social media formats are now also included among the researched media genres (e.g., Udupa 2016). Recently, for example, we find the first case studies with a clear focus on Facebook (e.g., Zeiler 2018b), Instagram and Twitter (both for first time in this volume, see Sundaram 2020), chat and messaging applications such as WhatsApp (for the first time in this volume, see De and Nandi 2020), live streaming on websites (for the first time in this volume, see Lazar 2020), and video games (Zeiler 2018a, 2014). These belong to the newer digital spaces which are now being tackled in research.

The only publication with an overview character in the emerging research field of digital Hinduism so far has been offered by Scheifinger (2015), in a book chapter discussing the Internet and Hindu traditions in historical perspective. The only existing monograph which claims the theme in its title (Balaji 2017) contains a mix of chapters from academic authors and non-academic authors with personal interests on the theme and has been criticized accordingly (e.g., Griswold 2018[1]). Last but not least, we also find a number of publications with various other foci than digital Hinduism which nevertheless contain some valuable information on selected aspects relevant to the theme. Some examples for this are the studies of Chaudhuri (2010) on Indian media and its transformed public, Sinha (2010) on merchandising diasporic Hinduism, Gajjala (2010) on digital Indian diasporas, Jacobs (2012) on Hinduism in a changing media context, Titzmann (2015) on the Indian online matrimonial market and Zeiler (2020) on cultural heritage and Indian video games.

The studies mentioned here do not constitute an exhaustive list but rather were chosen as examples to demonstrate the variety and range of existing research in the emerging but rapidly evolving field of digital Hinduism and the scattered nature of publications so far (see also Gittinger 2017; Scheifinger 2015). Fortunately, today the scholarship is expanding, with more and more researchers from diverse disciplinary backgrounds analyzing and discussing Hinduism in, and as related to, the ever-expanding digital media spaces and formats. The increasing importance of media, especially digital media including social media, for the shaping of Hindu beliefs and practices and the ongoing intertwining of digital media and religion worldwide are certain to boost the interest in the field even more. Future studies will continue to provide not only new case study material but also novel approaches, methods and theoretical frameworks.

The structure and content of this volume

It remains apparent that while contemporary Hinduism is massively (re) negotiated in and increasingly transformed by digital media on many levels, academic studies on this theme are still relatively few in number and scattered in different publication venues. In order to allow for a more comprehensive, overview picture of the recent complex developments, *Digital Hinduism* brings the latest work together in one coherent volume, thus highlighting and critically investigating the complexity and diversity of the field at the end of the second decade of the twenty-first century. While the major focus in *Digital Hinduism* is on case studies from India, in order to exemplify the geographical diversity of the developments the volume also necessarily includes book chapters on digital Hinduism beyond India, that is in the global Hindu diaspora (e.g., in the USA and Singapore). Methodically, *Digital Hinduism* unsurprisingly is a multidisciplinary volume.

This volume's chapters are arranged into three parts, according to key questions and main arenas of current negotiations in digital Hinduism. These parts are framed by an introductory chapter at the beginning and a critical reflection at the end. The individual chapters include case studies covering a wide variety of digital media genres (including websites, WhatsApp and various social media such as Facebook and Instagram), Hindu ritual and worship practices (including both long-established and widely popular practices, such as *pūjā*, *darśan* and pilgrimage, and new emerging practices which are facilitated or even induced by digital media, such as preaching through posting, liking or sharing deity images on Facebook), social and cultural themes and fields of negotiations (including the matrimonial market, celevision self-fashioning and cultural regrouping) and various geographical regions (including India, the USA and Singapore). Part 1 presents chapters which focus on negotiations of identity by discussing and analyzing case studies that especially highlight issues of perceived or aspired belongings to a certain community and finding one's place within existing groups or practices. Part 2 contains chapters which focus specifically on how Hindu religious authority is (re)negotiated in digital spaces, who grasps or is given the power to define important key issues and concepts in contemporary Hindu traditions, who (often very successfully) appropriates digital spaces in order to boost personal or institutional authority and which strategies are applied to do so. Part 3 concludes with chapters which specifically highlight processes of negotiating and contesting established Hindu practices and beliefs and which discuss and analyze debates in and as related to digital spaces.

This volume opens with an introductory chapter on digital Hinduism, providing a contextualization and an overview of the research existing to date, information on the volume's aim and structure, and an overview of the book's chapters. Part 1, "Who belongs? Identity and finding one's place", includes chapters on negotiations of identity in various digital media genres (including WhatsApp, websites and Facebook), fields of culture and religion (including festivals and the Indian matrimonial market) and geographical regions (including India and the Hindu diaspora in the USA). Aparajita De and Rajib Nandi in "Whats(up) with Hinduism? Digital culture and religion among Bengali Hindus" explore how the members of a WhatsApp group, formed by a Bengali Hindu community to celebrate various Bengali Hindu festivals, actively engage, using digital and mobile technologies, to create a cohesive community and shared Bengali Hindu identities through the celebration of religious festivals. The chapter also delves into how these constant interactions lead to immediate and personal experiences that overlap and are enmeshed with offline everyday experiences and religious practices. Fritzi-Marie Titzmann in "Hindu religious identification in India's online matrimonial market" examines Hindu religious aspects such as the specific components of the Hindu horoscope or caste which feature prominently on Indian matrimonial websites and are the markers that differentiate them from other global matchmaking portals. Her research is situated within the theoretical framework of the socio-constructivist mediatization approach and her case study reveals that while religious affiliation remains as a crucial aspect of partner selection, we often find varying and overlapping meanings of the term community, namely, as regional identity, caste group, sect or subcaste. Nicole Karapanagiotis in "Automatic rituals and inadvertent audiences: ISKCON, Krishna and the ritual mechanics of Facebook" examines the ways in which ISKCON devotees use digital media in their preaching / evangelizing efforts, in particular, the sharing of Krishna's digital images across websites and social media pages. The chapter argues that ISKCON devotees share Krishna's digital images because they believe them to possess what the author calls an *accidental power of conversion*, meaning that these images are believed to automatically rouse love of Krishna in the heart of anyone who views them, and that any act of spreading them (including liking or sharing them on Facebook) is itself an act of preaching. In the last chapter of this part, Juli Gittinger in "Cultural regrouping in the diaspora: Mediating Hindu identity online" proposes that cultural regrouping, a phenomenon that occurs when an immigrant or diasporic individual enters a location, setting or community that invokes the homeland in ways that prompt original, authentic or native cultural identities, now occurs in digital spaces. Using data from a survey of Hindus living in the USA, this chapter explores how non-resident Indians negotiate their cultural and religious identities in such spaces, and how connecting with such communities can reify national and cultural connections.

The volume's Part 2, "Who defines? Authority and appropriation", includes chapters which focus specifically on how Hindu religious authority is negotiated in digital spaces. Pramod K Nayar in "Authors, self-fashioning and online cultural production in the age of Hindu celevision" discusses the self-representations of three authors who have published extensive retellings of Hindu scriptural stories – Ashok Banker, Amish Tripathi and Devdutt Pattanaik. The chapter argues that they work within a dominant Hindu-visual cultural field and a sociopolitical ethos of a hypervisible Hinduism, producing a celevision in their self-representation through a careful process of ancestral self-fashioning. The chapter also reflects on new forms of the national popular and the mimetic capital that the authors' location at the intersection of the faith economy and the celebrity economy draws upon and generates. Dheepa Sundaram in "Instagram your Durga Puja! Social media, hashtags and state-sponsored cultural marketing" examines Facebook and Instagram posts that contain particular hashtags to show how the social media economy of likes and shares determines which hashtags (and therefore which posts) gain traction with users and how this is related to marketing religious products, increasing religious tourism and converting individual Instagram pages into makers of a cultural marketplace of mainstream Hindu traditions. The chapter argues that *branding* of the social media spaces produces a neoliberal commercial space in which niche products (e.g., marginalized groups such as casted groups or women) cannot employ digital tools such as the hashtag or social media sharing with the hopes of having the same impact as those sites which cater to majoritarian audiences. Knut A. Jacobsen in "Sāṃkhyayoga and the Internet: The website of a contemporary Hindu monastic institution" analyzes the websites of Kāpil Maṭh, a Bengali monastic institution, and their relation to the Maṭh's books and printed texts. The chapter argues that the sources of the webpages are mostly the printed texts of Kāpil Maṭh and that the website represents a continuation manifestation of the Maṭh's efforts of promoting the texts of their gurus through English translations and their ambitions of spreading the message of Sāṃkhyayoga. In their chapter "Mediatized gurus: Hindu religious and artistic authority and digital culture", Hanna Mannila and Xenia Zeiler study mediatized gurus in contemporary India, specifically by focusing on the interface of religious and art authority in Hindu contexts as related to digital culture. The chapter discusses a Hindu and a *kathak* dance guru's self-presentation on their respective website and argues that while these gurus use digital spaces to effectively construct a contemporary brand of themselves by combining selected traditional and innovative self-markers, these authority construction strategies are still largely based on conventional understandings of Hindu authority.

The volume's concluding Part 3, "Who debates? Contest and negotiation" contains chapters which emphasize especially the continuous debates and negotiations in online spaces. Vineeta Sinha in "The Internet: A new marketplace for transacting *pūjā items*" focuses on how the Internet has been appropriated and honed creatively by manufacturers, distributors and sellers of Hindu religious products and services. Analyzing the techniques and rationale through which these online businesses and service providers present, package and market their wares to and for online consumers, this chapter argues that the Internet can be viewed as yet another marketplace where *pūjā* things are advertised and available for purchase by consumers / devotees. Sravana Borkataky-Varma in "Taming Hindu Śakta Tantra on the Internet: Online *pūjās* for the goddess Tripurasundarī" explores whether online *pūjās* perpetuate normative understandings of Hindu Śakta Tantra or leave room for the esoteric aspects of the Śakta tradition to shine through, as well. The chapter compares the (visual and textual) representations and *pūjās* of the goddess Tripurasundarī in one exemplary temple, Kāmākhyā, and on four websites which offer online *pūjās*; accordingly, it asks if the goddess and her ritual are depicted online in a sweetened, mainstreamed and overall pacified version. Jesna Jayachandran in "New media and spiritualism in India: Understanding online spiritualism in convergence cultures" examines online spiritualism in the context of the rapid expansion of new media technologies in India by focusing on www.speakingtree.in, a digital venture of India's most circulated English newspaper, *The Times of India*. The chapter uses Hoover and Echchaibi's (2014) theory of a third space that emerges at the intersections of lived spiritual practices and emerging digital cultures to explore how participatory, networked and user-generated aspects foster the formations of an imagined online community, negotiations such as online seeking and other user-generated representations and strategies that build notions of online spiritualism. In the last chapter of Part 3, "Streaming the Divine: Hindu temples' digital journeys", Yael Lazar depicts the different digital journeys that temples navigate and the manner in which external forces shape these paths. The chapter investigates the motives of temples in adopting digital technologies, the various players involved and the dynamics of religion, media and commerce they exhibit. Through an exploration of the Live Darshan feature – online streaming of the statue – this chapter also highlights the involvement of a big Indian communications company in the digitization efforts of Hindu temples and its major impact on digital Hinduism. The volume concludes with a critical reflection by Heinz Scheifinger.

Overall, this volume presents a broad range of novel studies on the interrelations of digital media and Hinduism, exemplifying the intensity and variety of what constitutes digital Hinduism today and highlighting how and why digital spaces intensively contribute to shaping the constructions of Hindu beliefs and practices in contemporary culture and society. *Digital Hinduism* offers diversified yet systemized case studies and discussions from recent scholarship in the field, from both leading and emerging scholars, in a cohesive collection. Bringing this work together into a single volume will also allow for interdisciplinary reflection and interaction between South Asian Studies, Religious Studies, Communication and Media Studies, Asian Studies and, more broadly, Cultural Studies (and adjoining disciplines such as Anthropology and Sociology), in order to help map out future research agendas and implications in the study of digital religion at large.

Note

1 The reviewer, among other things, "raises questions of intent and bias ... throughout the collection" (Griswold 2018).

References

Babb, L. A. and Wadley, S. S., eds., 1995. *Media and the Transformation of Religion in South Asia.* Philadelphia: University of Pennsylvania Press.

Bachrach, E., 2014. Is Guruji Online? Internet Advice Forums and Transnational Encounters in a Vaishnav Sectarian Community. In: Sahoo, A. K. and de Kruijf, J. G., eds. *Indian Transnationalism Online – New Perspectives on Diaspora.* Farnham: Ashgate, 163–176.

Balaji, M., ed., 2017. *Digital Hinduism. Dharma and Disclosure in the Age of New Media.* Lanham: Lexington Books.

Campbell, H. A., ed., 2015. *Digital Judaism: Jewish Negotiations with Digital Media and Culture.* New York: Routledge.

Campbell, H. A., ed., 2013. *Digital Religion. Understanding Religious Practice in New Media.* London and New York: Routledge.

Campbell, H. A. and Lövheim, M., 2011. Studying the Online-offline Connection in Religion Online. *Information, Communication & Society* 14(8), 1083–1096.

Chaudhuri, M., 2010. Indian Media and Its Transformed Public. *Contributions to Indian Sociology* 44(1&2), 57–78.

Dwyer, R., 2006. *Filming the Gods: Religion and Indian Cinema.* London and New York: Routledge.

Gajjala, R., 2010. 3D (Digital) Indian Diasporas. In: Alonso, A. and Oiarzabal, P. J., eds. *Diasporas in the New Media Age: Identity, Politics, and Community.* Reno: University of Nevada Press, 209–224.

Gittinger, J., 2018. *Hinduism and Hindu Nationalism Online.* London and New York: Routledge.
Gittinger, J., 2017. Digital Hinduism. In: Coleman, T., ed. *Oxford Bibliographies in Hinduism.* New York: Oxford University Press. DOI 10.1093/obo/9780195399318-0178.
Grieve, G. P., 2016. *Cyber Zen: Imagining Authentic Buddhist Identity, Community and Practices in the Virtual World of Second Life.* New York: Routledge.
Grieve, G. P. and Veidlinger, D., eds., 2015. *Buddhism, the Internet, and Digital Media: The Pixel in the Lotus.* New York: Routledge.
Griswold, S., 2018. Review of Digital Hinduism: Dharma and Disclosure in the Age of New Media. *Reading Religion. A Publication of the AAR,* [online] 5 July. Available at http://readingreligion.org/books/digital-hinduism, accessed 15 May 2019.
Helland, C., 2010. (Virtually) Been There, (Virtually) Done That. Examining the Online Religious Practices of the Hindu Tradition: Introduction. *Online – Heidelberg Journal of Religions on the Internet* 4(1), 148–150.
Herman, Phyllis K., 2010. Seeing the Divine through Windows. Online Darshan and Virtual Religious Experience. *Online - Heidelberg Journal of Religions on the Internet* 4(1), 151–178.
Jacobs, S., 2012. Communicating Hinduism in a Changing Media Context. *Religion Compass* 6, 136–151.
Jacobsen, K. A. and Myrvold. K., eds., 2018. *Religion and Technology in India. Spaces, Practices and Authorities.* London and New York: Routledge.
Karapanagiotis, N., 2013. Cyber Forms, Worshipable Forms. Hindu Devotional Viewpoints on the Ontology of Cyber-Gods and -Goddesses. *International Journal of Hindu Studies* 17(1), 57–82.
Karapanagiotis, N., 2010. Vaishnava Cyber-Puja. Problems of Purity and Novel Ritual Solutions. *Online – Heidelberg Journal of Religions on the Internet* 4(1), 179–195.
Lal, V., 2014. Cyberspace, the Globalisation of Hinduism, and the Protocols of Citizenship in the Digital Age. In: Sahoo, A. K. and de Kruijf, J. G., eds. *Indian Transnationalism Online – New Perspectives on Diaspora.* Farnham: Ashgate, 121–143.
Lövheim, M., 2011. Mediatisation of Religion: A critical Appraisal. *Culture and Religion* 12(02), 153–166.
Mallapragada, M., 2012. Desktop Deities. Hindu Temples, Online Cultures and the Politics of Remediation. In: Dudrah, R., Gopal, S., Rai, A. S. and Basu, A., eds. *InterMedia in South Asia. The Fourth Screen.* London and New York: Routledge, 6–18.
Scheifinger, H., 2015. New Technology and Change in the Hindu Tradition. The Internet in Historical Perspective. In: Keul, I., ed. *Asian Religions, Technology and Science.* London and New York: Routledge, 153–168.
Scheifinger, H., 2014. Online Connections, Online Yatras. The Role of the Internet in the Creation and Maintenance of Links between Advaita Vedanta gurus in India and Their Devotees in the Diaspora. In: Sahoo, A. K. and de Kruijf, J. G., eds. *Indian Transnationalism Online - New Perspectives on Diaspora.* Farnham: Ashgate, 103–117.
Scheifinger, H., 2010. Internet Threats to Hindu Authority. Puja Ordering Websites and the Kalighat Temple. *Asian Journal of Social Science* 38(4), 636–656.
Scheifinger, H., 2008. Hinduism and Cyberspace. *Religion* 38(3), 233–249.

Sinha, V., 2010. *Religion and Commodification. Merchandising Diasporic Hinduism.* London and New York: Routledge.

Titzmann, F.-M., 2015. Media Mobility and Convergence within India's Matrimonial Market. In: Schneider, N. and Richter, C., eds. *New Media Configurations and Socio-Cultural Dynamics in Asia and the Arab World.* Nomos: Baden-Baden, 243–260.

Udupa, S., 2016. Archiving as History-Making. Religious Politics of Social Media in India. *Communication, Culture & Critique* 9, 212–230.

Udupa, S., 2015. Internet Hindus. New India's Ideological Warriors. In: van der Veer, P., ed. *Handbook of Religion and the Asian City. Aspiration and Urbanization in the Twenty-First Century.* Berkeley: University of California Press, 432–449.

Warrier, M., 2014. Online Bhakti in a Modern Guru Organisation. In: Singleton, M. and Goldberg, E., eds. *Gurus of Modern Yoga.* Oxford and New York: Oxford University Press.

Zeiler, X., 2020 forthc. Digital Humanities Practices and Cultural Heritage: Indian Video Games. In: Dodd, M. and Kalra, N., eds. *Exploring Digital Humanities in India.* London and New York: Routledge.

Zeiler, X., 2018a. Coding Comments on Gaming Videos: YouTube Let's Plays, Asian Games, and Buddhist and Hindu Religions. In: Sisler, V., Radde-Antweiler, K. and Zeiler, X. (Eds.). *Methods for Studying Video Games and Religion.* London and New York: Routledge, 189–204.

Zeiler, X., 2018b. Durgā Pūjā Committees: Community Origin and Transformed Mediatized Practices Employing Social Media. In: Simmons, C., Sen, M. and Rodrigues, H., eds. *Nine Nights of the Goddess. The Navaratri Festival in South Asia.* Albany: SUNY, 121–138.

Zeiler, X., 2018c. Indian TV Soaps and Gender Roles. Hindu Widows in Historical Texts and Contemporary TV Serials. In: Jacobsen, K. A. and Myrvold, K., eds. *Religion and Technology in India.* London and New York: Routledge, 95–111.

Zeiler, X., 2014. The Global Mediatization of Hinduism through Digital Games: Representation versus Simulation in Hanuman: Boy Warrior. In: Campbell, H. A. and Grieve, G. P., eds. *Playing with Religion in Digital Games.* Bloomington: Indiana University Press, 66–87.

Part 1

Who belongs? Identity and finding one's place

1 Whats(up) with Hinduism? Digital culture and religion among Bengali Hindus

Aparajita De and Rajib Nandi

Introduction

A few weeks prior to the Durga Puja[1] in 2017, one of the most important and widely celebrated festivals amongst Bengalis, outrage and protest in equal measure broke out in social media over an advertisement of JH Salon – a chain of salons owned by well-known hairstylist Jawed Habib. The advertisement, containing the tagline "Gods too visit JH Salon", was a cartoon illustration that depicted the goddess Durga with her four children – goddesses Saraswati and Laxmi, and gods Ganesh and Kartik – at the salon getting beauty treatments before the start of the festive season. Habib, a Muslim himself, not only faced severe criticism for insulting the Hindu gods and goddesses and hurting the sentiments of Hindus, on social media, in particular Facebook and Twitter, but one of his salons in Uttar Pradesh was even vandalized (IANS 2017). A case was registered against Jawed Habib, and subsequently he tendered a public apology (The Times of India 2017). Around the same time a YouTube channel called *Bong Eats* caused ire for posting an egg roll video as part of its Durga Puja special series (Bong Eats 2017), primarily because during this period[2] most Hindus, other than Bengalis, practice vegetarianism (Trends Desk 2017).

Interestingly, what followed was a debate in social media around the understanding and practice of Hinduism in India. Many Bengalis protested on both the issues, admitting that the community had a long-standing tradition of cartoons, funny illustrations and pop art around Durga Puja festivals, citing examples of the cover pages of *Anandamela*, an extremely popular children's magazine from Kolkata (BongHaat 2016). Others mentioned and tagged the popular animation series called the *Mahisasur Badh Pala* that depicts the eternal fight between the goddess Durga and the demon Mahisasur through cartoon animations (Anandabazar Patrika 2017). Bengalis also argued that festivities in Bengali culture meant having fun and good food. For many Hindu Bengalis, good food means both vegetarian and non-vegetarian food – primarily fish, eggs, chicken and mutton. Others talked of the diverse notions, meanings and practices of Hinduism and that Hinduism was never monolithic and homogenous in its practice, as believed and propagated by right-leaning groups (Tharoor 2018). These incidents bring to light the increasing visibility and coverage of religion in India, and rearticulations of how religion is being imagined in the public domain, particularly in the digital realm. It is a phenomenon which has been observed globally as an opposition to modernist assumptions of religion being vanquished from the public sphere (Hjarvard 2011; Knott, Poole and Taira 2013; Meyer and Moors 2006). More importantly, it draws our attention to the complex relationship that religion shares with media and digital media in particular.

The relationship between religion and technology, particularly the use of technology in religious practices in South Asia, hints at an underlying imagination of tension. By tension here we are not simply referring to the mediatized conflicts over the manner in which religion is discussed and who controls these representations of religion in the public domain (Cottle 2006; Hjarvard 2012). The tension here refers to the continued usage of digital and mobile technologies by communities for religion and religious practices that not only challenge but seem oppositional to the popular imaginations of the digital realm as necessarily modern, and secular sites of progress and religion as traditional and non-secular. Hjarvard (2011, 120) argues that "mediatization is about long term social and cultural change" that can be equated to the transformative processes of modernity – individualization, urbanization, globalization and secularization – and may, as we argue, transform religion and religious practices.

The attempt of this chapter is to gain a critical understanding of how religion, religious identities and practices are negotiated, appropriated and reworked in their relationship with digital technologies. In other words, the chapter attempts to unpack how Hindu religion and WhatsApp digital technology intersect and accommodate each other. It is unsurprising to find an array of films, television serials, animations, dedicated religious television channels, YouTube channels, Facebook pages, blogs and WhatsApp groups for virtual *darśans*,[3] *pūjā*[4] and rituals that underscore the complex intersections between religion and media. Many see the overall widespread visibility of religion, Hindu and otherwise, as a kind of revival of religion and an emergence of post-secular societies (Beckford 2012; Habermas 2006; Philpott, Shah and Toft 2011). The main question that we seek to raise in this chapter is as follows: Does the visibility, representation and discussion of religion in the public sphere go along with a greater engagement with religion in the everyday private sphere? Elsewhere, it has been noted that there has been a steady decline in church memberships and an overall decline in organized religion both at the individual and private levels (Hjarvard and Lövheim 2012). Based on these observations, we seek to unpack how entanglements of Hindu religion and digital and mobile technologies, namely, WhatsApp, have affected religious practices in everyday lives and in the private domain. Has digital and mobile technology been able to transform religious practices, giving birth to new techno-digital forms of Hinduism?

The chapter is based on digital ethnography of *Prantic Forever*, the WhatsApp group of the Prantic cultural society, a community organization which has been primarily hosting Durga Puja for about a decade in the residential locality of Indirapuram in Delhi – National Capital Region (Delhi-NCR).[5] Prantic as an organization is well known as it is regularly covered and visible in journalistic media (Prantic Media n.d.). Its Durga Puja has not only been awarded as one of the best Pujas in Delhi-NCR but has also been recognized as being inclusive in terms of including members from other regional communities living in Indirapuram (Ara 2017). For instance, events during Durga Puja showcase traditional arts and crafts of different regions across India, to highlight the participation of non-Bengali residents (Jha 2016; Maqsood 2017). The digital presence of Prantic is remarkable – the organization has Facebook pages, Twitter handles, websites, blogs and newsletters as well as several WhatsApp groups. The study presented here is based on material collected in 2016 and 2017. During this time, the digital ethnography of *Prantic Forever* was complemented with in-depth interviews of members and participant observation of the Durga Puja and other events organized by Prantic.

Hindu religion and digital media

Digital media and religion share a complex relationship, where the former is often imagined as ever fluid, evolving and an outcome of modernity itself as opposed to religion, which especially more traditional religious actors often perceived as consisting of an inflexible, unchanging repository of customs, rituals, beliefs and traditions. For example, Mr. Mukherjee, a retired officer of the Government of India and one of the earliest members of Prantic, opined:

> Can you really worship MaaDurga without actually touching her feet? Or without offering Pushpanjali or listening to the dhak, kasarghanta (drums, gong and bell)? Can seeing MaaDurga on T.V. and now on Facebook or WhatsApp create a similar feeling of bhakti (devotion)? I don't think so or at least for me one has to actually experience it. (Mukherjee, interviewed by the authors, Indirapuram, 14 November 2016)[6]

For some religious actors, the ruptures between technology and religion also rest on the supposed loss of actual physical, sensorial experience, and thereby a loss of meaning, as one is unable to internalize these experiences through the use of digital technology. Thus, virtual realities are sometimes envisioned as mechanically produced, disembodied spaces that are disconnected and disengaged from the real world (Bittarello 2008). Campbell (2010, 7), using Geertz's (1966) understanding of religion, argues that religion is a system of cultural practices that involves a "distinctive model of reality" that is based on making sense or meaning of everyday lifeworlds.

Digital media then becomes an integral part of religious life and practice as it goes on to produce these distinctive models of reality which are rooted in the actual physical world. The virtual world, as Radde-Antweiler (2008, 1) points out, emerges as an alternative space where people "meet, communicate and perform" social, cultural and religious activities irrespective of actual, physical or sensory experiences and also becomes a resource where one gains knowledge of one's culture and heritage and which "forms, modifies and creates new cultural structures".

Parama, one of our interviewees who moved from Kolkata to Delhi after her marriage a decade back and who teaches in a reputed private school, similarly informed us:

> Today in our busy lives it is digital media that has given us the opportunity to meet, greet and stay in touch.... To get to know new people, stay in contact with people/friends who go back to childhood. If you look at it a little differently we are also re-discovering our old friends in a new way through the digital world..... it's not just about rediscovering old friends in many ways we have rediscovered our culture and religion. You know you are doing a pūjā at home so there would always be an aunt or an elderly who would guide you and tell you exactly what rituals are to be followed. Now we just need to ask some of our friends in these groups. In fact we are asking both new and old friends about various things that we need to know.... and so many other countless experiences. This kind of communicating is so exciting, engaging and even comforting. I would say it is priceless!!! All thanks to technology and social media. (Parama, interviewed by the authors in Indirapuram, 11 December 2016)

Religion and religious practices have simultaneously shaped and, in turn, have been shaped by digital technologies and media – termed digital religion by Campbell (2012). Digital technology has provided a platform that enables and facilitates many to engage and practice religion, albeit differently from its earlier practices. Sudip, a software engineer working with a multinational IT firm, reflected a similar sentiment:

> [I]n a corporate job I simply cannot take leave for four days to celebrate Durga Puja like our fathers' used to in our childhoods. In fact, sometimes it becomes difficult to take even a day off whether it for Durga Puja or any other. Ordinarily we would take a day off visit a paṇḍāl (a temporary structure that is made to celebrate and perform Durga Puja) in our neighborhood, offer pūjā or go for a day of paṇḍāl hopping. Today because of social media we are more engaged and involved in the Durga Pujas. We get minute by minute update of the Pujas through social media. So whether we are at office, home or anywhere else we feel more connected and know when and what exact

> rituals are being performed. Irrespective of our geographical locations we become part of the Pujas. In fact at hindsight I think we are now aware...know in detail what many of the ritual entails and means. We did see them but today everything is video recorded or live streaming is done and a kind of on the spot documentation is done. You also get to see it and experience it at that very instance even if you may be on the go. (Sudip, interviewed by the authors in Indirapuram, Ghaziabad, 27 September 2017)

Interestingly, Sudip's narrative corroborates what Campbell (2010) argues is the essence of digital religion – a conceptual framework, she suggests, to critically understand how digital technologies and culture on the one hand, and religion and religious practices on the other hand, are co-constituted by one another. In a way it calls for an exploration of religion and religious practice in new technological contexts, moving away from earlier understandings of religion and digital media as binary opposites – that of the traditional vis-à-vis modern, or the real vis-à-vis the virtual. Sudip's narrative questions not just the binary constructions of the online and offline realms but also how experiences and practices are made sense of as well as the assumption that *real* religious practices resonate more profoundly than those that are mediated digitally. We argue that the digital technologies itself have evolved in such a manner that such divides have been blurred and have integrated the online with the offline, making possible for the digital experience to merge with the real embodied experiences.

Helland (2005, 1–2) is of the opinion that any conceptual framework to understand digital religion faces the challenge of a fast evolving technology which changes the digital forms of religion and the nature of digital engagement with religion. Helland's argument here has informed us in our selection of WhatsApp, a relatively new yet popular messaging application, and the digital engagement of its users with Hindu religion. It is equally pertinent to question and ponder on, as Helland (2000) does, what constitutes an act of religion, religious practice and experience in an online digital environment and on the methodological challenges in determining the authenticity of an act of religion, its experience and its practice due to its subjective nature. Here, its subjective nature is an indication of the need to understand digital religion within particular sociocultural contexts. Hoover (2012) stresses the need to reformulate and understand the making of religion by the digital and how the digital is used to explore, experience and make sense of religion in new ways. Thus, digital religion connects the technological with the sociocultural contexts on the one hand, and the online with the offline on the other hand. Both Campbell (2010) and Helland (2005) acknowledge and highlight the continuities, the blurring and blending rather than the ruptures between the online and the offline. Digital religion emerges as the third space that is born as a creole of online and offline practices of religion (Hoover and Echchaibi 2014). It reflects the social interactions in a digital environment that informs and is informed by society and its practices.

In September 2017, just before Durga Puja, a message was widely circulated on WhatsApp. The message basically commented on how the technology of radio and radio broadcasting had brought about a change in the manner Durga Puja is celebrated in contemporary Bengal. The message tried to highlight how changing technology transforms religious practices but, more importantly, also tried to warn that meanings and interpretations of religion are constantly transformed and contaminated rapidly in a technologically networked society. The message reads:

> Presently Mahalaya marks the beginning of Durga Puja which was not the original case. Mahalaya actually marked the last day of 'Pitripakhkha' when families would perform the ritual (tarpan) during the Sunrise in remembrance of their forefathers, which is not at all associated with Durga Puja. It was in 1932 that Indian Broadcasting service started the broadcast of 'Mahishasura Mardini'[7] on 'Shosthi' or the sixth day when actually the Durga Puja starts. However, from the following year they started broadcasting 'Mahisasura Mardini' on the early morning of Mahalaya. The purpose was to attract many listeners in the early morning of Mahalaya when they had already gotten up for the Mahalaya rituals. Since then Bengalis wrongly started associating Mahalaya as the start of Durga Puja. (personal communication in WhatsApp group Prantic Forever, 25 September 2017, 16:15)

Scholars of religion and media like Lundby (2009) and Hjarvard and Lövheim (2012) have long argued for mediatization of religion that tries to understand how it transforms religion in modern secular contexts. Hjarvard (2012, 25) further elaborates that digital media has become an integral part of our everyday lifeworlds, enabling greater "communication in flexible ways" in terms of acting as "in-here" resources at both individual and institutional levels. In other words, as we argue in this chapter, the interactive digital media give agency specifically to individual religious actors to express their notions of religion that is in tune with modern, secular and sociocultural contexts. Hjarvard has argued that the mediatization of religion does not transform uniformly; yet the role of media remains somewhat similar in terms of how it becomes an important source of information, experience and a means of circulation, and how it creates new social relations and cultures within the community.[8] One of our interviewees, Pradip, a banking executive in a private bank, explained that though he may be part of a WhatsApp group that organized Durga Puja, he never thinks of the group as solely religious. He explained:

> True the group organizes Durga Puja but it is not a religious group in the conventional sense. All of us, that is Hindu Bengalis together as a

community celebrate the Puja but if you look closely at the messages being exchanged you will find that they are about our everyday lives. Yes there will be some discussion on Puja, people will post messages with religious content – but they are about a larger philosophy. For example, someone may speak how to achieve a stress free life in our very busy, stressful lives. You know to find larger meaning of life. But at the same time you will find people posting jokes, or asking about a good doctor.... You may have seen it yourself that one of the members of Prantic recently passed away rather suddenly leaving behind a young family. Many of the group members personally visited giving them moral support and any other help that they may require. So you could say, we act as a support group extending our help and assisting one another in a small way. (Pradip, interviewed by the authors in Indirapuram, 14 January 2017)

Pradip's narrative refers to what scholars like Hjarvard and Lynch assert as the mediatization of religion that transforms religion within a larger secular modern discourse. It refers not to a new form of religion but to one which is rooted in changing and varied contemporary societal contexts (Hjarvard 2012; Lynch, Mitchell and Strhan 2011).

Contextualizing the *Prantic Durga Puja*

In recent years, the number of Durga Pujas in Delhi has phenomenally increased. While Delhi's oldest Durga Puja, the Kashmere Gate Durga Puja, turned 108 years in 2017, in the same year there have been almost 350 *paṇḍāls*[9] in the city (Sethi 2017). One such Durga Puja in Delhi-NCR is organized by Prantic, an organization formed by the local residents of Indirapuram and which has been awarded the first prize for its Durga Puja in 2016 in Delhi-NCR by the Bengali Association (Prantic Homepage n.d.). Given the large public presence and visibility of the Pujas organized by Prantic, it is not surprising that they are equally visible in the digital realm. They have a website (www.prantic.org/default.asp), blog (http://prantic.org/blog/), annual e-newsletter (www.prantic.org/Newsletter.asp), official and unofficial Facebook pages (www.facebook.com/pages/Prantic-Cultural-Society/818574868164996 and www.facebook.com/www.prantic.org), a Twitter handle (https://twitter.com/prantic_ncr) and WhatsApp groups. The Prantic blog page claims that "more than 175 member families living in Indirapuram are a part of the organization" (Prantic Membership n.d.). As of 24 April 2018 (10.00 am Indian Standard Time), the unofficial Facebook page had 62 likes and 1,233 visits, whereas the Prantic official Facebook page had 1,911 likes and 1,906 followers. The closed WhatsApp called *Prantic Forever* had 213 participants as of 24 April 2018. There are a few other WhatsApp groups run by Prantic as well, as a single WhatsApp group cannot accommodate more than 256 members at a time.

The official website of Prantic introduces itself as a group that was formed in 2008 by residents of Indirapuram, Delhi-NCR, who are charged with "firm commitment, religious faith and traditional grandeur" (Prantic Homepage n.d.). The chairperson of Prantic, Mr. Malay Kumar Majumder, further adds that the journey of the community started with the blessings of *Maa Durga* which only laid the basic foundations of Prantic. According to him, the strength of the community is its focus on the cultural values and traditions that enables one to embrace the positive aspects of the society (Majumder 2015). The website further highlights that Prantic not only organizes religious festivals but is also involved in organizing cultural events, education and social activities that promote and provide exposure to Bengali arts, music, language, literature, cuisine, culture, history and Indian heritage. It also supports various social causes for a better society like community services in the fields of healthcare, literacy training and a neighborhood improvement program. The website claims that the Prantic society aims to renew festive spirits through celebrations of Durga Puja, Laxmi Puja, Kali Puja, Saraswati Puja and other Pujas. The society also aims to bring the Bengali community of Indirapuram together through various social events like Annual Picnic, Poila Boisakh (Bengali New Year) and other activities/gatherings. Prantic is also committed to promoting the literary and cultural traditions of Bengal by organizing literary and musical fests (Prantic Homepage n.d.).

Interestingly, Prantic emphasizes the need to encourage and expose younger generations to the Bengali heritage and culture and initiated a program called *Esho Bangla Shiki* (come and learn Bengali) for young people. The website clearly states that the mission of Prantic is to promote a harmonious blend of diverse cultures and rich values with today's hi-tech, fast-paced, success-driven way of life: "We welcome people from every section of the society who want to share the bond and warmth together. We seek to build a great neighbourhood and provide a social platform to all our members" (Prantic Homepage n.d.).

The *Prantic Forever* WhatsApp and the celebration of Durga Puja

The WhatsApp group *Prantic Forever* was initially formed in 2015. The participants of the WhatsApp group mostly belong to the Bengali Hindu community living in the residential locality of Indirapuram, Delhi-NCR, and who are members of Prantic. Membership is given on the payment of annual fees and simultaneously one is inducted into the *Prantic Forever* WhatsApp group. In recent years, beyond the local Bengali community, a small number of people from Bihar, Orissa, Assam, Punjab and Uttar Pradesh who are keen to participate in the Durga Puja and live in Indirapuram have taken membership. After following this WhatsApp group as members for last two years, we detected that the purpose of this group is to update the group members about various religious and cultural festivals that are celebrated by Bengalis in general, and by Prantic in particular, and to remain connected to one another during the days of the festivals and for the rest of the year. Also we, as Bengalis and residents of Indirapuram, have been interacting and communicating with a number of Prantic members (from 2016 to 2018), both at community gatherings and through WhatsApp messages. The interviews with selected Prantic members, the general interactions with the members and the profiles of the members indicate strongly that the Prantic community is mostly from the educated middle-class population, working and living in Indirapuram, Delhi-NCR. Here, in defining the middle-class, we follow Säävälä (2003) and identify it as a group whose members are neither poor nor elite, have a basic level of economic security and well-being irrespective of their caste locations and education, live in middle-class residential areas, and considered mobile as they can move to categories of poor or elite. Thus, the group is marked by heterogeneity on the one hand, and upward mobility on the other (cf. Lutgendorf 1997). Hawley (2001) claims that since the 1950s, India has had a strong and influential presence of the middle class who are integrated into a globalized world that has set forth a chain of transformations that include religion as well. In many ways, the middle class stands at the intersection of modern and tradition, poor and elite, and creatively integrates these binaries. Thus, it becomes interesting and relevant to understand how the middle class negotiates and reworks religion and digital technologies.

The digital platform of WhatsApp was primarily selected as it has the features of a group chat where one can share messages, voice messages, photos and videos with up to 256 people instantaneously. WhatsApp also has an end-to-end encryption which means that all messages, photos, videos and voice messages are secured and remain within the group and cannot be accessed by non-group members (www.whatsapp.com/features/). The WhatsApp group *Prantic Forever* is a closed group based on membership in the Prantic cultural society. Thus, the group is more private in nature and yet has all characteristics of other digital platforms where the content is informative and is created and distributed instantaneously and spontaneously, irrespective of geographical location. The selection of WhatsApp is also due to its increasing popularity in recent years; in 2018, an estimated 200 million monthly active users of WhatsApp were found to be in India alone (FE Online 2018).

The chapter is based on multisite digital ethnography that focused mainly on the WhatsApp group but also took into account other online platforms of Prantic like its webpage, blog, newsletter, Twitter and Facebook pages. The period of study extends over a year, from August 2016 to November 2017, and covers the period of Durga Puja both in 2016 and 2017. The online ethnography was supported by offline ethnographic fieldwork and included personal interviews of WhatsApp group members. A total of ten WhatsApp members were selected based on their degree of participation in the WhatsApp group between 2016 and 2017. We also attended social and religious events organized by Prantic during the same period on the occasion of Bengali New Year, Saraswati Puja, introductory meeting on Mahalaya just before the Durga Puja and during the Durga Puja in 2017; we employed participant observations during these events to develop an understanding of the interconnections between the online and offline religious practices.

> I would suggest everyone to use the hashtag #PranticPujo17 on all their Facebook, Twitter, Insta posts n pictures, videos etc. We can create an amazing Social media community and we can enjoy all the posts just by clicking on the hashtag. (personal communication in WhatsApp group Prantic Forever, 26 September 2017, 15:04)

This message posted in the WhatsApp group during the Durga Puja of 2017 articulates specifically the creation of a community in social media through some of the popular social media platforms like Facebook, Twitter and Instagram. The narrative effectively places WhatsApp as more intimate and in the private domain that curates and controls what appears in other forms of social media. This very placing of WhatsApp creates a close-knit group of people who can freely interact unhindered by the expectations and norms that tend to govern behavior in the public domain, thereby creating a more informal, warm, personalized experience (Desai 2017). Subsequently, they go on to produce a sense of community and belongingness amongst the group members.

From *Team Prantic to Prantic Family*: The making of a community

Prantic as an organization claims, through its website and blog, to be acting like a bridge that aims to build relationships between people and to embark on a journey of togetherness in celebrating Durga Puja (Prantic Homepage n.d.). It does so rather effectively through its WhatsApp group where every detail of the Puja is shared; the efforts and struggles made toward organizing the Puja, as well as suggestions, advice and help are actively solicited. For example, each year, Prantic has to seek permission to organize and build its *paṇḍāl* for the Durga Puja from the owners of the ground, municipal authorities and law enforcement agencies. Seeking approval from different authorities is quite a difficult task. Often these struggles and the effort to overcome them go to the making of *us* and *Team Prantic* with a distinct sense of being part of a community:

> We are delighted to announce that PRANTIC will be celebrating 9th year of Durga Puja from 24th to 30th September, 2017. Shipra management has finally agreed to allocate us the same venue where we have

> celebrated the Puja for the last three years.....Vice President, Prantic Cultural Society. (personal communication in WhatsApp group Prantic Forever, 20 July 2017, 00:17)
>
> Relieved to know that we've got the same venue!! Congratulations to all of us at Team Prantic!! (personal communication in WhatsApp group Prantic Forever, 20 July 2017, 07:04)

Similarly, in 2017, due to the effects of demonetization[10] and a new taxing system called GST,[11] organizing funds were difficult and yet the members willingly accepted not only to increase membership contributions but to "explore all possibilities of getting funds from their known vendors / organizations / establishments" (personal communication in WhatsApp group Prantic Forever, 3 August 2017, 08:22) toward meeting the expenses of the Puja.

Through the interactions within the closed WhatsApp group, Prantic creates a bond among its members akin to a family. Often the word family is used in the messages to remind the members that Prantic is like a family and all members are the members of this big joint family. The WhatsApp messages are also posted to encourage and urge members to participate and perform. The following message in the group calls for cooperation and support from its members:

> Our group is big and growing bigger every day. But we are happy to see that all members are nicely knitted just like an Indian family. Each and everyone's contribution is required to run this family. The members interested to participate and volunteer in the forthcoming cultural program may kindly contact Mrs. D. S. at 98XXXXXX54. (personal communication in WhatsApp group Prantic Forever, 20 July 2017, 08:00)

On noticing the enthusiasm amongst members to participate, one member even commented that "Its so good to see the team spirit with great involvement and collaboration from all members...this only builds solidarity and showcases us as one big Prantic Family!!" (personal communication in WhatsApp group Prantic Forever, 3 August 2017, 09:08). Clearly, this constant communication and sharing of information is often perceived as being inclusive and accommodative of diverse people that cuts across caste, class and subregional differences within the larger Bengali community. Jayeeta, one of our interviewees and a volunteer in the Durga Puja, confessed that the camaraderie in the WhatsApp group overlaps and enmeshes with their offline everyday lives:

> After the Pujas we often meet for movies, lunches, addas (social gathering). In fact some of us also form our own smaller WhatsApp groups. It creates a strange kind of bond we meet both online and offline, talk to each other everyday. ... every moment sharing our lives,

> some happy moments and some of our tensions and worries. We share the same values, care for each other and form a support system for one another... its like one huge family – the Prantic family. (Jayeeta, interviewed by the authors in Indirapuram, 28 September 2017)

Centered on the celebration of Durga Puja and continued interaction on WhatsApp, the members develop a mutual feeling of empathy and togetherness based on their shared religious practices, values and common culture and heritage. The following narratives that were posted on Bijaya Dashami, the penultimate day of the Durga Puja, indicate it:

> We came to Delhi six years back. We were very depressed to leave Bangalore and apprehensive about life in Delhi. Right after we came here in August, we joined the Prantic family. The warmth love and affection of the members wiped away all of that as we were welcomed with open hearts. Today, Prantic is our 'Pran' (life) and we are very happy and proud to be a member of this family. (personal communication in WhatsApp group Prantic Forever, 30 September 2017, 19:04)
>
> Being married to a bong (Bengali) boy has given me the honour of getting associated with Prantic...but today after five years I have developed such a strong bond with everyone that I cant imagine a life without you all...thank you for all the love my extended Family!! ShubhoBijoya!! (personal communication in WhatsApp group Prantic Forever, 30 September 2017, 20:59)
>
> I agree and second with the feeling of belonging at prantic... Its not only a platform for our kids to learn about our culture but a community which is totally united and strongly bonded in its mission and extending a warm hand to all on board!! From its menu to its themes to the cultural evenings and everything else pushes us much closer to our heritage... our pride...and to become like a family. (personal communication in WhatsApp group Prantic Forever, 3 October 2017, 19:25)

The instant messaging in this WhatsApp group opens up a space for continuous interaction that creates a filial connection between members where they feel that they are engulfed in a large extended family and its warmth. This connection continues beyond the Durga Puja, and though messaging may not be as frequent, there is continued interaction and engagement with one another during the whole year. Relationships are built and consolidated around everyday needs. Often members post about needing a reference to good doctors, or looking for information about blood donation volunteers in an emergency situation. One of the authors posted a query in the group seeking information on Aadhaar enrollment center.[12] A number of members came forward with details of such centers. The WhatsApp group also organizes social awareness campaigns on governance involving young voters or cleanliness drives in the neighborhood that specifically include adolescents and young adults. The group often becomes an online forum for debates and discussions on a wide range of everyday emergencies that are faced by the members in their offline lives. Thus, on the one hand, the members may know each other better and create a bond over the celebration of Durga Puja, which, in turn, concretizes and reaffirms their shared religious beliefs and practices. On the other hand, it creates a sense of community that acts as a support system on which they can rely on for their everyday needs, anxieties and emergencies.

Absent in body, present in mind: Online remote participation

During the Durga Puja festivals, the WhatsApp group witnesses frenzied and hyperactive messaging that almost keeps the participants updated, minute-by-minute, regarding timings, the schedule of the cultural programmes and the lunch menu, accompanied with innumerable photographs and instant videos. This greatly enables the members irrespective of their actual physical geographical locations and their busy lives to be involved and to participate in the Durga Puja.

In the days leading up to the Durga Puja, something which can almost be called a countdown to Durga Puja takes place, with continuous and incessant posts like "Maaaschen…opekkhay 77 din" ("Maa Durga is coming…. 77 more days to wait") (personal communication in WhatsApp group Prantic Forever, 10 July 2017, 21:45). Pictures of the goddess Durga and *Sarodiya Subhechcha* (autumnal season's greetings) are sent just before the Puja, reflecting the excitement and *pujopujo* (festive) feeling that were similar to the childhood memories of Durga Puja, as Parama, one of our interviewees, claimed. Constant updates regarding the arrangements of the Puja and various announcements, such as on the theme of the Puja and the many cultural programs that will be performed, add to the atmosphere and excited expectation of the Pujas that are about to unfold in the days to come. It is interesting to note that through continuous updating and messaging in the WhatsApp group, a kind of momentum and excitement is created that encourages a regular online participation. The following series of conversations emphasizes this building of momentum and increased remote participation of the members of Prantic:

> Dear Member, This year through DURGA ABAHON 2017, we attempt to bring to life our rich fascinating heritage. There is history, architecture, art, sculpture, jewellery, costumes, instruments, tools, dances, music, paintings, and culture in our Puja *paṇḍāl*. We say….Come, see Bengal at its cultural, historical, and natural best! Enjoy its vibrant colours, across magnificent sweeps of time and space. Our this year Durga Puja theme "Our Heritage, Our Pride" is for everyone in Love with India! We look forward to your active participation in this auspicious

> occasion. Vice President, Prantic Cultural Society. (personal communication in WhatsApp group Prantic Forever, 12 August 2017, 22:37)

Another member responded immediately: "This moment is just too overwhelming... a whole year of waiting..!.. over!!" (personal communication in WhatsApp group Prantic Forever, 13 August 2017, 22:40).

Every year, a number of new members join Prantic just before the Durga Puja festival. In September 2017, a week before the actual Durga Puja festival began, Prantic organized an introductory meeting for its members on the auspicious day of Mahalaya. The gathering created a space for a round of interactions among the old and new members. The prime attractions of this gathering were the musical event and the food that was served on the occasion. The WhatsApp group was used to attract more people to join the gathering. The event also created a momentum for the main Puja event:

> We request all Prantic members to join us at the Mahalaya Program on Sunday at 7.30 PM. At the program melodious Bengali songs would be sung by the renowned artist AshisDey. The dinner menu would be Plain Rice, Muger Dal, Taler Bora, Mutton Rogonjosh, Sorshe Bhapa Illish, Kumroghonto – Iilish machermatha diye, Potol-bhaja, Kurkure-Aloo bhaja, Matar Paneer, chatni, papad, salad, sweets. (personal communication in WhatsApp group Prantic Forever, 14 September 2017, 21:25)

The WhatsApp messages continuously remind and keep the members updated about the preparations that go into the making of the Durga Puja, right from the making of the *paṇḍāl* to the bringing home of the idol, to the constant rehearsal practices by the members for the cultural events that take place every evening. In a way, the WhatsApp messaging connects the members not just with one another and the community at large, but also with the ritualistic performances of the Puja. The following message reminded the members of the commencement of Puja celebrations:

> Thank you all for joining the MAHALAYA 2017. Your presence made the evening a mega celebration. After a week, next Sunday, Chaturthi, 24–09–2017, Durga Puja Celebration starts at our Puja *paṇḍāl* with unveiling the face of Durga idol in the evening. (personal communication in WhatsApp group Prantic Forever, 17 September 2017, 12:00)

Messages, such as the one that follows, work as reminders to the members about the auspicious moment when the idol of Devi Durga will be installed at the *paṇḍāl*:

> It's time to bring Her home. It's time to blow conch to the fullest to announce Her arrival. It's time to welcome and seek Her divine blessings in our own Puja *paṇḍāl*. We shall be bringing Maa Durga Idol

tomorrow evening. We shall start with the idol from CR Park at 10.00 PM and expect to reach Puja venue at 10.45 PM. We welcome you all to join. (personal communication in WhatsApp group Prantic Forever, 21 September 2017, 15:46)

Within a few moments, a large number of members started responding and confirming their presence on the following day: "We will be very happy to join" (personal communication in WhatsApp group Prantic Forever, 21 September 2017, 15:50). Others requested to post images and videos because they could not be present at that auspicious moment: "Please post live videos for us who won't be able to attend the ceremony of Pratimabaran" (personal communication in WhatsApp group Prantic Forever, 22 September 2017,10:12).

Consequently, on the following day the WhatsApp group was filled with images and videos of the *pratimabaran* ceremony (ritual welcome for the goddess). One member wrote: "We are delighted to share these photographs of our MaaDurga and the Pandal. Our pandal and idol is the best in entire Delhi NCR" (personal communication in WhatsApp group Prantic Forever, 22 September 2017, 23:12).

The momentum, we argue, has been able to generate and arouse an interest and enthusiasm and a day-to-day online involvement in the events that lead to the Puja itself. In fact, in 2017, the venue of the Mahalaya gathering had to be changed as a larger number of families than originally anticipated confirmed participation. The momentum is further sustained during the Puja as messages are constantly posted informing the members of the start of the daily Puja and other ritual and festive details. Photographs and videos of the cultural programs are also posted, and so are the audience's reactions. Almost a minute-by-minute commentary is given in the WhatsApp group. For example, each morning a detailed daily program schedule is posted:

Dear Members, Please note the *Puja Timings*: Puja 8.30 AM, Pushpanjali 10.30 AM, Bhog 1 PM, Sondi Puja 7.06 PM to 7.54 PM, Aarti 8 PM. (personal communication in WhatsApp group Prantic Forever, 28 September 2017, 02:22)

Dear Members, Please note the timings of the cultural programme and the *Lunch Menu*: Loochi, Plain Rice + Ghee, Dry Aloo Gobi Masala, Thor Chechki, Chanar Kofta Dalna, Sukto, Chatni & Papad, sweets. **Morning Cultural Programme schedule*: 10.30 AM–1.30 PM. **Drawing Competition for kids followed by quiz competition for Prantic members. ***Evening Cultural Programme schedule*: (8 PM–10.30 PM) – Dhanuchi Nrityo: an extempore dance with the sacred incense burner; Dhaker Tale Komor Dole: dance performance with melodious songs by kids of Prantic; Anu-Rager Choya: a fascinating rendition of raaga based melodies by Prantic members. And finally,

> Jolly Mukherjee: India's King of Strings, with his bouquet of famous Bollywood hits. (personal communication in WhatsApp group Prantic Forever, 21 September 2017, 15:50)

Sudip, one our respondents, freely admitted that during earlier Durga Pujas, the family would just go out any day and do *paṇḍāl hopping* – that is go from one Durga Puja *paṇḍāl* to another. Now, they are more bound and involved in Prantic's Puja; if they have the time, they choose to actually go to Prantic's *paṇḍāl* rather than endless other unknown *paṇḍāls*. The feeling of being bound and involved comes through this unceasing engagement with the Durga Puja through messages in which the actual time of performing the rituals are continuously posted:

> Puja is delayed by few minutes. It will start soon. (personal communication in WhatsApp group Prantic Forever, 28 September 2017, 08:40)
>
> You may please watch the video of today's Puja and aarti. Pushpanjali will begin in any moment now. (personal communication in WhatsApp group Prantic Forever, 28 September 2017, 10:45)
>
> Pushpanjali started... (personal communication in WhatsApp group Prantic Forever, 28 September 2017, 10:58)

Members, for example, also post queries and request to delay the program in order to accommodate them:

> Till when the Pushpanjali will continue? I'll be reaching the venue in 10 minutes (WA Group- Prantic forever. 28/09/17, 11:37- +91 98XXXX XXX99) Or like the following one. Please accommodate my wife and son for pushpanjali. I am just dropping them at the venue in 2 minutes. (personal communication in WhatsApp group Prantic Forever, 28 September 2017, 11:50)
>
> Please post images and videos of Pushpanjali. I would like to offer my prayer by watching the video. (personal communication in WhatsApp group Prantic Forever, 28 September 2017, 11:52)

The members thank and applaud the Puja management group on successful completion of the festival: "The arrangements seem really good and really well coordinated and conducted. Kudos to the mgt and team" (personal communication in WhatsApp group Prantic Forever, 28 September 2017, 13:46).

The experience of the Durga Puja thus is not limited to being present in a particular place at a particular time. WhatsApp and the nature of interaction on it – the high traffic of information flow that is created and distributed in an equally hyper-fast manner – have enabled the members who could not be physically present to participate and engage remotely in the celebration of the Durga Puja. Thus, it highlights not only the interconnections but the blurring of boundaries between the real and the digital, the local and the translocal (Lövheim 2013). The technology of digital platforms has effectively blended lived and virtual realities. The digital platforms have made possible for one to be present in the real world and go online (virtual) or to be virtual but have access to and participate in the real world.

Conclusion

Digital technologies have facilitated its users to transcend the temporal, spatial and material boundaries and practice religion. The spectacular and elaborate Durga Puja celebrations that are ritually performed in public spaces in view of the entire community can now be easily experienced through smartphones, and WhatsApp in particular. Our case study has shown that while one may be away or busy, one may be simultaneously and constantly updated through text messages, photographs and videos referring to the performance of the rituals during Durga Puja. The instantaneous sharing of messages, videos and photographs contributes to create the liveness of the Durga Puja online. The members of the WhatsApp group *Prantic Forever* thus remain connected to the events of the Puja and are able to participate virtually in its collective performance through access to even minute details of the progression of events. Thus, it creates a feeling of collective participation between those who are present physically at the Durga Puja and those who are online.

Constant communication and intimate interaction over WhatsApp have led to a disembodied yet *in-the-moment* experience of Durga Puja. In other words, the *Prantic Forever* WhatsApp group primarily creates a momentum among its members and reconnects every member with the community. While it is still preferred to perform the customary rituals and be physically present within the community, the WhatsApp group facilitates to alternatively participate remotely and ultimately connects the community though digital means. The collective participation and continuous interaction during the Durga Puja between the WhatsApp members creates a sense of community and belonging. Continued interaction on WhatsApp beyond the Durga Puja further consolidates these feelings, particularly when members act as an online support system for offline everyday needs and emergencies. Thus, Bengalis living in the residential locality come together to celebrate Durga Puja, and organize themselves as a community digitally through WhatsApp.

Notes

1 Durga Puja is an annual Hindu festival that reveres the goddess Durga. Durga Puja is believed to be the greatest festival of the Hindu Bengali people, celebrated over a six-day period. It is celebrated to mark the victory of Goddess Durga over Mahishasur, a demon. The festival glorifies the triumph of good over evil. The primary goddess revered during Durga Puja is Durga, but her representations and celebrations feature other major deities of Hinduism such

as Lakshmi (goddess of wealth, prosperity), Saraswati (goddess of knowledge and music), Ganesha (god of good beginnings) and Kartikeya (god of war). All four of them are considered to be the children of Durga. For Bengalis, Durga Puja is not just a religious practice, but Durga is also considered the daughter of Bengal. Hence, Durga Puja also celebrates the annual visit of Durga with her children to her ancestral home, that is Bengal. This homecoming of the goddess creates an opportunity for Bengali people to reunite with their families and friends. See, for example, Zeiler (2018).

2 The Durga Puja festival is named differently and celebrated in different forms all across India and beyond, with Navaratri being the most popular name besides Durga Puja. The Bengali Durga Puja dates additionally coincide with the festival Dussehra, centered on god Ram. For many Hindu believers, this is a time of personal introspection and bodily purification, with many avoiding non-vegetarian food including meat, fish and eggs, but also refraining from onions, garlic, wheat and grains. The end of Navaratri and Durga Puja is further believed to mark an auspicious time for starting new activities or business ventures. See, for example, Subramaniam (1981).

3 Darśan refers to the seeing of a holy person or the image of a deity. See, for example, Scheifinger (2009).

4 Puja refers to the act of worship. See, for example, Herman (2018).

5 Delhi-NCR (National Capital Region) is a coordinated planning region centered on the National Capital Territory of Delhi in India. The region comprises of Delhi and parts of the states of Uttar Pradesh, Haryana and Rajasthan.

6 All interview quotes and WhatsApp message text quotes in this chapter have been translated from the original Bengali by the authors. Exceptions are a very few WhatsApp message texts which were circulated in English.

7 Mahishasurmardini, lit. the slayer of the demon Mahishasur, is another name for Durga. The Indian Broadcasting Company started broadcasting a musical drama entitled "MahisasurMardini" in 1932, which gained immense popularity among Bengali people in the following years. The program is equally popular today and broadcasted by All India Radio every year (Mitra 2017).

8 For details, see Hjarvard (2012, 26) and his usage of Meyrowitz's metaphor of media as a framework to analyze how media transforms religion in terms of it acting like a conduit, language and environment for change.

9 A *paṇḍāl* is a temporary fabricated structure. During Durga Puja, a *paṇḍāl* becomes a temporary venue of worship where people gather to celebrate and perform the Durga Puja festival.

10 On 8 November 2016, the prime minister of India had announced the demonetization of all 500 and 1,000 banknotes. The government claimed that the sudden action would curtail the black economy and crack down on the use of counterfeit notes to fund anti-people activity and terrorism. The sudden nature of the announcement and subsequent cash shortages in the following months created significant disruption throughout the economy, threatening economic output. Many experts opined against this program and claimed that a large number of economic activities got disrupted in India (e.g., Saikia 2016).

11 Goods and Service Tax (GST) is an indirect tax (also known as consumption tax) system that came into effect in India on 1 July 2017. The tax is levied on the sale of goods and services at every step in the production process. Some experts opined that the new tax system is complex in nature and unsettled the small businesses (Rao 2018).

12 Aadhaar is a 12-digit unique identity number for the residents of India. The number is generated based on their biometric and demographic data. The data are collected by the Unique Identification Authority of India (UIDAI), a

statutory authority established by the government of India. One needs to visit an Aadhaar enrollment center to enroll oneself. The enrollment became crucial for residents after the government urged to link the Aadhaar number with one's bank accounts.

References

Anandabazar Patrika, 2017. *Mahishasur Pala, Episode no. 14*, [YouTube] 18 September. Available at https://youtu.be/BRAWmxfTmKY, accessed 23 April 2018.

Ara, I., 2017. Flavours of Bengal in Durga Puja Celebrations at Indirapuram. *The Hindu* [online] 24 September. Available at www.thehindu.com/news/cities/Delhi/flavours-of-bengal-in-durga-puja-celebrations-at-indirapuram/article19744277.ece, accessed 15 August 2018.

Beckford, J., 2012. Public Religions and the Postsecular: Critical Reflections. *Journal for the Scientific Study of Religion* 51(1), 1–19.

Bittarello, M. B., 2008. Another Time, another Space: Virtual Worlds, Myths and Imagination. *Heidelberg Journal of Religions on the Internet* 3(1), 246–266.

Bong Eats, 2017. *Kolkata Egg Roll Recipe: DurgaPujo Special*, [YouTube], 31 August. Available at www.youtube.com/watch?v=84iZjEzqpRE, accessed 23 April 2018.

BongHaat, 2016. *Bengali Sharadiya Magazines 2016*, [Electronic print]. Available at https://in.pinterest.com/pin/557953841318299241/, accessed 23 April 2018.

Campbell, H. A., 2010.*When Religion Meets New Media*. London: Routledge.

Campbell, H. A., 2012. How Religious Communities Negotiate New Media Religiously. In: Cheong, P. H., ed., *Digital Religion, Social Media and Culture: Perspectives Practices and Futures*. New York: Peter Lang, 81–96.

Cottle, S., 2006. *Mediatized Conflict: Developments in Media and Conflict Studies*. Maidenhead: Open University Press.

Desai, S., 2017. The WhatsApp Group – India's emotional Pipeline? *The Times of India Blogs* [blog] 22 May. Available at https://blogs.timesofindia.indiatimes.com/Citycitybangbang/the-whatsapp-group-indias-emotional-pipeline/, accessed 22 April 2018.

FE Online, 2018. WhatsApp Now has 1.5 billion Monthly Active Users, 200 Million Users in India. *Financial Express*, [online] 1 February. Available at www.financialexpress.com/industry/technology/whatsapp-now-has-1-5-billion-monthly-active-users-200-million-users-in-india/1044468/, accessed 15 August 2018.

Geertz, C., 1966. Religion as a Cultural System. In: Banton, M., ed. *Anthropological Approaches to the Study of Religion*. London: Tavistock, 1–46.

Habermas, J., 2006. Religion in the Public Sphere. *European Journal of Philosophy* 14, 1–25.

Hawley, J. S., 2001. Modern India and the Question of Middle-Class Religion. *International Journal of Hindu Studies* 5(3), 217–225.

Helland, C., 2000. Online-Religion/Religion-Online and Virtual Communities. In: Hadden, J. K. and Cowan, D. E., eds. *Religion on the Internet: Research Prospects and Promises*. New York: JAI Press, 205–223.

Helland, C., 2005. Online Religion as Lived Religion: Methodological Issues in the Study of Religious Participation on the Internet. *Heidelberg Journal of Religions on the Internet* 1(1), 1–16.

Herman, P. K., 2018. Seeing the Divine through Windows: Online Puja and Virtual Religious Experience. *Online Heidelberg Journal of Religions on the Internet* 4(1). Available at https://heiup.uni-heidelberg.de/journals/index.php/religions/article/view/9390, accessed 15 August 2018.

Hjarvard, S., 2012. Three Forms of Mediatized Religion: Changing the Public Face of Religion. In: Hjarvard, S. and Lövheim, M., eds. *Mediatization and Religion: Nordic Perspectives*. Goteborg: Nordicom, 21–44.

Hjarvard, S., 2011. The Mediatization of Religion: Theorising Religion, Media and Social Change. *Culture and Religion* 12(2), 119–135.

Hjarvard, S. and Lövheim, M., 2012. Introduction. In: Hjarvard, S. and Lövheim, M., eds. *Mediatization and Religion: Nordic Perspectives*. Goteborg: Nordicom, 9–17.

Hoover, S., 2012. Foreword: Practice, Autonomy and Authority in the Digitally Religious and Digitally Spiritual. In: Cheong, P. H., Fisher-Nielson, P., Gelfgren, S. and Ess, C., eds. *Digital Religion, Social Media and Culture: Perspectives, Practices and Futures*. New York: Peter Lang, 6–12.

Hoover, S. M. and Echchaibi, N., 2014. *Media Theory and the Third Spaces of Digital Religion*. Boulder: Project Finding Religion in the Media. Available at https://thirdspacesblog.files.wordpress.com/2014/05/third-spaces-and-media-theory-essay-2-0.pdf, accessed 26 November 2017.

IANS, 2017. Jawed Habib Salon Vandalised in Uttar Pradesh after Durga Puja Caricature. *Hindustan Times*, [online] 9 September. Available atwww.hindustantimes.com/india-news/jawed-habib-salon-vandalised-in-uttar-pradesh-after-durga-puja-caricature/story-VLh4NsvaPLyqsXgZBLQAKL.html, accessed 23 April 2018.

Jha, V., 2016. Indirapuram Durga Puja to Show Diversity in Art Forms. *Hindustan Times*, [online] 26 September. Available at www.hindustantimes.com/noida/indirapuram-durga-puja-society-to-showcase-diversity-in-indian-arts/story-0k8wjb6DgvpswDNVRFw8NJ.html, accessed 15 August 2018.

Knott, K., Poole, E. and Taira, T., 2013. *Media Portrayals of Religion and the Secular: Representation and Change*. Farnham: Ashgate.

Lövheim, M., 2013. Identity. In: Campbell, H. A. ed. *Digital Religion: Understanding Religious Practice in New Media Worlds*. London: Routledge, 41–56.

Lundby, K., ed., 2009. *Mediatization. Concepts, Changes, Consequences*. New York: Peter Lang.

Lutgendorf, P., 1997. Monkey in the Middle: The Status of Hanuman in Popular Hinduism. *Religion* 27(4), 311–332.

Lynch, G., Mitchell, J. and Strhan, A., eds., 2011. *Religion, Media, and Culture: A Reader*. London: Routledge.

Majumder, M.K., 2015. *From the Chairman's Desk*. Available at www.prantic.org/letternew.asp, accessed 24 April 2018.

Maqsood, Z., 2017. BWW Previews: Prantic Cultural Society Celebrates Durga Puja at Indirapuram, UP. *India Broadway World*, [online] 22 September. Available at www.broadwayworld.com/india/article/BWW-Previews-PRANTIC-CULTURAL-SOCIETY-CELEBRATES-DURGA-PUJA-at-Indirapuram-UP-20170922, accessed 15 August 2018.

Meyer, B. and Moors, A., 2006. Introduction. In: Meyer, B. and Moors A., eds. *Religion, Media, and the Public Sphere*. Bloomington: Indiana University Press, 1–25.

Mitra, A., 2017. Mahalaya 2018: Eight decades on, Bengalis continue to tune in to "Birendra Krishna Bhadra" for Durga Pujo. *The Indian EXPRESS*, [online] 27 September. Available at http://indianexpress.com/article/lifestyle/art-and-culture/mahalaya-2017-eight-decades-on-bengalis-continue-to-tune-in-to-birendra-krishna-bhadra-4848287/, accessed 23 April 2018.

Philpott, D., Shah, T. S. and Toft, M. D., 2011.*God's Century. Resurgent Religion and Global Politics*. New York: WW Norton & Co.

Prantic Blog, n.d. *Prantic* [blog]. Available at http://prantic.org/blog/, accessed 24 April 2018.

Prantic Culture Society Facebook, n.d. *Prantic Cultural Society*, [Facebook]. Available at www.facebook.com/pages/Prantic-Cultural-Society/818574868164996, accessed 24 April 2018.

Prantic Facebook, n.d. *Prantic*, [Facebook]. Available at www.facebook.com/www.prantic.org, accessed 24 April 2018.

Prantic Homepage, n.d. Homepage – *Prantic Cultural Society Website*. Available at www.prantic.org/default.asp, accessed 23 April 2018.

Prantic Media, n.d. *Prantic Media Coverage*. Available at www.prantic.org/Media-Coverage.asp, accessed 23 April 2018.

Prantic Membership, n.d. *Prantic Membership*. Available at www.prantic.org/Membership.asp, accessed 23 April 2018.

Prantic Newsletter, n.d. *NEWSLETTER – PRANTIC DARPAN*. Available at www.prantic.org/Newsletter.asp, accessed 23 April 2018.

Prantic Twitter, n.d. *Prantic*. Available at https://twitter.com/prantic_ncr, accessed 23 April 2018.

Radde-Antweiler, K., 2008. Religion becoming Virtualised: Introduction to the Special Issue on Religion in Virtual Worlds. *Heidelberg Journal of Religions on the Internet* 3(1), 1–6.

Rao, M.G., 2018. GST: Need to Revisit the Complex System. *Financial Express*, [online] 3 April. Available at www.financialexpress.com/opinion/gst-need-to-revisit-the-complex-system/1119257/, accessed 24 April 2018.

Säävälä, M., 2003. Auspicious Hindu Houses: The New Middle Classes in Hyderabad, India. *Social Anthropology* 11(2), 231–247.

Saikia, B.S., 2016. Demonetization May Drag India behind China in GDP Growth, Rob Fastest-growing Economy Tag. *The Economic Times*, [online] 18 November. Available at https://economictimes.indiatimes.com/markets/stocks/news/demonetisation-to-drag-india-behind-china-in-gdp-growth-rob-fastest-growing-economy-tag/articleshow/55492970.cms, accessed 24 April 2018.

Scheifinger, H., 2009. The Jaganath Temple and Online Darshan. *Journal of Contemporary Religion* 24(3), 277–290.

Sethi, N., 2017. Theme? No Thanks. Delhi"s 108-Year-Old Durga Puja Sticks To Tradition. *NDTV*, [online] 25 September. Available at www.ndtv.com/delhi-news/durga-puja-2017-theme-no-thanks-delhis-108-year-old-puja-sticks-to-tradition-1754783, accessed 23 April 2018.

Subramaniam, K., 1981. *Ramayan*. Mumbai: BharatyaVidyaBhawan.

Tharoor, S., 2018. *Why I am a Hindu*. London: C. Hurst.

Times of India, 2017. *Celebrity Hairstylist Jawed Habib Trolled for Featuring Gods in ad*, [YouTube] 6 September. Available at www.youtube.com/watch?v=I-L81tcGzHM, accessed 23 April 2018.

Trends Desk, 2017. Bengali Vlogger Posts "Harmless Egg Roll Video", Gets Trolled for "Eating Meat during Navratri." *The Indian EXPRESS*, 14 September. Available athttp://indianexpress.com/article/trending/trending-in-india/bengali-vlogger-posts-harmless-egg-roll-video-4841966/, accessed 23 April 2018.

Zeiler, X., 2018. Durga Puja Committees. Community Origin and Transformed Mediatized Practices Employing Social Media. In Simmons, C., Sen, M., and Rodrigues, H., eds. *Nine Nights of the Goddess. The Navaratri Festival in South Asia*. New York: SUNY Press, pp. 121–138.

2 Hindu religious identification in India's online matrimonial market

Fritzi-Marie Titzmann

Introduction

For centuries Indian families have sought help from relatives, marriage brokers and later newspaper advertisements to marry their sons and daughters. They relied on kinship and caste networks, on marriage bureaus and on word of mouth. However, the global media age has opened up a whole new world of digital possibilities. The first India-based websites dedicated to matrimonial matchmaking, most prominently Shaadi.com, appeared on the World Wide Web in the late 1990s, and their popularity has increased ever since. Shaadi.com (2018) alone claims over 35 million members since its inception in 1996, and roughly 5 million successfully matched couples. While the medium is a new one, analyses attest that traditional patterns of finding a suitable match persist (Kaur and Dhanda 2014; Seth and Patnayakuni 2009; Shukla and Kapadia 2007; Titzmann 2014). Religious and caste affiliation and astrological details remain important factors of decision-making. Nevertheless, young users in particular transform the practice of partner search by blending these traditional criteria with individualistic expectations like personal compatibility. Situated within the theoretical framework of the socio-constructivist mediatization approach, this chapter examines the negotiations of Hindu religious identities in terms of search criteria and of self-description in matrimonial profiles. The affordances of an increasing digitalization and continuous processes of identity production significantly influence how users construct their self(ves) and represent themselves with regard to individual religious identification and group-based religious membership. Based on media content analysis of 200 user profiles and website design as well as around 30 qualitative interviews,[1] this chapter particularly interrogates how digital media usage impacts the category of caste by possibly reinforcing or diminishing its significance. The concept of media appropriation is applied in order to understand how the outcome of media consumption is decisively shaped by individual users' preferences and practices.

The mediatization of matrimonial matchmaking

I situate my study of the Indian online matrimonial market within the theoretical frame of mediatization, an approach that describes the growing impact that media has on culture and society. Mediatization is currently discussed in divergent ways as a meta-process of sociocultural change. Basically, the term describes an increasing influence of communication media on different social and cultural spheres (Hepp 2010, 2009; Kim 2008). Hepp's model of "media as moulding forces" (Hepp 2010) in conjunction with social change offers a suitable theoretical starting point. He names three dimensions of mediatization: individualization as social dimension, deterritorialization as a spatial dimension and an increasing immediacy as a temporal dimension (Hepp 2010, 71). Individualization as a dimension of social change and the trends of media usage are found in the following media content analysis. An increasing immediacy is primarily present in terms of changing forms of communication and technology. Communication with prospective candidates has become essentially quicker and more direct through the Internet, email and mobile phones than through middle-men such as marriage bureaus or advertising departments. The third dimension, deterritorialization, is extremely apparent as digital media is essentially characterized by its deterritoriality. Hepp's concept applies as far as transnationality and translocality are concerned but excludes the important factors of regionalization and localization or reterritorialization (Schneider and Gräf 2011). However, a medial trend toward regionalization reflects strongly in the digital matrimony landscape, as will be shown later.

The World Wide Web provides a complex picture of young Indians searching for life partners. The sheer fact that millions of profiles containing personal information are accessible via the Internet proves how significant mediatization is. The media permeate very intimate and personal domains and thereby impact on crucial social institutions such as marriage as well as on religious practice. In the context of arranging marriages, digitalization is not exactly a revolution but rather the most recent phase of mediatization and developments of increasing commercialization and professionalization over the last century. Matchmaking is a long-lasting tradition in South Asia and despite being the responsibility of family and community networks, there is a demand for middle-men and professionalized help as well. Marriage brokers came into the picture centuries ago, evolving into modern marriage bureaus and newspaper advertising in the nineteenth and twentieth century, and since the late 1990s, culminating in matrimonial websites (Titzmann 2014, 166f).[2] Pal (2010, 55) argues that matrimonial websites are comparable to social networking sites like Facebook or Orkut, Facebook's immensely popular predecessor in India which was shut down in 2014. The success of websites like Shaadi.com, one of the most popular Indian matrimonial websites, is based on a similar networking principle. While Pal correctly points out the similarity of high media mobility and interactivity, I prefer to contextualize both social media and matrimonial media within a general meta-process of medialization and increasing connectivity. The networking principle related to marriage matchmaking is not new at all. *Going through the family*, using caste associations or simply word of mouth are based on traditional and non-digital networks. The rise of online matrimonial websites is therewith part of a general boom that has taken place in the Indian media landscape since the 1990s, alongside economic liberalization and privatization (Munshi 2001, 79, Schneider 2014). Nevertheless, digitalization heralds a new matchmaking era. The Internet theoretically enables geographically unlimited partner search. The decisive difference to earlier methods is its interactivity, a key component of all branches of social media (Pal 2010). Partner search and communication work dialogically, and no other matchmaking medium has ever rendered immediate contact via chatting possible. Since other media formats continue to exist, the Internet forms the central point of a complex multimedia Indian marriage market. Apart from hosting matrimonial websites, the Internet is an important space of communication and hence serves as a virtual interface enabling cooperation between print media, caste communities, television and other matchmaking actors (Titzmann 2014, 167).

The concept of media appropriation provides an important theoretical framework enhancing the understanding of how the outcome of media consumption is decisively shaped by individual user's preferences and practices. In this way, the digitalization of matrimonial matchmaking neither promotes instant social change, nor does it simply reproduce existing patterns. "Appropriation holds that people actively select how functionality and social structures embedded in the technology are used, and that a given feature may be deployed in different ways depending on how it is appropriated" (Seth and Patnayakuni 2009, 331). Media content and its usage consequentially are localized in people's everyday life, and "technology is shaped and reshaped over time and may eventually reach a state of equilibrium where it becomes embedded in users' lives" (Seth and Patnayakuni 2009, 332).

A detailed analysis of matrimonial profiles offers remarkable insights into changing concepts of marriage, love and subjectivity. Religious identification is strongly interwoven with all aspects of marriage on the subjective as well as the community level. Hence, India's matrimonial market can be seen as a paradigmatic process of medialization. On the one hand, marriage as a central social event is being medialized. On the other, changing gender roles, social concepts and values are reflected in the design of websites and advertising as well as in user profiles. In addition, research of Indian matrimonial websites overlaps with multiple other issues; for instance, a global Indian online matrimonial market includes a strong transnational component. Finally, with regard to religious identification, matrimonial websites are interesting sources for observing the construction and mediation processes of community and belonging.

The Indian online matrimonial market: A brief overview

What I refer to as the contemporary Indian online matrimonial market describes a conglomerate of innumerable websites that cater to an assumed

Indian clientele including a transnational diaspora consisting of millions of people worldwide that identify as Indian or people of Indian origin. In 2014, *The Economic Times* estimated 3,100 registered matrimonial websites in India (Sengupta 2015), but global numbers are impossible to specify. Market research documents that classified markets have seen a significant growth in India and were valued at INR 896 crores (around USD 140 million) by December 2014 (IAMAI 2015, 8).[3] The online matrimony segment alone contributed to a huge 87% (IAMAI 2015, 8).[4] Hence, matrimonial media is an important and growing business branch as well. The online matrimonial market is big – and highly diversified. Websites offer matchmaking according to different criteria, the most important being language and regional affiliation as well as religion. The website BharatMatrimony.com was the first to develop this trend as business strategy. The portal consists of 15 regional subsites that are organized along linguistic lines such as TamilMatrimony, BengalMatrimony and MarathiMatrimony. Meanwhile, most other websites that are not already specialized on a certain community follow BharatMatrimony's pattern.

After these *general websites* (which contain profiles from people of diverse religious and regional backgrounds), the second large segment is made up of *websites catering to specific communities* or customers and are often defined along religious lines. Examples are SikhingYou.com[5] for Sikhs, Nikah.com for South Asian Muslims or TrinityMatrimony.com,[6] which focuses on Christians from the South Indian state of Kerala and thus combines regional and religious identification markers. Many portals have even specialized on distinct castes such as KutchiLohana.com[7] (for Kutchi Lohanas, a caste from the region of Kutch in Western India) or Brahmakshatriya Shaadi (for the BrahmKshatriya Sorathiya Vaishnavs, a Gujarati subcaste). The cited examples show that most caste groups are regionally specific as well.

The third segment offers what I call *social niche markets*. These include websites for clients seeking a second marriage, that is, divorcees and widowed people (e.g., SecondShaadi.com). Therewith, the founders tapped a new market, since remarriages, at least for traditional Hindus, and particularly for women, were a taboo for a long time, and are still not accepted all over India (Michaels 2005, 151f). Other websites target certain groups defined by age (e.g., 40plusMatrimony.com), economic class (e.g., EliteMatrimony.com) or health (e.g., portals for HIV positive people).

Keeping the overarching theme – and title – of this book in mind, I focus in the following on those aspects of matrimonial matchmaking that are crucial for people identifying as Hindu. This includes websites of all three segments, since the general websites such as BharatMatrimony.com or the very popular Shaadi.com are not religiously specific but do offer search criteria according to location, religion, language, profession, horoscope and so forth. In a different way from the already community-specific portals, these big websites afford multiple and very detailed search filters enabling results that include exclusively candidates of the same caste, sect,[8] subcaste and/or with a matching horoscope.

Religion and caste in the contemporary Indian Hindu matrimonial market

As noted earlier, religion is a key identity marker in the matrimonial market's differentiation. It is an important search and filter criterion and produces submarkets divided along religious lines. The distribution by religion among members on general Indian websites appears to have shifted from an overrepresentation of religious minorities – as generated by my analysis of profile samples from 2007 (Titzmann 2014, 262) – toward a higher representation of Hindus in recent years (Kaur and Dhanda 2014, 280). Since in their sample, the proportion of Muslim users was a little over half of their presence in the Indian population, Kaur and Dhanda (2014, 280) presume that Muslims may be posting exclusively on websites such as Muslim-Matrimony.com.

In Hindu contexts, the general objectives of a marital union are defined frequently by three aspects: *dharma*, the compliance of social duty; *prajā*, procreating and preservation of one's lineage; and *rati*, sexual fulfillment (Shukla and Kapadia 2007, 38). The hierarchically structured caste system constitutes an integral part of the socioreligious structure in most branches of what has come to be summarized under Hinduism. Michaels (2005, 166f) describes the social system as one of clearly demarcated extended families which are also understood as part of a caste group (*varṇa*), a subcaste (*jāti*) – that correlates with professional groupings – and a clan or kinship group (*gotra*). All three categories are integrated in Shaadi.com's profile mask. Similar to Michaels, the case study that I discuss later in this paper suggests that these terms are used interchangeably; the answer to the caste questions thus depends on the context:

> If an Indian asks another Indian about his caste (*jāti*), he usually wants to know his profession. If he knows this and nevertheless asks about caste, he generally wants to know the subcaste. If two Indians of the same subcaste ask each other about their caste, they possibly want to know the descent group. (Michaels 2005, 166)

A detailed discussion of the emergence and the nature of the caste system cannot be included in this paper due to spatial restraints.[9] Yet, the procreation and preservation of family lineage in the Hindu context always comprises questions of caste. For the purpose of this chapter, I discuss caste identity as an important socioreligious category without going into the depths of the system itself or the ritual duties and functions of certain castes or subcastes. Research reveals that marriage fulfills a dual function with regards to the Indian social structure. Firstly, it reproduces the institution of caste; secondly, it enables social mobility of groups and individuals (e.g., Hankeln 2008: 38f, Pfeffer 1985; Skoda 2002, 13ff). The latter is practiced widely in the form of hypergamy (i.e., a woman of lower status marries socially upwards) in North India (Skoda 2002, 15).

The digitalization of marriage matchmaking does not result in a remarkable deviation from these traditional patterns, but it creates new avenues of strengthening or rejecting the importance of caste through a wider choice of candidates. Thus, marriage concerns the commitment to a life partner as well as the preservation of cultural and caste differences and the reproduction of communities. Websites like CommunityMatrimony.com utilize India's accelerated social differentiation as its business model and invest in community as the strongest identity marker. In Indian English, the term community is commonly used not only for a group of people somehow linked to each other but also as a synonym for caste. The term caste, being negatively connoted through its long history of discrimination among certain classes, is rather avoided for reasons of political correctness.

CommunityMatrimony.com does not offer anything else other than caste-based marriage advertisement. While in 2012, the website's self-description partly concealed the caste aspect by emphasizing community,[10] six years later, the website's main page openly offers three different drop-down menus: Caste Based Matrimony Sites (around 300 different options), Religion Based Matrimony Sites (Christian, Kerala Christian, Muslim, Sikh, Jain, Buddhist), and Other Exclusive Matrimony Sites (Divorcee, Manglik,[11] 40Plus, Defence, Anycaste, Ability) (CommunityMatrimony.com 2018). A television commercial (Community Matrimony TV Commercial) additionally suggests that the website's business model targets parents as their prime audience. The television spot shows an Indian couple living in an unidentified Western country. The parents observe how their daughter passes by, sitting on a young, long-haired man's motorcycle. The shocking incident provokes an agitated discussion over the failure of not having found a suitable groom for the daughter from within the community. An acquaintance recommends checking out CommunityMatrimony.com for that matter.

CommunityMatrimony.com's marketing strategy is no isolated case. Concerning the question of caste in matrimonial media, existent research finds two contradictory patterns: the perpetuation of caste through matrimonial media and a diminishing social significance of caste.

Most research shows that caste endogamy is perpetuated through marriage advertisements in print media or online (e.g., Banerjee et al. 2009). The main reason might be what Seth and Patnayakuni (2009, 330) define as "affordance": a design that invites or leads users through subtle hints to act in a certain way. In the case of matrimonial media, users are asked to enter their caste as a major category in their profile mask; hence, it emphasizes caste as an important social criterion to be considered in matchmaking. Kaur and Dhanda (2014, 279) found as many as 248 available caste names in a drop-down menu for registrants to choose from, including castes among Hindus, Muslims, Christians and Sikhs. CommunityMatrimony.com, as stated earlier, lists around 300 caste names, mostly according to caste (*varṇa*) and subcaste (*jāti*). Similarly, Diminescu and Renault (2011, 687) describe that Indian matrimonial websites, through the numerous filter options along aspects such as religion or horoscope, are far more culturally specified than other standardized dating websites, for example, in the USA. Every piece of information, including leaving certain fields blank, contains codes that help to decipher the complex picture of a candidate's socioeconomic positioning. Consequentially, the authors indicate that "Shaadi[.com] promotes an 'Indo-centric' viewpoint and takes an active part in the construction of a society which, on a global level, is more and more 'caste ridden', more and more 'ethnicized'" (Diminescu and Renault 2011, 689). Thus, websites make it easy to practice caste endogamy, as they allow access to a greater number of individuals of the same caste. The greatest variety exists in Brahmin subcastes, where Kaur and Dhanda (2014, 279) registered around 30 subcastes in the drop-down menu. Brahmins, traditionally occupied as priests and scholars, represent the top of the Hindu caste hierarchy.

> While members from among all castes thus appear to have access to the net and are keen to use internet technology, the great variety of Brahmins reiterates the pattern whereby the educated and elite Brahmins have always been the first to access new channels of education and communication for upward mobility, while at the same time emphasizing and maintaining caste and class exclusivity. (Kaur and Dhanda 2014, 279)

Thus, marriage websites contribute to a horizontal strengthening of caste.

On the other hand, marriage advertisements with the remark "Caste No Bar"[12] increase, and Béteille (2011, 88) remarks that the function of caste decreases with regard to ritual significance, choice of profession or marriage. However, caste consciousness remains important as a social identity. Brosius (2010, 274) confirms that more marriages are based on young people's own choice and that economic position is the decisive factor in spouse selection. She yet warns to call this a rebellious development:

> Marriage candidates might have become smarter in choosing their future partner, and have more choice at their hands due to online marriage portals. But surveys have shown that 64 per cent men in Delhi favor intra-caste marriage and most urban youths want their parent's blessing as regards their choice. (Brosius 2010, 274)

These trends have little to do with belief in caste as a ritual identity, she argues, but rather function as an "emotional strategy of dealing with the flip side of mobility in the contemporary world" (Brosius 2010, 274). The traditionally important role of the family as a social unit further provides protection and functions as a safeguard for young people's life decisions. Postliberal India thus witnesses a simultaneous emergence of a cosmopolitan Indianness and a reassertion of traditional concepts like the joint family[13] or socioreligious identities. For instance, Brosius stresses the importance of arranged marriage in an urban and transnational context in the creation of a modern national identity. These aspects serve as markers of an Indian identity in a globalized context. And despite social change, she attests that "[f]amily, caste and religion still play a vital role in education, residential environments and for life-cycle rituals despite the privileging of merit over birth for life-conduct and upward mobility" (Brosius 2010, 330).

In the context of marriage arrangement, Seth and Patnayakuni (2009) observe gradual changes in the role of the family that result in a work division during the matchmaking process. The process of media appropriation is not linear and shows crucial intergenerational differences. The younger generation, being digital natives or at least more internet-savvy than their parents, usually take a proactive part in registering and personalizing their matrimonial profiles with descriptions of their character, preferences, dreams and expectations. Nevertheless, family members remain important consultants with immense influence on the decision-making process. The parents are often responsible to ensure that basic criteria of religion, caste, age, economic background and so forth are met by potential candidates (Seth and Patnayakuni 2009, 343). Therewith, the family continues to play two important gatekeeping roles:

> [T]he first is that of controlling the entry of new members into the family, especially the bride, and ensuring that they are compatible with the family's values and traditions. In its second role, the family perpetuates the caste, community and religious divisions in the society. (Seth and Patnayakuni 2009, 341)

Despite the continuing importance of the family, Sharma (2008) states that the construction of the self is crucial in the process of identity production enabled by digitalization. She focuses her research on the Indian diaspora in North America and suggests that information technology and matrimonial websites become "enablers of public discourse about issues of identity and community production" (Sharma 2008, 149). As already discussed, the design of matrimonial portals replicates caste practices through affordance. However, individual media appropriation allows for acceptance of rejection of casteism[14] (Sharma 2008, 150).

Negotiating Hindu identity online

The next part discusses a case study of profiles from Indian matrimonial websites. The analysis is enhanced by findings from field research that comprised interviews with users of online matchmaking portals and was undertaken between 2008 and 2012 in multiple Indian locations. Given that this book explores digital forms and practices of Hinduism, the central question revolves around the digital construction of identity, and in particular of a self, through the creation of a matrimonial profile. How do users construct their self(ves)? As Hindu, as caste member, as Indian, as traditional? The basic data consist of 200 analyzed matrimonial profiles posted on Shaad.com in 2007. These 100 male and 100 female profiles by people aged 20–25 years located in Mumbai were derived by default search. As already mentioned, religion is one of the key filters to organize one's search. Although the portal offers "no religion" and "spiritual" as alternatives to prevalent religious denominations, none of the 200 users chose these categories. Around 90% of the users in the sample mentioned their caste/sect which suggests caste's perseverance as an important criterion. Additionally, qualitative content analysis was employed to decode the free text posted in the female profiles of the sample. Among the generated coded categories were "religion" and "tradition and values". Interestingly, despite naming their religion and specifying their caste, comparably few women describe themselves in the free text as religious (19%). The self-descriptions rather fall under the category "tradition and values" (29%) in opposition to "modernity" (11%).[15] Again, in the personal interviews, religion was never mentioned specifically, but often circumscribed by terms such as "culture" or "values", thus diffusing notions of Indianness and (Hindu) religiosity.[16]

> What I feel is, being modern is good but then you should be into your culture. You should follow your cultural values and you should not forget that. (Chandani,[17] interviewed by the author in Ahmedabad, 3 February 2011)

Similarly, the description of partner preferences corresponds to the self-descriptions, with "religion" being mentioned by 9% and "tradition and values" by 20%. Overall, the free text analysis suggests a stronger emphasis on individual and personal criteria such as character, humor, vitality and hobbies. A third of all users within the sample expressed the desire to find a partner with corresponding religious background. However, the specification of the desired partner's caste affiliation disclosed a significant gender difference, with more female users specifying the desirable caste background.[18] These statistics suggest that the caste background is more relevant for women. But the data should be read within the context of a higher participation of third parties such as parents, siblings or friends. Shaadi.com's profile mask includes the field "posted by", which shows that only 47% of the female users created the profile themselves. Research suggests that the religious background is more important to elder family members. I hypothesize that what Seth and Patnayakuni (2009, 341) describe as the family's "gate-keeping role" reflects in my case study as well. In an interview with *Daily News & Analysis (DNA)* Vibhas Mehta, former director of Shaadi.com, confirmed, that "[w]hen parents are involved they do consider the caste factor" (Acharya 2007, 13).

Caste as a variable category of belonging

For the purpose of this chapter, I am particularly interested in the negotiation of caste as an allegedly specific component of Hindu religious identity. The drop-down menu of Shaadi.com's profile mask facilitated a quantitative analysis and generated four dominant interpretations of what users define as caste identity.

1 Regional affiliation
   Caste was often equated with regional belonging, indicated by the use of terms such as Punjabi, Gujarati, Sindhi or Maharashtrian.[19]
2 Caste groups
   Other users interpreted caste as one of the four *varṇas*, the traditional ranks or caste groups in the Hindu social system. They accordingly identified themselves as Brahmin, Kshatriya, or Vaishya. The fourth rank, Shudra, was not mentioned in a single profile. Probably users used other categories of membership (e.g., regional) to not emphasize their low social rank according to the caste system.
3 Sect
   Another interpretation corresponds with the term sect, and was primarily applied by non-Hindu users. Hence, Christians identified as Protestant, Catholic, Born Again or Pentecost; Muslims as Sunni, Shia or Dawoodi Bohra; and Jains as Digamber or Shwetamber. Some Hindus used a categorization in the same sense, describing themselves as either Shaiva or Vaishnava.[20]
4 Subcaste
   The fourth pattern only applied to Hindu profiles, where a specific subcaste – in the sense of *jāti* – is mentioned (although Shaadi.com offers a separate field for subcaste), such as "96 K Konkanastha"[21] or "CKP".[22] This pattern was most commonly used by ritually high-ranking subcaste members. Ritually high-positioned castes are supposedly more eager to ensure endogamy in order to secure their status which also reflects in the maximum number of subcastes being listed under Brahmin, according to Kaur and Dhanda (2014).

Hence, caste as a category is ambiguous, and belonging and identity are defined in highly individual and diverging ways. Puri's (1999) sample of 54 urban Indian women revealed in a similar way how they identified ambiguously and with overlapping markers of religion, ethnicity, region and language. For instance, a woman described her caste simultaneously as Roman Catholic and Goan Brahmin, blending Christian religiosity (Roman Catholic) with regional (Goa) and caste (Brahmin) identities (Puri 1999, 17).

Membership of certain communities defined by religion, clan or lineage plays a very important role in the construction of the self, as shown by the profile analysis. But the respective categories of affiliation are not always comparable. Michaels (2005, 160) affirms this assumption by stating the almost inflationary use of the term for "so many social units – endogamous groups, a category of such groups, a system of social organization – that it is almost better to give it up altogether". This impression is further reinforced by the fact that many non-Hindus filled in their caste as well – opposed to the presumption of caste being an exclusive feature of Hinduism. In fact, no significant difference was detected between Hindu and Muslim users. Both considered the category Caste/Sect with almost the same frequency. Against this background, the importance of caste, as suggested by the high percentage of people mentioning it in their profiles, appears to be diffused. Similar to the equation of religiosity and alleged Indian culture and values, the assumed importance of caste was, during the interviews, only partially confirmed and the interviewees rather circumscribed caste with community.

Interviewees on community

The analyses of self-representation and interviews are examples of media appropriation and identity production as well as constructions of the self. Corresponding to Hepp's (2010) dimensions of mediatization, all three perspectives generate a clear trend of individualization regarding media usage, socioreligious identification and individual self-representations. However, parallel developments of the marriage market's fragmentation – in terms of regionalization and religious differentiation – reflect in the analyzed data as well. Both trends combined give the impression of a simultaneous strengthening of ethnolinguistic/religious identification and a growing importance of the individual. These developments might seem incompatible, but individualization and increasing agency can occur within traditional concepts as well. The key term holding these conflicting notions together is compatibility. The majority of the interviewed women listed a mix of emotional and social motives driving them to focus on a partner with a coinciding socioreligious background. The desire for compatibility generally extends to a "shared culture", as one interviewee explained:

> Getting into a family whose cultural background, religious background I already know, it is just easier for me to adapt and for them to have me in the family. (Bhavna, interviewed by the author in Mumbai, 24 November 2011)

Another woman called it "comfort of the same community" and stated:

> [i]n our society which is so fragmented and so different, like different languages and different food cultures, that becomes quite a comforting

thing. (Sonia, interviewed by the author in Mumbai, 29 November 2011)

In these narratives, community is defined by shared culture, religion, language and food. This indicates possible understandings of community along similar lines as the four variations of caste discussed earlier, but may be extended to other demarcations such as urban/rural locations or social class.

Conclusion: New media and religious identification

I have argued that the term community deserves particular attention as it is employed by users to circumscribe diverse religiously defined (Hindu) identities. By emphasizing community membership through the preselection of search criteria and drop-down menus, caste as a category is being reinforced. While the case study confirms religious affiliation as a crucial aspect of partner selection, it reveals varying and often overlapping meanings of the term community, namely, as regional identity, caste group, sect or subcaste. Hence, the data also show caste as a fluid category that is subject to interpretation. Caste as an important criterion for marriage matchmaking neither disappears, nor does digitalization simply perpetuate the existing patterns. In Sharma's (2008, 150) words, "matrimonial websites allow a fusion of tradition with technology in which there is a simultaneous opening up of possibilities within highly specific cultural constraints".

Other religious aspects such as the specific components of the Hindu horoscope feature prominently on Indian matrimonial websites and are the markers that differentiate them from other global matchmaking portals. Further remarkable is an intergenerational shift concerning media appropriation. While most individuals seek advice from their extended families during the partner search, profiles with higher external participation contain stronger emphasis on religion and caste in particular. This points toward the continuing rôle of the family as gatekeeper for community identity. Therein the findings connect to other areas of research on digital Hinduism by showing parallels to Bachrach's (2014) study of online advice forums of the Hindu sect Vallabh Vaishnava. She concludes that the Internet renders a continuation of offline practices possible in virtual space – in her case study the devotee–guru relationship and forms of proselytization like pilgrimages – thereby enabling young and diasporic devotees to rediscover what they assume to be tradition and adjusting it to modern and/or diasporic circumstances (Bachrach 2014, 169). These developments mirror the aforementioned observations on the digitalization of matchmaking in many ways. Similar to what I have termed intergenerational difference in the use of new media, Bachrach notes demographic change through the employment of new media. The mostly diasporic users of the analyzed discussion forums are mainly young and male, whereas Indian offline devotees are mainly elderly and female (Bachrach 2014, 172). This is an interesting parallel since marriage matchmaking in South Asia is traditionally in the hands of elderly female family members, while a gradual shift toward stronger initiative from young people is a clearly visible trend.

The combined data from online analysis and field research have shown that each single user of online matrimonial media thus employs the search and filter mechanisms afforded by the respective medium individually according to their personal requirements with regard to self-representation as well as their constructed desirable partner. The online manifestations of these negotiations thus reflect varying forms of media appropriation and constructions of the self, enabled by technology and medialization. Digital Hinduism features as a cross-cutting theme in so far as religious (self-) identification is, to some extent, demanded through the design of online matrimonial media. Hence, Hindu users are urged to digitally negotiate their religious belonging.

Notes

1 The major field research for a larger project on matrimonial media was carried out between 2010 and 2012. The analyzed user profiles were derived in 2007.
2 For a detailed description of predigital matchmaking methods, see Titzmann (2014, 158–167) and Majumdar (2004).
3 The IAMAI report is no longer online. Last accessed 17 April 2018. Internet content is dynamic and continuously evolving and changing. This provides a major challenge for research based on online data as sources may disappear over time. Wherever this is the case, the last date of access is indicated.
4 The source is no longer online. Last accessed 17 April 2018.
5 The source is no longer online. Last accessed 10 January 2013.
6 The source is no longer online. Last accessed 10 January 2013.
7 The source is no longer online. Last accessed 10 January 2013.
8 Sect is used as a category to describe religious denominations within the major religions, such as Catholic/Protestant Christians, Sunni/Shia Muslims or Shaiva/Vaishnava Hindus.
9 For an introduction to the Indian social system, see Michaels (2005, 159–200); see Béteille (2011) on the politicization of the caste system and Skoda (2002) on caste practices, with special reference to marriage rules.
10 "In India it is still believed that marriage within the community is healthy, happy and strengthens the bond within the community. CommunityMatrimony.com is a union of over 350 community matrimony sites catering to the unique needs of various communities" (CommunityMatrimony.com 2012).
11 Manglik refers to people born in an astrological constellation connected to the planet Mars deemed unfavorable for marriage; if two mangliks marry, the negative effects are believed to cancel each other out.
12 It means that caste matching will not be the crucial factor in considering a prospective marriage match. Candidates from different castes too will be considered.
13 For a detailed discussion of the conceptualization of the Indian joint family, see Uberoi (2003).
14 Casteism denotes the adherence to the Hindu caste system as well as prejudice or discrimination on the grounds of caste. Sharma refers to the first meaning.
15 See Titzmann (2014, 244, 259) for the complete analysis of free texts in female users' self-descriptions.

16 Except for two Jains, all interviewed users identified themselves as Hindu.
17 All interviewees' names were changed to protect their identity.
18 In all, 47% of the female users wanted a partner with a specific caste background, identical or similar to their own caste, whereas only 34% of male users specified the desired caste background. Twenty years earlier, an analysis of newspaper matrimonial advertisements in *Samaj* yielded similar results. In all, 42% mentioned a desired caste affiliation and only 14% indicated "Caste no bar" (Choudhury, Choudhury and Mohanty 1995, 350).
19 Punjab, Gujarat and Maharashtra are Indian states, whereas Sindh is a Pakistani province, but a significant number of Sindhis live in India as well.
20 These denominations are derived from the two great traditions in contemporary Hinduism. Shaivas worship Shiva as the highest god, whereas Vaishnavas relate to the god Vishnu.
21 96 K Konkanastha denotes a Brahmin subcaste whose members originally hail from the Konkan coast and today live predominantly in Maharashtra. Members are also called *Chitpavan* Brahmins.
22 Chandraseniya Kayastha Prabhu. CKP is a *Kşatriya* subcaste whose members live predominantly in Maharashtra.

References

40plusMatrimony.com, 2019. *The No.1 Matrimony Site for the 40Plus*. Available at www.40plusmatrimony.com, accessed 14 August 2018.

Acharya, P., 2007. Demand for Dowry Is Less and Less In Big Metros: Vibhas Mehta, Business Head of Shaadi.Com, In Conversation with Preety Acharya. *DNA (Daily News & Analysis)*, 13.

Bachrach, E., 2014. Is Guruji Online? Internet Advice Forums and Transnational Encounters in a Vaishnav Sectarian Community. In: Sahoo, A. K., and de Kruijfeds, J. G., eds. *Indian Transnationalism Online. New Perspectives on Diaspora*. Farnham/Burlington: Ashgate (Studies in Migration and Diaspora), 163–176.

Banerjee, A., Duflo, E., Ghatak, M. and Lafortune, J., 2009. *Marry for What: Caste and Mate Selection in Modern India*. Cambridge and MA (NBER Working Paper Series), 14958. Available at www.nber.org/papers/w14958, accessed 17 April 2018, 1–65.

Béteille, A., 2011. Caste and the Citizen. *Science and Culture* 77(3–4), 83–90.

BharatMatrimony.com, 2019. *Matrimony, India Matrimonials, Matrimonial Sites, Marriages, Brides*. Available at www.bharatmatrimony.com, accessed 15 August 2018.

Brahmakshatriya Shaadi, 2019. *Online Dating at Brahmakshatriya*. Available at www.brahmakshatriya.com, accessed 14 August 2018.

Brosius, C., 2010. *India's Middle Class: New Forms of Urban Leisure, Consumption and Prosperity*. New Delhi: Routledge.

Choudhury, B., Choudhury, R. K. and Mohanty, S., 1995. Mate Selection through Mass-Media Aid. *Man In India* 75(4), 339–354.

CommunityMatrimony.com, 2012/2018. *Community Matrimony*. Available at www.communitymatrimony.com, accessed 12 December 2012/18 April 2018.

CommunityMatrimony.com, 2019. [video] *Community Matrimony TV Commercial*. Available at www.youtube.com/watch?v=UVPhdOBk2kM, accessed 16 April 2019.

Diminescu, D. and Renault, M., 2011. The Matrimonial Web of Migrants: The Economics of Profiling as a New Form of Ethnic Business. *Social Science Information* 50(3–4), 678–704.

EliteMatrimony.com, 2018. *Elite Matrimony*. Available at www.elitematrimony.com, accessed 15 August 2018.

Hankeln, M., 2008. *India's Marriages Re-arranged: Changing Patterns among the Urban Middle Class*. Saarbrücken: VDM.

Hepp, A., 2009. Transculturality as a Perspective: Researching Media Cultures Comparatively. *Forum: Qualitative Social Research*, [e-journal] 10(1). Available at http://nbn-resolving.de/urn:nbn:de:0114-fqs0901267, accessed 10 October 2010.

Hepp, A., 2010. Mediatisierung und Kulturwandel: Kulturelle Kontextfelder und die Prägkräfte der Medien. In: Hartmann, M. and Hepp, A., eds. *Die Mediatisierung der Alltagswelt. Festschrift zu Ehren von Friedrich Krotz*. Wiesbaden: Verlag für Sozialwissenschaften, 65–84.

IAMAI, 2015. *Digital Commerce*. Internet and Mobile Association of India. March 2015. Available at www.iamai.in/sites/default/files/research/pdf/IAMAI%20Digital%20Commerce%20Report%202014_90.pdf, accessed 17 April 2018.

Kaur, R. and Dhanda, P., 2014. Surfing for Spouses: Marriage Websites and the 'New' Indian Marriage? In: Kaur, R. and Palriwala, R., eds. *Marrying in South Asia: Shifting Concepts, Changing Practices in a Globalising World*. New Delhi: Orient BlackSwan, 271–292.

Kim, Y., 2008. Introduction: The Media and Asian Transformations. In: Kim, Y., ed. *Media Consumption and Everyday Life in Asia, vol. 1*. New York: Routledge, 1–24.

KutchiLohana.com. Available at www.kutchilohana.com, accessed 10 January 2013.

Majumdar, R., 2004. Looking for Brides and Grooms: Ghataks, Matrimonials, and the Marriage Market in Colonial Calcutta, Circa 1875–1940. *The Journal of Asian Studies* 63(4), 911–935.

Michaels, A., 2005. *Hinduism. Past and Present*. New Delhi: Orient Longman.

Munshi, S., 2001. Marvellous Me: The Beauty Industry and the Construction of the 'Modern' Indian Woman. In: Munshi, S., ed. *Images of the 'Modern Woman' in Asia: Global Media, Local Meanings*. Richmond: Curzon, 78–93.

MuslimMatrimony.com, 2019. *Muslim Matrimony*. Available at www.muslimmatrimony.com, accessed 15 August 2018.

Nikah.com, 2019. *Muslim Matrimony*. Available at https://nikah.com, accessed 14 August 2018.

Pal, J. K., 2010. Social Networks Enabling Matrimonial Information Services in India. *International Journal of Library and Information Science* 2(4), 54–64.

Pfeffer, G, 1985. Formen der Ehe: Ethnologische Typologie der Heiratsbeziehungen. In: Völger, G. and v. Welck, K., eds. *Die Braut: Geliebt, verkauft, getauscht, geraubt. Zur Rolle der Frau im Kulturvergleich*, vol. 1. Köln: Ethnologica, 60–71.

Puri, J., 1999. *Woman, Body, Desire in Post-colonial India: Narratives of Gender and Sexuality*. New York: Routledge.

Schneider, N.-C. and Gräf, B., 2011. Introduction. In: Schneider, N.-C. and Gräf, B., eds. *Social Dynamics 2.0: Researching Change in Times of Media Convergence: Case Studies from the Middle East and Asia*, Berlin: Frank & Timme, 9–26.

Schneider, N.-C., 2014. Medien in Indien. *Zwischen Globalisierung, Ausdifferenzierung und bedrohter Glaubwürdigkeit*. Bundeszentrale für politische Bildung. Available at www.bpb.de/internationales/asien/indien/44549/medien, accessed 10 March 2015.

Secondshaadi.com, n.d. *Second Shaadi*. Available at www.secondshaadi.com, accessed 14 August 2018.

Sengupta, D., 2015. Matrimonial Sites Witness 50–100% Surge in Demand for Match Making. *Economic Times*, [online] 21 March. Available at https://economictimes.indiatimes.com/small-biz/startups/matrimonial-sites-witness-50-100-surge-in-demand-for-match-making/articleshow/46641762.cms, accessed 10 April 2018.

Seth, N. and Patnayakuni, R., 2009. Online Matrimonial Sites and the Transformation of Arranged Marriage in India. In: Romm-Livermore, C. and Setzekorn, K., eds. *Social Networking Communities and e-dating Services: Concepts and Implications.* Hershey: Information Science Reference, 329–352.

Shaadi.com, 1996–2019. The No.1 Matchmaking, Matrimony & Matrimonial Site. Available at www.shaadi.com, accessed 14 August 2018.

Shaadi.com, 2018. *Celebrating 21 Years of Innovation.* Available at www.shaadi.com/introduction/index/celebrating-n-years, accessed 17 May 2018.

Sharma, A., 2008. Caste on Indian Marriage dot-com: Presence and Absence. In: Gajjala, R. and Gajjala, V., eds. *South Asian Technospaces.* New York: Lang, 135–151.

Shukla, S. and Kapadia, S., 2007. Transition in Marriage Partner Selection Process: Are Matrimonial Advertisements an Indication? *Psychology and Developing Societies* 19(1), 37–54.

SikhingYou.com. 2013. Available online at www.sikhingyou.com, accessed 10 January 2013.

Skoda, U., 2002. *Forever yours: Mobility and Equilibrium in Indian Marriage.* New Delhi: Mosaic.

Titzmann, F.-M., 2014. *Der indische Online-Heiratsmarkt. Medienpraktiken und Frauenbilder im Wandel.* Berlin: Frank & Timme.

TrinityMatrimony.com. 2013. Available at www.trinitymatrimony.com, accessed 10 January 2013.

Uberoi, P., 2003. The Family in India. Beyond the Nuclear versus Joint Debate. In: Das, V., ed. *Oxford India Companion to Sociology and Social Anthropology.* Delhi: Oxford University Press, 1061–1103.

3 Automatic rituals and inadvertent audiences

ISKCON, Krishna and the ritual mechanics of Facebook

Nicole Karapanagiotis

Introduction

I remember clearly the day I arrived in ISKCON Mayapur to conduct fieldwork on the International Society for Krishna Consciousness (ISKCON). In the early evening hours, just before I walked into my guest room in the Conch Building, I recall looking out of the window in amazement at my room's close proximity to the temple. As I pensively unpacked my bags for my week-long stay during the cold winter week of the Christmas holidays, I remember hearing reverberating all around me – from the temple and from the streets, and into my guestroom – the loud and upbeat chanting of Krishna's names. As I stood in my room listening, I remember feeling palpably the devotional draw of the place, understanding why so many pilgrims would travel from so far to immerse themselves in the place which, at that moment, felt to be the devotional heart of ISKCON. But these feelings of peace and joy also shared a space in my experience with an anxious fear: a fear that I might never be able to fall asleep during my stay in Mayapur. Because this, as it turns out, is exactly what happened: the joyfully loud chanting of Krishna's names continued throughout the night and into the early morning not only on my first day there, but on every day during my stay. And after several days of my stay had passed, I understood the meaning behind something I had been told about Mayapur before I visited. Mayapur, I was told, is a "special place" because it is a place "where you can't help but hear the names of Krishna at all moments...even if you don't want to hear them, you will".[1]

Within ISKCON Mayapur, one can, in fact, hear a near continual chanting of Krishna's names from almost every corner of the walled complex. This chanting can be heard not only from the temple, but also from a chanting hut (*bhajan kuṭīr*)[2] on the premises, which features a staged, 24-hour-a-day continuous *kīrtan*.[3] It can also be heard, most prominently, from the chanting groups (known as *saṅkīrtan parties*) that dance through the streets of the complex numerous times a day, singing the famous *mahāmantra* with the accompaniment of musical instruments, microphones, large portable speaker systems and, often, large groups of pilgrims as well (Figure 3.1).

Figure 3.1 ISKCON Mayapur chanting group. Groups are known as *saṅkīrtan* parties. A *saṅkīrtan* party moves along the streets of ISKCON Mayapur, singing the *mahāmantra*. Musical instruments – including *karatālas* (cymbals), a harmonium and a *mṛdaṅga* drum – accompany the singing, all of which play loudly over a large speaker that sits in the bicycle's basket. ISKCON Mayapur, 22 December 2015. Photograph taken by author.

The practice of singing the names of Krishna in the form of a congregational and public chant is called *saṅkīrtan* (lit. to sing or praise loudly). As Delmonico (2007, 549) writes:

> *Kirtana* means "praising" or "glorifying," and *sankirtana* means loudly praising or glorifying. *Sankirtana* often takes the form of the congregational singing of Krishna's names with the accompaniment of various kinds of musical instruments (drums, cymbals, harmoniums, and so forth). As the singing becomes emotionally charged, various kinds of dancing often break out as well. *Sankirtana* is generally a public performance, in that it is often carried out in public areas such as the streets and the squares of villages, towns and cities.

In traditional ISKCON theology, the power of *saṅkīrtan* has a twofold basis. Primarily, its power derives from the fact that devotees believe that

Krishna himself is present in the holy name.[4] As Delmonico (2007, 550) puts it, devotees believe that "by vocalizing or even just remembering his names, one is brought into the presence of Krishna himself". This view is derived from the *Bhaktirasāmṛtasindhu* of Rupa Goswamin, for example, verse 1.2.233 (as well as the *Padma Purāṇa*), wherein it is stated that "the holy name is the giver of wishes; it is the embodied form of consciousness itself; it is whole, pure, and eternally unbound. The holy name and named (Krishna) are identical" (*nāma cintāmaṇiḥ kṛṣṇaścaitanyarasavigrahaḥ/pūrṇah śuddho nityyamukto'bhinnatvānnāmanāmiṇoḥ// iti/*). The Vrindavan Goswamins referred to this idea as *Nāmanāminoradvaita* or *Nāmanāminorabheda*, "the nondifference between the Named One and the Name" (Hein 1994, 21). In fact, "Jīva Goswāmin in his *Bhagavata-Saṁdarbha* states the main point bluntly: *bhagavat-svarūpam eva nāma*, 'The Name is the very essence [or embodied form] of the Lord'" (Hein 1994, 21). Echoing these Vaishnava theologians who came before him, A. C. Bhaktivedanta Swami Prabhupada – the founder of the ISKCON movement – himself, on numerous occasions, remarked about the equivalence of Krishna's name and Krishna's very self: "The holy name of Kṛṣṇa", he said, "is as good as Kṛṣṇa Himself. Since Kṛṣṇa and His holy name are identical, the holy name is eternally pure and beyond material contamination. It is the Supreme Personality of Godhead [*Puruṣottama*] as a transcendental vibration" (Prabhupada 1973a, 7.74 [purport]).

Besides the belief that the names of Krishna are non-different from Krishna's very form or *svarūpa* itself, there is another dimension of *saṅkīrtan* that contributes to its perceived power within the ISKCON movement. This dimension has to do with *saṅkīrtan*'s purported capacity to ritually affect not only those actively engaged in the singing, but also those who passively hear it: even those – and perhaps especially those – who do so inadvertently. This is a ritual feature of *saṅkīrtan* that Swami Prabhupada explained in his lectures. For example, in a 4 January 1973 lecture, he told his devotees that their *saṅkīrtan* efforts can save all livings beings, even animals. "Everyone can hear", he (Prabhupada 1973b) said:

> Even they [who] do not understand what is Hare Kṛṣṇa, if you chant loudly Hare Kṛṣṇa, even the ants and insect who is hearing, he'll be delivered, because it [the Name] is spiritual vibration. It will act for everyone ...Just like fire. The fire will act, either you are human being or insect. If you touch fire, it will do its work. Similarly, Hare Kṛṣṇa mahā-mantra is transcendental vibration. When we chant loudly, anyone who hears—it doesn't matter whether he's man, animal, tree, insect—anyone who will hear, he'll get profit. This is transcendental vibration.

Put differently, ISKCON devotees believe that, despite the intention (or even understanding) of the audience, *saṅkīrtan* has the power to automatically affect those who hear it, even those who do so passively or inadvertently. In this regard, devotees often compare *saṅkīrtan* to medicine, which works to cure disease irrespective of a patient's intentions.[5] *Saṅkīrtan* is, for these reasons, an example of a type of ritual within ISKCON that I call an "automatic ritual".[6]

Within ISKCON, there are a number of such "automatic rituals", or rituals that devotees believe have the power to affect the public automatically, or inadvertently, and without their intention. For example, Zeller (2012) and King (2012) have written about one such ritual in ISKCON, namely, the eating of *prasādam*. *Prasādam* is food that, having been offered to Krishna, devotees eat and then serve to others. Devotees believe that Krishna eats food that is offered to him, and in so doing touches it with his grace – a grace that automatically moves the heart of anyone who eats it, regardless of their intention. Besides *saṅkīrtan* and *prasādam*, another ritual in ISKCON that works on a similar mechanism is the ritual of *rathayātrā*: a practice wherein an embodied form of Krishna (*mūrti*) is brought to the public streets and wheeled around on a chariot, with the belief that anyone who sees this form (even if unwittingly) will develop a seed of love for Krishna in their hearts (Dāsa 2008). ISKCON is a proselytizing religion, which means that devotees actively aim to bring converts into their movement. What is powerful about these automatic rituals, therefore – according to ISKCON devotees – is that they put the public in a position to be preached to without their signing up for it. That is, they allow the public to become *inadvertent recipients* of ISKCON's proselytizing efforts: to be preached to without their even knowing it.

In this chapter, I will explore one of ISKCON's newest forms of ritual practice, namely, the posting of Krishna's digital images on Facebook. I will argue that though it is a historically new practice in ISKCON, it is nonetheless an example of an automatic ritual, because, like ISKCON's other automatic rituals, it sets people up to be *inadvertent recipients* of ISKCON's preaching. This argument requires some degree of setup to get off the ground, so I will build it over the next few sections. I will begin, however, with a brief discussion of the ISKCON movement.

The International Society for Krishna Consciousness (ISKCON)

ISKCON is a Vaishnava (Vishnu- or Krishna-centered) religious movement that has its roots in the Bengali Vaishnava form of Hinduism known as Gaudiya Vaishnavism. Like all Gaudiya Vaishnavas, ISKCON devotees trace their tradition back to the sixteenth-century Bengali saint Chaitanya – a key Hindu religious figure who promoted the ecstatic worship of god Krishna through the practice of *saṅkīrtan* (the public chanting of Krishna's names).[7]

Though there are many schools of Chaitanya Vaishnavism, ISKCON devotees trace their particular lineage to Chaitanya through Bhaktisiddhanta

Saraswati (1874–1937): the Bengali-born son of prominent Vaishnava intellectual Bhaktivinoda Thakura (1838–1914). Bhaktisiddhanta Saraswati was the guru of A. C. Bhaktivedanta Swami Prabhupada (1896–1977), the founder of the ISKCON movement. In 1965, Swami Prabhupada left his home in India and boarded a freight ship to the United States. In so doing, he was executing the wishes of Bhaktisiddhanta Saraswati: he traveled to the United States because he hoped to start a worldwide devotional movement (ISKCON). He believed this movement would bring not only global love of Krishna, but also an end to the myriad of miseries he believed plagued the Western world.

Arriving in New York City in 1965, Swami Prabhupada was able to draw American youth to the ISKCON movement in droves.[8] Today, ISKCON enjoys widespread global success. ISKCON's official 50th anniversary commemorative piece, *The Hare Krishnas: Celebrating 50 Years* (Goswami and Devi Dasi 2016), reports that as of July 2016, there are 650 ISKCON centers, temples, schools and colleges worldwide. Besides centers, temples and educational institutions, ISKCON also owns and manages 110 worldwide vegetarian restaurants, as well as 65 farms and eco-villages. What is more, ISKCON devotees run an estimated 3,600 home study (*bhakti vṛkṣa*) groups each week, as well as a number of regular programs at universities and colleges, parks and other public meeting spaces (Goswami and Devi Dasi 2016).[9] Besides the many global centers and programs that it runs, ISKCON is also flourishing in terms of its number of worldwide practitioners. According to ISKCON's most recent official report, 95,000 people have taken formal initiation into the movement since 1966 (Goswami and Devi Dasi 2016, 6), though ISKCON's Governing Body Commission (GBC) estimates that the actual number of people who worship at ISKCON each year is around nine million (and many on the GBC feel this number is conservative).[10]

The main reason why ISKCON has had such widespread global success has to do with the fact that Swami Prabhupada encouraged an intense evangelism amongst his disciples. This preaching imperative remains a central tenet of the movement today, and contemporary devotees base much of their religious praxis on preaching: that is, in trying to spread love of Krishna worldwide. There are a number of ways in which devotees enact this imperative today: ranging from book distribution (also called *saṅkīrtan* within ISKCON), *rathayātrās* (public chariot processions) and also public preaching programs.[11] Many of these preaching strategies can be grouped as automatic rituals. This evangelism includes ISKCON's newest automatic ritual, sharing Krishna's digital images on Facebook.

Krishna and Krishna's images within ISKCON

In order to explain posting Krishna's digital images on Facebook as a type of automatic ritual, it is first necessary to explain what exactly ISKCON devotees believe Krishna's digital images to be. This requires that we first understand how they see Krishna.

Within ISKCON, Krishna is defined to be the "Supreme Personality of Godhead". Though this translation to English is perhaps a bit awkward, it is a direct translation of the Sanskrit term *Puruṣottama*: that Being, depicted in the 15th chapter of the *Bhagavadgītā*, who is identified as the *Ultimate Person* because he is beyond both the changing (*kṣara*) and unchanging (*akṣara*) dimensions of existence: "*dvāv imau puruṣau loke kṣaraścākṣara eva ca/ kṣaraḥ sarvāṇi bhūtāni kūṭastho'kṣara ucyate*" (Bhagavadgītā 15.16) "*...yasmāt kṣaram atīto'ham akṣarād api cottamaḥ/ ato'smi loke vede ca prathitaḥ puruṣottamaḥ*" (Bhagavadgītā 15.18).[12]

In understanding Krishna as the "Supreme Person", those within the ISKCON movement mean two things. First, following Prabhupada's teachings, Krishna as the Supreme Person is understood to be the *cause of all causes*: the ultimate and original Being from whom and because of whom all else has emanated. But ISKCON's theology of Krishna's divine personhood is a complex one, one which freely interweaves Krishna's supremacy on the one hand, with his intimacy on the other. Far more than a distant, primeval God, ISKCON devotees believe Krishna to also be a being embodied in a human-like form: one whose life stories (*līlās*) they can trace, whose birth place they can locate, whose bodily form they can artistically depict and, most importantly, whose love and friendship they can palpably feel in a daily, intimate and life-altering personal relationship. This personal relationship that Krishna grants to his followers, devotees believe, is an act of his grace and mercy. Out of love, they believe, Krishna the Absolute comes to inhabit a personality with whom his devotees can lovingly relate: someone they can think of, remember, talk to and even cook for (see Deadwyler 1985; Valpey 2006).

The primary way in which Krishna graces devotees and allows them to have a personal relationship with him is by descending as materially embodied, three-dimensional forms, known as *mūrtis* (or in ISKCON, as *deities*). Within ISKCON, the *mūrti* or deity is typically housed in the temple, though many devotees also have *mūrtis* in their homes. Typically made of clay or stone, the *mūrti* is understood to be a living and embodied form of Krishna: Krishna's gracious and willful descending of himself as tangible materiality so as to facilitate a close relationship with his devotees. Through his *mūrti* forms, Krishna takes on a materially intimate existence: one that his devotees can see, touch, tend to and lovingly care for. According to William H. Deadwyler, a prominent ISKCON devotee-scholar,

> God descends as the *arcāvatāra* at the request of his pure devotee to aid those less advanced in the removal of their ignorance. In his *arcā* form God graciously comes to dwell among us, to be visible even to materially limited senses, and to allow the devotees to become totally absorbed in body, mind, and senses in the devotional service of the Lord. (Deadwyler 1985, 82)

For ISKCON devotees then, the *mūrti* is not merely a representation or symbol for Krishna – the *mūrti is* Krishna (see Deadwyler 1985; Valpey 2006). As Prabhupada himself said,

> never think of the Deity as made of stone or wood. Every worshipper must remember that Kṛṣṇa is personally present [as the Deity]. He is simply kindly presenting Himself before us in a way so that we can handle Him. That is His mercy, otherwise He is unapproachable. (Deadwyler 1985, 83)

ISKCON devotees believe that because these *mūrtis* are Krishna himself, being in their presence – and seeing them and being seen by them (*darshan*) – is a ritual act of great significance (see, e.g., Eck 1996). In fact, devotees believe that seeing a *mūrti* form of Krishna does something to the heart of the viewer – changing it – and moving it (evermore) toward love of Krishna. What is more, many devotees believe *darshan*'s ritual power works automatically – that is, in the same way as that of *saṅkīrtan*. This makes sense given the parallels between *saṅkīrtan* and *darshan*: in *saṅkīrtan*, the public encounters a sonic form (*mūrti*) of Krishna, and in *darshan*, they encounter a material form (*mūrti*) of him.

With the advent of new digital technology, many ISKCON devotees have come to believe that Krishna can be fully manifest as digital forms (*mūrtis*) as well (Karapanagiotis 2018).[13] ISKCON devotees use a number of texts to justify this position, including – most prominently – the *Bhāgavatapurāṇa*[14] and the *Bhagavadgītā*.[15] They also cite a number of personal religious beliefs based on the teachings of Swami Prabhupada and the corpus of texts from which he drew. For example, devotees have told me that "Krishna is there in the online photos",[16] and that the Vedic scriptures elucidate this by

> giving the example of the sun. The rays of the sun are equal to the sun—in every situation, whether it is a palace or a filthy place, wherever they shine, the rays shine equally. Similarly, Krishna is absolute, so he can relate to a person from several different levels. This can be from a photograph, the computer, the temple, everywhere his mercy is there.[17]

This view was even expressed by the head *pujārī* (priest) at ISKCON Mayapur:

> we consider that the same Krishna is in the temple, in the home, in photographs on the computer. The difference is only the schedule that they live by. At the temple they have a strict schedule you know, and in the home they follow the householder schedule. But we consider them equal, it is the same person. They are all considered different forms of the Lord we worship.[18]

That Krishna's digital images are full forms of him (*mūrtis*) is a view that devotees consistently expressed to me in my conversations with them throughout the United States and India. For this reason, in the remainder of this chapter, I will refer to these digital images as *digital forms*.

Because ISKCON devotees believe that digital forms of Krishna are full forms of him, many of them also believe that taking their *darshan* (digital *darshan*)[19] works automatically to rouse love of Krishna in the hearts of those who view them, just as this love is automatically roused in viewers' hearts by seeing Krishna's other material forms (*darshan*) or hearing his sonic forms (*saṅkīrtan*).[20] As one administrator at ISKCON of New Delhi put it:

> It comes to a similar analogy that Srila Prabhupada's guru, Bhaktisiddhanta, he has given that in the *bhakti* tradition, we say that names of the Lord are equal to the Lord himself. They are non-different. So that's why we go out on the *saṅkīrtan* —we do the *kīrtan* on the streets so that when I chant on the street you may hear it. So basically it is helping you. So similarly, [although] you can come to the temple and see the lord, there is also other form of the lord which shows the compassionate nature of Krishna and through this form we bring Krishna to others. So someone can see this online photograph of Krishna and have some sort of change occurring inside from seeing this form of the Lord. It comes to a similar analogy.[21]

Since many ISKCON devotees believe that seeing a digital form of Krishna can automatically rouse love in viewers' hearts, they post Krishna's digital forms on a number of ISKCON's websites, as well as ISKCON's video channels and television channels (Karapanagiotis 2018). The goal is to provide members of the public with as much opportunity as possible to see these forms and take Krishna's digital *darshan*.

Posting Krishna's digital forms on Facebook

Despite the fact that the digital forms of Krishna that are posted on ISKCON's websites, video channels and television channels are believed to have the potential to automatically generate love of Krishna in the hearts of those who view them, ISKCON devotees believe that the preaching potential of websites, video channels and television channels is limited. This is because the setup of these sites is such that members of the public must actively (i.e., intentionally) make their way to these sites and channels in order to see Krishna's digital forms that are posted there. This requires not only that these members of the public already know about these sites and channels, but also that they take the time and the initiative to seek them out. Because the social media site Facebook works in a different way, it is the preferred digital form posting site for ISKCON devotees.

Facebook is the world's most ubiquitous social media site. Though it started off as a platform designed exclusively for college students, its going public in 2006 "led to a large influx of high school students and younger teens, as well as adult users of the site" (Johns 2012, 151–152). In July of 2010, Facebook had over a half a billion users (Johns 2012, 152); as of 2017, it was approaching almost two billion (Fiegerman 2017).

As a social media site, Facebook is popular because it allows its users to post photos and other images, status updates, news articles, videos and various other forms of media. The audience for this sharing is one's circle of Facebook friends: a group of people, large or small, with whom the user has agreed to share her various media on the site. As a social media site, however, Facebook is not just for viewing (and/or reading) the media of one's circle of friends; rather, the site also allows for users to *respond to* what their friends post. For example, users can *react or emote* to their friends' posts by *liking* them, *loving* them, responding with *surprise*, as well as a variety of other emotional responses. More than this, users can also *comment on* their friends' posts: offering enthusiastic support, making witty remarks and/or posing questions, replies or responses to other commenters. Finally, friends can also *share* the media that they see on Facebook: that is, if one sees on her Facebook feed that one of her friends has posted an interesting story, beautiful image and so forth, she can share – that is, repost – that story, image and so forth for her own circle of friends to see. In this regard, Facebook is a dynamic site, allowing users to re-share and re-mediate content as they fancy.

Though Facebook users can see, comment on and share the media that their friends post on the site, their friends' content is not the only media that users can see. Rather, given the site's algorithm design, Facebook users can often also see, read and watch the media *that their friends like, comment on and so forth*. In other words, if I am friends with user X on Facebook, then not only can I see all of the media that user X posts on the site, but I can often also see the media that user X *likes, comments on and so forth*. This means that if user Y posts a picture, video and so on on Facebook that user X likes, then I have a good chance of also seeing user Y's picture, video and so on *even if user Y is not my friend on the site*. In this regard, the viewership radius for Facebook media is extremely wide, with users being able to see media that extends beyond just that posted by their own friends.

It is this wide viewership radius of Facebook that makes it ISKCON devotees' preferred site for posting digital forms of Krishna. Further, it is this particular feature of the site that allows the posting of Krishna's digital forms on Facebook to be an example of an automatic ritual. This is because it gives ISKCON preachers the chance to turn a wide (and often unwitting) public into *inadvertent recipients* of their preaching. Many ISKCON Facebook administrators discuss this. As one ISKCON Facebook administrator in Vrindavan put it:

> I am using Facebook page for preaching. I am using Facebook page to preach because we don't just share, but sometimes others they also share our photos on Facebook. So we get normally like eighty shares everyday on photos. Eighty to one hundred shares. So suppose you are not related to ISKCON, and are not in ISKCON, and you see some of these deity photos that are shared by the others. And you see some deity photos, like photos of Krishna Balarama. So then you see like, ok, this photo is interesting, and you get inspired. Krishna is in the photos there, so there are so many people who doesn't even know what it is, who doesn't know who is Krishna, they get inspired by looking at the photos that are shared by the others and from that they start coming to the temple and becoming interested in devotional life.[22]

This administrator is not (just) talking about the inspiration that people get from seeing the photos that he himself shares on Facebook. Rather, he is discussing the photos of Krishna that people see because *others* shared his photos, and the inspiration and love that they draw from seeing them. Put simply, for him as a preacher, the beauty of posting Krishna's digital forms (these photos) on Facebook has to do with the fact that he can reach people who are not his Facebook friends: that is, he can reach a wide audience of unwitting people who never signed up to be preached to. This view was expressed by a number of other Facebook administrators in ISKCON. As an administrator in Delhi put it:

> People relate to Krishna on many, many levels. Our deities are beautiful, so many people actually relate to the deities. So by sharing these photos every time on Facebook, we are actually helping people relate to the form of the lord. And, ya know, people are looking for that. But also, let's say I share to my friends who are 1,000 friends, and you are one of those friends. If you are also one of those similar minded people [who relate to the deities] and basically you get attracted to it, then you will also share it. So then it becomes a whole chain that's being created because eventually one thing leads to another and one of your friends sees it and also he becomes attracted. And then he might inquire ok why do you worship, how do you worship. So Facebook works like this.[23]

As can be seen from this statement, like the previous one, the perceived benefit of preaching via sharing Krishna's digital forms on Facebook is that this ritual is automatic: not only do the temple's 1,000 friends see the digital forms of Krishna that the temple administrators share, but if any of these 1,000 friends share, like or comment on these forms, *then their friends might also see them*. And they see them despite the fact that they didn't sign up to see them or volunteer to see them. Just like the people who, sipping their afternoon tea at a roadside tea stall, might inadvertently hear a *saṅkīrtan* as it passes by them on the road, users on Facebook might similarly encounter a form of Krishna as they are going about their ordinary Facebook business: watching videos, catching up with friends or arguing about politics. And if they encounter a form of Krishna, many devotees believe, love of Krishna will necessarily grow in their hearts even if they don't intend it to. For many ISKCON devotees, therefore, posting digital forms of Krishna on Facebook is a perfect form of preaching.

Conclusion

Throughout this chapter, I have argued that as one of ISKCON's newest ritual practices, posting digital forms of Krishna on Facebook is a fresh ritual spin on an old theme: namely, it is ISKCON's latest example of an automatic ritual. As I have defined them, automatic rituals in ISKCON are those that are perceived to work by virtue of the fact that they set up audiences to be inadvertent recipients of ISKCON's preaching: in particular, by placing these audiences in contact with forms of Krishna. Just like *saṅkīrtan* is an automatic ritual insofar as it sets up unwitting audiences to encounter a sonic form (*mūrti*) of Krishna on the streets, so too does posting Krishna's digital forms on Facebook set up unwitting audiences to encounter digital forms (*mūrtis*) of Krishna. These Facebook audiences consist of the people who see Krishna's digital forms on their Facebook feeds simply because their friends have liked or otherwise reacted to (or shared) them. In this chapter, therefore, my aim was to showcase the ways in which ISKCON's traditional ritual logics are being amended to new media ritual forms. If one goal of ISKCON preaching is to reach as many audiences as possible, then ISKCON devotees are successfully using Facebook in order to greatly expand the possible pools of inadvertent recipients of their preaching. In fact, if friends of friends of friends of ISKCON administrators can now see forms of Krishna on Facebook without ever having signed up or intending to do so, then it seems that the sky is the proverbial limit for how many people might one day become inadvertent recipients of this preaching.

In repurposing an old theology with a new ritual form, ISKCON devotees have greatly expanded the potential radius for who might get to be an audience of their preaching. Besides this, however, it is interesting to consider for a moment whether they might also have expanded the parameters of who is considered a preacher. Put simply, if many ISKCON devotees believe that the spreading of Krishna's forms to the public is an act of preaching because these forms rouse love of Krishna in the hearts of anyone who encounters them, is it the case that these devotees believe that *anyone* who shares these forms is a preacher? If so, might this include those people on Facebook who share Krishna's digital forms with their friends simply by *liking* them or *commenting on* them, thereby causing them to show up in their friends' Facebook feeds? In other words, is there room in ISKCON theology for inadvertent preachers just as there is room for inadvertent recipients of preaching? By way of an answer, it would certainly seem to be the case that there is such room, given ISKCON's broader conceptual framework. In fact, anthropologist Malcolm Haddon has argued that "by the 'transcendental' logic of Hare Krishna theology", it is probable that even "ethnography 'of' *sankirtana* [is] also a 'form of' *sankirtana*" (Haddon 2013, 251). But what is far more interesting than tracking the specific theological answers to these questions will be to examine the ways in which ISKCON devotees *operationalize them* over time, incorporating them into the logics of traditional ritual practices and using them to innovate the design of ever more new ritual forms. And this innovative spirit is, after all, at the heart of the ISKCON project. "Prabhupada", devotees say, "used all of the technology available to him" so that he could best spread the ISKCON movement "according to time, place, and circumstance" to people all over the world.[24] As such, devotees say that they are committed to doing the same. As one high-ranking ISKCON administrator put it,

> if there is the Internet, let me use it for Krishna. If there is Facebook and Instagram and things that I don't even know what they are, let me use them for Krishna. Is there a way to use them for Krishna?[25]

Though it is too early to tell of all the ways in which ISKCON devotees will use these various platforms for Krishna, it is nonetheless an exciting time for scholars of Hinduism, of religion and new media and of ISKCON as we await the amalgamation of theological and ritual possibilities as ISKCON devotees combine their movement's own interest in innovation to preaching with the latest innovations in digital media and technology. The possibilities are endless.

Notes

1 Personal communication via Skype with ISKCON devotee, 1 July 2015. This chapter reflects a small part of a multiyear, multisited and multimodal ethnography that I conducted on the ISKCON movement in India and the USA during 2014–2017. During this time, I conducted a number of formal and informal interviews with devotees, administrators and gurus in the ISKCON movement. I also engaged in much informal conversation with them, and spent much time with them in their homes, temples and at other events and settings in locations including Delhi, Mumbai, Vrindavan, Mayapur and others in India, and New Jersey, Philadelphia, Washington, D.C., and others in the USA. I am thankful to all of the devotees who graciously gave their time and good spirits during my research. I have omitted all devotees' names in this chapter to retain their anonymity. Finally, in this research, I have also worked with a number of primary source texts. All translations in this chapter (from Sanskrit and Hindi) are mine.

2 Italics and diacritical marks have been used for Hindi and Sanskrit words throughout this chapter. However, diacritics have been omitted for commonly used words (such as *darshan* and *bhakti*) as well as for proper and personal names (such as Gaudiya and Prabhupada).

3 Sources note that there has been a continuous, 24/7 chanting of Krishna's names in this hut since 1990, even during the 1999, 2000 and 2006 years when Mayapur was hit with devastating floods. See ISKCON Mayapur.

4 ISKCON devotees cite numerous texts for this belief, principally ISKCON founder Swami Prabhupada's various purports on the *Bhāgavata Purāṇa* (known in ISKCON as the *Śrīmad Bhāgavatam*) as well as the *Śikṣāṣṭakam* of Chaitanya. See Prabhupada (1974). For the *Śikṣāṣṭakam,* see Dimock (1999, *Antya Līlā*, chapter 20). Various pdfs of Prabhupada's translation of the *Śikṣāṣṭakam* are available online. See, for example, Prabhupāda (1968). For more discussion, see Delmonico (2007) and Hein (1994).

5 The following conversation appeared in an article in the *Back to Godhead* magazine, the main periodical of the ISKCON movement. In this conversation (Dasa 2006), a devotee recalls a conversation that he had with his barber: a man named "Alex."

> "Alex had seen groups of people chanting on the streets, and he asked, 'Is chanting all that your religion does? Don't you do welfare or anything like that?'
>
> 'We do welfare work,' I responded, 'but it's welfare for the soul.'...I told him that the chanting itself is the greatest welfare, because it invokes the presence of the Lord in the form of His name. When we chant in public, everyone who hears is benefited by association with the Lord. Thus, *sankirtana* is welfare.
>
> [Following this], Alex said that he didn't want to offend me, but he had noticed that many people who see the Hare Krishna chanting groups don't understand what we're doing. He asked, 'How is that welfare, if they don't understand?'
>
> I explained that the effect of the chanting doesn't depend on our understanding. I used the example of a medicine we take to cure a disease. We swallow the pills, but we don't need to know how they act. After some time, the medicine takes effect, and the disease goes away. Similarly, the chanting acts to cure the soul of its disease, which is bondage to maya."

6 David L. Haberman (2014) developed the idea of "accidental ritualists": individuals who unknowingly perform religious rituals, yet who, by so doing, inadvertently reap transformative results. As Haberman notes, "more important than any other factor—such as intentionality" for those who are accidental ritualists, "ritual action itself is identified as the transformative agent...physical imitative action itself is clearly endorsed, regardless of knowledge or intention. Putting the body in the physical groove of ritual action is lifted up as foremost among the possible transformative elements" (Haberman 2014, 154).

7 Chaitanya believed Krishna's names to be sonic forms of Krishna himself.

8 Many books discuss the early years of ISKCON and its official founding in the USA. These include Rochford (1985), Squarcini and Fizzotti (2004), Dwyer and Cole (2007) and Bromley and Shinn (1989).

9 This magazine is the official commemorative periodical for the 50th anniversary of ISKCON, and is produced by ISKCON Communications International. It contains a set of statistical data for the movement, data which contain both the most recent and the most accurate statistical counts for the movement, according to ISKCON's International Minister of Communications Governing Body Commissioner.

10 Personal communication via Skype with ISKCON's International Minister of Communications Governing Body Commissioner, 30 January 2017.

11 This account is also given in Karapanagiotis 2018.

12 Prasad 1995. Though many Vaishnavas interpret *Puruṣottama* to mean the Supreme Being whose body subsumes both the changing (*kṣara*) and unchanging worlds (*akṣara*), the traditional ISKCON gloss on *Puruṣottama* tends to highlight Krishna's transcendental superiority over the *kṣara* and the *akṣara*, rather than his ontological inclusion of them.

13 Many Hindus, not just devotees in ISKCON, hold this position. For a broad discussion of positions on this issue, see Karapanagiotis (2013). This present chapter, however – like Karapanagiotis 2018 – discusses only the viewpoints of ISKCON devotees, not Hindus more generally.
14 Several devotees cite verse 11.27.12 of the *Bhāgavata Purāṇa*. This verse states *śailī dārumayī lauhī lepyā lekhyā ca saikatī/ manomayī maṇimayī pratimāṣṭavidhā smṛtā* (Goswami and Shastri 2003): "It is taught that embodied forms (*pratimā* [like *mūrtis*]) are of eight types: those made of stone, wood, metal, plaster, paint (or drawing), sand, mind (*manomayī*), and jewels". Devotees noted that digital images of Krishna are like those made of paint (or are made of paint).
15 Some devotees explained to me their belief that the very first *śloka* of the *Bhagavad-Gītā* predicts the use of the webcam to broadcast digital forms of Krishna remotely.
16 ISKCON Vrindavan Facebook Administrator. *Personal Interview of ISKCON Vrindavan Facebook Administrator.* Interviewed by Nicole Karapanagiotis. [in person], Vrindavan, 7 January 2016.
17 ISKCON Delhi Facebook Administrator. 2015. *Personal Interview of ISKCON Delhi Facebook Administrator.* Interviewed by Nicole Karapanagiotis. [in person] Delhi, 31 December 2015.
18 ISKCON Mayapur Head *Pujārī*. 2015. *Personal Interview of ISKCON Mayapur Head Pujārī.* Interviewed by Nicole Karapanagiotis. [in person] Mayapur, 24 December 2015.
19 Digital darshan can be defined as an "online reconfiguration of the Hindu ritual tradition of darshan", which "harnesses Web technologies and network space to represent [or foster] the act of seeing the sacred image" (Mallapragada 2010, 114). Besides Mallapragada (2010), there are a number of important works on digital *darshan*. See Herman (2010), Karapanagiotis (2013) and Scheifinger (2008, 2009, 2010).
20 Though all ISKCON devotees with whom I have worked agree that digital forms of Krishna are full, and ontologically real forms of him (*mūrtis*), not all devotees believe that digital forms automatically rouse love of Krishna in all viewers. In particular, there is a subset of ISKCON devotees who believe that digital forms of Krishna do not work to rouse love of Krishna in those identified as "western newcomers". For a full discussion of the complexities of this issue, see Karapanagiotis (2018).
21 ISKCON Delhi Facebook Administrator. 2015. *Personal Interview of ISKCON Delhi Facebook Administrator.* Interviewed by Nicole Karapanagiotis. [in person] Delhi, 31 December 2015.
22 ISKCON Vrindavan Facebook Administrator. *Personal Interview of ISKCON Vrindavan Facebook Administrator.* Interviewed by Nicole Karapanagiotis. [in person], Vrindavan, 7 January 2016.
23 ISKCON Delhi Facebook Administrator. 2015. *Personal Interview of ISKCON Delhi Facebook Administrator.* Interviewed by Nicole Karapanagiotis. [in person] Delhi, 31 December 2015.
24 Personal communication via phone with ISKCON devotee, 16 July 2014.
25 Personal communication via Skype with ISKCON's International Minister of Communications Governing Body Commissioner, 22 July 2014.

References

Bromley, D. G. and Shinn, L. D., eds., 1989. *Krishna Consciousness in the West.* Lewisburg: Bucknell University Press and Associated University Presses.

Dasa, D., 2006. Sankirtana: Welfare for All Beings. *Back to Godhead*, [online] September/October. Available at http://btg.krishna.com/sankirtana-welfare-all-beings, accessed 28 May 2018.

Dāsa, Ravīndra Svarūpa (W. Deadwyler), 2008. Śri Chaitanya at Ratha-Yātrā and God's Unrestrained Kindness. *Journal of Vaishnava Studies* 17(1), 43–56.

Deadwyler, W. H. III (Ravīndra-svarūpa dāsa), 1985. The Devotee and the Deity: Living a Personalistic Theology. In: Waghorne, J. P. and Cutler, N., eds. *Gods of Flesh, Gods of Stone*. New York: Columbia University Press, pp. 69–87.

Delmonico, N., 2007. Chaitanya Vaishnavism and the Holy Names. In: Bryant, E. F., ed. *Krishna: A Sourcebook*. Oxford and New York: Oxford University Press, 549–575.

Dimock, Jr., E. C. 1999. *Caitanya Caritāmṛta of Kṛṣṇadāsa Kavirāja: A Translation and Commentary*. Cambridge: Harvard University Press.

Dwyer, G. and Cole, R. J., eds., 2007. *The Hare Krishna Movement: Forty Years of Chant and Change*. London and New York: I. B. Tauris.

Eck, D. L., 1996. *Darśan: Seeing the Divine Image in India*. New York: Columbia University Press.

Fiegerman, S., 2017. *Facebook Is Closing in on 2 Billion Users*. Available at http://money.cnn.com/2017/02/01/technology/facebook-earnings/index.html, accessed 22 June 2018.

Gosvāmin, R., *Bhaktirasāmṛtasindhu*, 2003. *The Bhaktirasāmṛtasindhu of* Rūpa Gosvāmin. Translated with Introduction and Notes by D. L. Haberman. New Delhi and Delhi: Indira Gandhi National Centre for the Arts and Motilal Banarsidass Publishers.

Goswami, C. L. and Shastri, M. A., 2003. *Śrīmad Bhāgavata Mahāpurāṇa (With Sanskrit text and English Translation) Part—II [Book Nine to Twelve]*. Gorakhpur: Gita Press.

Goswami, M. and Devi Dasi, K., eds., 2016. *The Hare Krishnas: Celebrating 50 Years*. Potomac: ISKCON Communications International.

Haberman, D. L., 2014. The Accidental Ritualist. In: Penkower, L. and Pintchman, T., eds. *Hindu Ritual at the Margins: Innovations, Transformations, Reconsiderations*. Columbia: University of South Carolina Press, 151–165.

Haddon, M., 2013. Anthropological Proselytism: Reflexive Questions for a Hare Krishna Ethnography. *Australian Journal of Anthropology* 24(3), 250–269.

Hein, N., 1994. Chaitanya's Ecstasies and the Theology of the Name. *Journal of Vaishnava Studies* 2(2), 7–27.

Herman, P. K., 2010. Seeing the Divine through Windows: Online Puja and Virtual Religious Experience. *Online—Heidelberg Journal of Religions on the Internet* 4(1), 151–178.

ISKCON Delhi Facebook Administrator, 2015. *Personal Interview of ISKCON Delhi Facebook Administrator*. Interviewed by Nicole Karapanagiotis. [in person] Delhi, 31 December 2015.

ISKCON Mayapur, 2012. *ISKCON Mayapur Campus*. Available at www.mayapur.com/visit-mayapur/places-to-visit/iskcon-mayapur-campus/, accessed 26 May 2018.

ISKCON Mayapur Head *Pujārī*, 2015. *Personal Interview of ISKCON Mayapur Head Pujārī*. Interviewed by Nicole Karapanagiotis. [in person] Mayapur, 24 December 2015.

ISKCON Vrindavan Facebook Administrator, 2016. *Personal Interview of ISKCON Vrindavan Facebook Administrator.* Interviewed by Nicole Karapanagiotis. [in person], Vrindavan, 7 January 2016.
Johns, M. D., 2012. Voting "Present": Religious Organizational Groups on Facebook. In: Cheong, P. H., Fischer-Nielsen, P., Gelfgren, S. and Ess, C., eds. *Digital Religion, Social Media and Culture: Perspectives, Practices, and Futures.* New York: Peter Lang Publishing, 151–168.
Karapanagiotis, N., 2013. Cyber Forms, *Worshippable Forms*: Hindu Devotional Viewpoints on the Ontology of Cyber-Gods and Goddesses. *International Journal of Hindu Studies* 17(1), 57–82.
Karapanagiotis, N., 2018. Of Digital Images and Digital Media: Approaches to Marketing in American ISKCON. *Nova Religio: The Journal of Alternative and Emergent Religion* 21(3), 74–102.
King, A. S., 2012. Krishna's Prasadam: "Eating our way back to godhead". *Material Religion* 8(4), 440–465.
Mallapragada, M., 2010. Desktop Deities: Hindu Temples, Online Cultures and the Politics of Remediation. *South Asian Popular Culture* 8(2), 109–121.
Prabhupāda, A. C. Bhaktivedānta Swāmī, 1968. (From: "Teachings of Lord Caitanya, 1968). "*Śrī Śikṣāṣṭakam (Caitanya Mahāprabhu): The Eight Instructions of Lord Śrī Caitanya Mahāprabhu.*" Available at www.prabhupada-books.de/chaitanya/siksastakam_en.html, accessed 27 May 2018.
Prabhupada, A. C. Bhaktivedanta Swami, 1973a. *Śrī Caitanya-Caritāmṛta of Kṛṣṇadāsa Kavirāja Gosvāmi: Ādi-līlā Volume Two "Lord Caitanya Mahāprabhu in the Renounced Order of Life" with the original Bengali text, Roman transliterations, synonyms, Translation and Elaborate Purports.* New York, Los Angeles, London, Bombay: The Bhaktivedanta Book Trust.
Prabhupada, A. C. Bhaktivedanta Swami, 1973b. "The Nectar of Devotion – Bombay, January 4, 1973." *Lectures: Vaniquotes.* Available at https://vaniquotes.org/wiki/If_you_chant_loudly_Hare_Krsna,_even_the_ants_and_insect_who_is_hearing,_he'll_be_delivered,_because_it_is_spiritual_vibration._It_will_act_for_everyone, accessed 28 May 2018.
Prabhupada, A. C. Bhaktivedanta Swami, 1974. *Śrīmad-Bhāgavatam: With the Original Sanskrit Text, Its Roman Transliteration, Synonyms, Translation and Elaborate Purports by His Divine Grace A.C. Bhaktivedanta Swami Prabhupada Founder-Acarya of the International Society for Krishna Consciousness.* [e-book] Los Angeles: Bhaktivedanta Book Trust. Available through http://vanisource.org/wiki/Srimad-Bhagavatam, accessed 4 August 2018.
Prasad, R., 1995. *The Bhagavad-Gītā.* Delhi and Fremont: Motilal Banarsidass and The American Gita Society.
Rochford, E. B. Jr., 1985. *Hare Krishna in America.* New Brunswick: Rutgers University Press.
Scheifinger, H., 2010. Om-line Hinduism: World Wide Gods on the Web. *Journal for the Academic Study of Religion* 23(3), 325–345.
Scheifinger, H., 2009. The Jagannath Temple and Online Darshan. *Journal of Contemporary Religion* 24(3), 277–290.
Scheifinger, H., 2008. Hinduism and Cyberspace. *Religion* 38(3), 233–249.
Squarcini, F. and Fizzotti, E., 2004. *Hare Krishna.* Torino: Elle Di Ci, Leumann.

Valpey, K. R., 2006. *Attending Kṛṣṇa's Image: Caitanya Vaiṣṇava Mūrti-Sevā as Devotional Truth*. London and New York: Routledge.

Zeller, B. E., 2012. Food Practices, Culture, and Social Dynamics in the Hare Krishna Movement. In: Cusack, C. M. and Norman, A. eds. *Handbook of New Religions and Cultural Production*. Boston: Brill, 681–702.

4 Cultural regrouping in the diaspora

Mediating Hindu identity online

Juli L. Gittinger

Cultural enclaves and ethnic communities are found in big cities across the USA. One crosses over into a Little Vietnam or Chinatown and sees storefronts or signs in foreign languages, grocery stores stocked with traditional ingredients of the region, ethnic restaurants and newsstands stocked with media in the native language of the community. There may be a local mosque, temple or church that reflects that neighborhood's population. In these enclaves, immigrant communities can encounter cultural resources that assist in the mediation of diaspora identities.

When native culture is no longer confined to the singular geographical place of the motherland, digital space presents itself as an ideal site for the recovery of and connection with other members of the diasporic community with whom they imagine a cultural kinship. This is what I term *cultural regrouping*. Cultural regrouping refers to the phenomenon that occurs when an immigrant or diasporic individual enters a location, setting or community gathering which invokes the native or homeland in an effort to remind oneself of their original, authentic or native cultural identity, and where one can be among other community members who share that identity.

This chapter will consider the role of digital media in the process of *cultural regrouping* for the Hindu diaspora in the USA. This work draws from research done over a three-year period, from 2014 to 2017, and from over 250 surveys (given online, with both open and multiple choice questions) inquiring how Hindus of various generations and backgrounds use digital platforms and tools, including social media, websites and smartphone apps. I posit that for Hindus living in the USA – particularly for those who do not live in or near a local diaspora community – the Internet plays an important role in mediating cultural and religious identity. Websites and social media are important tools for connecting to Hindu communities online, especially for those living outside urban centers. Clusters of websites that act as a sort of *virtual ethnic neighborhood*, virtual temples or rituals, and social media that facilitate transnational connections all contribute to the ways in which Hindus in the USA can regroup with their culture and/or religion.

Although my larger body of research more fully examines Hinduism online and how Hindus around the world encounter culture/religion on the web, this study will focus on the Internet use, and the mediation of identity through representation, communities and information usage. I am using the term *mediation* as a way to look at the intervention of communication and media in the process of culture-making (or culture regrouping). Mediation, in this discussion, refers to the process of reconciling the host (US American) culture and identity with the diasporic identity, which may be "imagined" in the sense that Benedict Anderson uses (Anderson 1983). That is to say, a sense of belonging and community is forged through media as its members identify as having shared experiences, culture, symbols and histories.

Digital diasporas

The term *diaspora* has been problematized in South Asian studies, frequently reduced to a simplification that describes any immigrant community or racial minority group living in countries other than their native origin. It is worth noting that the designation *Indian diaspora* is a rather broad category and not particularly useful for a serious investigation beyond its general designation. The terms *non-resident Indian* (NRI) and *person of Indian origin* (PIO) imply a coherence of identity where there is instead a diverse range of ethnic groups (Tamil, Punjabi, Gujarati, etc.), not to mention religious and linguistic diversity. Therefore, Indian-American ethnicity is actually a collection of ethnicities that are not bound by indigenous coherence, but rather exist as an imposed "groupness" from within and without (Adams and Ghose 2003, 415). The common bond across the community is a broad cultural understanding of India, and ties to the motherland itself.

To better define this term, Steven Vertovec (1997, 278) argues that diaspora has three nuances. The most common application of the term is diaspora as a *social form*, referring originally to the Jews' traumatic exile form the homeland. The word subsequently took on a negative imbuement, being associated with forced displacement, loss and alienation (Vertovec 1997, 278). Thus, the social aspects of diaspora may include the process of becoming scattered, living as a community in foreign lands, the maintenance of collective identity, the idea of a shared experience or "ethnic myth" of common origin and the maintenance of ties with the homeland (Vertovec 1997, 278–279). Vertovec notes that most work done on South Asian communities relates diaspora to this social form.

The second application of diaspora is as a *type of consciousness*, or awareness of a multilocality. This approach puts greater importance on the experience narratives, states of mind and a sense of identity (Vertovec 1997, 281). What is often described as diaspora consciousness refers to a distinct type of awareness produced by transnational communities. This awareness is marked by a dual or paradoxical nature which is aggregated negatively by discrimination or exclusion, and positively through the identification with historical heritage or by contemporary global, cultural or political forces (Vertovec 1997, 281). This is analogous to W. E. B. Dubois' (1903) concept of "double consciousness", which relates to an idea of simultaneity – of past and future experienced in the present, and of the simultaneous cognizance of memory and promise.[1]

Lastly, there is an approach to diaspora as a mode of *cultural production* that is related to globalization and "the world-wide flow of cultural objects, images and meanings resulting in variegated process of creolisation, back-and-forth transferences, mutual influences, new contestations, negotiations and constant transformations" (Vertovec 1997, 289). In this approach, identity is constituted, produced and reproduced fluidly to create categories of ethnicity. Vertovec (1997, 290) notes that the primary channel for this flow of cultural experience and transformation of diasporic identity is global media and communications.

> Complex transnational flows of media images and messages perhaps create the greatest disjunctures for diasporic populations, since in the electronic media in particular, the politics of desire and imagination are always in contest with the politics of heritage and nostalgia. (Appadurai and Breckenridge 1989, iii)

I am particularly interested in this third approach to diaspora, especially the production and reproduction of transnational social and cultural phenomena, as it is closely related to the process of globalization (Appadurai and Breckenridge 1989, 19).

Anthony Giddens defines globalization as an intensification and compression of time and space, resulting in a simplification of culture because of its removal from local contexts. Regarding migrant communities, Giddens (1990, 18–19) describes the process as a tearing away of space from place, through the fostering of relations between "absent others" which are distant from another location's face-to-face interaction: "In conditions of modernity, place becomes increasingly phantasmagoric". The web and digital technology have transformed the complex relationships between the local and global, thereby becoming integral to the globalization process. Thanks to the processes of cultural globalization, diasporas are able to create and maintain meaningful networks across great distances, whether bound by nation, language, ethnicity, religion, ideology or histories (Gillespie 2002, 173). Yet, how diasporas are maintained and experienced are deeply dependent on the ability to access and use these technologies.

The Indian population is one of the fastest growing ethnic groups in the USA, running third after Mexican and Chinese immigrants. According to a 2010 US Census report titled "The Asian Population", the Indian population grew from ~1.6 million to ~2.8 million at a growth rate of 69.37% increase since 2000. They represent more than 16% of the Asian-American community, following Chinese-Americans and Filipino-Americans. The largest Indian-American populations (in order) are in California, New York, Texas, New Jersey and Illinois, and they are the highest earning migrant group, largely employed in engineering and technology companies. They have the highest educational levels of all ethnic groups in the USA.[2]

Yet, as Vinay Lal (e.g., 1999) observes, Indian-Americans understand themselves as the *invisible* minority. In the Unites States, the word Asian has more Sinic connotations than Indic, and the word "Indian" is often the term for Native American. Indian-Americans are neither black nor white (as opposed to the United Kingdom where they are considered black), and as a brown ethnic group they exist in a much higher economic tier than Latinx in the USA. I would further suggest that Hinduism has something to do with this *invisibility*, as it is not a religion that is perceived as threatening either to Christianity or to secular government.[3]

There are over 390 Hindu temples in the USA (list of all Hindu temples in the USA). Religion is frequently used as an ethnic symbol in the diaspora (e.g., Eck 2007), and the role of temples is not only for hosting events such as weddings, funerals or holidays, but they also acts as an important locus of community. This function greatly increases in migrant communities, where the temple both acts as place for worship and ritual and as a symbol of intensified cultural identity. Bhardwaj and Rao (1998) have studied the regrouping process of Hindu immigrants in America, stating, "Ethnic regrouping in the diaspora tends to occur around religious and other cultural symbols of the land of origin" (Bhardwaj and Rao 1998, 125). They identified several sites of religious activity as part of that process, including the family altar, interfamily religious meetings, prayer houses and community centers, gurus and teachers from India, connections with sacred sites in India and so forth (Bhardwaj and Rao 1998, 126). The role of the temple in America, they note, differs greatly from that in India. Unlike temples in India, the American counterparts often have developed Sunday schools, summer camps, language and culture instruction for children, and often sponsor local educational activities. Many become involved in community humanitarian activities, much like a Christian church, and thus it is no longer only a center of worship (Bhardwaj and Rao 1998, 141). The wider outreach of the Hindu temple in America reflects the general need in the diasporic community for multiple opportunities of engaging with one's culture, in manners which are compatible with the social mores of the dominant culture (US American). Most temples have a website indicating information about the organization and promotion of events.

Instances of *cultural regrouping* can also happen outside religious institutions. A good example of this is found in campus student organizations, such as a South Asian Students' Association or Hindu Students' Council. Regrouping also happens in camps or schools which teach in native languages. Holiday festivals in particular are a very public demonstration of regrouping; often open and inviting to non-community members, it provides a way to both share culture with outsiders and proudly demonstrate its traditions or visual symbols through affirmation of the ethnic community.

As I observed in the introduction, the *ethnic village* functions as an important gathering point for immigrants. With designations such as a Chinatown, Little India, Little Italy and so forth, these neighborhoods often serve as a short-term means of adjusting to a new location – especially when there is a disjunction from the place of origin or when retaining ties to the homeland presents difficulties (Hiller and Franz 2004, 735). Within an ethno-cultural enclave, outward markers of the native culture – such as language, dress, imported products and groceries – are seen and easily recognized.

Such visual cues are also utilized in online spaces designed to appeal to the diasporic web-user, thereby creating virtual Indian neighborhoods through collections of links to books, clothing, matrimonial and astrological services, temples and news sites – many of which are easily marked with recognizable images of deities, cultural symbols (like the OM or lotus) or the Indian flag. *The Hindu Universe* (hindunet.org) is one such website that I have analyzed in detail, categorizing it as a *portal* – that is, a hub that has organized thousands of hyperlinks into categories which parallel the stores and sights encountered in an ethnic neighborhood (see Gittinger 2015). Food, sundries, clothing, ritual items, music or DVDs and newspapers in native languages are all available in such digital neighborhoods and are found via hyperlinks on hindunet.org. The website also has links for history, literature, tourism and e-rituals. In this way, such portal websites act as virtual ethnic neighborhoods and function for cultural regrouping.

According to Adams and Ghose (2003, 415), NRIs maintain such websites "for the purposes of cultural preservation and the maintenance of ethnic identity, and to support cosmopolitan, intercontinental lifestyles and consumption habits". Material culture in general – such as traditional clothing items, jewelry, food items, music, videos and books – supports the continuation and preservation of traditional constructions of community, personal identity and embodiment, and online availability to such items via shopping sites such as *utsavfashion.com* or *sareeka.com*, thereby slowing or negotiating the assimilation process (Adams and Ghose 2003, 429). Prominent websites like *hinduonline.co* and *hindunet.org* are two of the most popular specialized sites in assisting NRIs with the preservation of cultural knowledge and spiritual practices.

From statistics (see endnote 2) we can postulate that because Indian migrants have higher education and household incomes — thereby socioeconomically well established as middle class — they are more likely to have integrated technology into their daily lives both through exposure in their education and through economic ability to acquire the access. As my own research revealed, however, not all diaspora communities use the Internet differently than their counterparts still in the homeland. As such, they have the opportunity to encounter others in the immigrant or diaspora community through digital media or through portals which act as virtual ethnic neighborhoods. It is in this way we can begin to think about the spatial dimensions of transnational communities online as exemplary of globalization.

The survey: How Hindu NRIs use the web

Methodology

The starting point for my research began with a collection of online surveys. One of the initial questions with which I was concerned was how Hindus living in the USA are encountering Hinduism online. This was inspired, in no small part, by an article titled "Google has replaced your grandparents' wisdom", which ran in 2013 on the website of feminist e-magazine *Jezebel* (Davies 2013). The article posited that, in our cyber age and with ease of information access, we no longer ask our parents or grandparents about things that we can easily find online. If Google – or more accurately, the web –has replaced the elder generation as a source of information about tradition and culture, then we can posit that some of the community interaction which contributes to cultural and religious identities is also taking place online. To explore this idea, I created a survey asking Hindu Americans how they encountered religion and culture online, and if it was relevant to their identity as a Hindu.

I made some very careful considerations in constructing the survey. It was anonymous (although there was an option to provide an email for further questioning) and brief (less than 20 questions). I also circulated the link on social media, including Reddit, Facebook and Twitter. The survey was circulated through South Asian Student Organizations from cooperating universities in New York, Texas, California and Illinois (states with densest Indian populations), and was also promoted through the list-serv of the Hindu Temple of Central Indiana, which caters to a geographically and ethnically diverse diaspora community in the Midwest. I gathered a total of 289 respondents, which was fruitful in that it gave me a better picture of how younger Hindus in particular might be encountering their traditions online –although many of my respondents were older as well.

I have given the statistics as percentages rounded up/down from the nearest decimal, and noted the number of respondents who skipped a particular question when it occurred. My email correspondents (about 90 in total) were numbered for my records and are referred to by their assigned numbers for anonymity (for example, "respondent 4").

In analyzing the data, I considered how the respondents' use of online resources contributed to the mediation of their cultural and/or religious identities as Hindus –that is, the effect of the medium on structuring or constructing such identities. I used both quantitative and qualitative methodologies, analyzing survey figures on what forms of media are used and how, as well as further exploring conclusions drawn from the numerical data in the form of interviews and longer survey responses. I considered generational differences in my statistics, as well as provided the number of comments provided by my respondents through email correspondence. My conclusions came largely from the written responses and anecdotes which gave personal perspectives on how the respondents personally negotiate and relate their identities in digital spaces. Personal narratives provided insights into experiences and expectations of online communities, from which I was able to extrapolate conclusions about the role digital media is playing in these processes of regrouping.

Findings

I found the best way to analyze the responses was to sort them by their status as visiting, first generation, second generation or third generation. In all, 45% (129 respondents) of those surveyed were in the USA on visa or exchange, 42% (121 respondents) were first generation, that is, born in India but moved here with their family at some point, and 12% (35 respondents) were second generation, born in the USA to parents who migrated from India. Very few of those surveyed were third generation (4 respondents, at 1%), but that is consonant with US census data (Hoeffel 2012) which show that prior to 1980, Indian immigrants were quite low but are almost doubling per decade since. According to this brief, the following figures reveal a dramatic increase in the last generation: in 1990 there were 815,447 Indian immigrants in the USA, doubling in 2000 at 1,678,765, and again in 2010 at 2,843,391.

Occupations and discipline majors were diverse, with IT, medicine and engineering having the highest numbers, though respondents also included lawyers, homemakers, humanities students and blue-collar occupations. I had 96 respondents (33%) who were 21 and under, 89 respondents (31%) aged 22–29 years, 51 (17%) between age 30–39 and 54 (19%) that were 40 and over. Sixty-five percent were male, 34% were female and ~1% identified as non-binary/other.

Access to the web was mostly through personal computer or smartphone. As websites frequented on a daily basis (respondents could check as many as applied), Email, Google and YouTube topped the rotation across the survey pool, with news sites and other interests having smaller frequency (Figure 4.1). These are consistent with how Americans across the board use the web – Google, YouTube, Gmail and Yahoo! Mail were consistently among the top eight sites accessed in 2017 (Top Websites n.d.).

Social media may play an important role in *cultural regrouping*, allowing for transnational communities to form and maintain contact with friends and family members who still live in South Asia. While Facebook remained fairly ubiquitous (Figure 4.2), WhatsApp was a more popular choice than Snapchat and Instagram (67.7% using WhatsApp).[4] The popularity of WhatsApp in India is due to the fact that the smartphone, for many Indians,

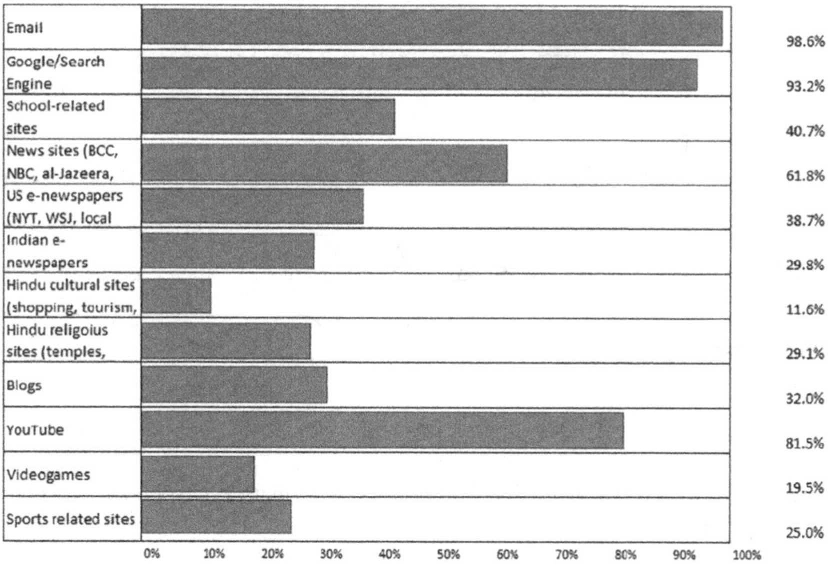

Figure 4.1 "What sites do you frequent on a daily basis? Check all that apply" (278 responded, 11 skipped question).

was their first (and remains their only) computer. It also does not require a network connection (3G for example), but can instead rely upon local Wi-Fi. US Americans' chat preferences, in environments where personal computer ownership has been much higher and for a longer period of time, reflect the interfaces of their established social media networks like Facebook or Twitter. "In India, there's less legacy clutter and people are picking the best software — the ad-free, easy to use, well-designed WhatsApp" (McMillan 2014). WhatsApp has an estimated 200 million users in India, so it is no surprise that it remains a favorite among Indian immigrants in the USA.

I followed up with several survey respondents who voluntarily provided their email for further correspondence, and asked them if social media and online communities gave them any sense of belonging to their ethnic, religious and/or cultural group:

> *Respondent 8*: "I feel connected ethnically, to my Telegu culture, through some social media accounts. However, I don't use social media or online communities to connect with my religion (I usually talk to my family)".
>
> *Respondent 13*: "Every now and then I will read a blog about being Indian-American and what that identity means for different people and read about their experiences...However, when I do read them (ex: a Buzzfeed article on being Indian American), it makes me feel good to know that I can connect with the experiences of other Indian Americans

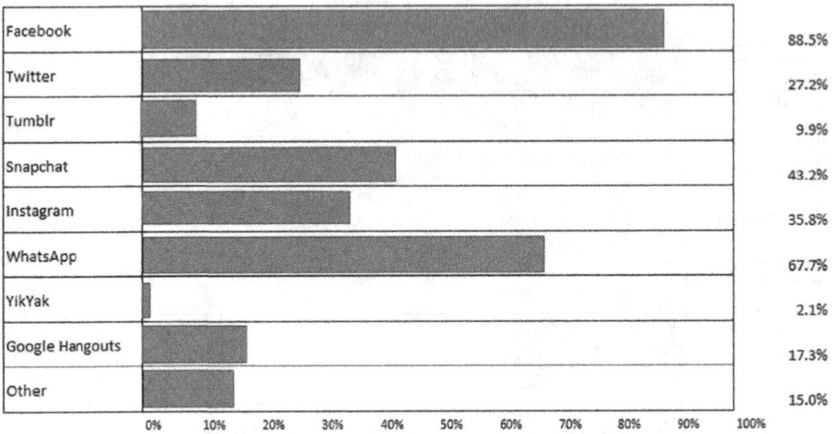

Figure 4.2 "Which social media/chat/messaging formats do you use?" (276 responded, 13 skipped the question).

and that here are commonalities in our experiences. It makes me feel connected to others and not alone".

Respondent 21: "Yes in a religious sense. Culturally or ethnically I'm not super well connected, but the Internet has proven to be a fantastic resource to learn more about my particular path within Hinduism".

Respondent 34: "Yes, as an American Hindu convert living in the south it gives me the community aspect that's hard for me to obtain".

Respondent 36: "Many times I feel we can celebrate or commiserate together".

Respondent 51: "Actually the Internet helps me feel more in tune to myself. I am able to find people who had the same struggle of not being able to take Indian food to school for lunch or had to explain that while the Color Run is fun, it is not Holi. Growing up and Indian-American, your life is almost entirely bound by the hyphen. Toss in the fact you're usually the only Hindu in the room and that makes it all the more difficult since you don't get to have the 'White Wedding' or understand a lot of the religious meaning behind Western history. It's really hard growing up in two distinct societies and the Internet is an escape for that".

Respondent 57: "Social media accounts run by Indians/Hindus allow me to feel included in a bigger group. The ability to share/express thoughts regarding our culture, political opinions, etc. with those that are like us (though they are not near us) is very helpful".

Respondent 58: "Yes since I am away from home, this way I have people I can talk to even when I am not home".

Respondent 62: "My connections to the temple and the events that are going on there is only possible because of electronic information.

> The constant connection to others in my religious and cultural group via electronic media (WhatsApp and Facebook) keeps me updated on current issues in India and locally that I would not otherwise be aware of. It has deeply enriched my sense of belonging".

Not all of my survey-takers felt that social media was beneficial:

> *Respondent 22*: "No, because the South Asian space is too highly fragmented, and the only online communities that can attract enough participation to be worthwhile are those that include communities as disparate as Muslim Pakistanis and South Indian Tamil Brahmins, and a wide range of other groups. It gives some limited sense of community, but within the group are sub-groups that are trying to differentiate themselves from other sub-groups, so there is nothing to belong to".
>
> *Respondent 42*: "Social media makes religious or ethnic groups worse".
>
> *Respondent 80*: "Yes, they remind of important festivals and events. But they can also provoke unnecessary radicalism which must be carefully thought upon, and could be misleading for some people. I have seen a lot of messages and posts shared without understanding the context".

As any social media user will attest to, platforms such as Facebook and Twitter have both positive and negative aspects: on the plus side, being connected to friends and family and finding good information or resources; the downside being that public forums are subject to *trolling* and can quickly degenerate into hostile environments, or that reposting articles or images without context quickly spreads misinformation. Those that found social media beneficial, however, repeatedly found the ability to connect over long distances, being part of a community or sharing experiences as a religious or ethnic minority to be a source of comfort. One of the most consistent themes across the personal responses and correspondence was that among online Hindu communities, there was a shared idea of commiseration — that the experience of being Hindu in America was similar and relatable between other web users.

Another interesting set of data from my survey was borne out of the article I cited earlier, "Google has replaced your grandparents' wisdom" (Davies 2013). I gave the subjects categories in which they could say they would either go to their parents or go online first to inquire about a range of religious-, cultural- or identity-related topics (Table 4.1).

Across the board, respondents preferred to rely on family for information about tradition –recipes, holidays and religion. Second generation, arguably more *Americanized*, had higher percentages here, suggesting a need to connect or regroup through more authentic channels. Some topics, like sexuality and politics, were those in which the participants preferred to be engaged through online communities or websites rather than through

Table 4.1[5] Are you more likely to ask a *family member* or to do an *Internet search* to find out about the following topics

Family/ Internet	*A* F/I (%)	*B* F/I (%)	*C* F/I (%)	*D* F/I (%)	*E* F/I (%)	*F* F/I (%)	*G* F/I (%)
Visa/non-US citizen	69/31	58/42	14/86	95/5	52/48	12/88	36/64
First generation	67/33	60/40	35/68	81/19	53/47	9/91	41/39
Second generation	82/18	93/7	36/64	92/8	87/13	24/76	57/43

A. A traditional recipe
B. A question about religion
C. Opinions on Indian political issues
D. How to celebrate a traditional holiday
E. Personal issues with ethnic/religious identity
F. Sexuality/gender issues
G. Indian historical events (partition, emergency, etc.)

family. This could suggest a tension between a more progressive liberal culture of the USA versus a more religious conservative outlook in the household. The second generation had an exceptionally high percentage of those who preferred to go to family to ask questions about religion (93%, compared to 58%60% with other generations). I found this intriguing, because this would certainly be the most online generation (see Prensky 2001).Three respondents in this group had provided their email, so I asked them about this:

> *Respondent 8*: "When I was little I didn't like being different. I tried to dress and wear my hair like all the other girls in my class, and I really liked celebrating American (Christian) holidays because they were so big commercially and everyone participated. Now (in college) I am really trying to reconnect with my culture, and I am proud to celebrate holidays with my family. It feels brave to be 'different' in this time with politics and everything, so I have become more serious with my religious outlook and relied a lot upon my parents for guidance on how to be a Hindu woman in this modern world. You can't get that online".
>
> *Respondent 55*: "My parents were born in America and are completely 'American' as far as culture goes. They go to the temple for festivals and holidays, but we don't do much day to day things that might seem traditional Hindu (I'd classify us as 'secular' Hindus). My older brother even had a civil wedding in the courthouse. But I started to feel like part of me was missing when I was a teenager, and I started researching Hinduism online and reading things, but that wasn't very helpful because there is a sort of generic Hinduism out there. So I started talking to my grandparents about religion, and they were very

supportive. I went with them to the temple, and took a class on the Gita which really sold me. Culture is something I can get online, but religion needs personal connection. I feel like this is something that you can only get handed down from family, and I'm glad I had my grandparents as a resource for this".

Respondent 89: "I was never very interested in being 'hindu' when I was in school, and my parents did not pressure me to participate in traditions other than Durga Puja, which is a big deal in Bengal. Now that I'm in my twenties, I feel a strong need to reconnect with this part of who I am. I am a technie, and I belong to several social communities online for Bengalis in the west, but to learn about religion I felt it would be more authentic to ask my parents. When I look at how Hinduism is portrayed on websites, it is usually very Vaishnav. My family is Bengali and our 'kuladevi' is Durga, and what is online is really different from things I have learned in my family. I never read the Bhagawad Gita, for example, but I have read from the Devi Mahatmya online, which is a text that celebrates Durga as the primary goddess. So I am using the Internet for that part. But the true religious instruction (about ethics, rituals, and devotion) is coming from my family".

The conclusion I draw from these numbers and conversations is that given a choice, religion is something one still learns in the family, even if online tools or resources may be used to supplement this information. While culture may be gleaned from a number of resources and influences, religion, it seems, remains something that is taught person-to-person. We can focus on the numbers of those who preferred web-source information, however, as a statistic worth considering on its own. It is clear that the Internet is playing an active role across the board – albeit at different levels – in cultural negotiations.

I am also interested in how NRIs represented themselves online, and if it was important that they identified as Hindu or Indian on the web, or if they preferred anonymity – making their ethnic or cultural background not apparent. This could be demonstrated through choice of avatar, online name/handle, membership to certain groups or through their social media postings (Table 4.2).

The first generation appears to be fairly enthusiastic about showing off their ethnic/cultural identity online, but was also the only generation that had a notable number who chose anonymity. As first-generation individuals, they straddle the Americanized/immigrant line more clearly, and thus may feel social prejudices more keenly as they negotiate their identity online and offline.

These figures also suggest that the second generation felt their ethnic identity was important enough to reveal it to some degree online, but not to the point of emphasis or anonymity. A possible conclusion could be that the more removed they are from the memory of the homeland, the more

Table 4.2[6] When you are online, how important is it that you retain your cultural identity?

	Visa/non-citizen (%)	*First generation (%)*	*Second generation (%)*	**Third generation (%)*
Very important, I am clearly Hindu and/or Indian	3.2	27.6	10.3	50
Somewhat important. I don't hide it, but I don't make a point to emphasize it.	42.6	39.5	59.5	50
Not important; I construct a fairly generic identity online that could be anything	52.21	19.4	30.2	0
I deliberately choose anonymity and hide my cultural background online.	2.0	13.5	0	0

important this identity becomes to them (also suggested in the Table 4.1 data). If this is a correct assumption, then this is consistent with what is often called "symbolic ethnicity", a theory put forth by sociologist Mary Waters (1990, 164–166) in which she questions the process of claiming an ethnic label among middle-class Americans. Referring specifically to white Americans, ethnic identity is a symbolic, personal choice and does not influence daily life:

> It does not determine where you will live, who your friends will be, what job you will have, or whether you will be subject to discrimination. It only matters in voluntary ways — in celebrating holidays with a special twist, cooking a special ethnic meal...remembers a special phrase or two in a foreign language. (Waters 1990, 147)

In his book *American Karma*, Sunil Bhatia employs the concept of symbolic ethnicity as a heuristic device in his study of American Hindus, positing that the claim to Indianness enhances the belonging to a community while at the same time highlighting individualism:

> Indian migrants counter their assignations of otherness by invoking the discourse of sameness, equality, and universal humanity to define their sense of identity. Their assertions of self, through the frame of universal humanity, do not mean that they are erasing their ethnicity or sense of "being Indian." Rather, they want to invoke their Indian ethnicity

without having to feel that displaying their Indianness will have negative costs. (Bhatia 2007, 25)

As Bhatia's research explores, Indian migrants are more comfortable with highlighting their cultural identity than racial identity in order to avoid the stigmas that people of color have in the USA. Again, as Indians have some of the highest education and highest household income in the USA, they fit the *model minority* and *invisible minority* archetypes.

Finding Hinduism online

My larger body of research involves Hinduism online – how it is presented, encountered and consumed worldwide – and central to that thesis are questions of authority and authenticity. To claim that there is such a thing as *authentic Hinduism* is problematic on many levels, among other things, because of the sheer diversity and scope of what we colloquially term Hinduism. Whether it is a Western scholar, a Hindu practitioner or a curious Internet surfer, the way we encounter Hinduism online is shaped by global discourses of religion, pervasive Orientalism and colonial scholarship.[7] Therefore, I found it useful to ask my survey respondents about how, in their opinion, Hinduism is represented on the web.

The consensus among the majority of my respondents was that the web ultimately fails to capture the wide range of traditions and variances among Hindus. Disparate languages, regional practices and social divisions were among the reasons given for why Hinduism remains a difficult tradition to represent online. One person even said, "I think we should stop using the word Hindu and Hinduism" (respondent 2). Western and Orientalist perspectives were also blamed:

> *Respondent 22*: "It is represented almost solely through the western lens, which treats it as 'other' and focuses on discrete elements of it, such as multiple deities, or yoga, or ritual, without looking at it as the non-concrete system of beliefs and philosophy it is. And, frankly, tried to understand it in a rather simplistic and amateurish way".
>
> *Respondent 25*: "No, I believe it is negatively portrayed with a focus on caste and 'exotic' rituals and no mention of the philosophical aspects".
>
> *Respondent 50*: "I personally feel that Hinduism amongst Westerners is essentially boiled down to a statement like the following 'Oh yeah that religion with a bajillion gods and that elephant dude'".

There were some other concerns as well:

> *Respondent 5*: "I think there are many sites which claim to answer all your questions about Hinduism, and I think that is very misleading. There is a trend to think about Hinduism in the context of the

Abrahamic religions, like identifying the 'Hindu Bible' and rituals similar to baptism and how to convert. But since there is no mention of a Hindu identity until the age of colonizers, this is very misguided. Any attempt to find or understand 'true Hinduism" just further legitimizes a skewed identity thrust upon an entire, diverse community. I don't think the problem lies in the Internet, but in the historic construction of "The Hindu" which is completely created and unfortunately adopted. When attempting to explain Hinduism online, the conversation is framed by Judeo-Christian thoughts of what is or isn't important to a religion. Is there a solution to this? I don't know. Regardless of its less-than-optimal origins, the word Hindu has come to mean so much to the people within the community that it cannot simply be rejected as a colonial construction".

Respondent 8: "I do think Hinduism is accurately represented, however there are specific issues I find with discussions about Hinduism. One that bothers me the most, is the Hindu symbol, the Swastika, which is interpreted as an anti-Semitic symbol. Instances like this make me feel like there is still a little misunderstanding when it comes to how Hinduism is represented on the Internet".

Respondent 46: "I think it isn't really represented accurately. I feel like advocate of Hindutva and Hindu nationalism are the dominant voices of Hinduism online — there doesn't seem to be much of a space for liberal/progressive Hindus, aside from small community groups like the Sadhana Coalition of Progressive Hindus".

Respondent 51: "Most of what I see of Hinduism online is said by Hindus, making it quite accurate. However the stereotypes I see on TV are only slightly accurate. I mean there is a reason they became sterotypes [sic]! The religion is so complex and hard for the average American to understand since it breaks a lot of the religious barriers set in other religions, making it hard for Hinduism to be portrayed entirely accurate by a western perspective".

Overall, it seemed that Hinduism's issues with representation extend beyond the digital medium, but the Internet certainly exacerbated these issues – especially regarding misinformation and what may be termed ideologies. One could make the argument – and indeed a few of the respondents did just this – that Hinduism is always changing and adapting, and this fluidity not only works well with digital media, but means that the idea of the so-called authentic, true Hinduism (as Hindu nationalist organizations would claim exists) is a moving target that will never be struck.

Finally, I included a question about whether or not respondents had ever used *e- pūjā* or *e- darśan* websites or smartphone apps.[8] *Pūjā* is a prototypical Hindu ritual in which the deity is believed to be present in the image/icon, during which time they are treated like an honored guest: bathed, adorned with flowers, offered incense and food as well as songs and prayers. *Darśan* is part of the *pūjā* ritual, although can be performed on its own; *darśan* means seeing, and being seen by, the deity (Eck 2007). This eye contact is important and can be done via electronic devices.

Seventeen percent of the respondents reported that they had used such electronic tools to aid ritual practice (or in some cases, this was the only opportunity they had for such practice, living far from a Hindu community/temple). Several of these respondents provided their emails for further follow-up, and I asked for more detail on how and why they used these apps.

> *Respondent 14*: "As I am in college now, I am not used to performing a ritual or singing a prayer without my mom with me. So, when there is a festival I usually check for the prayer on Youtube and I will listen to it. Also, I use Skype sometimes to be virtually a part of my hometown's puja".
>
> *Respondent 15*: "When my grandmother was alive, she wasn't able to make it to major places of pilgrimage like she used to when she was younger. Live streaming darshans worked well for her, and I was happy to partake as well. On a similar note, I do puja with family who are far away but are streaming, or in cases where I'm sick and cannot attend, or cannot take days off of work. Two years ago, I was busy on janmaastami, but streamed the puja while working on my computer.
>
> [Also,] I live in NYC, and the nearest temple that isn't like a cult is out in Flushing. It's definitely a hike. It's also a South Indian temple. I am modh brahmin, and it's also a family tradition to venerate Sarasvati, so I tend to do darshan online for events particular to those deities as it's more convenient. It certainly helps that there is a lot of room to philosophically justify it fitting into Hinduism, but in general, it's better than nothing".
>
> *Respondent 59*: "I work nights and also I live a bit out in the sticks, about 3 hours to the nearest temple and Hindu community. I have only done puja rituals with my parents in India, so I'm not comfortable doing them on my own here [in the US]. But I do darsan every day even sometimes on work breaks (I use Om Namah Shiva app). It is calming and helps me focus and I even use the mantra counter".

As scholars Nicole Karapanagiotis (2010, 2013) and Heinz Scheifinger (2010, 2013) have noted in their research, Hinduism's adaptability lends itself well to electronic media, and the divine is understood to be ontologically present in the image during *pūjā/darśan* – whether the image is a color lithograph, a statue or an electronic image. According to some religious actors, it is therefore consonant with Hindu theology that the divine is present in everything, including the web. As many users have stated in the reviews of such apps (there are dozens of *pūjā* and *darśan* apps available on GooglePlay and iTunes), the portability and ability to do ritual on one's own schedule are highly valued, as well as features which have recordings of mantras and prayers, or verses in a number of languages to read. Other electronic methods of religious practice include watching a live stream feed from your favorite temple (in the USA or in India), Skyping family during a ritual or virtual pilgrimage (also offered on a number of sites).

Conclusions

As Peter Mandaville (2001, 178) argued in an early study of Muslims online, "diasporic media can and should be understood as much more than simply a means by which information of interest to a given community can be exchanged, or a means for communicating", but rather to understand "media as spaces of communication in which the identity, meaning and boundaries of diasporic identity are continually constructed, debated and reimagined". In other words, we have passed up the era of computer-mediated communication as central feature of the Internet, to the more spatial understanding of the Internet with its online neighborhoods, self-expressions and multimodal features – a digital world in which geographic borders are irrelevant.

As my study reveals, Hindus in the USA are indeed using digital media for *cultural regrouping*. Internet use allows them to be less reliant upon fellow migrants locally (a difficulty for those in less urban regions) and develop social networks that extend beyond their geographic proximity. The efficiency and breadth of the digital diaspora relies upon both participation and upon access. In order for a diaspora to express its digital identity, it must have access to digital communication platforms such as the Internet – an easy task in the USA where Hindus occupy mostly middle- and upper-class economic tiers and where Internet saturation is at 89% as of 2018 (Pew Research Center, 2018).

Generally speaking, my respondents showed an enthusiasm for engaging with and representing their culture online, while not completely rejecting offline family input on certain topics. They are aware of the inherent perils of the medium (misinformation, bias and Western perspectives), but still utilize it as a resource or even as a vehicle for religious practice. Communities seem to be an important feature, linking families, friends and organizations across transnational boundaries. Virtual *neighborhoods* or portal-like websites with hyperlinks can offer goods and services much in the way that an ethnic neighborhood does, and print media (news, magazines, religious texts) are available in a number of languages on the web. This would suggest that there is a balance being struck between the local and global, between interpersonal and impersonal and between migrant and native identities – the traditional balancing act of diasporic identity, only now facilitated by digital media and globalization.

I found the tools used in this research to be effective, both for general numerical data and for more personal accounts and responses. Digital ethnographies and survey research have become important tools for religious studies, although their methodological approaches and applications are still evolving (see, e.g., Cheruvallil-Contractor 2016; Hine 2015). Understanding how religion and culture are *encountered* or *consumed* online is an important part of any analysis which seeks to engage religion, globalization, Orientalism or cultural studies in the age of the World Wide Web. The mediation of identity is also part of that equation; therefore, surveying diaspora communities about their online behavior is a step toward understanding how religion and culture are shaped by new technologies.

The question I would raise at this point is whether or not NRIs or PIOs are using the Internet much differently than other citizens in the USA. Instead of asking how migrants are negotiating religious or cultural identity online, a better question might be about how religion and culture are negotiated online *in general*. This broader question is well traversed in current scholarship, although studying the symbols and cultures of the *other* may be easier simply because it appears more visible. As Lisa Nakamura (2002, xii) has argued already a decade and a half ago, "the Internet is a place where race happens".[9] Most certainly, the Internet is a place where cultural and religious identities happen as well.

Notes

1 With regard to diaspora, Benedict Anderson (1983, 24) discusses the simultaneity of two identities within a singular imaginary: (1) "time" of the nation is eternal and has always been, a promise to be fulfilled in the future and representing an unbroken line of historical narrative, and (2) a "homogenous empty time" in which simultaneity is transverse, cross-time, "marked not by prefiguring and fulfillment, but by temporal coincidence, and measured by clock and calendar". Anderson is drawing heavily from Walter Benjamin's (1986) concept of Messianic time, in which there is a simultaneity of past and future in an instantaneous present. In this sense, it could be argued that diasporic communities collectively negotiate the eternal, intrinsic qualities of how they imagine their past, and the modern temporal qualities of the promised future.

2 In 2016, the median household income including all sectors of the USA was $56,277 per year, and 30.3% have a bachelor's degree or higher, while 37% are employed in professional or managerial jobs as reported in the US Census (ACS 2016). Asian Americans in general have higher number compared to other ethnic groups, but Indians top the numbers among immigrant communities: 73% have bachelor's degree or higher and 66.3% are employed in professional or managerial jobs (27% in Information Technologies); they have a median household income of $83,000 (Migration Information Source 2008, Richwine 2009).

3 Indian-Americans represent a diverse religious spectrum; Pew Research Center reports in 2012 that 51% were Hindu, 18% Christian, 10% Muslim, 5% Sikh, 2% Jain and 10% were unaffiliated (Pew Research Center 2012, 16).

4 According to a Pew Survey of 1,520 adults in the USA, Facebook was also top, but followed by Instagram, Twitter and Pinterest (Pew Research Center 2016). Unlike in the USA, WhatsApp has its biggest market in India, with an estimated 200 million monthly active users as of 2017 (Singh 2017).

5 272 responded, 17 skipped the question. None of the four "third generation" subjects answered this question.

6 271 responded, 18 skipped the question. Only two of the four "third generation" participants answered.
7 At the scholarly level, this has been a popular subject of inquiry. Arising from a symposium titled "Who speaks for Hinduism?", the *Journal of the American Academy of Religion* devoted an entire issue to this very subject in 2000. See the pieces by Brooks, Hawley, Lopez and Smith.
8 For more on the fascinating practice of *e-puja*, see Karapanagiotis (2013) and Scheifinger (2013).
9 Nakamura's study of the discursive and rhetorical production of racial categories in cyberspace (what she terms "cybertypes") is a thoughtful investigation of how race is created, delineated and recognized through the language of the Internet. She notes that being ascribed a particular race or ethnicity is already a disorienting position, but being typed as such in cyberspace is "doubly disorienting" (2002, xv).

References

ACS, 2016. *US Census, American Community Survey (ACS)*, 2012–2016 ACS 5 Year Data Profiles. Available at www.census.gov/acs/www/data/data-tables-and-tools/data-profiles/2016/, accessed 1 July 2018.

Adams, P. C. and Ghose, R., 2003. India.com: The Construction of a Space between. *Progress in Human Geography* 27(4), 414–437.

Anderson, B., 1983. *Imagined Communities*. London: Verso.

Appadurai, A. and Breckenridge, C. 1989. On moving targets. *Public Culture* 2, i–iv.

Bhardwaj, S. and Rao, M., 1998. The Temple as a Symbol of Hindu Identity in America? *Journal of Cultural Geography* 17(2), 125–143.

Bhatia, S., 2007. *American Karma: Race, Culture, and Identity in the Indian Diaspora*. New York: New York University Press.

Brooks, D. R., 2000. Taking Sides and Opening Doors: Authority and Integrity in the Academy's Hinduism. *Journal of the American Academy of Religion* 68(4), 817–829.

Cheruvallil-Contractor, S. and Shakkour, S., eds., 2016. *Digital Methodologies in the Sociology of Religion*. London and New York: Bloomsbury Press.

Davies, M., 2013. Google Has Replaced Your Grandparents' Wisdom. *Jezebel*. Available at https://jezebel.com/5987837/google-has-replaced-your-grandparents-wisdom, accessed October 2016.

Du Bois, W. E. B., 1903. *The Souls of Black Folk*. New York: Dover Publications.

Eck, D. L., 2007 [2000]. *Darśan: Seeing the divine image in India*. Delhi: Motilal Banarsidass.

Giddens, A., 1990. *The Consequences of Modernity*. Stanford: Stanford University Press.

Gillespie, M., 2002. Dynamics of Diasporas: South Asian Media and Transnational Cultural Politics. In: Stald, G. and Tufte, T., eds. *Global Encounters: Media and Cultural Transformation*. Bedfordshire: University of Luton Press, 173–195.

Gittinger, J. L., 2015. Hindu Diaspora as 'Virtual Community': Digital Neighborhoods, Electronic Transnationalism. *Symposia: The Journal of Religion* 7, 1–16.

Hawley, J. S., 2000. Who Speaks for Hinduism – And Who Against? *Journal of the American Academy of Religion* 68(4), 711–720.

Hiller, H. H. and Franz, T. M., 2004. New Ties, Old Ties and Lost Ties: The Use of the Internet in Diaspora. *New Media and Society* 6, 731–752.

Hindu Online. Available at http://hinduonline.co, accessed 1 December 2017.

The Hindu Universe. Available at http://hindunet.org, accessed 1 December 2017.

Hine, C., 2015. *Ethnography for the Internet: Embedded, Embodied, and Everyday*. London and New York: Bloomsbury Press.

Hoeffel, E. M., Rastogi, S., Kim, M. O. and Shahid, H., 2012. The Asian Population: 2010. Census Briefs. *US Census*. Available at www.census.gov/prod/cen2010/briefs/c2010br-11.pdf, accessed 1 July 2018.

Karapanagiotis, N., 2010. Vaishnava Cyber-puja: Problems of Purity and Novel Ritual Solutions. *Online-Heidelberg Journal of Religions on the Internet* 4(1), 179–195.

Karapanagiotis, N., 2013. Cyber Forms, Worshipable Forms: Hindu Devotional Viewpoints on the Ontology of Cyber-Gods and-Goddesses. *International Journal of Hindu Studies* 17(1), 1–26.

Lal, V., 1999. The Politics of History on the Internet: Cyber-diasporic Hinduism and the North American Hindu Diaspora. *Diaspora: A Journal of Transnational Studies* 8(2), 137–172.

List of all Hindu Temples in the USA. 2016. *USATemples.com*. Available at www.usatemples.com/blog/list-of-all-hindu-temples-in-usa/, accessed 1 March 2016.

Lopez, D. S., 2000. Pandit's Revenge. *Journal of the American Academy of Religion* 68(4), 831–835.

Mandaville, P., 2001. Reimagining Islam in Diaspora: The Politics of Mediated Community. *Gazette (Leiden, Netherlands)* 63(2–3), 69–186.

McMillan, R., 2014. You May Not Use WhatsApp, But the Rest of the World Sure Does, *WIRED* Magazine. Available at www.wired.com/2014/02/whatsapp-rules-rest-world/, accessed 1 November 2017.

Migration Information Source, 2008. *Indian Immigrants in the US*. Available at www.migrationpolicy.org/article/indian-immigrants-united-states-0/, accessed 1 November 2017.

Nakamura, L., 2002. *Cybertypes: Race, Ethnicity, and Identity on the Internet*. New York and London: Routledge.

Prensky, M., 2001. Digital Natives, Digital Immigrants Part 1. *On the Horizon* 9(5), 1–6.

Richwine, J., 2009. Indian Americans: The New Model Minority. *Forbes*. Available at www.forbes.com/2009/02/24/bobby-jindal-indian-americans-opinions-contributors_immigrants_minority.html, accessed 1 August 2017.

Sareeka.com, 2019. *Online Indian Ethnic Wear Store*. Available at www.sareeka.com/, accessed 1 July 2018.

Scheifinger, H., 2010. Internet Threats to Hindu Authority: Puja-ordering Websites and the Kalighat Temple. *Asian Journal of Social Science* 38(4), 636–656.

Scheifinger, H., 2013. Hindu Worship Online and Offline. In: Campbell, H. A., ed. *Digital Religion, Understanding Religious Practice in New Media Worlds*. New York: Routledge, 121–127.

Singh, M., 2017. Guess WhatsApp's Biggest Market? India. *Mashable*, [online] 24 February. Available at https://mashable.com/2017/02/24/whatsapp-india-200-million-active-users/#lxUlMx5LPsqm, accessed 1 March 2018.

Smith, B. K., 2000. Who Does, Can, and Should Speak for Hinduism? *Journal of the American Academy of Religion* 68(4), 741–749.

Pew Research Center, 2012. *Asian Americans: A Mosaic of Faiths*. Washington: Pew Research Center. Available at http://assets.pewresearch.org/wp-content/uploads/sites/11/2012/07/Asian-Americans-religion-full-report.pdf, accessed 1 May 2018.

Pew Research Center, 2016. *Social Media Update 2016*. Washington: Pew Research Center. Available at www.pewinternet.org/2016/11/11/social-media-update-2016/, accessed 2 January 2017.

Pew Research Center, 2018. *Internet/Broadband Fact Sheet*. Washington: Pew Research Center. Available at www.pewinternet.org/fact-sheet/internet-broadband/, accessed 1 February 2018.

Top Websites. n.d. Available at www.quantcast.com/top-sites/, accessed 1 July 2017.

The Asian Population – 2010 Census Briefs, 2012. *US Census*, March. Available at www.census.gov/prod/cen2010/briefs/c2010br-11.pdf, accessed 1 November 2016.

Utsav Fashion. 2016. Available at www.utsavfashion.com/, accessed 1 July 2016.

Vertovec, S., 1997. Three Meanings of "Diaspora", Exemplified among South Asian Religions. *Diaspora: A Journal of Transnational Studies* 6(3), 277–299.

Waters, M. C., 1990. *Ethnic Options: Choosing Identities in America*. Berkeley: University of California Press.

Part 2

Who defines? Authority and appropriation

5 Authors, self-fashioning and online cultural production in the age of Hindu celevision

Pramod K. Nayar

Introduction

Ashok Banker, Amish Tripathi and Devdutt Pattanaik are Indian authors who have mined the *Ramayana*, the *Mahabharata* and, overall, Hindu mythology to produce a series of novels, adaptations and commentaries. They rank among the highest selling authors in India today, with translations into multiple languages. This chapter takes as its case studies the websites of the three authors (Banker n.d.b; Pattanaik n.d.a; Tripathi 2018b). It seeks to unpack the ideologies encoded through a close reading of their strategies of impression-management and self-representations vis-à-vis their repackaged Hindu cultural productions. To this end, it unravels the discursive strands within their representations.

That religion is integral to any definition we might make of the public sphere today is now a given (e.g., Campbell and Golan 2011). This public sphere is at once offline and online with a constant interplay between the two, and social media in particular contributing in significant ways to its very making. The making and dissemination of online religious content, memberships and exchanges are central to the discussions of religion in the digital age, and frame the arguments stated later in the chapter. As commentators often note, the circulation of texts and images online does not imply a *religious public* as much as a public that discusses the legitimacy and competing forms of religious belief and practices (Fader and Gottlieb 2015, 776). Further, online Hinduism and its representations or cultural texts cannot be separated from the spectacular, hypervisible Hinduism in contemporary India. For purposes of this chapter, I use the term *public sphere* to signify the *demos* of democratic India, constituted occasionally by rational debate but also through the consumption of texts and discourses, as Novetzke argues (2016). The public sphere, with the numerous discourses contesting for space, is made of competing legitimacies – for instance, of secularism and right-wing (both Hindu and Muslim) belief systems – and their chosen forms of representations.

I propose that online self-representations and presentations of these authors intersect with an increasingly Hindu-hegemonic visual and cultural field in today's India, and contribute to it as well. Further, because these authors also function as cultural commentators through their blogs, public appearances and journalism, their online work must be located in a transmedial context of speeches, fiction-writing, public engagements, fan cultures and exchanges by these authors.

My first argument is that these three authors embark on a project of self-fashioning through a careful engagement with a Hindu ancestry and tradition. Second, this self-fashioning is linked to, and manifests as, their literary location within scriptural-mythological narrative even as they adapt these older narratives for their purposes, and thus constitute a part of Hindu cultural production today. Finally, I argue that the three authors appropriate and leverage existing conditions in which spectacular, hypervisible Hinduism is writ across the cultural landscape. The result is: each author is able to generate a celevision in the self-representation.

Ancestral self-fashioning

The significance of this self-fashioning in contemporary India is in terms of its contribution to the making of a specific public sphere. While the works of these authors are constituted by and constitutive of the public sphere and of reading publics, their online self-representations calls for a more nuanced manner of studying the contours of this public sphere. The Internet itself has been described as a public sphere (Papacharissi 2002). However, we now know that the digital world is always already linked to the offline or material spaces, and they mutually influence, impact and even determine each other. This means the writings around Hinduism by these authors, based on textual appropriations, and their self-representations are part of a continuum marked by the revival of Hinduism in the form of Hindutva (the ideological position espoused by Hindu right-wing parties that argues for the supremacy and superiority of an alleged non-diversified Hindu way of life, and seeks to impose Hinduism as the *national* identity for India, and socio-cultural-political expression of this belief). The larger point, for purposes of this chapter, is online or digital Hinduism as manifest in these web presences and self-presentations.

Authors reworking Hindu epics and mythologies undertake a specific form of self-fashioning, one that, adapting Vokes (2008), I term "ancestral self-fashioning". Vokes (2008, 347), examining photographs of individuals dying of AIDS in Africa, describes the photographic albums as "victim's life history … better understood as an act of self-making, one that is specifically oriented toward this idea of how that person might 'continue to live on' after his death". Vokes' emphasis is, of course, on the victim's *intended* continuity of life in association with the survivors by documenting, in a move akin to what Hirsch (1992–93) termed *postmemory*, familial linkages and ancestry via memory *objects* and artifacts. I appropriate the term to describe the self-fashioning of a group of authors whose self-fashioning is clearly aligned, in terms of their self-representation, with ancestry – a term

I take to mean not just family lineage but also cultural and religion-based identitarian genealogies.

Amish Tripathi, or *Amish* as he signs his name on the books' covers, in his first step toward this ancestral self-fashioning, positions his name and photograph on a backdrop that resembles an ancient scroll (Tripathi 2018b). The yellow-brown scroll has religious – Hindu – symbolism and the mantra *Om Nama Shivaya* is inscribed throughout. Amish's own name and photograph occur in the midst of this set of inscriptions. The contemporary font of Amish contrasts sharply with the Sanskrit letters of the chant, and Amish in a suit poses in the backdrop of ancient symbolism. Further, halfway down the homepage (Tripathi 2018b), there are endorsements from persons who are perceived by many as authorities on Hinduism – a fact that additionally connects Amish to Hindu ancestry: "Archetypal and stirring… Amish's books unfold the deepest recesses of the soul" – Deepak Chopra; "India's First Literary Popstar" – Shekhar Kapur. Amish, we are told, "worked for 14 years in the financial services industry before turning to full-time writing", and is a graduate of the prestigious Indian Institute of Management, Calcutta.

Devdutt Pattanaik adopts a different strategy. His website (Pattanaik n.d.a) opens on a photograph of Pattanaik himself, with some words of self-description scrolling across, of which one (as of date) is *Mythologist*. The opening page lists his newest essays. On the left is an image of a woman holding a lamp, apparently symbolic of praying. The woman is clearly marked, with the *bindi* (forehead mark), as a Hindu woman. It also tells us that he is "trained in medicine" and has worked in the "healthcare and pharma industries before he focused on his passion full time" (http://devdutt.com/about). Ashok Banker is described on his opening page as "India's epic storyteller".

Two features of Amish's self-presentation stand out. First, Amish as a name and author, it suggests, is located on and in a palimpsest of older texts. Second, his contemporaneity seems to draw upon for sustenance and identity, on older names and chants. Thus, contemporary words, as Amish writes them, are the parole of the much older langue embodied in the chants and symbolisms.

Pattanaik's self-description as a mythologist rather than an author, or novelist or storyteller, presents him in a unique style (I do not recall anybody in contemporary India who has styled himself/herself this way): of a man connected to his past and cultural heritage. His work, we are informed, is on "the relevance of mythology in modern times" (a phrase that occurs quite a few times on the website, Pattanaik n.d.b). Pattanaik presents himself as a man who links past and present and, more importantly, demonstrates how the past – mythology – is relevant in domains such as "management, governance and leadership" (Pattanaik n.d.b). His specialization is, as the website suggests, lectures to corporates on "Leadership topics based on Indian way (adapted to audience need)" (Pattanaik n.d.c).

The word *epic* which immediately recalls the Hindu texts *Ramayana* and *Mahabharata* enables Banker to present himself as not only one who tells epic stories, but one whose stories ought to resonate for those readers who *know their epics*. *Epic* is the link between Ashok Banker in contemporary India and the ancient world of the *Ramayana* and *Mahabharata*.

All three authors locate contemporaneity in their narrative and cultural genealogies: Hindu symbolism, Hindu prayers, Hindu myths and Hindu narrative modes. Vokes (2008, 349–350) has argued that:

> ... the family portrait shot also contributed to these effects [a new regime of seeing and new forms of personhood], by further casting this newly contrived individual in a particular way: as the outcome of a specified nuclear family, itself the product of a broader, and peculiarly linear, family history.

I propose that a similar set of effects is generated by these authors in the process of their self-fashioning. First, ancestral self-fashioning generates a regime of *seeing* and receiving the authors as linked to, descended from and drawing upon older genealogies, texts and traditions. The works of these authors are self-conscious adaptations and retellings of earlier, authorized by Hindu institutions, textual – both oral and printed – traditions, a significant point in terms of the cultural (re)production of Hinduism online to which I shall return for a different reason later. Second, and related to the first, the ancestral self-fashioning positions the author – Banker, Pattanaik and Amish – as the product of a specific family history: a larger Hindu family history that is *not* restricted to a bloodline (Banker incidentally identifies himself as "Born and brought up in a multi-racial, multicultural Christian family in India" in his longer bio-note on his website, see Banker n.d.a). That is, the author here does not restrict or define his identity in terms of a biological family line but rather a cultural genealogy of the larger *Hindu family* where the textual inscriptions – their writings – are to be read as reiterations of the family-line. The anastomosing line is not between individuals or individual families but diachronic in terms of inheritances. The insistence on the textual traditions – mythology, stories, epics – in the three authors' self-fashioning might then be read as Miller (1995) interpreted the *line* (as *linum*, *linen*, implying textual weaves) in *Ariadne's Thread: Storylines* as a textual line (of composition), a weave and a lineage. It is therefore clear that all three authors explicitly situate themselves within Hindu textual traditions. However, they do not remain entrenched within this.

The contemporary nature of their identities has to be emphasized. The bio-note that says Amish has a finance and management background or that Devdutt trained in medicine imply their this-worldliness, so to speak. Thus, it is their unique ability to merge (temper?) their heritage and cultural affiliations with the contemporary disciplines, fields and professions – from pharma and from finance – that add to their aura. They occupy more than one field. They come with different trainings and skill sets, and cannot be reduced, therefore, to the mere fact of birth in a Hindu family or Indian setting. That is, their interest in mythology or Hindu heritage may be read as proceeding from a multifaceted, highly skilled intellect rather than from blind belief. Bringing different trainings and skills to the task of rendering Hinduism into readable stories is different from doing so just out of belief.

Cultural production of Hinduism, online

When these authors present themselves as located within a tradition of scholarship and writing, they adapt these older narratives for their purposes. First, the authors and their texts are "multimarketable" (Murray, cited in Ponzanesi 2014, 110), taking recourse to multiple modes of validating their cultural claims and their cultural products. Thus, blogging and tweeting enables the authors to connect to their readers. Amish wishes his readers via his tweet and his website on festive occasions (e.g., "This #RamNavami may lord Ram bless you with happiness, strength and success", Tripathi 2018c). A community of readers is addressed through the multiple forms of communication and exchange facilitated by social media. The forging of this community has, in some cases, an interesting dimension: readers and fans are asked to design a book cover for Amish's forthcoming (at the time of writing) book. The readers are encouraged to write to the authors, respond to them and interact with them ("Amish loves to interact with his readers", says his website, Tripathi 2018c). Thus, readers are co-opted, however nominally, into the *making* of the book and the author-aura: it is the production of a cultural text that includes the novel or book, the community of readers and fans around the book and the persona of the author. Cultural production, therefore, works at the level of participatory authorship and co-creative networks around the texts, which are themselves, as we know in the case of the epics, believed to have had multiple authors and editors. It is therefore possible to see these cultural texts – author websites – as sites of cultural production that adapts older traditions of textual productions.

The presentations of these authors also imply a country of readers waiting for these kinds of adaptations. In the case of Amish, we are repeatedly told of the phenomenal sales of his books, and numbers are scattered about in the commentaries, interview sound-bites and web-info, all suggesting that the contemporary reader has embraced him in a big way. We are also, finally, introduced to the multimodal dissemination of his work: the first ever YouTube trailer created for a book, "movie-like big-budget trailers" in theaters, a music album, among other "innovative" (the term used by the voiceover in the video on Amish's website, Tripathi 2018d) marketing strategies. Bollywood stars such as Amitabh Bachchan, Kajol and Akshay Kumar appear in clips endorsing the books. We see a similar rhetoric of grand success in the case of Banker too.

Second, in terms of reception, the cultural texts around epics, mythologies and storytellers as represented on the author websites offer a different role for the authors. Novetzke (2013, 138) proposes an "anamnetic authorship" in the case of Indian-Hindu saint-poets like Namdev, where later poets added their own compositions, verse and performances (since these songs were sung in public) *in his name*. Various later compositions, then, accrued to the signature of "Namdev" (Novetzke 2013, 138–139). More importantly, an authorship "collapsed, articulated and differentiated in ways that appear purposeful and collectively enacted" enabled the making of a "public memory" of Namdev (Novetzke 2013, 139). Novetzke (2008, xii–xiii) argues that such efforts on the part of authors are indicative of the desires of an audience for a specific textual history. If all memory is social, as theorists of memory have argued, then a text that appropriates earlier memories encoded in their texts like the *Ramayana* and *Mahabharata* generates a specific public around these connected (past-present) memories. Thus, the author-websites are spaces where authorship is located within the cultural genealogies but in the process also generate, through their appeals to and interactions with the audience as mediators for social and cultural memories around folk, legend and other such older texts in the tradition.

Third, Hinduism is (re)produced online through these authors' websites when the older stories are repurposed in the marketing brochures, images and book notices. More importantly, the (re)productions of iconic images on these websites must be seen as integral to the marketing of specific *models* of Hindu gods, legends and heroes.

The emphasis on muscled gods in the case of both Rama and Shiva, in calendar art and other mass-circulated image forms as has been argued (Jain 2007; Lutgendorf 2003), on the cover images of Amish's books is a particular model of Hindu divinity visible after the late 1980s. The gods are clearly defined in martial terms, sporting bodies that are toned and fit. Kajri Jain in fact proposes that the Ayodhya campaign of the late 1980s[1] would not have been possible without the "lean, active, hungry, fighting, and laboring" of the Bollywood superstar of that time: Amitabh Bachchan (Jain 2007, 340). Jain's argument refracts depictions of Hindu gods of that age via a Bollywoodization of the male body, where all heroes – gods and humans – sport a specific look and physique. This argument retains considerable purchase even today, with the six-pack male Bollywood star becoming the standard of male appeal. The continuity from the 1980s may therefore be seen in both – the contemporary male star body and the representations on the author websites under consideration here.

Fourth, the websites and their cultural production are examples of contemporary (postcolonial) India's adaptation of its historical, mythological and religious pasts into the digital age of global business and capital. But preceding all this is the success story. Adaptation, as Hutcheon (2006) defines it, is both process and product. It is an acknowledged transposition of a recognizable other work or works, a creative *and* an interpretive act of appropriation/salvaging and an extended intertextual engagement with the adapted work (Hutcheon 2006, 8, emphasis in original). What online self-representations and marketing rhetoric of these authors work to achieve is precisely these three. The works are clearly, from their very title and synopsis as presented on the authors' websites, situated in a well-known tradition: the "Shiva Trilogy" and the "Ram Chandra Series" (Amish); "Shivaji", "Maurya", The *Mahabharata* Series and The *Ramayana* Series (Banker); *My Gita*, *Sita* (Pattanaik). Then, these are made relevant and appealing to the contemporary right away, suggesting a creative interpretation (or *applicability*) of the textual tradition. This is particularly true in the case of Devdutt Pattanaik whose book titles advertised on the website are "The Talent Sutra", "The Leadership Sutra", "The Success Sutra". The titles themselves indicate the appropriation of older texts and argumentative, philosophical and political systems (*sutras* in Sanskrit are collections of aphorisms or rules). The adaptation of religious figures and legends for the purpose of success in the (neoliberal) corporate world as the larger goal of Pattanaik is very clear from the slides and links on his website (Pattanaik n.d.a) to his talks, corporate guru role, advice books and columns. The tagline on the website reads: "I help leverage the power of myth in business, management, and life".

Effective transcoding, therefore, of myths, says Pattanaik, is what he does. Here the story is not being shifted into another medium (book to film), but from one context to another, so that the context changes the story's interpretation (Hutcheon 2006, 7–8). Thus, Pattanaik is describing a transcoding where the cultural information – or culture *as* information – is being transcribed from one code language (religion, belief systems, faith, mythologies) into another (business). This transcoding, as Crewe (1997) has demonstrated in the case of Haraway's work on cultures of science, ensures that Pattanaik's cultural production (of myths and stories) is presented, implicitly, as narrowing the gap between the culture of religion and the culture of everyday business and politics.

The process of transcoding enables Pattanaik to position himself within Hinduism but distancing himself from Hindutva. He claims that Hindutva is one version of Hinduism, and currently the dominant one. He then goes on to claim:

> Hindutva follows a linear Western template just like Marxism, secularism, and liberalism, ideologies it holds in deepest contempt. This means, both see themselves as objective and scientific and seek the truth, and are disturbed by ideas such as existence of multiple myths that are true for some but not all. Both find the present imperfect and problematic. Both yearn for solutions and seek perfection through human intervention in one lifetime. Thus, both use words like mission, destination and revolution. Both display messianic certainty and a sense of urgency. Both harbour a saviour complex! While Marxism, secularism

> and liberalism seek to save the world by reforming what they see as an unfair past, Hindutva seeks to save the world by reclaiming what it sees as Hinduism's glorious past destroyed by Muslims and Christians and now, Marxists-secular-liberal forces that it bundles into one group. Both are combative, constantly seeking and finding villains to annihilate and establish their righteous heroism. Both despise alternate points of view. Neither likes diversity and seeks to contain it within a larger single homogenous discourse, like nationalism, or human rights. Both are embedded in anger, and seek justice. One can argue that Hindutva marks the semitisation of Hinduism, for linear thought is the hallmark of Abrahamic mythology, while Hinduism is rooted in cyclical structures. (Pattanaik 2016a)

When read alongside his attempt to relocate Hindu mythology within the safer domain of (neoliberal) business and corporations, recasting them in the language of success, wealth and leadership, Pattanaik's cultural production of Hinduism has smoothly segued into the new world order, as he seeks to maintain a careful distance from the much-criticized Hindutva. That Pattanaik also speaks of subjects that are taboo to Hindutva – such as lesbianism – on his website (Pattanaik 2017) is also a matter of interest, and indicative of his attempts to avoid the label *right-wing Hindu*. Pattanaik is also careful to present himself as critical of hegemonic discourses, moral policing and any kind of fundamentalism. In a 2016 piece archived on his website (https://devdutt.com/articles/modern-mythmaking/from-macaulay-to-frawley-from-doniger-to-elst-why-do-many-indians-need-white-saviours.html), referring to the controversy around Wendy Doniger's book on Hinduism, Pattanaik has several things to say. He first notes:

> In order to appreciate the writings of Donger or Pollock, it is important to remind ourselves that they are highly successful American professors in American universities and this has as much to do with their ability as scholars as it has to do with their shrewd ability to negotiate successfully through the worldview of American education … they need to indulge the America's saviour complex if they need a share of the shrinking funding… their writings are at pains to constantly point how privileged Hindus have been "othering" the Dalits, Muslims and women, using Sanskrit, Ramayana, Mimamsa, Dharmashastras, and Manusmriti. (Pattanaik 2016b)

"All this activism", he notes, "in the guise of academia causes the Hindutva lobby to bristle" (Pattanaik 2016b).

Pattanaik then turns to those American scholars who have written more favorably about Hinduism. He says:

> If we attribute strategy to the works of Doniger and Pollock, the same needs to be done to the works of Elst and Frawley. Both are catering

> to a vast latent need of privileged Hindus to feel good about themselves. ... After having been at the receiving end of Orientalist and Marxist criticism since the 19th century, privileged Hindus have not developed requisite skills in the field of humanities to launch a worthwhile defense. (Pattanaik 2016b)

He then concludes by stating that we have to shake off this obsession with Euro-American academia:

> The Hindutva obsession (raga, in Sanskrit) for Elst and Frawley, and the revulsion (dwesha, in Sanskrit) for Doniger and Pollock, is mirrored by the liberal-secular obsession with Doniger and Pollock and their revulsion for Elst and Frawley. In doing so, these White Knights have transplanted Euro-American valorisation of intellectual combat into Indian soil, seeking one truth (scientific objectivity) over multiple truths (anekantavada of Jainism, for example). Thus we find in India the Euro-American Left's war against religion, and the Euro-American Right's Crusade against Muslims. ... If we have to truly be decolonised, and truly swadeshi, be it the MK Gandhi or the Rashtriya Swayamsevak Sangh variety, we have to overcome our inferiority complexes, and without succumbing to chauvinism, realise that we Indians, with all our shortcomings, do not really need Europeans and Americans to tell us what Hinduism, Sanskrit or Vedas were, are, or should be. (Pattanaik 2016b)

Pattanaik calls for dialogue, conversation and not simply argument: "We have bought into the fantasy that being an 'argumentative Indian' in a spirit of rancor is a marker of scholarship" (Pattanaik 2016b). This effective rejection of both fundamentalist and academic debate enables Pattanaik to convey the sense of one who is taking neither a left liberal nor a Hindutva position.

Both Pattanaik and Amish primarily speak of mythology. For instance, in a video on Amish's site, "The Journey of the Shiva Trilogy" (Tripathi 2018e), the voiceover refers to *our ancestors*, while the still images in the video depict the Hindu god Shiva's muscular arms. There are questions enunciated in the voiceover such as "what if their [the gods'] life is their message?". The blurring of myth and religion serves the purpose well here, for it locates these authors in the gray area, as storytellers and chroniclers but not necessarily *Hindu* writers.

Ashok Banker concludes his longer bio-note (Banker n.d.a) with the statement "... he determined that he would grow up without such biases and prejudices against any religion, community or nationality and would never espouse any one faith or group all his life". He thus distances himself from his vast oeuvre of Hinduism-driven texts. More importantly, Banker ensures he has espoused the right causes. His website (Banker n.d.a) says:

> He is a home-maker, feminist, animal lover, and actively supports the marginalised, QUILTBAG, neurodiverse, disabled, and #ownvoices.

> Born and brought up in a multi-racial, multicultural Christian family in India, he does not follow a religion nor does he identify with any one culture or community. (For example: He is **not** a Hindu and does not celebrate or observe Hindu practices, rituals, customs or festivals.) His view on God (any god) is DGAF. His politics are left of left liberal, somewhere between anarchy and communism; he identifies most closely with the intellectual views of Arundhati Roy. He believes Black Lives Matter. He does not tolerate or accept social injustice, hierarchical structures, binary gendering, 'Othering', or systemic and endemic biases such as racism, sexism, misogyny, bigotry, patriarchy, and casteism.

On Amish's website self-introduction (Tripathi 2018f), we are told about Amish: "Amish's unique combination of crackling story-telling, religious symbolism and profound philosophies has made him an overnight publishing phenomenon, with spiritual guru Deepak Chopra hailing Amish's books as 'archetypal and stirring'".

Explicitly referring to his religious symbolism, supplemented by Deepak Chopra (the USA-based spiritual guru of Indian origin,) description, the bio-note, however, positions Amish as not just a *Hindu* novelist but a philosophical one. The author, we are told, subscribes to philosophies, in the plural, suggesting a more eclectic and variegated foundation, and not just a Hindu one. Deepak Chopra's labeling of Amish as "archetypal" (www.authoramish.com/homepage/) is more complicated given its three foundational meanings. It suggests a purity of person/persona that chimes easily with the Hindutva agenda of and insistence on purity. Then, it also suggests a standard or template that others may follow or emulate. Third, in Jungian terms, it suggests a universality. Whether this is meant to suggest that the Hinduism-inspired Amish is a prototype/standard author whose concerns and themes are universal is a moot point, but if it were so indeed, the meanings one takes away from "archetype", then Chopra is implying a certain universality to Hinduism itself.

In his 2 March 2017 *Telegraph* essay, "A Patriotic Manifesto" (The modern Indian: Amish 2017), linked from his website, Amish declares that true patriotism is "love towards all who live here". Yet again, although he employs terminology from Hinduism – *swadharma* (purpose and action in accordance with one's own nature) and *rajdharma* (duty toward the land/others) – Amish is careful to not speak of religious identities and instead focuses on "all who live here". Similarly, Amish is careful to not insist on a monolithic Hinduism either. In an interview linked from his website (Dixit and Padmar 2016), he states "there are hundreds of versions of *Mahabharata*, *Ramayana*, and all other scriptures, and they are all different. We have to believe which version brings us peace, just like how I chose the version of mythology that suits me for my stories". Amish's statement brings to mind the furor over A. K. Ramanujan's essay "Three Hundred Ramayanas" which was withdrawn from the Delhi University syllabi due to protests by Hindutva groups in 2011 (Vijetha 2016). The insistence on plurality and multiple interpretations is welcome, of course, in Amish's statement.

Cumulatively, these instances from the online cultural productions of Hinduism-driven texts offer us several insights. There is indisputably a major revival of cultural productions around Hindu texts, myths and stories. The leveraging of this for larger discursive purposes – such as the insistence on speaking of true patriotism (Amish) or corporate strategies (Pattanaik) or tolerance (Banker) – suggests that any outright endorsement of Hindu fundamentalisms is kept out of the visible persona of the authors.

Authors in the age of Hindu celevision

Having noted the self-fashioning of authors and their cultural production of Hinduism online, I now turn to the making of celebrity Hindu authors in the age of "celevision". Kavka (2016, 297) uses the term "celevision" to describe a media context that enables "seeing celebrity through a range of platforms, channels and interlinked delivery mechanisms", and elaborates:

> Celevision, then, articulates the multiplication of screens on which celebrity can appear, as well as the sociotechnological interconnection of spaces in which these screens function. At the same time, celevision is an outgrowth of the transformations to television itself, both to its technology and its culture. Celevision thus names the everyday circulation of celebrity through the extensions of television culture as supported by the spread of screen technologies. (Kavka 2016, 297)

Kavka is pointing to the convergence of media technologies that ensure the connection of spaces – from newspapers on the web to author websites – in which the author appears.

The appearance of these authors on YouTube (linked from their websites) is arguably the first major move toward celebrification in the age of new media. YouTube itself hosts channels like RajshriKids (Rajshri Kids 2009) which carries numerous stories in animation form from the *Ramayana, Mahabharata, Panchatantra* and others (it also carries Christmas stories, and the famous Akbar-Birbal tales). Apps that enable one to listen to prayers are also increasingly available (e.g., the BalVihar app). These apps, channels and online resources should be seen as part of the socio-technological contexts in which authors such as Banker and Pattanaik flourish.

Nanda has argued in *The God Market* (2009) that there is an increasing Hindu religiosity in India in the face of globalization. If globalization is driven, as Manuel Castells (1996–1998) has argued, by Information and Communications Technologies (ICTs), then the responses to globalization make use of the same ICTs. This means, the interconnection of spaces – from the temples to the markets to the screens – is to be seen as facilitating technologies of religiosity. Banker and others are responding not merely to the arrival of new technologies for the transmission of their work but to a transformation of public culture itself, with doses of religion, spiritual advice and myths and stories drawn from scriptural traditions (what I am calling *technologies of religiosity*). The celevision experience of Banker's website or Amish's interview with Smriti Irani, a minister in the Indian government, on YouTube (linked from his website, Tripathi 2018a) might then be read as the distribution of televisual content about Hinduism across multiple sites and screens.

The authors, therefore, only leverage existing conditions in which Hinduism is across screens and sites, to generate a celevision. As Kavka (2016, 302) puts it, "the figure and role of the star that sustains and is sustained by the dispersed television apparatus". If we see celevision as an apparatus that carries Hinduism across screens, sites and peoples, then what unites the screens is also the star author.

The star author, such as Amish, in representations of muscular deities such as Rama or Hanuman, is appropriating and participating in what I have termed at the beginning of this chapter, spectacular and hypervisible Hinduism, especially after the election of Narendra Modi as prime minister in 2014. With more cut-outs, posters and processions during Hindu festivals, arches on the roads and temple rituals with amplified music than ever before, Hinduism is a spectacle, a public event. My use of the term hypervisible signifies the unavoidable persistence of Hindu icons in all public spaces, the frequent debates around secularism *versus* Hinduism and a *Hindu India,* and the insertion/assertion of Hindu motifs – whether in the form of scriptural texts or songs in schools, yoga or dress codes. Freitag (2003, 389) has argued that acts of seeing become acts of *knowing* as consumers and viewers impute new meanings to familiar messages. Civil society's informal activities – as opposed to the state's – writes Freitag, especially in the realm of popular visual culture, often challenge the actions of the nation-state. Earlier in this same essay, Freitag (2003, 371) argues that traditional art or performance is fine-tuned to accommodate the new. If we think of the visual field of statues, cut-outs, arches and processions that constitute contemporary spectacular Hinduism, we see how, *contra* Freitag, it supplements the present state's ideology. Digital Hinduism embodied in author websites, blogs and tweets is therefore part of this *Hindu* celevision and popular visual culture rather than a distinct entity or process. The authors revive the textual traditions and repurpose the older tales in the form of adaptation and storytelling to appeal to the new.

Marshall (2006, 637–638), writing about celebrity culture, has argued that "there has been an explosion of presenting one's self online in the most public way". My point is, the *public way* in contemporary India is one associated most closely with a Hindu idiom, and representational regimes across media reenact and repurpose this idiom – which is what we see Banker, Pattanaik and Amish doing.

The author in the age of Hindu celevision is at once a means of cultural capital and a marketable commodity, as Moran (2000, 6) argued about star authors in America. Moran (2000, 8), following Barthes, refers to the "complicated relationship between cultural authority and celebrity visibility in the representation of famous authors". When Pattanaik's blog and online self-representations, like Amish's journalism, serve the purpose of cultural commentary – from patriotism to lesbian art – then the celebrity status is assured, and the author may be said to have arrived. Writing books around Hindu texts and then using them as launchpads for cultural commentary, tweeting greets on Hindu festival days and lecturing on Hinduism-based recipes for professional wealth and success lend Banker, Amish and Pattanaik both the cultural authority and celebrity visibility. The former comes from their drawing upon Hinduism, the latter comes from the insistence of cultural production, both online and offline.

Conclusion

Chris Rojek (2001, 58) has argued that "post-God celebrity is now one of the mainstays of organizing recognition and belonging in a secular society". But what is also fascinating is the celebrity status of those authors who organize this recognition and do so by returning to ancient religious texts. What Banker, Pattanaik and Amish achieve is a celebrity status that stems from being glossily packaged conduits and mediating devices for these ancient texts and stories. Many of these stories are already well known to Hindu audiences, but the repackaging of popular and populist tales into epic generates a form of the national popular.

Such a national popular – and one *must* qualify the national as exclusionary, because here it is a Hindu popular that takes on the role and status of/as an *Indian* one – builds on a celebrity connection and identification with both the author and the epic characters being repackaged. A commonplace and routine devotion to the latter can serve to produce the fandom for the first. If religion provides coherence and direction, then Banker, Pattanaik and Amish instrumentalize such a coherence, and in the process direct the audience toward their own works.

It would be interesting and challenging to explore the charisma around these authors. I forward, by way of a conclusion but also as a possible future course of study, a brief point. The charisma of these authors, demonstrated at the crowded book launches and a fan following of common readers and Bollywood superstars, relies upon the mediated self-representation as well as the charisma-effect of working with gods, demons and mythic heroes. That is, Banker, Amish and others generate their charisma through an investment in and drawing upon the ready mimetic capital available in India's god tales and the now-dominant god market. Mimetic capital refers to "a stockpile of representations, a set of images and image-making devices that are *accumulated*, 'banked', as it were, in books, archives, collections, cultural storehouses, until such time as these representations are called upon to generate new representations", as Stephen Greenblatt puts it in *Marvelous Possessions* (1991, 6, emphasis in original). Mimetic capital can be banked upon because of a very specific feature of celebrity culture: iterability. In this case, the author becomes the instrument of this iterability wherein a *recognizable* god-figure is being re-presented.

To phrase it differently: Banker, Pattanaik and Amish participate in the faith economy *even as* they re-represent the set of images and stories that is at the core of this economy – its mimetic capital – within the celebrity economies of television, book production and fandom.

Note

1 This refers to the Bharatiya Janata Party's nationwide campaign to muster support to (re)build a temple in Ayodhya, at the place where they believe that Rama was born, and where a mosque built by the Mughal Emperor Babar stood till 1992, when the party-led masses destroyed it.

References

Banker, A. K., n.d.a. *Welcome to Ashok's World.* Available at www.ashokkbanker.com/, accessed 11 July 2018.

Banker, A. K., n.d.b. *About.* Available at www.ashokkbanker.com/home/about/, accessed 11 July 2018.

Campbell, H. and Golan, O., 2011. Creating Digital Enclaves: Negotiation of the Internet among Bounded Religious Communities. *Media, Culture, & Society* 33(5), 709–724.

Castells, M., 1996. *The Rise of the Network Society. The Information Age: Economy, Society and Culture Vol. I.* Cambridge and Oxford: Blackwell.

Castells, M., 1997. *The Power of Identity. The Information Age: Economy, Society and Culture Vol. II.* Cambridge: Blackwell.

Castells, M., 1998. *End of Millennium. The Information Age: Economy, Society and Culture Vol. III.* Cambridge: Blackwell.

Crewe, J, 1997. Transcoding the World: Donna Haraway's Postmodernism. *Signs: Journal of Women in Culture & Society* 22(4), 891–905.

Dixit, M. and Padmar, D., 2016. Past in the present. *The Hindu*, [online] 20 December. Available at www.thehindu.com/todays-paper/tp-features/tp-metroplus/Past-in-the-present/article16908700.ece, accessed 11 July 2018.

Fader, A. and Gottlieb, O., 2015. Occupy Judaism: Religion, Digital Media, and the Public. *Anthropological Quarterly* 88(3), 759–793.

Freitag, S., 2003. The Realm of the Visual: Agency and Modern Civil Society, In: Ramaswamy, S., ed. *Beyond Appearances? Visual Practices and Ideologies in Modern India.* New Delhi: SAGE, 365–397.

Greenblatt, S., 1991. *Marvelous Possessions: The Wonder of the New World.* Chicago: University of Chicago Press.

Hirsch, M., 1992–93. Family Pictures: *Maus*, Mourning, and Post-Memory. *Discourse* 15(2), 3–29.

Hutcheon, L., 2006. *A Theory of Adaptation.* New York and London: Routledge.

Jain, K., 2007. *Gods in the Bazaar: The Economies of Indian Calendar Art.* Durham, NA: Duke University Press.

Kavka, M., 2016. Celevision: Mobilizations of the Television Screen. In: Marshall, P. and Redmond, S., eds. *A Companion to Celebrity.* Malden: Wiley-Blackwell, 295–315.

Lutgendorf, P. A., 2003. Evolving a Monkey: Hanuman, Poster Art, and Postcolonial Anxiety. In: Ramaswamy, S., ed. *Beyond Appearances? Visual Practices and Ideologies in Modern India.* New Delhi; London: Sage, 71–112.

Marshall, P. D., 2006. New Media – New Self: The Changing Power of Celebrity. In: David Marshall, P. D., ed. *The Celebrity Culture Reader.* New York: Routledge, 634–644.

Miller, J. H., 1995. *Ariadne's Thread: Story Lines.* New Haven: Yale University Press.

Moran, J., 2000. *Star Authors: Literary Celebrity in America.* London: Pluto.

Nanda, M., 2009. *The God Market: How Globalization is Making India More Hindu.* London: Random House.

Novetzke, C. L., 2008. *History, Bhakti and Public Memory: Namdev in Religious and Secular Traditions.* Ranikhet: Permanent Black.

Novetzke, C. L., 2013. *Religion and Public Memory: A Cultural History of Saint Namdev in India.* New York: Columbia University Press.

Novetzke, C. L., 2016. *The Quotidian Revolution: Vernacularization, Religion, and the Premodern Public Sphere in India.* New York: Columbia University Press.

Papacharissi, Z., 2002. The Virtual Sphere: The Internet as a Public Sphere. *New Media & Society* 9(4), 1–24.

Pattanaik, D., n.d.a. *Devdutt Pattanaik.* Available at http://devdutt.com/, accessed 11 July 2018.

Pattanaik, D., n.d.b. Bio. Available at http://devdutt.com/about, accessed 11 July 2018.

Pattanaik, D., n.d.c. Speaker. Available at http://devdutt.com/speaking, accessed 11 July 2018.

Pattanaik, D., 2016a. *The Impact of Abrahamic Mythology.* Available at https://devdutt.com/articles/applied-mythology/society/the-impact-of-abrahamic-mythology.html, accessed 11 July 2018.

Pattanaik, D., 2016b. *From Macaulay to Frawley, from Doniger to Elst: Why do Many Indians Need White saviours?* Available at https://devdutt.com/articles/modern-mythmaking/from-macaulay-to-frawley-from-doniger-to-elst-why-do-many-indians-need-white-saviours.html, accessed 11 July 2018.

Pattanaik, D., 2017. *How to Spot a Lesbian in Sacred Indian Art.* Available at https://devdutt.com/articles/applied-mythology/queer/how-to-spot-a-lesbian-in-sacred-indian-art.html, accessed 11 July 2018.

Ponzanesi, S., 2014. *The Postcolonial Cultural Industry: Icons, Markets, Mythologies.* London: Palgrave-Macmillan.

Rajshri Kids, 2009. *Rajshri Kids.* Available at www.youtube.com/user/RajshriKids, accessed 11 July 2018.

Rojek, C., 2001. *Celebrity.* London: Reaktion.

The modern Indian: Amish, 2017. A Patriotic Manifesto. *The Telegraph*, [online] 2 March. Available at www.telegraphindia.com/1170302/jsp/opinion/story_138412.jsp, accessed 11 July 2018.

Tripathi, A., 2018a. *Author Amish*. Available at www.authoramish.com/news-n-media-about-author/, accessed 15 April 2019.

Tripathi, A., 2018b. *Homepage*. Available at www.authoramish.com/homepage/, accessed 11 July 2018.

Tripathi, A., 2018c. *Readers Hub*. Available at www.authoramish.com/readers-hub, accessed 11 July 2018.

Tripathi, A., 2018d. *Shiva Trilogy Videos*. Available at www.authoramish.com/shiva-trilogy-videos/, accessed 11 July 2018.

Tripathi, A., 2018e. *The Immortals of Meluha*. Available at www.authoramish.com/the-immortals-of-meluha/, accessed 11 July 2018.

Tripathi, A., 2018f. *About Amish*. Available at www.authoramish.com/news-n-media-about-author, accessed 15 April 2019.

Vijetha S. N., 2016. Historians Protest as Delhi University Purges Ramayana Essay from Syllabus. *The Hindu*, [online] 18 October. Available at www.thehindu.com/news/national/Historians-protest-as-Delhi-University-purges-Ramayana-essay-from-syllabus/article13372074.ece, accessed 11 July 2018.

Vokes, R., 2008. On Ancestral Self-Fashioning: Photography in the Time of AIDS. *Visual Anthropology* 21, 345–363.

6 Instagram your Durga Puja! Social media, hashtags and state-sponsored cultural marketing[1]

Dheepa Sundaram

Introduction

Since the early part of the twenty-first century, scholars have investigated the Internet as a new landscape for religious expression, ritual and salvation (e.g., Brasher 2001; Campbell 2005, 2010, 2013; Grieve 2016; Helland 2002; Højsgaard and Warburg 2005; Radde-Antweiler 2006). Heidi Campbell defines digital religion as "not simply refer[ring] to religion as it is performed and articulated online...[but also] how digital media and spaces are shaping and being shaped by religious practice" (Campbell 2013, 1). Recent studies in Hindu online ritual consider, for example, how virtual worship practices both resemble and alter the traditional surroundings / liturgical context of *yajñā* (fire ritual) and *pūjā* (worship) (e.g., Scheifinger 2010). More notably, they highlight the considerable growth in what we can perceive of as industry through various virtual media (e.g., Gittinger 2018; Karpanagiotis 2010; Radde-Antweiler and Zeiler 2019). The popularity of social media platforms as spaces for religious community and networking has introduced a new set of "publics [that] are now active in the production, circulation, imbrication, selection, and re-making of 'the religious' and the 'spiritual'" (Hoover 2012, xii). Stewart Hoover suggests that digital spaces do not operate as competition for traditional religious spaces but, rather, relocate religious authority "in a different place than the past" (Hoover 2012, xii). Doing so creates what he terms a "horizontal inventory" of sources in which tradition and innovation exist side by side, empowering those who access this inventory to contribute and critique it in the context of lived experience and practice (Hoover 2012, xii).

Such digital platforms also become the center of a debate regarding access and accessibility. While many Hindu worship platforms and websites focus on offering convenience and ease of service, this access still seems to disinclude those already excluded from the material sacred spaces – that is, marginalized castes, in some cases women or those from marginalized social communities. Unlike in material sacred spaces such as temples, where such disinclusion is direct and public, virtual spaces devoted to Hindu rituals, ideas, deities and temples do not bar participation from any group.

However, user-language and references as well as webhosts and social media platforms are mainly directed toward an upper-caste and financially stable community. Social media posts most often function as virtual references (as in the case of Durga Puja posts) for rituals or celebrations taking place in material spaces. In this way, they reify any restrictions on these spaces faced by marginalized groups. Thus, accessibility to online worship modules requires more than just permission: financial means, Internet access and, notably, the representation of minoritarian views, rituals, traditions and so forth often prove to be insurmountable hurdles for members of marginalized groups (Mallapragada 2010). Apps and social media overall broaden accessibility by lowering costs and allowing users to be connected to such platforms through mobile devices. However, as state actors begin promoting the use of social media as a way for users to experience a religious festival such as Durga Puja virtually, these spaces among other things also become cultural marketing platforms designed to increase state capital. For instance, user-generated content collected through the *share pūjā* button on the West Bengal tourism app *Sharadotsav* produces a digital image canon that reifies the dominant Hindu narrative regarding Durga's killing of Mahisasura.[2] The Adivasi (first-dwellers) Asur community, found predominantly in the states of Bengal and Jharkhand, trace their lineage to Mahisasura and view Durga Puja festivities as a time of mourning the loss of their great king. Many Asurs also see Durga as a symbol of caste discrimination and part of the systemic eliding of indigenous and non-majoritarian cultures, histories, traditions and beliefs. Thus, this collection of images is linked to hashtags such as #durgapuja and #biswabangla when posted to individual Instagram accounts. These hashtags include those suggested by the state tourism board including links to the West Bengal Tourism Ministry (WBT) and its corporate partner Biswa Bangla.

This chapter examines how hashtags convert social media posts into cultural products that must compete to ensure that their meanings are linked to the virtual semiotic thread and seen by other users. Using Walter Benjamin's (1969) concerns regarding the *fascist salvation* of mass media, which champions opportunity rather than accessibility, I argue that social media platforms (e.g., Instagram and Facebook) reinforce casted Hindu traditions as an unmarked *normal* by encouraging communal insularity through cultural marketing. Examining Facebook and Instagram pages of individual users as well as those of state actors and non-governmental organizations during Durga Puja in West Bengal, I demonstrate how particular hashtags (#durgapuja, #westbengaltourism, #biswabangla, #mahisasura/#mahisasur, #asurking and #casteviolence) garner meaning and gain traction with users in the social media economy of likes and shares. In this context, hashtags create meaning by first collecting semiotic currency through the various likes, shares and posts that use a particular hashtag. A particular narrative, through a saturation of posts as well as likes and shares, directs the trajectory of meaning, subordinating all other meanings. When this occurs, these subordinate meanings are, essentially, delinked from the semiotic thread of the hashtag in the public platform and relegated to localized, insular networks in which users share the hashtag with like-minded individuals. Thus, in the libertarian space of social media, the alternative narrative held by the Asur community regarding the killing of Mahisasura has little to no ability to use the hashtag to advance their ideas.

I have organized this chapter as follows. I begin with a brief methodology and discussion of the social media platforms examined, followed by background and context on the development of the WBT and Biswa Bangla. The next section details the globalization processes often applied to online religion - disembedding and deculturation and the process of unmooring that takes place when a public ritual like Durga Puja is transformed for social media consumption. To show how this works, the subsequent section explains how hashtags function as a semiotic technology which is subject to market dynamics in order to produce a virtual information highway through social media channels. Analysis of specific examples from Instagram posts as well as the WBT website for Durga Puja, wbtourismpuja.in, demonstrates how WBT converts Durga Puja into a saleable asset by orchestrating a social media marketing campaign. The final section demonstrates how social media operate as cultural marketing platforms that elide the voices of marginalized groups who are unable to change the meaning trajectory of the hashtag because of a lack of social market share. The conclusion spotlights what I call the tyranny of hashtags and the unspoken alliance that emerges between state interests, majoritarian beliefs and social media technologies to produce a virtual market space in which individuals are granted access rather than true accessibility to market their ideas.

Methodology

The data for this chapter will be taken from an Asur Facebook page titled *Asur Adivasi Wisdom Documentation Initiative*, an activist Instagram account @indian.feminist as well as selected posts from the thousands of Instagram posts which include the hashtags #durgapuja, #durga, #mahisasuramardini, #mahisasura, #wbtourism and #biswabangla. I analyze a select number of Instagram posts by users that appear on the first page of search results within Instagram for #durgapuja, #mahisasura / #mahisasur, #westbengaltourism, #biswabangla and #asurking. I focus on posts with high share rates to demonstrate how they steer the meaning to these hashtags. To show how these social media sites become cultural marketplaces, I will also examine how posts link to particular corporate and government sponsors to both self-brand while also directing users to particular cultural products that then become icons and, in a sense, part of a digital image canon. In addition to the aforementioned hashtags, I performed searches on Instagram for #casteviolence coupled with #mahisasura / #mahisasur to show how initial pages of results yield posts which reify the mainstream Hindu narrative of Durga's killing of Mahisasura. I also examine the West Bengal Tourism Department's Instagram campaign to market Durga Pujas by using hashtags to link their project to their cultural product store – Biswa Bangla. Finally, I examine two social media pages (@indian.feminist on Instagram and *Asur Adivasi Wisdom Documentation Initiative* on Facebook) which focus on Durga Puja as a day of mourning for Asurs. Analyzing their use of the hashtags #casteviolence and #mahisasura to demonstrate how the number of followers and likes does not necessarily guarantee traction; rather, hashtags use a saturation of posts to create aggregate meanings. Since Asur Adivasi or indigenous communities have a rather modest Instagram presence, I offer a brief look at their Facebook page (*Asur Adivasi Wisdom Documentation Initiative*), its followers and the traction of the hashtags they use. It is important to note that Facebook and Instagram often attract different sets of users. This research does not explore the difference in demographics of these sites. Rather, the focus remains on how hashtags work through a social capitalistic algorithmic model that attaches meaning by aggregating likes and shares to produce a virtual semiotic pathway. However, I will show that hashtag semiotic networks also subordinate less popular meanings, effectively making them invisible within these social networks.

Background and context: West Bengal tourism department and Biswa Bangla

In 2013, the West Bengal TMC (Trinamool Congress) government, led by Chief Minister Mamata Bannerjee, committed to a platform of development and modernization led by a push for a more robust digital and social media presence. Social media accounts are used by the state to market Bengali culture as a sign of economic prosperity, to potential corporate investors in the state. In addition to a separate website (West Bengal Tourism Puja 2016) for Durga Puja, the government launched contests for photo submissions through their private limited corporation, Biswa Bangla, while also organizing parades for *paṇḍāls* (temporary worship structures that include a tableau with the main statue) who were winners in various categories of the Biswa Bangla Sharad Samman established in 2014 (All India Trinamool Congress 2014). Founded in 2014, Biswa Bangla is the corporate arm of the Government of West Bengal's tourism initiative. It highlights a "social business" approach that focuses on "creating entrepreneurs out of artists, and bringing back economic self-reliance to the bottom of the pyramid" (Biswa Bangla 2014).

Durga Puja in Bengal provides an excellent example of how app engagement is integrated into the government's agenda of capitalizing on worship through tourism and the subsequent sale of relevant products. By asking users to share photos through social media and use particular hashtags, West Bengal Tourism becomes the curator of a living digital canon of Durga Puja, one that operates through the social capitalism of hashtags. Additionally, since social media worship platforms have become an important tool for various religious and political groups (e.g., government entities, religious organizations and political parties), when tourism sites crowdsource photos of a ritual, they effectively become unwitting partners in an advertisement campaign for a particular brand of Hinduism – one that can be marketed globally, to both modern and traditional groups. Most importantly, such a campaign offers support for a fiercely nationalist identification which dovetails with a majoritarian vision of Hindu-ness. Indeed, mobile, web-based and virtual platforms offer users new, creative ways to engage with religious traditions, practices and canons while also shaping them.

State and center government initiatives within India, in general, and particularly in West Bengal, that seek to promote cultural artisans have been a part of development programs for several years. In 2006, the Government of India enacted the Micro, Small and Medium Enterprises Development (MSMED) Act to provide loans and financial support to small and medium business ventures (MSME 2018). This organization combined several smaller initiatives including The Ministry of Small Scale Industries and Agro and Rural Industries (SSI and ARI) which were created in October 1999. Amending the Government of India (Allocation of Business) Rules from 1961, ARI and SSI were merged into the MSME. In 2013, Chief Minister Mamata Banerjee folded the loss-bearing West Bengal Handicraft Corporation founded in 1976 into a new MSME corporative initiative called Biswa Bangla (Dutt 2016). Biswa Bangla's success, where other similar initiatives failed, comes from the incorporated social media campaign, linking the corporation to efforts to promote religious tourism within the state. Offering a marketing platform to artisans and traditional Bengali handicrafts, Biswa Bangla fulfills a vital role in preserving cultural practices. However, using a corporate entity as a cultural repository necessitates the use of marketing techniques to promote traditions, rituals and artisans. Doing so makes the corporate arm of WBT the arbiter of what constitutes authentic Bengali / Hindu culture. When WBT launched a social media campaign using Biswa Bangla to promote Durga Puja products in 2014, this corporate entity instantly became an authority of what constitutes authenticity in this space. More recent WBT social media campaigns in 2016–2018 to increase tourism, utilize Biswa Bangla to help "West Bengal become a preferred tourism and tourism-related investment destination by leveraging its unique geographical setting along with its various tourism-related assets" (Department of Tourism Government of West Bengal 2016).[3] Moreover, the website notes that the WBT is committed to "develop necessary infrastructure and promote tourism in an integrated manner which will…bring in more investment and further the socio-economic goals of the Government" (Department of Tourism Government of West Bengal 2016). The discussion of infrastructure, tourism and development in these contexts follows a narrative tale of the mythological landscape of Bengal including being the traditional home of the Hindu goddess Durga.

Perusing the separate West Bengal website for Puja tourism, these *assets* clearly include the Pujas which Bengalis see as most important, Durga and Kali Puja (West Bengal Tourism Puja 2016). Under the tab *Holiday Specials,* users can choose a variety of ways to participate in the worship festivities including Puja packages (West Bengal Tourism Puja 2016). Adherents who purchase these packages can embark on a tour of *pūjā paṇḍāls* or temples and various outlets to purchase traditional foods and other cultural products (e.g., clothing, ritual supplies, idols of the goddess, pamphlets with stories about the goddess and her family) often sold by government stalls or Biswa Bangla stores (West Bengal Tourism Puja 2016). Users are also asked to visit wbtourismpuja.in to learn about how and where to enjoy Durga Puja in various sites in Bengal, with specific cities such as Kolkata having spin-off sites and hashtags (West Bengal Tourism Puja 2016). Visitors to the website are encouraged to download government-sponsored apps as well as visit specific linked pages to the police department, Biswa Bangla, to help navigate the mass of *paṇḍāls*, food stalls and other celebratory activities taking place (West Bengal Tourism Puja 2016). These apps also received wide media coverage including in Condé Nast's travel page briefly causing wbtourismpuja.in to trend on Twitter in September 2017 (Agarwal 2017). By increasing their social media footprint, WBT fosters virtual cultural marketplaces through which users can self-brand and participate in a purchase-based method of affirming their Bengali / Hindu identity.

Disembedding, globalization and the making of cultural marketplaces

The concept of *disembedding* coined within globalization circles refers to the cultural unmooring process that occurs as religious praxis moves into the unfettered global marketplace. Olivier Roy (2013, 7–8) suggests that this process first requires "deculturation" or the "loss of social expression of religion" coupled with a simultaneous "market of different religious products" which results in a homogenizing and standardizing of belief and praxis. In this vein, the recent WBT media campaign that encourages religious tourism by asking adherents to "Share Your Durga Puja" through the *Sharadotsav* app using particular hashtags including #durgapuja, #westbengaltourism and #biswabangla, spotlights such partnerships between state actors and corporate sponsors (Agarwal 2017).[4] These partnerships help convert social media sharing into cultural marketing by asking users to hashtag corporate entities such as Biswa Bangla as well as state sponsors in order to gain benefits (e.g., winning a photo contest, being featured on the WBT website and winning Biswa Bangla Sharad Samman awards) (wbtourism 2017).

Within the world of business and marketing, cultural marketplaces and the concept of cultural marketing have been seen as the method by which to gain a "competitive advantage" and make brands more relatable and effective in drawing in new consumers (Fields 2014). With the advent of online and virtual commercial platforms, marketing strategies targeting a particular cultural demographic must also consider the economy of sociality that determines whether a product will gain market share (Fields 2014). Moreover, the culture of sharing that now characterizes social media platforms such as Facebook, Twitter and Instagram becomes integral to "how online social interaction should be conducted" (Dijck 2013, 46). Jose van Dijck (2013, 46–47) argues that Facebook sets the standard for new business models that privilege sharing over user privacy, making "formatted content, governance policies, and business models...prime tools for intervention". Van Dijck (2013, 68) suggests that Twitter, though initially founded as a microblogging platform for "promoting user connectedness", gradually "transmuted into an information network exploiting user connectivity". In this way, the predictive analytics that govern sharing and trending aim to "capitalize on the flow of tweets rushing though its veins" (Dijck 2013, 69). Van Dijck's study does not consider Instagram, founded in 2010, as it was still a relatively new social media platform. My work seeks to build on van Dijck's critical history by considering hashtag sharing through Instagram, which is the most rapidly growing social media platform within India, with nearly double the number of users since 2015, most of these being upwardly mobile and economically stable (Economic Times Bureau 2015). Both state and individual pages within Instagram use hashtags to create what Roy (2013, 8–9) terms "closed communities with a universalist vision of religion" that trade "cultural depth" for a "reduced set of religious markers" relegating the diversity of traditions to a luxury that is only available once a unified identity is accepted. In this case, by asking users to combine #durgapuja with #biswabangla, in effect, legitimizes Biswa Bangla as an authentic source of Hindu culture and also indelibly links Durga to Bengali identity. Furthermore, these hashtags work together to form a digital meaning chain that cements the narrative of Durga's killing of Mahisasura as the victory of good over evil as the unmarked norm to which all other interpretations are subordinate.

Walter Benjamin (1969) cautions that mass production of art, by way of new media such as the photograph, could result in a loss of *aura*, an *authenticity* that comes with the unique difference of each artistic creation. He contrasts this *authentic consumption* with *mass absorption* of mechanically reproduced art. Benjamin (1969, 226) concludes by saying mass production will become a "salvation of Fascism", giving the masses "not their right, but their chance to express themselves", dovetailing with the aims of the modern cultural marketplace.

Benjamin's (1969) concerns regarding the loss of aura and the advent of fascist populism are well founded when considering how social media platforms function as cultural marketplaces predicated on shared interests. Marketing products to these social media communities has increasingly become a part of how these platforms operate (Dijck 2013). In India, marginalized groups are often restricted from accessing temples and discouraged from participating in rituals in material sacred spaces. Thus, while increased access through such platforms contributes to democratizing the sacred, it also participates in a homogenizing of Hindu-ness, an important aspect of religio-centric nationalist revival in Hindu right politics (Mallapragada 2010). Platforms such as Instagram and Facebook increasingly gravitate toward religious insularity, reifying shared values rather than building communal bridges. Removing the restrictions and the *aura* of the physical space of the temple, social media operate as cultural marketplaces for Hindu ideas, traditions and practices. In this way, virtual platforms unmoor Hindu practices from the mores of purity, pollution and caste discrimination that dominate material sacred spaces, transforming them into identitarian discourses instead. Within these spaces, like-minded individuals share news, ideas and events, echoing a shared ideological positionality. Since these spaces utilize shared interest and values to build social networks, they remain marginally accessible for resistance to majoritarian views. This is largely a result of how these networks are formed through the use of hashtags which garner meaning through the economy of sharing posts. This lack of accessibility is compounded by the marketing of cultural products geared toward majoritarian Hindu communities such as ritual supplies, idols and images.

Hashtag currency and social media markets

Hashtags operate as social currency, allowing users to both self-brand and promote corporate sponsors and their products as we see with the so-called social media influencers who become emblems of this process (Gotter 2018) – this is true also for #biswabangla on Instagram (Biswa Bangla 2014). The media campaign asking users to "*Share your Durga puja!*" was launched in 2017 by WBT in order to capitalize on the state's hottest commodity - Durga Puja (West Bengal Tourism Puja 2016). This website functions as digital canon of the Durga Puja experience in West Bengal by encouraging adherents to share pictures on the WBT webpage or on their own Instagram account with the hashtags #wbtourism, #durgapuja2017 and #sharadotsav2017. These hashtags operate as part of a larger cultural marketing campaign launched by WBT to promote authentic Bengali traditions and arts (United News of India 2018a). Collecting these images into a user-generated digital corpus that appears to be state-sanctioned reinforces majoritarian narratives of Hinduism. Since hashtags operate through likes and shares, this type of capitalist cultural transaction perpetuates minority status for groups traditionally disadvantaged in material sacred spaces (e.g., women, non-*savarṇa* castes[5] and Adivasi communities).

> At one level, the intervention is that the computer, like preceding mass-produced calendar art technologies, is extending the reach of the

> sacred image... it is [also] important to point to the democraticizing potential of the virtual sacred image and consequently, digital darshan... Online darshan delinks the temple institution historically erected on caste and gender oppression from the practice to 'see and be seen by the deity' (Eck 3); new barriers (such as lack of network access) notwithstanding, it is significant that digital darshan opens up the space for historically marginalized Hindu subjects to renegotiate their relation to sacred space-time and divine presence. (Mallapragada 2010, 12)

Mallapragada's arguments concerning accessibility of these sites provide an important foundation for considering the rise of social media platforms catering to religious and spiritual communities. She makes the point that such new media potentially democratize Hinduism by offering access to sacred spaces for historically marginalized Hindu subjects (2010). I suggest that new media spaces afford the opportunity for increased access and participation, but not necessarily the *right* to advance their ideas. These spaces are not necessarily democratic; rather, they operate as libertarian spaces in which everyone is offered the same access, although not necessarily the same traction for their ideas. In this forum, the semiotic currency of hashtags is not reliant on the intended meaning, but rather on the connotational meaning (Zappavigna 2018). The process of connotation within hashtag semiotic networks occurs through an aggregation of significations. Ultimately, the *signified* meaning emerges as the one which dominates most posts, relegating less popular meanings to a position of virtual obscurity. Hashtags produce meaning through market share that form semiotic virtual meaning strings that compile meanings. When users attempt to steer this meaning-making process in a new direction (i.e., create a new semiotic trajectory for the hashtag), they require social currency or market share for the meaning they wish to circulate (Roy 2013). Examining the use of hashtags during Durga Puja in 2017 and 2018 through both state and individual users on Instagram, attempts by marginalized groups to reclaim hashtags such as #mahisasura / #mahisasur and remain *visible* virtually, require having more posts and *shares* for these hashtags than those using #mahisasuramardini. Searches on Instagram for the hashtag #mahisasura invariably lead the user to posts with images of Durga killing Mahisasura. In order to find any pages devoted to the story of the Asur community, the user must search for a specific site by name, such as #indianfeminist.[6]

Durga Puja in West Bengal shows how social media and app interfaces both support state interests in wider access for marginalized groups to sacred spaces through virtual means and corporate sponsorship, while also operating as cultural marketplaces that homogenize worship practices by converting Hindu rituals and holidays into saleable products. Fostering a virtual community of *savarṇa* Hindus through hashtags and messaging, social media platforms unwittingly produce networks of cultural support for the echo-chamber extremism that fuels Hindutva (Hindu-Nationalist)-inspired militant iterations of Hindu values.[7] In essence, the extensive social media presence of WBT reveals features of an emerging Hindu *brand* that can be marketed globally while unwittingly dovetailing with the ethno-national, identitarian political project of the Hindu right.

In 2017, WBT shared an invitation to their Instagram account for a Durga Puja photo contest sponsored by Biswa Bangla, suggesting users can "win fabulous prizes by simply clicking [their] favourite Durga puja" (wbtourism 2017). The contest rules asked users to download the *Sharadotsav* app and then use the *share pūjā* option to post Puja pictures from one's mobile phone. Users are also asked to tag photos with #sharadotsav. The pictures are entered into the Biswa Bangla photo contest while also becoming a part of the WBT website wbtourismpuja.in which collects Puja images. Other contests ask users to post pictures with particular hashtags in order to earn a featured position on the WBT website or Instagram page @wbtourism (wbtourism 2017).

Biswa Bangla also offers the Biswa Bangla Sharad Samman award to the best *paṇḍāls* in several categories (All India Trinamool Congress 2014). Expanding the number of categories and awardees each year since its inception 2014, the 68 winners of these various awards in 2017 were invited to a carnival sponsored by WBT to showcase their award-winning idols parading them enroute to their immersion in the Hooghly river (IANS/Express Photo 2017). Program organizers claimed that in addition to the 20,000 onlookers on the parade route, over five million users watched the live streaming of the event on the WBT social media pages (IANS/Express Photo 2017). One of the *paṇḍāls* featured in the parade the previous year boasted having "not one clay Asura, but nine live Asurs…in an attempt to familiarise Calcuttans with [the Asurs] and their history" (Biswas 2016). However, this is not the narrative that emerges from this event. Sushma Asur, an Asur invited to participate who claimed she was duped about the *paṇḍāl* organizer's intentions, explains "This duping is yet another instance of the historical whitewashing of Asur cultures, rituals and beliefs that have been going on for far too long" (Biswas 2016). Thus, it is the vision of Durga Puja as a celebration for everyone which persists, ironically, strengthened through attempts to complicate this narrative. The social media marketing of the photo contests and parades shows how the WBT uses Biswa Bangla to legitimize and shape a majoritarian Hindu view of Durga Puja as a fundamental aspect of Bengali identity. It also demonstrates how hashtags not only operate as currency, but also as curators of information, sculpting a crowdsourced narrative. They are used to cull posts that reflect what the state views as authentic Bengali identity. In doing so, the state arbitrates what constitutes being a Bengali by producing a digital corpus of Puja images that reify tribal King Mahisasura as a villain and the Hindu goddess Durga as a heroine. While this post by @wbtourism on Instagram received only 21 likes and two shares, it gains traction through the included hashtags (e.g., #biswabangla, #wbtourism and #durgapuja), which extend the reach of this post to other social media platforms as well as other users within those platforms.

When searching for images using #mahisasur or #mahisasura, most often images depicting Mahisasura's death at Durga's hand appear. In an Instagram image and post (Dash 2017) which depicts a black and white artistic rendering of Durga's victory, the included hashtags function in two ways. First, they help define the image for the public; second, they ensure that adherents viewing this page understand the importance and impact of the image. These hashtags determine the virtual semiotic path this image takes within social media platforms as well as the Internet as a whole, determining which meanings will become prominent and which will remain as niche significations without the social marketing power to become part of the main semiotic thread. For example, this image shows how marginalized perspectives like the Asurs are often muted on social media. This image is one of several depicting Durga's killing of Mahisasura that include #Mahisasura. The hashtags associated with this post are: #Goddess #Demon #Good #Evil #Shakti #Form #Supernatural Power #Devine #Durga #Mahisasura #Painting #Black & White #Pattachitra #Depiction #Art form #Detail #Victory #Triumph #Femine power #Mother #Religious #Hinduism #Energy source #Bhubaneswarbuzz #Theperceptivelens #Raghurajpur #TheCraftvillage #Puri #Odisha #Culture #Tradition (Dash 2017). The mixing of sacred imagery with the promotion of particular websites (bhubaneswarbuzz.com) as well as the use of #mahisasura coupled with #good and #evil effectively mutes efforts by Instagram users such as @indian.feminist from redirecting the hashtag meaning trajectory.

When examining the initial page of results from an Internet search on Google, Duckduckgo and Bing for Instagram posts using #mahisasura / #mahisasur coupled with #casteviolence, one of the first posts shows users donning costumes for a *Yakshagana* performance (a traditional folk theater from Karnataka) to reenact the dominant Durga Puja narrative. The user has 3,000 followers on his Instagram page, and this particular post has 73 likes and no shares. The post also includes the following caption, "I am not a monster I am just ahead of the curve #yakshagana #mahisasur #theasurking #latepost in love with this role" (Mr. Joker 2018). Also, the costumes show how depictions of Mahisasura are nearly always as a dark-skinned individual while Durga is represented as fair-skinned (Mr. Joker 2018). The color contrast is not accidental. Rather, it speaks to the larger concerns surrounding caste and class that continue to undergird what functions as a brahmanized social Hinduism.

The next example does not come from Instagram, but rather from a Facebook post (Asur Adivasi Wisdom Documentation Initiative 2018) shared by the *Asur Adivasi Wisdom Documentation* Initiative Facebook page. It should be noted that the posts on this page do not have hashtags, making it difficult for them to participate directly in the meaning-making chain that hashtags produce. I discuss this page to demonstrate the limited social media presence of the Asur communities as well as their limited resources. For example, one recent post on the page asks for donations to pay for the webhosting fees for a related website asurnation.in so that the site can be revived (Asur Adivasi Wisdom Documentation Initiative 2018). Several posts on the page discuss the recent court case filed by several Asur communities against majoritarian Hindu communities in Jharkhand and Bengal, filed to redress their concerns regarding the portrayal of their ancestor Mahisasura (Asur Adivasi Wisdom Documentation Initiative 2018). There are also many images and posts regarding Mahisasura, but two of these posts are particularly interesting. One depicts him as an indigenous king, dressed simply with a turban and loin cloth and with a muscled body and darker skin (Asur Adivasi Wisdom Documentation Initiative 2018). The post, written in Hindi, tells a story of how an Asur from the Netarhat incurred the anger of a *pandit* (learned man, often also ritual specialist) who asked why the Asur continued to denigrate Durga. The Asur explains that just as the *pandit* had the right to recite stories from Hindu epics, the Asurs had a right to their stories regarding their ancestor, Mahisasura (Asur Adivasi Wisdom Documentation Initiative 2018). In another image taken from a news article shared on the Asur Facebook page (Asur Adivasi Wisdom Documentation Initiative 2018), Mahisasura resembles a Hindu idol, light-skinned, bedecked in gold and dressed in colorful attire with an ornate crown (Biswas 2016). Both images clearly foreground Asurs' concerns about caste inequality and the brahmanization of the Durga Puja while seeking to create a resistant and heroic image of Mahisasura. The light-skinned idol of Mahisasura, which resembles a Durga *paṇḍāl*, also displays two framed photos of B. R. Ambedkar, a champion of Dalit rights and author of anti-caste provisions in the Indian constitution. The Asurs use each of these images of Mahisasura to show how their social marginalization is reified through Durga Puja.

The image of Mahisasura as caste hero was also shared on Instagram by @indian.feminist, an account with 3,200 followers on Instagram. This page is a subaccount of a website feminisminindia.com which has a substantial following on Twitter (30,900 followers, Feminisminindia c), Instagram (28,400 followers, Feminisminindia b) and Facebook (65,717 followers, Feminisminindia a). While @indian.feminism uses hashtags with the post #dalit and #casteviolence that link to activist accounts such as @ dalitfeminist and @feminisminindia which include posts that discuss other incidents of caste-based clashes as well as those which spotlight the inequality and brutality often faced by Adivasi and non-*savarṇa* communities, the original post about Mahisasura is not shared to either of these sites. The inclusion #casteviolence along with the hashtag #durgapuja is an attempt to alter the semiotic trajectory of the dominant narrative to include the Asur reading of this story. When compared with resistant demonstrations taking place in material spaces, such acts of resistance in the virtual cannot have the same impact. Since hashtags work through a market model which crowdsources meaning linked through virtual share networks, the resulting semiotic composite meaning uses the volume of posts, shares, likes and so forth to determine which meanings are important and those that can be ignored or discarded. In this case, the original post on @indian.feminist had 58 likes and three shares when it was posted on 17 September 2017 (Indian.Feminist 2017). Even with the boost of specific hashtags linking to other sites focused on caste struggles and minoritized communities within South Asia with much larger followings, the post received no traction (feminisminindia 2017, dalitfeminist 2017). Most notably, a web search for #durgapuja and #mahisasura did not readily bring up either Instagram account without scrolling through several pages. Instead, the most prominent results brought up several images of Durga Puja celebrations reifying the majoritarian Hindu narrative of the victory of good over evil. Even searches within Instagram for #casteviolence, both separately and combined with #mahisasura, bring up posts that either focus on other incidents of caste violence or, in the case of #mahisasura, posts focus on Durga Puja. In other words, despite having a significant number of followers, these posts were unable to infiltrate the hashtag semiotic network because those who liked the post were likely involved in social media groups which agreed with this position. Therefore, sharing the post may have been redundant or unnecessary. The few shares of the post did not garner enough interest or spark a significant number of similar hashtags or posts to alter the meaning of #durgapuja.

It is clear that the number of followers of a site do not determine the traction of hashtags but rather the visibility of the posts themselves. When considering who uses #durgapuja, social media markets treat these hashtags as representative of the majoritarian narrative of Durga's killing of Mahisasura. In this context, the ideas expressed in the @indian.feminist post cannot access the semiotic virtual highway produced by a hashtag with the same hope of exposure as the user sharing their Durga *pandal* hopping experience. This muting effect of minoritarian ideas is furthered by the state's exhortation that users share their *paṇḍāl* pictures with the #durgapuja.

Thus, this state-sponsored photo-sharing campaign helps fashion a *saleable* Hindu identity which is disseminated through social media platforms. This unmarked category of *Hindu* reproduces majoritarian narratives steeped in orthodox views of caste and class that mark sacred material spaces. Moreover, *Vedicizing* of the social media marketplace has unintended consequences through the tyranny of market dynamics. This process produces a virtual commercial space in which niche products (e.g., Adivasi communities, marginalized caste groups and women) cannot employ tools such as the hashtag or social media sharing with the hopes of having the same impact as those sites which cater to wealthier, *savarṇa* audiences.

Instagram culture and the tyranny of hashtags

Social media platforms inform and help produce a number of publics or social spaces in which religious communities operate. While many of these communities are socially rather than religiously oriented, a shared set of beliefs and traditions are often what binds these virtual communities in which users rarely have physical contact with each other. In this section I want to consider how social media hashtags produce cultural marketplaces that both democratize access and contribute to a digital image canon of Hindu praxis. Hashtags function as a "semiotic technology" that "can enact a metadiscourse" (Zappavigna 2018, 15). As both "inward and outward facing metadiscourse", hashtags function as "multimodal discourse markers" that mark other posts in the social network while creating meaning within the host post (Zappavigna 2018, 16). This marking of other posts functions as a sort of ranking system through which the information contained in these network posts informs the host post in so far as they are deemed relevant by the algorithm.

My examination of selected Instagram posts using hashtags linked to WBT social media pages and official website as well as the Facebook page for the Asur community *Asur Adivasi Wisdom Documentation Initiative* shows how virtual semiotic networks enact a metadiscourse which reinforces a majoritarian Hindu view by reifying minoritarian discourse markers within the main semiotic network produced by a hashtag. The lack of an Instagram account as well as frequent calls for donations to support their linked website and foundation suggests a lack of public interest and/or awareness for the Asur Adivasi project. Instagram accounts working to counter majoritarian narratives on Adivasi traditions such as @dalitfeminist and @indian.feminist as well as Facebook community group pages dedicated to Adivasi concerns such as *Adivasi Resurgence*, despite maintaining comparable numbers of followers, get little traction for their posts via hashtags. More notably, their attempts to retool the meaning trajectories of hashtags such as #durgapuja and #mahisasura largely fail since hashtag meanings gain traction by accumulating social currency through likes and shares. Furthermore, self-branding plays an important role in promoting these norms. Posts from personal Instagram accounts that share Durga *paṇḍāl* pictures and wish to participate in the Durga Puja social media photo contest are required to use particular hashtags designated by West Bengal tourism. When doing so, these users link their images and interpretations of Durga Puja to the semiotic network. The sheer volume of these posts which often also reproduce majoritarian Hindu tropes through subsequent hashtags and comments (e.g., good vs. evil, #mahisasuramardini, etc.) effectively creates an unassailable meaning trajectory that produces #durgapuja and #mahisasura as signifiers of the mainstream narrative of Durga's triumph over the evil Mahisasura. In analyzing these posts in terms of language, aesthetics of tradition and imagery, it becomes clear that they are mostly invested in promoting themselves as part of a mainstream Hindu community.

While material space protests often force confrontations between the state and the resistance movement, these efforts are essentially muted on social media and limited by the tyranny of hashtag currency. For example, Asur protests and court filings have received moderate media coverage, state responses, as well as statements of solidarity from student groups that view this as a caste violence concern. Bharatiya Janata Party legislator Smiti Irani's widely panned suggestions that the protests are anti-Hindu helped enhance coverage of the issue. Web searches for *mahisasura* on various platforms such as Google, Duckduckgo and Bing include results for news articles and blog posts detailing the 2016 court actions taken by Asur communities in Jharkhand and parts of Bengal in filing an FIR (first action report) against majoritarian Hindu communities for slandering their ancestor (Biswas 2016). Other efforts to draw attention to Mahisasura and his importance to the Asur community include the *Adivasi Resurgence* and *Asur Adivasi Wisdom Documentation Initiative* which seek to record Asur oral histories and support Adivasi and Asur rights as well as the social media presence of @dalit.feminist and @indian.feminist. Coordinated attempts within the Asur community to have Durga Puja recognized as a day of martyrdom for Mahisasura and to mark the holiday as brutal reminder of the caste violence have been championed by Jawaharlal Nehru University (JNU) student protesters of Durga Puja as a *casteist holiday* (Biswas 2016). When asked if their protest was disputing a widely held belief of Durga as the slayer of the demon Mahisasura, the students explained that this holiday was really about the celebration of caste violence and should be renamed to reflect this injustice (Biswas 2016). Ultimately, the Asur resistance narrative does not have the same access to the cultural marketplace of social media hashtags as *savarṇa* communities, limiting their message to circulation within like-minded identitarian social media circles.

Conclusion

Social media publics and counterpublics are formed through various interactions between corporate, social and, in some cases, state entities (Jackson and Welles 2015). Often these interactions focus on economic development and growth. The West Bengal government tourism campaign launched in 2017, again more successfully in 2018, results in a carefully curated digital collection of a mainstream vision of Durga Puja, perfect for marketing as a tourist package. In the case of WBT, the government sought to maximize cultural resources to improve tourism and encourage economic investment. Analysis of Instagram hashtags used by the West Bengal tourism department, Biswa Bangla, as well as individual Instagram pages, reveal the complicated, fraught alliance between religious traditions / practices and commerce in a globalized, virtual market. In this context, hashtags become culture markers and marketers of majoritarian views, ideas and belief traditions through social media platforms. When state actors and corporate partners use hashtags to promote cultures traditions as products, as we see with WBT's campaign to promote Puja tourism, these entities become arbiters of what constitutes authentic Bengali culture, history and tradition. This confluence of consumerist imperatives with religious tourism results in a homogenizing of Hindu-ness within virtual spaces, creating a social media image canon which reinforces a casted, Hindu identity. Thus, as user-generated posts link state interest with commercial ones within social media markets, the resulting digital corpus of posts supports a vision of India rebranding as a Hindu nation by selling and profiting from its own cultural products.

The generative process of meaning-making in social media settings takes place through the proliferation of hashtags, shares, likes and other media sharing through users. This meaning-making process is unique in that it is predicated on whether a particular meaning has the market share to become viable. Hashtags are thus dynamic signifiers with multiple-meaning threads to which they can attach along with the potential to *go viral*. However, in order to *trend*, a hashtag must be posted and shared by a large volume of users within a short time to be recognized as such by social media platform algorithms. Thus, when hashtags *trend*, they also flood the platform with the most widely shared, associated meanings, effectively erasing alternative and resistant meaning-threads by relegating them to smaller, insular social media circles. This is clear from my searches on Instagram performed during Durga Puja in 2017 and 2018 for #mahisasura which produced several hundred users sharing mainstream Hindu-centric visions of Durga's victory over Mahisasura. Only specific searches for sites such as @feminisminindia, @dalitfeminist and @indian.feminist lead users to posts using #mahisasura to highlight Durga Puja as a day of mourning for the Asur community. As niche cultural products, these sites remain hidden within the hashtag meaning string, as their narrative lacks the necessary volume of likes and shares to overtake the majoritarian view.

Within material spaces, Asur resistance movements are recognized by state apparatuses. In these cases, they are subject to traditional news media coverage, making their alternative discourses describing Mahisasura as a wrongfully maligned ancestor, visible within the public record. However, social media spaces make this type of recognition for such resistance more difficult, as now the state participates not as arbiter, but as marketer. State actors intervene by treating religious festivals as tourism opportunities and use virtual media technologies to help users navigate the mass chaos of the *paṇḍāls* and celebrations (Singh 2019). By asking users to "share their pujas" to the state website, WBT becomes the curator of a neo-*bhadralok* vision of Hinduism while remaining the authority providing access to public spaces and civil rights (West Bengal Tourism Puja 2016).[8] Further, WBT sees these platforms as a way to deepen West Bengal's economic footprint and enhance its reputation as a state that is friendly to development and investment. Indeed, TMC internal publications describe the Biswa Bangla corporation as a state-funded corporation founded to protect and promote Bengali culture while providing an economic platform for the sale of indigenous arts and handicrafts (All India Trinamool Congress 2014). However, the rapid expansion of Biswa Bangla coupled with its intimate participation in marketing its products to users through contests and other advertisements on the various web and social media platforms of the West Bengal tourism department demonstrates the shift in the role of the state when mediating social and religious dissent (United News of India 2018b). While the state may continue to intervene in direct and indirect ways in material spaces either to protect or to punish resistance movements, in the social media world, they become virtual *middlemen* focused on an economic motive while also (perhaps unwittingly) composing a user-generated collage of images that effectively functions as a digital image canon of *savarṇa* Bengali Hinduism. In the libertarian space of social media hashtags, this becomes the only meaning that has the capacity to circulate.

The WBT social media campaign is part of a broader push across India for state actors to forge close links with private investors, corporate sponsors and individual consumers. Prime Minister Narendra Modi's focus on *yoga* while in office offers an example of this type of state-sponsored cultural marketing that advances the desires of majoritarian communities by flattening "cultural depth" through economic partnerships with non-state entities (Roy 2013). Modi's desire to rebrand *yoga* as not only Indian, but Hindu, began with a push for International Yoga Day as the overarching theme of his inaugural UN speech on 27 September 2014. In 2017, he dedicated a 112-foot statue of Shiva as the first *yogi* (Adinatha) in Coimbatore, Tamil Nadu, that was commissioned by Jaggi ("Sadhguru") Vasudev's *Isha Foundation*. In this context, *yoga* operates as the cultural product, marketed as a foundational Indian practice that is simultaneously linked to Hindu ideals. Moreover, despite Isha Foundation's official status as a secular organization, its funding and defending of a Hindu religious statue provides an apt example of how both state and non-state actors foster a popular religious nationalism aided by globalizing commercial forces, rather than countered by them.

In a neoliberal marketplace of hashtags and *SEOs* (Search Engine Optimization companies) that traffic in the currency of clicks, likes, shares and links, resistant narratives like that of the Asurs struggle to receive exposure. This capitalist model of information sharing benefits Hindutva groups within India by turning social media into virtual cultural markets in which users and state and non-state actors co-constitute a globalized, cosmopolitan Hinduism palatable to *savarṇa* communities while ostensibly providing broad access to the sacred. However, if these spaces reproduce a majoritarian narrative without providing reference to alternative versions, as in the case of the Asur community's characterization of the Durga Puja as the

Martyrdom of Mahisasura, they reinforce a *Vedicized* Hinduism, rooted in casted traditions and values. In this context, expanded social media marketing by state and non-state actors increases the state economic footprint while producing a corporate-sponsored cultural repository of majoritarian Hindu traditions that effectively elides minoritarian beliefs, traditions and history.

Notes

1 The phrase "Instagram your Durga Puja" is not used directly by the West Bengal Tourism Department (WBT). Rather, I use it to characterize WBT's efforts to create a social media corpus of images designed to further their goal of making use of *indigenous resources* to encourage investment and development in the state. These efforts seem to be working; since on 2 April 2019, following the recommendation of Sangeet Natak Akademi, India's center government declared Durga Puja as their nomination to UNESCO to be designated a "Heritage Tradition" (Panja 2019).

2 Durga Puja is a festival that celebrates the goddess' defeat of Mahisasura, an indigenous king who becomes the buffalo demon. For most Hindu adherents, this ritual marks the triumph of good versus evil. However, several Asur Adivasi (first dweller) communities see this festival as an insult to their ancestor Mahisasura who they describe as a good king of whom the *devas* (Hindu deities) become jealous. Envious of Mahisasura's rapport with his people, the *devas* asked the Hindu deities Brahma, Vishnu and Shiva to create goddess Durga to first tempt Mahishasura and then kill him.

3 The tourism-related assets refer to Kali and Durga Puja.

4 It should also be noted that the Sharadotsav app is only available through Android platforms. A forthcoming work on Jain religious apps notes that the majority of these only appear on Android platforms (Vekemans 2019). Android has 97% of the market share in India according to a Strategy Analytics report in 2016 (Nair 2016). This is largely because of the cost of procuring an Apple device remains prohibitively high (Nair 2016). When considering the Android versus Apple disparity in the context of social media, somewhat of a paradox emerges. Instagram is the fastest growing social media platform in India, with 38% of Indian Instagram users owning cars, implying they are economically better off than most of the population (Economic Times Bureau 2015). Rajeev Nair's analysis suggests that the majority of this group would also be Android users, but it would likely also include the 3% of Apple users in the country (2016). In essence, a small group of wealthy, likely upper-caste users, which the WBT would be targeting, cannot access this app. It will be interesting to see if they develop an Apple version of the Sharadotsav app in their efforts to expand their Puja tourism marketing strategies.

5 The term *savarṇa* references majoritarian Indian groups that are recognized, promoted and advantaged by social, political and civic institutions.

6 A web search for #theindianfeminist instead of #indianfeminist takes you to a different account in which these posts do not appear.

7 The term *Hindutva* literally means *Hindu-ness*. It refers to ideologies, political groups and social movements that believe India is a Hindu nation. Thus, these groups view all Indians, regardless of religious affiliation, as originally *Hindu* in terms of culture and tradition.

8 The Bhadralok is a reference to the Bengali elites that emerged as a sort of aristocratic class during colonial rule (1757–1947).

References

Adivasi Resurgence, 2019. *Adivasi Resurgence*, [Facebook] 4 January. Available at www.facebook.com/adivasi.resurgence/, accessed 1 March 2019.

Agarwal, P., 2017. What's the Best Durga Puja Pandal in Kolkata? There's Now an App for That. *Condé Nast Traveller*, [online] 18 September. Available at www.cntraveller.in/story/best-pujo-pandal-kolkata-theres-now-app/?utm_source=Daily&utm_medium=email, accessed 4 March 2018.

All India Trinamool Congress, 2014. *Biswa Bangla Sharad Samman – Celebrating Durga Puja Worldwide*. Available at http://aitcofficial.org/aitc/biswa-bangla-sharad-samman-celebrating-durga-puja-worldwide/, accessed 6 April 2018.

Asur Adivasi Wisdom Documentation Initiative, 2018. *Asur Adivasi Wisdom Documentation Initiative*, [Facebook] 8 November, 27 November. Available at www.facebook.com/pg/WeAsurAdivasi/posts/?ref=page_internal, accessed March 3 2019.

Benjamin, W., 1969. Work of Art in the Age of Mechanical Reproduction. In: Arendt, H., ed. *Illuminations*. New York: Schocken Books, 219–226.

Bhubaneswar (Buzz), 2015. Bhubaneswar Buzz-Dream to see Odisha as Top Travel Destination in India. Available at www.bhubaneswarbuzz.com/, accessed 15 April 2019.

Biswa Bangla, 2014. Biswa Bangla Where the World Meets Bengal. Available at www.biswabangla.in/, accessed 24 January 2018.

Biswas, S., 2016. For the Asurs of Bengal, Durga Puja is the Time to Celebrate the 'Demon God' Durga Slayed. *Scoop Whoop*, [online] 7 October. Available at www.scoopwhoop.com/For-The-Asurs-of-Bengal-Durga-Puja-Is-The-Time-To-Celebrate-The-Demon-God-Durga-Slayed/#.385itgp7n, accessed 3 March 2018.

Brasher, B., 2001. *Give Me that Online Religion*. San Francisco: Jossey-Bass.

Campbell, H., ed., 2013. *Digital Religion: Understanding Religious Practice in New Media Worlds*. London and New York: Routledge.

Campbell, H., 2005. *Exploring Religious Community Online*. Bern: Peter Lang.

Campbell, H., 2010. *When Religion Meets New Media*. London and New York: Routledge.

Dalitfeminist, 2017. *Dalitfeminist*. [Instagram]. Available at www.instagram.com/dalitfeminist/?hl=en, accessed 1 December 2017.

Dash, S., 2017. *Dashraman*. [Instagram], 29 September. Available at www.pikdo.me/media/BXorgpThxTB, accessed 1 December 2017.

Department of Tourism Government of West Bengal, 2016. *Mission of West Bengal Tourism Department*. Available at www.wbtourismgov.in/home/mission, accessed 18 March 2018.

Dutt, I., 2016. Mamata wipes out losses from Manjusha, Tantuja, *Business Standard*, [online] 11 July, Available at www.business-standard.com/article/economy-policy/mamata-wipes-out-losses-from-manjusha-tantuja-116071100026_1.html, accessed 27 April 2018.

Economic Times Bureau, 2015. Most Instagram Users in India Upwardly Mobile: Study. *Economic Times*, [online] 19 November. Available at https://economictimes.indiatimes.com/tech/internet/most-instagram-users-in-india-upwardly-mobile-study/articleshow/49838905.cms, accessed 20 April 2018.

Feminisminindia, 2017a. *Feminisminindia*. [Facebook]. Available at www.facebook.com/feminisminindia/, accessed 1 December 2017.

Feminisminindia, 2017b. *Feminisminindia*. [Instagram]. Available at www.instagram.com/feminisminindia/?hl=en, accessed 1 December 2017.

Feminisminindia, 2017c. *Feminisminindia*. [Twitter]. Available at https://twitter.com/FeminismInIndia?ref_src=twsrc%5Egoogle%7Ctwcamp%5Eserp%7Ctwgr%5Eauthor, accessed 1 December 2017.

Fields, R., 2014. Culture as Competitive Advantage for Marketers. *Forbes*, [online] 7 April. Available at www.forbes.com/sites/onmarketing/2014/04/07/culture-as-competitive-advantage-for-marketers/#8e8c8ec7a13c, accessed 6 April 2018.

FII Feminism in India, 2019. Feminism in India | Intersectional Feminism—Desi Style! Available at https://feminisminindia.com/, accessed 15 April 2019.

Gittinger, J., 2018. *Hinduism and Hindu Nationalism Online*. London and New York: Routledge.

Gotter, A., 2018. The Marketer's Guide to Instagram Hashtags. *Snappa blog*, [blog] 2 January. Available at https://blog.snappa.com/instagram-hashtags/, accessed 23 April 2019.

Grieve, G., 2016. *Cyber Zen: Imagining Authentic Buddhist Identity, Community and Practices in the Virtual World*. London and New York: Routledge.

Helland, C., 2002. Surfing for Salvation. *Religion* 32(4), 293–302.

Højsgaard, M. and Warburg, M., eds., 2005. *Religion and Cyberspace*. London and New York: Routledge.

Hoover, S., 2012. Foreword. In: Cheong, P. H., Fischer-Nielsen P., Gelfgren, S. and Ess, C., eds. *Digital Religion, Social Media, and Culture: Perspectives, Practices, and Futures*. Bern: Peter Lang, vii–xii.

IANS/Express Photo, 2017. Durga Puja 2017: Kolkata's Pujo Ends with a Grand Carnival. *The Indian Express*, [online] 4 October. Available at https://indianexpress.com/photos/lifestyle-gallery/durga-puja-2017-kolkata-pujo-carnival-process-u-17-fifa-football-tableaux-photos-4873849/, accessed 4 April 2018.

Indian.feminist, 2017. *Indian.feminist*, [Instagram] 27 September 2017. Available at www.instagram.com/indian.feminism/p/BZkrKfgnfty/, accessed 1 December 2017.

Jackson, S. and Welles, B., 2015. Hijacking #myNYPD: Social Media Dissent and Networked Counterpublics. *Journal of Communication* 64(6), 932–952.

Karpanagiotis, N., 2010. Vaishnava Cyber-Pūjā: Problems of Purity and Novel Ritual Solutions. *Online Heidelberg Journal of Religions on the Internet* 4(1), 179–195.

Mallapragada, M., 2010. Desktop Deities: Hindu Temples, Online Cultures, and Politics of Remediation. *South Asian Popular Culture* 8(2), 109–121.

Ministry of Micro, Small, and Medium Enterprise (MSME), 2018. *FAQ*. Available at https://msme.gov.in/faq, accessed 12 April 2019.

Mr. Joker, 2018. *Mr. Joker_puddin115*. [Instagram] 10 January. Available at http://hotsta.net/media/1689030137380689056_3850273839, accessed 7 August 2018.

Nair, R., 2016. *Handset Country Share: India Smartphone Vendor and OS Marketshare: Q2 2016*. India: Strategy Analytics. Available at www.strategyanalytics.com/access-services/devices/mobile-phones/handset-country-share/market-data/report-detail/india-smartphone-vendor-and-os-marketshare-q2-2016#.V6PVpvmANBd, accessed 3 April 2017.

Panja, P., 2019. Bengal Elated as Durga Puja Nominated for UNESCO 2020 List of Cultural Heritage. *The Statesman*, [online] 2 April. Available at www.

thestatesman.com/bengal/bengal-elated-as-durga-puja-nominated-for-unesco-2020-list-of-cultural-heritage-1502742432.html, accessed 8 April 2019.

Radde-Antweiler, K., 2006. Rituals Online: Transferring and Designing Rituals. *Online Heidelberg Journal of Religions on the Internet* 2(1), 54–72.

Radde-Antweiler, K. and Zeiler, X., eds., 2019. *Mediatized Religion in Asia: Studies on Digital Media and Religion*. London and New York: Routledge.

Roy, O., 2013. *Holy Ignorance: When Religion and Culture Part Ways*. London: Oxford University Press.

Scheifinger, H., 2010. Hindu Embodiment and Internet. *Online Heidelberg Journal of Religions on the Internet* 4(1), 196–219.

Singh, V., 2019. Mixing Heritage with Festivities to Promote Tourism in Bengal: An Enchanting Pleasant Voyage. *Media India Group*, [online] 2 March. Available at https://mediaindia.eu/tourism/mixing-heritage-with-festivities-to-promote-tourism-in-bengal/, accessed 14 April 2019.

United News of India, 2018a. Biswa Bangla: Bengali Handicrafts Go Global. *United News of India*, [online] 21 August. Available at www.uniindia.com/biswa-bangla-bengali-handicrafts-go global/states/news/1326048.html, accessed 4 April 2019.

United News of India, 2018b. Bengal Govt Branding Durga Puja Festivals in Other Countries. *United News of India*, [online] 29 September. Available at www.uniindia.com/bengal-govt-branding-durga-puja-festival-in-other-countries/states/news/1364495.html, accessed 1 March 2019.

Van Dijck, J., 2013. *The Culture of Connectivity: A Critical History of Social Media*. London: Oxford University Press.

Vekemans, T., (2019). From Self-learning Pathshala to Pilgrimage App: The Expanding World of Jain Religious Apps. In: Fewkes, J. H., ed. *The Anthropological Study of Religious and Religion-themed Mobile Apps*. Palgrave-Macmillan, pp. 1–22.

Wbtourism, 2017. *Wbtourism*. [Instagram] 21 September. Available at www.instagram.com/p/BJTB9qZAJsg/?utm_source=ig_web_copy_link, accessed 23 November 2017.

West Bengal Tourism Puja, 2016. *Mission*. Available at https://wbtourismpuja.in/home/links_sites, accessed 24 January 2018.

Zappavigna, M., 2018. *Searchable Talk: Hashtags and Social Media Metadiscourse*. London: Bloomsbury.

7 Sāṃkhyayoga and the Internet

The website of a contemporary Hindu monastic institution

Knut A. Jacobsen

In 2008, Scheifinger noted that there was "an extremely large number of websites which have content regarding Hinduism and this number is increasing exponentially" (Scheifinger 2008, 233) and argued that "cyberspace is not only compatible with Hinduism, but actually well suited to it" (Scheifinger 2008, 247). However, the study of Hinduism and the Internet developed late, and "up until 2007 there was no published academic work which focused upon the relationship between Hinduism and the Internet" (Scheifinger 2015, 159). Research on the Internet and the numerous Hindu groups and phenomena has since touched especially upon such issues as *pūjā* and *darśan* as Hindu online rituals (Karapanagiotis 2013; Scheifinger 2008, 2012a, 2012b), on the use of the Internet to promote Hindu traditions and institutions (Scheifinger 2012a), on the Internet and global Hindu networks (Jacobs 2012), the Internet and change in Hindu pilgrimage rituals (Jacobsen 2018a), the Internet and the Hindu diaspora (Therwath 2012; Zavos 2015) and, in the last years, increasing attention has been given to the Internet and Hindutva and the Hindu right (Mohan 2015; Therwath 2012; Udupa 2015).

However, less attention has been paid to presentations of Hindu monastic institutions on the Internet, and there are only few studies on the phenomenon of yoga[1] on the Internet (Broo 2012, 18). This chapter tries to make a small contribution to these fields of study: monastic institutions, yoga and the Internet. It analyzes the web pages of the Sāṃkhyayoga institution of Kāpil Maṭh, one of the earliest institutions emerging as part of the modern revival of the *Yogasūtra* in nineteenth-century Bengal. The teaching of Kāpil Maṭh is based mainly on the Sāṃkhyayoga commentary tradition on the *Yogasūtra* and on the Sāṃkhya philosophy. The Kāpil Maṭh and its branches are probably the only living monastic Sāṃkhyayoga tradition in India, and it is certainly the only Indian monastic Sāṃkhyayoga tradition with a significant presence on the Internet. In this chapter I analyze the presentations of the institution, its teachings and its practices on its web pages based on the methods of hermeneutics and close reading of these pages. The article additionally builds on research of Kāpil Maṭh's many book publications, field research and numerous visits to the Kāpil Maṭh monastery in Madhupur in the last 20 years (see Jacobsen 2018b).

The layout of the web pages of Kāpil Maṭh was changed in 2016, and the old pages have been removed from the Internet; however, all the textual material of the old pages as well as the photo documentation were included in the new web pages. During the fall of 2017 and in winter 2018, the texts and number of web pages were continuously updated and expanded, and this will probably continue.

Kāpil Maṭh and its web pages

Kāpil Maṭh is a Bengali Sāṃkhyayoga institution, but none of its web pages are in Bengali. All of Kāpil Maṭh's web pages are in English. The choice of the English language for the web pages may indicate that they are primarily intended to reach out to Indians beyond Bengal and perhaps to a non-Indian global English-speaking audience. The web pages are probably aimed at presenting Sāṃkhyayoga and the Kāpil Maṭh tradition to outsiders and are not used or intended primarily for communication to the Bengali disciples of the Maṭh. The purpose is most likely to attract some attention beyond Bengal, and probably also international attention to the Sāṃkhyayoga teaching and the Kāpil Maṭh institution. The web pages make it possible to maintain a presence in a global context, and the web pages most likely result in a few people making contact and a few visits.

However, Kāpil Maṭh in the last decades has been a very quiet place with few visitors. One reason for the quietude is the unique feature of cave dwelling and the inaccessibility, most of the time, of the guru of the Kāpil Maṭh. The guru most of the time lives isolated in an artificial cave (referred to as *guphā*), a building without an entry and exit door. The founder Hariharānanda Āraṇya (1869–1947) started this cave dwelling, and when Hariharānanda Āraṇya died in 1947, his disciple Dharmamegha Āraṇya (1892–1985) became the new guru and moved into the *guphā*. He was followed by Bhāskara Āraṇya (b. 1942) who is the current (2018) guru. The web pages do not elaborate on the meaning of the cave, but cave dwelling gives associations to the idea dominant in modern yoga of *real* yogis living in caves in the Himalayas.[2] The guru Bhāskara Āraṇya has lived in the *guphā* for decades, but there are no longer any other monks associated with the Maṭh. Maintaining the heritage of Hariharānanda Āraṇya and Dharmamegha Āraṇya has become a foremost task of Kāpil Maṭh. Kāpil Maṭh is a small institution, and it values solitude and silence. The total number of followers is small. The ultimate goal of Sāṃkhyayoga is isolation from matter (*prakṛti* and its products) and other selves (*puruṣa*s). When the central values are solitude and silence, the institution, having been able to remain small, is a sign of success, and this point reminds us that there are other measurements of success than attracting a large number of followers, which are often used as the main sign of success of modern yoga gurus.

The Kāpil Maṭh represents an institutionalization of some important nineteenth-century views on Yoga that promoted the ancient sage Kapila as the world's first philosopher and as the founder of both philosophical systems Sāṃkhya and Yoga and suggested that the teaching of the Buddha was based on Sāṃkhya. Kapila was revered as the first human to realize liberation from rebirth in *saṃsāra* and the person who showed that salvific liberation was possible for all humans to attain. According to this view, all religions were dependent on him (see Jacobsen 2018b, 35–51). One section of the website, namely "Maharshi Kapila the great sage", is devoted to Kapila and depicts a painting of him in the iconographic style of the Kāpil Maṭh tradition. He is in *samādhi* (yogic concentration) surrounded by a tiger and a deer, who are under the influence of his mastery of *ahiṃsā* (non-injury), resting next to him. The mantra of Kāpil Maṭh is printed above the picture: "*Om ādividuṣe kapilāya namaḥ*, Our homage to Kapila, the first wise one". The web page "Maharshi Kapila the great sage" (Samkhya-Yoga n.d.d) states that:

> Samkhya preached by Kapila has been the backbone of all religious tenets of this world. The eternal spirituality which has been the source of joy and relief for billions of individuals since time immemorial has its origin in Kapila. There has been no greater saviour in this world than him, nor can there ever be. The lofty spirit of Buddhism too is based on Samkhya principles.

The web page additionally informs that the text is "taken from *Samkhya Across The Millenniums* by Samkhya-yogacharya Swami Hariharananda Aranya", which shows the close connection between the web pages and the published texts of Kāpil Maṭh (see Āraṇya 2005).

The Kāpil Maṭh is a Bengali institution and with supporters mainly from Bengal. This small Bengali monastic institution is centered in the small town of Madhupur, now in Jharkhand. Until 1912, Madhupur was part of the Bengal Presidency. In the late nineteenth and early twentieth centuries, many wealthy *bhadralok* ("respectable people", a class of prosperous or well-educated Bengalis, mainly upper caste Hindus, emerging in the colonial period) families from Kolkata built second homes in Madhupur, which they visited for their summer and winter vacations.[3] Many of the followers of Kāpil Maṭh today are descendants of families who had second homes in Madhupur and paid regular visits to the Maṭh during their vacation time and took initiation as lay disciples (Jacobsen 2018b). Besides the Bengali followers, there is also a group of Hindi-speaking followers of the teaching and practice of the Kāpil Maṭh tradition based in Sarnath, in Uttar Pradesh. This tradition was started by Omprakāś Āraṇya, who was a disciple of Dharmamegha Āraṇya. However, the Kāpil Āśram in Sarnath does not have web pages.

Hariharānanda Āraṇya, the founder of the Kāpil Maṭh, was from Howrah, next to Kolkata. He was born in 1869 in a *zamindār* (land owner) family, and started a university education in Kolkata, but became disillusioned. He knew Sanskrit, and learning about Sāṃkhyayoga, he became a *saṃnyāsin* (renunciant) in 1892, withdrew from society and lived isolated in the Barabar Hills outside the city of Gaya for several years (1892–1898). Hariharānanda Āraṇya revived the ancient Sāṃkhyayoga tradition, that is, the Yoga tradition promoted in the *Pātañjalayogaśāstra*, as the foundation of a monastic institution (Jacobsen 2018b). *Pātañjalayogaśāstra* is the name of the combined *Yogasūtra* and its commentary text, the *Yogabhāṣya*. Both the *sūtra* and the *bhāṣya* texts were probably written by the same author (Bronkhorst 1985; Maas 2013), who referred to himself as Patañjali. The Yoga system of religious thought is considered one of the six systems of classical Hindu philosophy and is often joined with another of the six systems, the Sāṃkhya system, and the two systems together are referred to as Sāṃkhyayoga. However, Yoga was originally part of the Sāṃkhya system of philosophy, and it was considered a separate system probably only in the twelfth or thirteenth centuries. The term Sāṃkhyayoga is also a name of this tradition of Yoga. The founder of Kāpil Maṭh realized that the *Yogasūtra* as well as the whole *Pātañjalayogaśāstra* was a Sāṃkhya text and that Sāṃkhya and Yoga promoted closely related philosophies, and he attempted to bring them together as the basis for a living *saṃnyāsin* practice. For Hariharānanda Āraṇya, Sāṃkhya was a theory about the world, and the theory of Yoga described in the *Yogasūtra* and the *Yogabhāṣya* presented the means to realize the truth of Sāṃkhya. About the relationship between Sāṃkhya and Yoga, the Kāpil Maṭh web page "Samkhya-Yoga" (Samkhya-Yoga n.d.a) states:

> Samkhya and Yoga are not mutually exclusive systems of philosophy inasmuch as both the systems accept the twenty-five principles or Tattvas. While Samkhya represents the theoretical basis of the psychology of liberation, Yoga concerns itself with the practices for attaining that objective. There is, therefore, no fundamental difference between the two.

Sāṃkhya analyzes the world into 25 *tattva*s (principles), and, according to Āraṇya, Yoga describes the method to realize these *tattva*s, which ultimately leads to the realization of the last two *tattva*s, the 24th *tattva, prakṛti* and the 25th *tattva, puruṣa*, which causes release from rebirth. The Kāpil Maṭh web page "Samkhya Philosophy" (Samkhya-Yoga n.d.e) stresses that these *tattva*s are not theoretical or abstract constructs but "real entities which can be directly apprehended". But they cannot be apprehended by everyone according to this web page, only "by yogins or serious aspirants with proper knowledge, discipline and training". The web page also has an illustrative map of the *tattva*s.

Yogasūtra is the most celebrated text of modern yoga, but even though the text promotes a form of Sāṃkhya philosophy, the popularity of the *Yogasūtra* did not give rise to a great Sāṃkhya revival. The philosophical systems of Sāṃkhya and Yoga (Sāṃkhyayoga) had disappeared from India as living systems, and there were no Sāṃkhyayoga monastic institutions when in the nineteenth century the text of *Yogasūtra* started to receive new attention. Western Orientalists and Theosophists in Bengal, and later Bengali paṇḍits and other intellectuals, became interested in the text, and this became the beginning of a Yoga renaissance, which created modern yoga. At this time, there were no communities of Sāṃkhyayogins; in fact, the Orientalists could not find a single person in Bengal who was a specialist in the Yoga philosophy of the *Yogasūtra*. The situation was similar for Sāṃkhya. The *Yogasūtra* was not at this time the main text of any communities of Sāṃkhyayogins. However, many had become curious about the text, not only Orientalists and Theosophists, but increasingly also Sanskrit paṇḍits and other Indian intellectuals. Many of the yogins of India were at the time looked down upon as mostly dishonest, uncultured and as belonging to low caste (White 2014). Haṭhayoga was associated with these yogins, and many of those who became interested in the *Yogasūtra* considered Haṭhayoga a mistaken form of yoga, and Haṭhayoga only later became part of the yoga renaissance. Those who became interested in the *Yogasūtra* thought that this text represented a different culture of yoga than the one found among these contemporary low-caste yogins. The *Yogasūtra* was thought to represent a philosophy associated with the ancient Sanskrit tradition, which had gained an enormous status partly due to the Orientalists' interest in the ancient texts. In addition, a large number of texts from ancient India were now becoming available as printed books. Modern Hinduism is very much a product of the printing press and the availability of these printed books, and so is the Sāṃkhyayoga tradition of Kāpil Maṭh. *Yogasūtra* became elevated as representative for romantic notions about ancient India typical of the Orientalists and Theosophists, a romanticism which became shared among some of the Indian elite and was important also for mobilizing opposition to the British colonialist ideology. Because of the interest in the *Yogasūtra* by Western Orientalists and Theosophists, the famous monk Vivekānanda was asked to give a lecture series on the text when he stayed in the USA. It was his lectures on the *Yogasūtra* given in the USA in 1894–1895 that were published in 1896 as *Rāja-Yoga*. Modern yoga is often considered to have begun with the publication of this book, a translation of the *Yogasūtra* with a non-traditional commentary. Kāpil Maṭh is a revival of Sāṃkhyayoga orthodoxy and does not consider reform or social service to have anything to do with real yoga. As pointed out earlier, the Kāpil Maṭh institutionalized nineteenth-century interpretations of yoga and has no connection to the traditions of modern yoga that focused on body postures.[4] Notably, *āsana* (body posture) is not even mentioned on the Kāpil Maṭh web pages. In the book publications of Hariharānanda Āraṇya, obsession with *āsana*s is condemned (see Jacobsen 2018b). The response of the Kāpil Maṭh tradition to the obsession with *āsana*s in modern yoga is that those attracted to Sāṃkhyayoga have perfected *āsana* in their previous lives and need now only practice meditation.

In Sāṃkhyayoga, Yoga means control of the mind. On the Kāpil Maṭh web page "Yoga – What it is and what it is not" (Samkhya-Yoga n.d.h), Yoga is defined as "The ability to stop at will the fluctuations or modifications of the mind which is acquired through constant practice in a spirit of renunciation". For this to be Yoga, the purpose for stopping "the fluctuations or modifications of the mind" has to be to attain *kaivalya*: "True Yoga is practiced with a view to attaining salvation", it is stated at the same web page. The salvific goal in Sāṃkhyayoga is separation. In contrast, modern yoga has focused on Vedānta and the idea of yoga as union of the individual soul and the divine. The idea of yoga as union is omnipresent in modern yoga; the word yoga is also mostly interpreted in modern Hinduism to mean *union*. However, according to Sāṃkhyayoga, yoga in the *Pātañjalayogaśāstra* means concentration and not union, and the goal of the Sāṃkhyayoga philosophy is separation of consciousness from matter, *puruṣa* from *prakṛti*. The strong focus in modern yoga on physical exercises (body postures) and on union is not found in the *Yogasūtra*, but these modern traditions of yoga nevertheless claim that the *Yogasūtra* is the foundation text also of their yoga. Thus, in modern yoga, an ancient Sāṃkhyayoga text has been appropriated to support ideas which are not found in the text, and which are quite opposite to the philosophy of Sāṃkhyayoga, which is at the foundation of the text. The Kāpil Maṭh tradition constitutes a corrective to this development. The founder of the Kāpil Maṭh, Hariharānanda Āraṇya, by accessing the Sāṃkhyayoga textual tradition realized the discrepancy between the teachings of Sāṃkhyayoga and other forms of yoga, and he understood these other forms of yoga as mostly misguided (Jacobsen 2018b). He wanted to revive Sāṃkhyayoga orthodoxy as a monastic practice. The Kāpil Maṭh is not a reform movement, but presents itself as a revival of the original Yoga teaching. But how did he learn about Sāmkhyayoga according to the Kāpil Maṭh web pages? How did this revival of Sāṃkhyayoga come about?

The web pages of Kāpil Maṭh and the origin of Āraṇya's Yoga

How do the Kāpil Maṭh web pages present the origin of the Kāpil Maṭh tradition? The basic view as stated in one of the Kāpil Maṭh web page Samkhya-Yoga (Samkhya-Yoga n.d.a) is:

> In course of time, Samkhya gradually lost its place as the prime philosophy of India. One reason of its decline was the absence of a worthy acarya (spiritual teacher) matching the stature of the early Masters. In recent times Samkhya-yogacarya Swami Hariharananda Aranya with his lifelong ardent practice and brilliance was able to revive Samkhya with the aid of his own spiritual realization.

The origin of the Kāpil Maṭh tradition is stated to be Āraṇya's own realization of the reality of Sāṃkhya. No oral tradition or teacher of Āraṇya is mentioned in the Kāpil Maṭh web pages "Acharyas of Kapil Math" (old web page: Samkhya-Yoga n.d.g; new web page: Samkhya-Yoga n.d.c). On the biography of Hariharānanda Āraṇya, on the web page "Swami Hariharananda Aranya/Acharyas of Kapil Math" (old web page: Samkhya-Yoga n.d.g; new web page: Samkhya-Yoga n.d.c), we read about his six years in Barabar Hills:

> Swami Hariharananda Aranya (1869–1947) spent six years of his early monastic life in utter seclusion in the caves of Barabar Hills, Bihar, India. His possessions were the barest minimum, even for a Sannyasin. He devoted the whole time to gain the mastery over his mind, which is Yoga. Having attained his goal, he returned to the world of men. Continuing the secluded and austere lifestyle and intense spiritual practice he began disseminating the message of Samkhya-yoga through books in Bengali and Sanskrit.[5]

The source of Āraṇya's authority is, according to this description, his ability to endure extreme solitude and his Yoga practice. A more detailed description of the origin of his Sāṃkhyayoga is found on another website of the Kāpil Maṭh, called "About us". Here (Samkhya-Yoga n.d.b) the source of his Sāṃkhyayoga teaching is said to be "a copy of an ancient text on Samkhya-yoga in a library". This page, "About us" (Samkhya-Yoga n.d.b), states that Hariharānanda Āraṇya:

> ...came from an educated middle class background in Bengal. In his student days, he felt the urge to renounce the world and don the robe of a Sannyasin. In his search he met many spiritual adepts but was not fully satisfied until he chanced upon a copy of an ancient text on Samkhya-yoga in a library. It resulted in his leaving the home, taking the vow of a Sannyasin and taking up the life of a mendicant. He ultimately landed up in Barabar hills in an uninhabited forested tract near Gaya. The caves were curved out of solid rock in the days of emperor Asoka, especially for accommodating hermits. He stayed there for six long years from 1892 to 1898 in utter seclusion. His possessions were the barest minimum, even for a Sannyasin. A resident from the nearest village trudged miles to bring his lone meal everyday. He devoted the whole time to gain mastery over his mind, which is Yoga. Having attained his goal, he returned to the world of men. He continued the same secluded austere lifestyle and intense spiritual practice in places like Tribeni in Hoogly district in West Bengal, Varanasi, Hardwar, Rishikesh and the Himalayas and finally decided to settle down at Madhupur, Jharkhand (formerly Bihar), India.

The origin of the monastery in Madhupur is accounted for on the website in the "About us" section (Samkhya-Yoga n.d.b) in the following way:

> He had already began disseminting [sic] the message of Samkhya-yoga through books in Bengali and Sanskrit. Emanating from his own experience it was unique, logical and penetrating. Attracted by his unique personality some genuine seekers found him out in the small town of Madhupur, Jharkhand, India and one of them volunteered to build a suitable house containing an artificial cave as the permanent home of the Master. Thus did Kapil Math come into existence. First a dwelling, and an artificial cave with its one and only entrance permanently blocked, where the Master spent the rest of his life. The Math was built adjacent to the 'cave' to house his followers who responded to his call for accepting Samkhya-yoga as the only aim in their lives.

In this narrative of the story of Hariharānanda Āraṇya and Kāpil Maṭh, the origin of Āraṇya's Sāṃkhyayoga is clearly stated. He was a religious seeker, but was not satisfied with the teachers he encountered. He then saw a book in a library which led him to Sāṃkhyayoga. It says correctly that Āraṇya had an educated middle-class background, that he had been a student, that he chanced upon a copy of an ancient text on Sāṃkhyayoga in a library, that he became a *saṃnyāsin* and that he stayed six years in Barabar Hills. The only other person mentioned in Barabar Hills is a "resident from the nearest village" who "trudged miles to bring his lone meal everyday" (Samkhya-Yoga n.d.b). After leaving Barabar Hills, he traveled for some years and stayed for a long time in Triveni, but settled finally in Madhupur where the Kāpil Maṭh was established. One devotee funded the building of a suitable house containing an artificial cave as the home of Āraṇya where he spent the rest of his life with the only entrance permanently blocked.

Neither the Kāpil Maṭh web pages nor any printed books or booklets of the Kāpil Maṭh identify the title of the ancient text on Sāṃkhyayoga, which Āraṇya found in a library. However, during one of my many stays in Kāpil Maṭh between 1999 and 2018, I asked the current guru Bhāskara Āraṇya about this book, that caused Āraṇya "leaving the home, taking the vow of a Sannyasin and taking up the life of a mendicant" ("About us"). Āraṇya kept the book all his life. The copy is still in the Kāpil Maṭh in Madhupur, and when I asked to see it, Bhāskara Āraṇya immediately fetched it and allowed me to examine it (see Jacobsen 2018b, 79–80). This book is a Sanskrit text in Devanāgarī, published in Calcutta in 1890 (dated *saṃvat* 1947). The title of the book is *Yogadarśanam*, and it contains four texts, the *Yogasūtra* and the three commentaries *Yogabhāṣya*, *Tattvavaiśāradī* and *Ṭippaṇa*. The title page of the book reads: *Yogadarśanam: Bhagavanmahāmunipatañjalipraṇītam; Nikhilatantrāparatantrapratibha; Vācaspatimiśraviracitatattvavaiśāradyākhyavyākhyābhūṣitamaharṣikṛṣṇadvaipāyanapraṇītabhāṣyā 'laṅkrtam; Srīmadudāsinasvāmibālarāmeṇa viṣamasthalaṭippaṇanirmāṇa-purahsaraṃ susaṃskrtam*. Kalikātā: Vyāptiṣṭamisanayantra, 1890 (*saṃvat* 1947).[6] In English translation the title reads

> The philosophy of Yoga (*Yogadarśana*) made by the great sage Patañjali, adorned with the commentary with the name *Tattvavaiśāradī* composed by Vācaspatimiśra, decorated with the *Bhāṣya* made by the great sage Kṛṣṇadvaipāyana and beautifully adorned with the gloss printed underneath by Udāsina Bālarāma.

The book contains the four texts *Yogasūtra*, the *Vyāsabhāṣya*, Vācaspati Miśra's *Tattvavaiśāradī* and Udāsina Bālarāma's *Ṭippaṇa* on the *Tattvavaiśāradī*, which are the texts considered the main sources for Harjharānanda Āraṇya's Yoga (Jacobsen 2018b, 79–82).

Āraṇya's restart of Sāṃkhyayoga orthodoxy has sometimes been misunderstood, and several researchers seem to have believed that Āraṇya's Sāṃkhyayoga represented an oral transmission of Sāṃkhyayoga going back centuries, perhaps even an original lineage going back to Patañjali himself. J. N. Farquhar seems to have thought that Āraṇya was the last in a long lineage of Sāṃkhya *saṃnyāsins* (Farquhar 1920, 289; Jacobsen 2018b, 2). Farquhar noted that he had met a Sāṃkhya *saṃnyāsin* in Kolkata. He wrote: "Sāṅkhya sannyāsīs are now so rare that it is of interest to know that, as late as 1912, a learned Sāṅkhya yati named Svāmī Hariharānanda was alive and teaching in Calcutta" (Farquhar 1920, 289). By using the phrase "as late as 1912", Farquhar seems to indicate that Āraṇya came from a larger premodern tradition of Sāṃkhya that was on the verge of dying out, and that Āraṇya was one of the few, or the last one left (Jacobsen 2018b, 2). However, another researcher has recently made the same claim, but now not based on any personal encounter but only with reference to a web page address of Kāpil Maṭh. David Gordon White, in his book *The Yoga Sutra of Patanjali: A Biography*, argues that Pātañjala Yoga was a dead tradition in nineteenth-century Bengal, but makes one exception, the Yoga tradition of Hariharānanda Āraṇya. According to White, during his stay in Barabar Hills from 1892 to 1898, Āraṇya received instruction from a Sāṃkhyayoga teacher "who, as he claimed, belonged to a lineage extending back to Patanjali himself" (White 2014, 224). White refers in the footnote only to a web page of Kāpil Maṭh as the source for the information he is providing: "'Biography of Hariharananda,' found at the 'Kapil Math' website, www.samkhyayoga-darshana.com" (White 2014, 247, n19).

That Hariharānanda Āraṇya's Yoga philosophy appears classical and orthodox as if coming from an oral lineage tradition of Yoga going back to the time of Patañjali and preserved in caves in the Himalaya, as some mistakenly claim (White 2012, 12, 2014, 223–224), is probably because of Āraṇya's lifestyle and because Āraṇya's Yoga was based on the texts which, according to Orientalists, constituted the "core textual complex" of Yoga philosophy (Larson 2008, 70–71). Through the detailed study for years as a *saṃnyāsin* of the texts of *Yogadarśanam* and other texts that were available, Hariharānanda Āraṇya, with his excellent understanding of Sanskrit, gained a deep and detailed understanding of the classical Sāṃkhyayoga tradition. He applied this teaching to his Yoga practice and his own writings and translations. Thus, he revived an orthodox Sāṃkhyayoga tradition based on the study and contemplation of the philosophical texts. It is well known in the Kāpil Maṭh tradition that one *saṃnyāsin* named Trilokī Āraṇya initiated Hariharānanda Āraṇya into the state of *saṃnyāsa* in the town of Triveni in Bengal, but also that no teaching took place. Trilokī was a silent *saṃnyāsin* and no words apparently were exchanged. The meeting lasted only a few hours, or perhaps one day, and took place in Triveni, north of Kolkata. Adinath Chatterjee has in the "Preface" to the *Yoga Philosophy of Patañjali and the Bhāsvatī* described how this encounter took place and stated the source of Āraṇya's Sāṃkhyayoga: "It is difficult to explain the phenomenon that was Swāmī Hariharānanda Āraṇya. He met his Guru only briefly and after his initiation as a Saṃnyāsin he chanced upon an old text of Sāṃkhyayoga in a library" (Chatterjee 2000, xviii). The only place in Hariharānanda Āraṇya's writings where Trilokī Āraṇya seems to be mentioned is in a poem. This poem, in Sanskrit and printed in Bengali letters, appeared in the dedication to his text *Sāṃkhya Prāṇatattva* published in 1902, in which a *paramparā* (lineage, tradition) of Sāṃkhyayoga is presented. This poem is, as far as I know, the only place Āraṇya refers to Trilokī Āraṇya. To my knowledge, he does not mention or elaborate on Trilokī Āraṇya anywhere else in his many published writings. The poem is most likely a piece of fiction, and it was perhaps even intended as such (see Jacobsen 2018b, 72–79 for a discussion). Āraṇya did not refer to this fictional *paramparā* again, and in the *ślokas* (hymns) recited every day in the Kāpil Maṭh tradition, the Sāṃkhyayoga *paramparā* consists only of the authors and names from the ancient textual tradition of Sāṃkhya and Yoga, and, in addition, the Buddha (see Jacobsen 2018b, 155–176).

The origin of the Kāpil Maṭh tradition is associated with books and printed texts. Āraṇya was proficient in Sanskrit and his main teacher was a Sanskrit book publication, the *Yogadarśanam*. Sanskrit books and nineteenth-century Orientalists' knowledge and ideas about ancient India provided access to the classical Sāṃkhyayoga textual tradition. The web pages of Kāpil Maṭh reflect this heritage. Hariharānanda Āraṇya wrote a number of books in Bengali and Sanskrit. The texts are translations, commentaries, a fictional autobiography and a number of essays on themes of Yoga and Sāṃkhya. The second guru wrote a number of letters, and some of his speeches were published. The current guru has been involved in the project of publishing English translations of all the significant texts of Hariharānanda and Dharmamegha Āraṇya. He has written prefaces to a number of the English translations. The Kāpil Maṭh is an intellectual and textual tradition that emerged as part of modernity in Kolkata and was brought about by the availability of printed books (see Jacobsen 2018b). This information is available on the web pages of Kāpil Maṭh and the same information is provided in the books and booklets of Kāpil Maṭh. There is no contradiction between the web pages and the printed texts of Kāpil Maṭh. In fact, the sources of most of the web pages are the printed texts of Kāpil Maṭh, and many of them contain excerpts from the Maṭh's book publications. However, in the printed text are more details, especially detailed instructions for practice (see Jacobsen 2018b: 124–146), which are absent from the web pages. Likewise, personal letters and instructions, as well as the *stotra*s (hymns of praise), are missing from the web pages. The web pages give mostly very limited information. The detailed descriptions of the Kāpil Maṭh tradition are found in the printed material.[7] In other words, the main differences between the web pages and their published books are the amount of information and the type of information. The content of the books can be divided into Sāṃkhya and Yoga philosophy, instructions in Yoga practice, descriptions of life and rituals of Kāpil Maṭh, personal letters and observations, fictional writings of Hariharānanda Āraṇya and *stotra*s. The main emphasis on the web pages is the teaching, information about the gurus, some information about the Maṭh and visual material. The main ritual practice, the daily singing of Sāṃkhyayoga *stotra*s (see Jacobsen 2018b, 153–176), is not presented nor is the fictional work or personal descriptions and observations. On the web pages is general information that the Kāpil Maṭh probably hopes will create some curiosity and interest. The web pages are probably intended to function as advertisements for the Maṭh.

Speed of communication and ease of access

In 1997 when I first contacted the Kāpil Maṭh to organize a visit, I sent a letter in the mail, and it took weeks for the return letter to arrive. The only written information about Kāpil Maṭh easily available was a short one-page appendix in an indological book (Larson 1979, 278). A few of the books about the founder Hariharānanda Āraṇya were available in book stores. Two books had been translated into English and published by Indian publishers, one published by Calcutta University Press in 1963, *The Yoga Philosophy of Patañjali* (Āraṇya 1981),[8] and another, *The Sāṃkhya Sūtra of Pañcaśikha and the Sāṃkhyatattvāloka* by Motilal Banarsidass (Āraṇya 1977a, 1977b). Two other texts in English translations were published by the Kāpil Maṭh, *The Sāṃkhya Catechism* (Āraṇya 1935) and Dhamamegha Āraṇya, *Epistles of a Sāṃkhyayogin* (Āraṇya 1989). Some had been translated into Hindi, but the other texts were in Bengali or Sanskrit and not available outside of Bengal and Madhupur. Currently, information about Kāpil Maṭh is easily available on the Internet. Speed of communication and ease of access are great changes caused by the Internet. However, the guru does not use a phone or computer, and for the disciples to communicate with him, they have to come to Kāpil Maṭh in Madhupur and meet him in person on one of the first five days of the Bengali months on which he is available at the opening window of the cave.

The Kāpil Maṭh has had web pages since 2003.[9] The purpose of these web pages seems to be to inform the non-Bengali world about the existence of Kāpil Maṭh and to propagate its Sāṃkhyayoga teaching. The main function of the pages is to provide information. A difference between the published texts and the web pages is the visual material. The web pages contain a large number of photos of the gurus and the institutional life of Kāpil Maṭh. In addition, video material was included in January 2018.[10] The videos available in January 2018 were of the buildings and gardens of Kāpil Maṭh. No people or activities were shown. It gave the experience of virtually being there when the place is empty, which it is most of the time during the days the guru is unavailable. People come to the Maṭh only on those few first days of the eight months of the year when the guru meets disciples in the window opening of the *guphā*. A few more people come during the festivals, but it is only during the Kapil *utsav* (festival to celebrate Kapila) in December that there are several hundreds. During that festival, local people from Madhupur come, among other things, likely because of the free food. The videos show that a main focus of Kāpil Maṭh currently is on the preservation of its own tradition. The material and visual dimension of the monastery has been expanded, and the texts of the gurus have been translated into English and published by the Maṭh.

Reestablishing the Sāṃkhya doctrine in the world

The language used at Kāpil Maṭh is Bengali. The web pages are intended to provide information to non-Bengalis. The purpose seems to be similar to the English language translations published by Kāpil Maṭh. The Sāṃkhyayoga institution of Kāpil Maṭh possesses a strong textual tradition, and much of its efforts over the last two decades have been on promoting the texts of the gurus through English translations. The Kāpil Maṭh is promoting the philosophical traditions of Sāṃkhya and Yoga as interpreted and practiced by its gurus. The web pages are comparable to the first major English language publication of Kāpil Maṭh, *The Sāṃkhya Catechism*, published in 1935, which was intended to present the Sāṃkhyayoga teaching of Hariharānanda Āraṇya for an international audience. In the preface to *The Sāṃkhya Catechism*, it says that the purpose of the book is to present Sāṃkhyayoga "as it is understood by those to whom it is a living system … to those who do not know Indian languages well" (Āraṇya 1935, iii). *The Sāṃkhya Catechism* mainly describes theories of Sāṃkhya and Yoga, and little is said about practice. Several of the Kāpil Maṭh web pages are based on or are direct quotations from *The Sāṃkhya Catechism*. The web page "Summary of Samkhya teaching" (Samkhya-Yoga n.d.f) is as a whole a quotation from *The Sāṃkhya Catechism*.

The Kāpil Maṭh has had great ambitions for spreading the message of Sāṃkhyayoga. An important lay member of the Maṭh, Ram Shankar Bhattacharya (2003, 152–153), wrote, addressing the members of Kāpil Maṭh:

> It is our responsibility to make people, both within and outside the monastery aware of the new landmark established by Ācārya Swāmijī [Hariharānanda Āraṇya] in the study of Sāṃkhya-yoga system, and we should not spare any effort to work in this direction, according to our individual disposition. Whether it is through study, meditation or practice, we should keep alive the tradition of Sāṃkhya-yoga initiated by Ācārya Swāmījī.

Bhattacharya (2003, 153) concluded that:

> Together we can work to re-establish the Sāṃkhya doctrine in the modern world, which is in search of a philosophy, fully comprehensible in all respects, empirically valid, free from blind superstition and emotionalism and unclouded by an excess of *rajas* and *tamas* elements.

This shows that members of the Kāpil Maṭh institution have had ambitions of spreading the message of Sāṃkhyayoga to the world. The web pages can be seen as a continuation of *The Sāṃkhya Catechism* and manifesting the same intentions and hopes of Kāpil Maṭh, formulated by Bhattacharya, of reestablishing the Sāṃkhya doctrine in the world.

Conclusion

This guru institution of Kāpil Maṭh differs markedly from many of the modern Hindu guru movements, which are often associated with Hindu nationalism or movements associated with capitalism and market strategies (Pandya 2016). Neither service to the Indian nation (Beckerlegge 2003) nor the idea of marketable salvation goods (Redden 2005) is part of this institution. The Kāpil Maṭh institution seems to contradict much that has been written about contemporary guru movements in India, which often emphasize success, Hindu nationalism, capitalism and the market and New Age spirituality. Typically, academic articles on the guru phenomenon deal with the most successful gurus whose disciples often exaggerate their success. While Hinduism as such is not a missionary religion, gurus do compete for adherents, and the number of adherents is often used as a measure of attainment and success. However, most Hindu gurus probably do not attract a large following, and most gurus are not able to establish institutions that last longer than the lifetime of themselves and their own devotees. It is the largest and most successful guru institutions that also attract most academic research. Kāpil Maṭh has none of these features. It has not repackaged Sāṃkhyayoga to suit modernity (see Pandya 2016, 224), but the disciples of Kāpil Maṭh emphasize the difficulty both of understanding the teaching and of practicing it. The number of followers has been stagnant for some time. Having a great number of devotees is often considered the sign of success of modern gurus and guru movements (see Lucia 2014; Singleton and Goldberg 2014), but in Kāpil Maṭh, the emphasis is on solitude and silence (see Jacobsen 2018b, 156–157).

The relationship between gurus and disciples is a personal relationship. The disciples can approach the guru with questions about spiritual development but also about all other kinds of problems regarding work and family life. The guru is supposed to advice in all kind of matters, and the relationship between guru and disciple can be a lifelong one. Hindu ascetics have often been quick in adopting new communication technologies such as mobile phones and email. The guru of Kāpil Maṭh has not adopted any of these means of communication. To have a personal relationship, one has to meet the guru, but if the purpose is to get some basic information about some of the main teachings of Kāpil Maṭh, their web pages can be read. However, the development has not been from oral tradition directly to web pages. Before the Internet, the teachings of many gurus, including the gurus of Kāpil Maṭh, were available in booklets or books, texts either written by the guru or in hagiographical descriptions of the life and the teachings. The Internet in the discussed case study has therefore come as an addition to the printed books that already were available. It could, however, also be argued that the Internet has influenced the distribution of books. It has made the books more easily available, as Internet book stores like Amazon have made books from all over the world, even books published by small monasteries in India, more easily available globally. In the case of Kāpil Maṭh, the Internet seems to be an extension of the written text of books and booklets rather than an expansion of the oral tradition. More than a century ago, book printing had started in India to make both ancient and modern teachings more easily available. In nineteenth-century India, book printing had an enormous influence in making available the teaching of Indian ancient traditions and increasingly their interpretations by contemporary gurus. The websites of many religious institutions have now become an additional source.

Notes

1 In this chapter I use capital letters (Yoga) for the philosophical system, and non-capitals (yoga) for other forms of yoga and the modern practice.

2 Joseph Alter writes: "The sage lost to the world in the Himalayas is an extremely powerful reference point in the search for authentic Yoga, and it is a reference point that has played an important role in the development of modern Yoga" (Alter 2004, 17).

3 L. S. S. O'Malley in his *Bengal Distcrict Gazetteers, Santal Parganas*, published in 1910, noted that the town had "a growing reputation as a health resort among the Bengali community. A number of new houses have consequently been built in recent years by residents of Calcutta and other places" (O'Malley 1910: 268–269).

4 Modern yoga combined this elevated status of the *Yogasūtra* with various forms of influences from traditions of sports and physical health such as modern body-building and forms of gymnastics, which had little connection to the *Yogasūtra* and its Sāṃkhyayoga philosophy. Because of this interest in sports, many traditions of modern yoga have a strong focus on *āsana*, body postures. They constructed yoga as a tradition of sports, but nevertheless sought to connect their yoga to the *Yogasūtra* as the foundation of yoga.

5 This text is from the old web pages of Kāpil Maṭh and found in the web archive at https://web.archive.org/web/20110202181158/www.samkhyayoga-darshana.com/, accessed 2 February 2011. The same text is found on the new web pages at www.kapila.math.com/acharyas-of-kapil-math/, accessed 6 January 2018.

6 This is the same copy of the text that John Haughton Woods used of for his translation of the *Pātañjalayogaśāstra* with the *Tattvavaiśāradī* published in 1914 (Woods 1914).

7 For an overview of the printed texts of Kāpil Maṭh, see Jacobsen (2018b, 209–213).

8 This book was republished in an American edition by State University of New York press in 1983.

9 The earliest web page available on the web.archive.org is from August 2003. See https://web.archive.org/web/20030628122357/www.samkhyayoga-darshana.com:80/, accessed 20 July 2018.

10 The material is available at www.kapilmath.com/videos-of-kapil-math-campus/, accessed 16 January 2018.

References

Alter, J. S., 2004. *Yoga in Modern India: The Body between Science and Philosophy*. Princeton: Princeton University Press.

Āraṇya, H., 1935. *The Sāṃkhya Catechism. Compiled from Sāṃkhya Praśnottarmālā, Karmatattwa and other works of Kāpil Math*, translated by S. V. Brahmacārī. Madhupur: Kapil Maṭh.

Āraṇya, D., 1989. *Epistles of a Sāṃkhya-Yogin*, translated by Adinath Chatterjee. Madhupur: Kāpil Maṭh.

Āraṇya, H., 1977a. *The Sāṃkhya Sūtra of Pañcaśikha and Other Ancient Sages*. In: *The Sāṃkhya Sūtra of Pañcaśikha and the Sāṃkhyatattvāloka*, Book I, translated by J. Ghosh. Delhi: Motilal Banarsidass.

Āraṇya, H., 1977b. *Sāṃkhyatattvāloka*. In: *The Sāṃkhya Sūtra of Pañcaśikha and the Sāṃkhyatattvāloka*, Book II, translated by J. Ghosh. Delhi: Motilal Banarsidass.

Āraṇya, H., 1981. *Yoga Philosophy of Patañjali*, translated by P. N. Mukerji, 3rd ed. Calcutta: Calcutta University Press.

Āraṇya, H., 2005. *Sāṃkhya Across the Millenniums*. Madhupur: Kāpil Maṭh.

Beckerlegge, G., 2003. Saffron and Seva: The Rashtriya Swayamsevak Sangh's Appropriation of Swami Vivekananda. In: Copley, A., ed. *Hinduism in Public and Private*. New Delhi: Oxford University Press, 31–65.

Bhattacharya, R. S., 2003. In Remembrance of Reverend Swāmī Dharmamegha Āraṇya. In: Āraṇya, Dharmamegha. *So We Have Heard (Iti Śuśruma)*. Madhupur: Kāpil Maṭh, 139–153.

Bronkhorst, J., 1985. Patañjali and the Yoga Sutras. *Studien zur Indologie und Iranistik* 10, 191–212.

Broo, M., 2012. Yoga in Cyberspace? The Web Pages of Yoga Studios in Turku/Åbo. *Approaching Religion* 2(2), 18–26.

Chatterjee, A., 2000. Preface to the Fourth Edition. In: Hariharānanda, Ā., ed. *Yoga Philosophy of Patañjali with Bhāsvatī*. Calcutta: University of Calcutta, xvii–ix.

Farquhar, J. N., 1920. *An Outline of the Religious Literature of India*. London: Humphrey Milford/Oxford University Press.

Jacobs, S., 2012. Communicating Hinduism in a Changing Media Context. *Religion Compass* 6(2), 136–151.

Jacobsen, K. A., 2018a. Pilgrimage Rituals and Technological Change: Alterations in the Shraddha Ritual at Kapilashram in the Town of Siddhpur in Gujarat. In: Jacobsen, K. A. and Myrvold, K., eds. *Religion and Technology in India: Spaces, Practices and Authorities*. London: Routledge, 130–145.

Jacobsen, K. A., 2018b. *Yoga in Modern Hinduism: Hariharānanda Āraṇya and Sāṃkhyayoga*. London: Routledge.

Karapanagiotis, N., 2013. Cyber Forms, Worshipable Forms: Hindu Devotional Viewpoints on the Ontology of Cyber-Gods and -Goddesses. *International Journal of Hindu Studies* 17(1), 57–82.

Larson, G. J., 1979. *Classical Sāṃkhya*, 2nd ed. Delhi: Motilal Banarsidass.

Larson, G. J., 2008. Introduction to the Philosophy of Yoga. In: Larson, G. J. and Bhattacharya, R. S., eds. *Yoga: India's Philosophy of Meditation*. Delhi: Motilal Banarsidass, 21–159.

Lucia, A., 2014. Innovative Gurus: Tradition and Change in Contemporary Hinduism. *International Journal of Hindu Studies* 18(2), 221–263.

Maas, P. A., 2013. A Concise Historiography of Classical Yoga Philosophy. In: Franco, E., ed. *Periodization and Historiography of Indian Philosophy*. Vienna: Sammlung de Nobili, Institut für Südasien-, Tibet-, und Buddhismuskunde der Universität Wien, 53–90.

Mohan, S., 2015. Locating the 'Internet Hindu': Political Speech and Performance in Indian Cyberspace. *Television & Media* 16(4), 339–345.

O'Malley, L. S. S., 1910. *Bengal District Gazetteers: Santal Parganas*. Calcutta: The Bengal Secretariat Book Depot.

Pandya, S. P., 2016. 'Guru' Culture in South Asia: The Case of Chinmaya Mission in India. *Society and Culture in South Asia* 2(2), 204–232.

Redden, G., 2005. The New Age: Towards a Market Model. *Journal of Contemporary Religion* 20(2), 231–246.

Samkhya-Yoga, n.d.a. *Samkhya-Yoga*. Available at www.samkhyayoga-darshana.com, accessed 16 January 2018.

Samkhya-Yoga, n.d.b. *About us*. Available at https://web.archive.org/web/20110202181158/ www.samkhyayoga-darshana.com/, accessed 16 January 2018.

Samkhya-Yoga, n.d.c. *Acharyas of Kapil Math*. Available at www.kapilmath.com/acharyas-of-kapil-math/, accessed 5 May 2018.

Samkhya-Yoga, n.d.d. *Maharshi Kapila the Great Sage*. Available at www.samkhyayoga-darshana.com/maharshi-kapila-the-great-sage/, accessed 16 January 2018.

Samkhya-Yoga, n.d.e. *Samkhya Philosophy*. Available at www.kapilmath.com/samkhya-as-a-philosophy/, accessed 1 November 2018.

Samkhya-Yoga, n.d.f. *Summary of Samkhya Teaching*. Available at www.samkhyayoga-darshana.com/2016/05/11/summary-of-samkhya-teachings/, accessed 11 January 2018.

Samkhya-Yoga, n.d.g. *Swami Hariharananda Aranya*. Available at https://web.archive.org/web/20110202181158/ www.samkhyayoga-darshana.com/, accessed 5 May 2018.

Samkhya-Yoga, n.d.h. *Yoga – What It Is and What It Is Not*. Available at www.samkhyayoga-darshana.com/2016/05/27/yoga-what-it-is-and-what-it-is-not/, accessed January 16, 2018.

Scheifinger, H., 2008. Hinduism and Cyberspace. *Religion* 38, 233–249.

Scheifinger, H., 2012a. Internet. In: Jacobsen, K. A., Basu, H., Malinar, A., and Narayanan, V., eds. *Brill's Encyclopedia of Hinduism, Volume IV*. Leiden: Brill, 700–706.

Scheifinger, H., 2012b. Hindu Worship Online and Offline. In: Campbell, H. A., ed. *Digital Religion: Understanding Religious Practice in New Media Worlds*. London: Routledge, 121–127.

Scheifinger, H., 2015. New technology and Change in the Hindu Tradition: The Internet in Historical Perspective. In: Keul, I., ed. *Asian Religions, Technology and Science*. London: Routledge, 153–168.

Singleton, M. and Goldberg, E., eds., 2014. *Gurus of Modern Yoga*. Oxford: Oxford University Press.

Therwath, I., 2012. Cyber-*hindutva*: Hindu Nationalism, the Diaspora and the Web. *Social Science Information* 51(4), 551–577.

Udāsina, B, ed., 1891. *Yogadarśanam: Bhagavanmahāmunipatañjalipraṇitam; Nikhilatantrāparatantrapratibha; Vācaspatimiśraviracitatattvavaiśāradyākhya vyākhyābhūṣitāmahārṣikṛṣṇadvaipāyanapraṇītabhāṣyā 'laṅkrtam; Srīmadudāsinasvāmibālarāmeṇa viṣamasthalaṭippaṇanirmāṇapuraḥsaraṃ susaṃskrtam*. Kalikātā: Vyāptiṣṭamisanayantra.

Udupa, S., 2015. Internet Hindus: Right-Wingers as New India's Ideological Warriors. In: van der Veer, P., ed. *Handbook of Religion and the Asian City*. Berkeley: University of California Press, 432–450.

White, D. G., 2012. *Yoga in Practice*. Princeton: Princeton University Press.

White, D. G., 2014. *The Yoga Sutra of Patanjali: A Biography*. Princeton: Princeton University Press.

Woods, J. H., [1914]1988. *The Yoga System of Patañjali Or the Ancient Hindu Doctrine of Concentration of Mind*, translated by James Haughton Woods. Cambridge: The Harvard University Press.

Zavos, J., 2015. Digital Media and Networks of Hindu Activism in the UK. *Culture and Religion* 16(1), 17–34.

8 Mediatized gurus

Hindu religious and artistic authority and digital culture

Hanna Mannila and Xenia Zeiler

Introduction

This chapter studies mediatized gurus in contemporary India, specifically by focusing on the interface of religious and artistic authority in Hindu contexts as related to digital culture. Historically, a guru was perceived and represented as personified Hindu authority. This high regard later also came to include other fields of culture than religion, for example, the arts – dance gurus have been, and to some degree still are, granted a comparable position and status in Indian society as Hindu gurus. The guru is still a central figure in Indian society, but increased levels of education, secularization and globalization have led people, including disciples of spiritual and dance gurus, to start to question their previously unquestioned authority. For example, very few dance students nowadays are willing to dedicate their entire life to serving their guru and fulfilling their wishes without questioning. Nevertheless, open confrontations with the guru are still rare. The aim of this chapter is thus to demonstrate how gurus construct their authority in an online environment. This is done by analyzing the websites of a Hindu guru and a guru of Indian *kathak* dance, the main classical dance form in the Hindi / Urdu speaking area of North India, and their respective interactions with digital media.

Today, the Internet and social media offer important ways for various professionals to reach out to potential audiences and customers, and in the case of gurus of religion and art, also disciples. The purpose of being present on various media platforms such as personal websites, Facebook, Instagram and YouTube is to promote the professional or a guru and ultimately increase his or her fame and income, yet these various platforms function in different ways and may have different audiences. The focus of social media sites tends to be on the present, what happened a few days ago, or what will happen in the near future. Furthermore, in the case of dance gurus, whose audience often consists of friends, professional acquaintances and fans, the roles of professional and private selves are also overlapping, causing a "blurring of boundaries between public and private communication" (Bakardjieva 2005, cited in Thumim 2012, 147).

In comparison, the websites of religious and artistic gurus appear to have a different focus and serve a partially different purpose. An initial analysis of guru websites reveals that they seem to serve as a multimodal form of online curriculum vitae, providing basic information - mainly the guru's religious experiences and actions in the case of religious gurus, and their education or training in the case of dance gurus, as well as major achievements. In both cases, this is done through text, images and sometimes videos. In terms of crossover of professional and public selves, websites tend to offer presentations that are more thoroughly thought than, for example, quick posts on social networking sites, which may include holiday photos and other posts unrelated to the individual's role as a guru. A website does not allow viewers to interact in the same way as in social media, where many of the posts are intended to receive likes and other reactions from the followers. Website interaction is often limited to the visitor choosing which links of the content banner to click on. There is usually no way of commenting on the content, other than by sending a message to an email address or using the form provided on the contact page of the website. Rather than focusing on the present, near future or recent past, as is usually done, for example, on Facebook, websites tend to be about superlatives, presenting the professional – or the guru, in this case – in relation to his or her best and most important achievements, rather than the latest ones.

This may partly be because the two media function differently: websites are more difficult to update (indeed, many gurus may not be able to do it for themselves), whereas Facebook is quick and easy to use. As Thumim (2012, 154) points out, "self-representation is *not ever* free of mediation, but is *always* mediated differently in different settings". Therefore, authority may also be constructed in different ways, depending on the context. This chapter discusses the various strategies employed in constructing the guru's authority on his or her website.

The chapter begins with defining and discussing mediatization and gurus. This is followed by a case study of the website of the Hindu guru Radhe Maa, as an example of Hindu religious authority self-presented in digital culture. Then, the main case study of this chapter focuses on the website of art gurus, namely, of guru Munna Shukla of Indian classical *kathak* dance. As is the case with Hindu traditions, the guru is of great importance in most Indian classical dance and music traditions. The respective case studies thus provide an example for a Hindu guru's website and a *kathak* dance artist website, along with analysis of the various strategies used for the construction of their authority through that multimodal medium. The chapter concludes with a brief summary and a discussion of our findings.

Mediatization and gurus

Mediatization as an approach and concept to study the interrelation of media and society first rose to prominence especially in Media and

Communication Studies, but by now has gained influence in numerous disciplines which are interested in the study of media, culture and society overall. Today, we find two distinguishable mediatization approaches or traditions: the institutionalist and the social-constructivist traditions. The institutionalist tradition regards media as an independent social institution with its own set of specific, institutionalized rules (e.g., Hjarvard 2013). In contrast to this, the social-constructivist tradition highlights the interrelation of media and the construction of reality (e.g., Couldry and Hepp 2016). Mediatization in this approach is defined as a metaprocess that shapes modern societies alongside other sociocultural processes such as globalization:

> Today, we can say that mediatization means at the least the following:
>
> a changing media environments …
> b an increase of different media …
> c the changing functions of old media …
> d new and increasing functions of digital media for the people and a growth of media in general
> e changing communication forms and relations between the people on the micro level, a changing organization of social life and changing nets of sense and meaning-making on the macro level. (Krotz 2008, 24)

This approach also necessarily means a shift from media-centered to actor-centered research. Instead of concentrating on the effect of one media genre on actors, mediatization research in this tradition focuses on actors (individuals or groups of individuals) in their mediatized worlds. In our chapter, we align with the social-constructivist tradition. As a methodical consequence, our chapter takes one religious guru and one art guru as a starting point for investigation and looks into their mediatized practices, especially vis-à-vis self-staging and self-advertisement on their personal websites. This means that we are particularly interested in deciphering how personal websites, in contrast to social media such as Facebook or Twitter, are employed by these gurus in order to construct, display and widely disseminate their authority and, related to that, their identity and status.

While the two mediatization traditions still diverge on certain points, more recently they have come to agree on basic aspects of the definition of mediatization (e.g., Lundby 2009). Currently, the theoretical and methodical approaches of mediatization are established especially in European and partly North American academia, and they have primarily been applied to case studies from these regions. For geographical contexts beyond these, including but not limited to South Asia, mediatization has yet to be applied on a broad scale (an exception for Asia is, e.g., Radde-Antweiler and Zeiler 2019). More research is much needed in order to widen the scope of varied case studies and offer more diversified analyses and material, which will in turn allow for expanded theorizing. It is very likely that mediatization is influenced, if not determined (to varying degrees), by regional cultural and social specifics (e.g., Zeiler 2019). Our chapter on mediatized gurus, both religious and art gurus, in contemporary India aims to point out some of these specifics.

Within the collection of heterogeneous religious traditions called Hinduism, the presence of gurus is often a common denominator between diverse traditions. Gurus and guru-like figures are also present in traditions outside the religion proper, such as Indian classical music and dance, although it should be kept in mind that performing arts traditions often are or have historically been linked to religious and ritual practices. Many religious and art traditions have recently entered the online environment, and, with them, so have their gurus. The word guru literally means heavy (with knowledge or authority) or a person with weight – thus, an elderly and respectable person. It is a masculine word, and therefore it originally referred to men only, but nowadays female teachers can also be called gurus. The word guru began to be used in the sense of a spiritual teacher gradually in the Upanishadic texts during the first millennium BCE. However, the guru institution is based on an even older Vedic institution of *ācāryas*, that is, Brahmin teachers of the Vedas. Both terms – *ācārya* and guru – are still in use, and sometimes used interchangeably, but in general *ācārya* refers to a teacher of some codified religious tradition with authoritative knowledge of its scriptures, whereas a guru may or may not belong to a particular sect or lineage. A guru may gain his spiritual authority, for example, through claimed self-realization rather than scholarly knowledge of scriptures; thus, anyone who can attract followers and disciples can become a guru. If the guru does belong to a lineage (*paramparā*) instead of being an individual self-proclaimed guru, and especially if the role of a guru is inherited (as in the case of a family of religious specialists or dancers), then acknowledgment and reverence of the lineage, that is, the chain of gurus and especially the first and most important gurus within the tradition, are usually of great importance; it is considered essential to preserve the tradition and pass it down to the next generation as it was received from the previous gurus (for a more extensive treatment on Hindu gurus, see Jacobsen 2012; Smith 2003, 167–180). This is also reflected in online media (for example, on the gurus' websites). Whereas self-declared gurus focus on promoting themselves and their own ideas (see, for example, Radhe Maa), on the websites of gurus belonging to a particular *paramparā* (e.g., the Vaishnava *Puṣṭimārga*), the ancestral or previous gurus and their teachings are usually acknowledged.

Traditionally in the *ācārya* and guru institutions, the disciple would stay with his teacher for several years until his training was completed (*gurukula*, lit. the guru's family and home, comprising residential education). This *gurukula* system is still considered the ideal situation for both spiritual and artistic training: the aim is to spend as much time as possible with the guru, either in an *āśram* or at the guru's home or institute. Nowadays, it is even possible to spend time with the guru while abroad, for example, through conversations, *satsang* (religious gathering), or dance and music lessons on various online platforms, such as Skype. Living with the teacher or spending time with him served the purpose of what nowadays would be called holistic education, allowing the disciple to not only learn the knowledge and skills needed in the profession but the entire lifestyle. This applies equally to religious specialists, dancers and musicians.

Today, the skills would ideally also include the use of new media. Yet, while there are some *kathak* gurus who can by example teach their students how to use social media for self-promotion, more often it is the students who act as their guru's social media assistants, maintaining their websites or social media accounts for him or her. This can be seen as a form of *sevā*, the disciple's service to the guru. In religious traditions, the guru is often seen as the representative of god on earth, or sometimes even as the god himself. Therefore, *gurubhakti* - the disciple's devotion toward the guru as a god-like figure - is understood as essential; it also involves the unquestioned authority of the guru. The concept of *darśan* is an important part of *bhakti*, referring to "the act of seeing a deity or a spiritually important person *and*, possibly more importantly, positioning oneself for being seen by that deity or person" (Valpey 2012). The gaze of the deity or a spiritually powerful person constitutes a powerful, possibly protective or curative, blessing (Gonda 1969, 57–59 in Valpey 2012). Apart from the gaze, the guru may bless his disciples through words or touch: by touching the feet of the guru the disciple not only shows respect to the guru but also receives his or her blessings. Both *darśan* and the blessings of a guru are still important aspects in spiritual and artistic traditions, and today these can be performed online.

Hindu gurus: Radhe Maa's website

Radhe Maa is a self-declared "Hindu spiritual teacher and guru from India" who has been active especially in the field of *sevā* (lit. service) "to all sentient beings as a means of self-purification for those aspiring for divine grace" (RadheMaa n.d.a). While her website (available in both English and Hindi) provides the basic expected information (a short biography, some quotes, her teaching philosophy, etc.), it is the pronounced emphasis on *sevā* that dominates. For example, the landing page (RadheMaa n.d.a) right in the beginning informs: "Serve not to change the world but your self," "Service to sentient beings is service to God," and "Work performed in a spirit of service becomes pure." This emphasis on *sevā* runs throughout the entire website, which also has a designated section called Seva Initiatives (RadheMaa n.d.b) of the Shri Radhe Guru Maa Charitable Trust (headed by her), which lists and describes in detail the numerous public appearances of Radhe Maa and her charity events and projects. These include, for example, a donation of equipment for disabled persons, a blood donation initiative and a distribution of "sewing machines to women with the intention of empowering them to channelize and run a livelihood for themselves" (RadheMaa 2019a). The website also has numerous embedded videos, which show her in various contexts related to charity (for example, speaking during celebrations and events and handing out donations). Only a small number of videos depict her in more traditional spheres often perceived as guru domains: for example, giving blessings to devotees, joining in temple rituals (*āratī*), singing religious songs and dancing while immersed in a dance in a trance-like state (Radhe Maa Ji Anomal Vachan & Bhajan 2017).

It is instantly visible that the main authorizing factor employed on her website to construct Radhe Maa as a guru figure is the (spiritually induced) element of *sevā*. At the same time, *sevā* is depicted as the main identity code for Radhe Maa. On the website, it is neither her religious education which authorizes her (on the contrary, her bibliography states that she has no religious education but has always been close to god) nor specific powers; instead, *sevā* is depicted as what she teaches, lives and embodies overall. Additionally, it is notable that this *sevā* is constructed in a specific way. Unlike more traditional understandings of *sevā* mainly (though not exclusively) centered on service to a deity or a respected person (in particular, one's parents), Radhe Maa's *sevā* is declaredly (and almost exclusively) centered on charity work:

> **Twenty Seven years of selfless service**
> Radhe Maa has inspired Millions of followers in the country and abroad to share what they have with the less fortunate through health camps, and donations of books, medicines and clothes. Several old age homes, orphanages and institutions for people with special needs. benefit from these initiatives.
>
> Radhe Maa inspires her followers to take their love for God beyond the temple to the community through service to all beings. You can also be a part of these initiates by volunteering your time to the seva efforts and through donations of, food, clothes, and medicines. (RadheMaa n.d.a)

Related to this charity focus, in all her media coverage (Radhe Maa is widely active on digital media – apart from the extensive website she has her own YouTube channel, a Facebook page, a Twitter handle and an Instagram account) it is strikingly apparent that Radhe Maa constructs herself as a blend of a very modern and a traditional Hindu guru at the same time. For example, on the one hand, she has been photographed combining flashy sunglasses with her characteristic red clothes and gold jewelry, or she has co-organized a charity event on her birthday with the Lions Club Delhi (RadheMaa 2019b). On the other hand, she adheres to some more traditional elements, which are perceived by many devotees as characteristic of a guru: for example, she teaches (i.e., she spreads her sayings) and she always carries a trident as a visual symbol of her closeness to god. Her embracing of digital media is rooted in the understanding that "Technology should be used as a tool to make us better human beings" (RadheMaa n.d.c). While the website does not state who is practically in charge of her online activities, it is very likely that media-savvy devotees (as in many other cases, such as in the later discussed case of *kathak* gurus) are authorized by the guru herself to take care of these.

Not surprisingly, like any personal website (which by definition is constructed and fed – or, at the very least, authorized – by the very person promoted on the website), Radhe Maa's website gives no indication of controversial – that is, unwelcome – issues or themes. In fact, Radhe Maa has been subject to several controversies in the Indian press over the years, to the extent of being called "'Godwoman' of Controversies" (Ghosh 2015). While at first glance it may seem harmless to be accused by the press of, for example, "dancing to Bollywood songs" or being "pictured in western clothes, notably a red mini-skirt" (Ghosh 2015), such information could be considered disreputable by some of the self-declared guru's target audience. Radhe Maa's website (as well as her other media accounts) avoids such themes, and thus it succeeds in constructing and portraying a rather flawless, selfless and mankind-serving figure of religious authority, embedded in traditional Hindu values and successfully and effectively transferring them into the twenty-first century.

Kathak gurus: Guru Munna Shukla's website

Kathak is one of the eight dance forms currently recognized as Indian classical dance. Their roots can be traced back to the classical period of Indian history, for example, through the similarity of some of their techniques with the dance technique described in the *Nāṭyaśāstra* (ca. 400 CE). These dance traditions have connections to Hindu religious and ritualistic practices, especially various *bhakti* traditions, but *kathak* also evolved in the competitive environment of the Mughal and Hindu courts in North India, which encouraged the refinement of the technique (for the history of *kathak*, see, for example, Walker 2014 and Chakraborty 2008, and for history, technique and repertoire, see Kothari 1989). The concept of classical dance also tends to include the notion that the technique is so challenging that accomplishing the art requires several years of intensive training under a guru through the co-called guru-*śiṣyaparamparā* (lit. teacher-disciple-tradition), a personal and intimate relationship between the teacher and his (nowadays also her) disciple [on guru-*śiṣya-paramparā*, see, for example, Prickett 2007 (*kathak* and *bharatanatyam*), Grimmer 2011 (Karnatic music) and Neuman 1990 (Hindustani music)]. Traditionally in performing arts traditions, the guru was often a family member or a more distant relative or a person from the same caste. In *kathak*, there is a strong emphasis on the lineage of gurus (*gharānā*, lit. household, lineage with a distinct style of *kathak*) and an aim to preserve the stylistic features of the lineage as pure as possible (for the *gharānā* system in Hindustani music, see Neuman 1990). Currently, some of the most notable gurus of *kathak* are Pandit Birju Maharaj (Lucknow *gharānā*), Pandit Rajendra Gangani (Jaipur *gharānā*) and Pandit Ravi Shankar Mishra (Benares *gharānā*). The heritage was passed down mainly within the male lineage and, until recently, the women of those families were not allowed to perform in public. The art form was also taught by the male gurus to courtesans (and by the courtesans to their daughters and other courtesans), who did perform in public. However, especially after the decline of the courtesan culture in India during the British rule, the male gurus of the hereditary *kathak* families have been considered the owners of the heritage, even though there have been some notable non-hereditary female gurus from the mid- twentieth century onward (e.g., Kumudini Lakhia and Rohini Bhate).

Based on Weber's (1958) categories of authority – rational-legal, traditional and charismatic authority – that of *kathak* gurus appears to be of the traditional and / or charismatic type: the role of the guru may be inherited but also earned through personal charisma, talent, skill and knowledge. In the following case study, the focus is on one hereditary guru and the strategies of authority construction on his website. The website analysis includes reflections based on observations and interviews during my (Mannila's) active fieldwork periods in India in 2015–2017 as well as my experiences as a *kathak* student, teacher and performer during the past 20 years.

Kathak Guru Munna Shukla

Guru Munna Shukla (b. 1943) comes from a family of hereditary *kathak* dancers of the Lucknow *gharānā*. Munna Shukla represents perhaps the last generation of hereditary *kathak* gurus, who were able to completely immerse themselves only in dance and music and who seem to be nothing but dancer-musicians. Thorough understanding of not only dance but also music was and is essential for *kathak* dancers, but according to what I have observed in my fieldwork, few *kathak* dancers nowadays possess such thorough knowledge because many dancers have to divide their time between, for example, university education and *kathak* (many professional *kathak* dancers have university degrees in sciences or other subjects not directly related to dance). Social media also demands more and more time from the younger dancers and gurus, whereas the older gurus, including Munna Shukla, do not necessarily spend any time online, as their students or family members often do the social media work for them.

After a preliminary content analysis of a sample of ten websites of *kathak* dancers, Munna Shukla's was chosen for discussion here as an example of a website or a traditional *kathak* guru. Munna Shukla's website is very clear and easy to navigate; it has a clearly labeled content banner with eight titles, with a content typical to *kathak* artist websites. His hereditary dance background shows in the content of the website, as it includes textual and visual representations of some traditional notions of the *kathak* guru tradition. On the website, various strategies of authority construction are employed: Perhaps the most obvious ones include the listing of the guru's greatest achievements such as performances at prestigious events and venues in India and abroad, major productions, awards and reviews in newspapers, some of them by famous dance critics. These are all similar strategies to what one might expect to see in an artist's curriculum vitae anywhere in the world. Apart from these universally typical strategies, there are also some culture-specific ways of constructing authority: for example, the artist is presented as an ideal guru in photographs and verbal descriptions of him, and there is a strong emphasis on the lineage of the artist's gurus, who in this case are the guru's relatives.

The landing page of Munna Shukla's website (GuruMunnaShukla n.d.a) has a black and white photo of Munna Shukla in a dance pose, wearing a traditional white dance costume. The overall background of the website is black and the text fonts are green and gray. To the upper right of the photo, there is an excerpt taken from a review (discussed later in the chapter) with the name Pandit Munna Shukla highlighted in yellow. To the lower right is a link titled Enter. Clicking this takes the viewer to the Home page (GuruMunnaShukla n.d.b). The title of the entire website, which appears on every individual page, is Guru Munna Shukla. Here we see the first and most obvious way of ascribing authority to, and/or claiming authority, as a guru: simply the use of the word guru as a title preceding the name of the artist, instead of choosing to use only the name or some other title, for example *pandit* (lit. learned, scholar, teacher), which is also commonly used, or perhaps *Kathak* Artist, all of which would give a slightly different impression. Rather than emphasizing his role as a performing artist or choreographer, here the emphasis is on the person being presented as a revered teacher, with 'guru' having stronger connotations of a spiritual teacher than *pandit*, which refers to a master of some field of knowledge. Munna Shukla seems confident enough to be publicly called and calling himself guru, whereas younger *kathak* dancers may prefer being presented as performing artists and might hesitate to refer to themselves as a guru. The title 'guru' is usually earned through work and achievements, and over time. Even though the students of younger dance artists may call their teacher guru-jī (a typical honorific way of addressing the guru by students), it may take longer for the wider audience to see the dancer as a guru. The emphasis on Munna Shukla as a guru may stem from the fact that the website was likely authored by one or more of his disciples. The voice of the student becomes obvious in some places, for example, in the way Munna Shukla is referred to as "guru-ji" on The Guru page (GuruMunnaShukla n.d.c): "Guru-ji's total commitment and dedication has been the inspiring force behind them [the students]". The word 'guru' even appears in the domain name of the website: www.gurumunnashukla.com.

The Home page of the website (GuruMunnaShukla n.d.b) has a content banner with links to eight areas Home, History, The Guru, Kathak Baithak, Legacy, Reviews, Productions and Contact. The layout is simple and clear. The black background gives a somber atmosphere, and with the dance photos on a black background, it is almost as if one is watching a dance performance in a black box theater space. On the Home page (GuruMunnaShukla n.d.b), there is another photo (this time in color) of Munna Shukla wearing a white *kathak* costume and a longer excerpt of the review (the same review which appeared on the landing page) by the famous Indian dance critic and scholar Dr. S. K. Saxena. The text serves as an introduction to the guru:

> The Kathak maestro, Pandit Munna Shukla, is an admirable three-in-one: a large hearted, self effacing and very effective teacher; an excellent performer himself even at present age; and a prolific creator of radically new dance numbers which no where spill over the Kathak idiom...

Here again, the guru's authority is first shown through the titles given to him, initially as *maestro* – for some reason choosing the Italian word rather than the English master – and then a Hindi word *pandit*, meaning roughly the same thing. The description of "three-in-one", that is, teacher, performer and choreographer, is something that is expected of all mature *kathak* artists nowadays. But not all traditional gurus are excellent choreographers, and therefore the text seems to aim at mentioning all the traits of an ideal guru. The fact that this piece of text was written by Dr. S. K. Saxena gives extra weightage to it. It is worth noting that "a prolific creator of radically new dance numbers" (GuruMunnaShukla n.d.b) does not refer to anything quite as radical as what might be the case when talking about Western contemporary dance. This phrase makes more sense when put in the context of the discourse within the *kathak*: there is a constant debate about how important it is, on the one hand, to preserve the tradition ("nowhere spilling over the *kathak* idiom", GuruMunnaShukla n.d.b) and, on the other hand, to also be innovative in order to attract students from every new generation, so that the dance form does not become a "museum piece" – an expression sometimes used when criticizing the strictly traditional approach to performing *kathak* and other classical dances (see, e.g., Bhide 2017, Ratnam 2000). Thus, there is a need to emphasize both tradition and innovation, not to appear backward and stagnant. Also, while the traditional guru-disciple tradition is often seen as the only way to master the art, at the same time, its strictest form (including accepting the unquestioned authority of the guru and even worshipping the guru as a god-like figure) may be off-putting to some students with a more modern upbringing. Therefore, it may be significant that Munna Shukla is described as "a large hearted, self effacing and very effective teacher" as well as "a simple, gentle and affable person" (GuruMunnaShukla n.d.b).

Apart from the introductory review by Dr. Saxena (the website is not clear about where this text was taken from), there is an entire page dedicated to reviews, some of them by more authoritative figures than others. This aforementioned text must have been considered important, because it appears in three different places on the website: on the landing page (GuruMunnaShukla n.d.a) the Home page (GuruMunnaShukla n.d.b) and the Reviews page (GuruMunnaShukla n.d.d).

Blessings through the lineage

It is customary in India for younger or junior persons to ask for blessings from their elders or seniors, especially gurus of both religion and performing arts. In a sense, it is the guru's duty to give his blessings to those who seek them. The act of touching the guru's feet is a gesture of both respect toward the guru as well as a sign of seeking his or her blessings. In the context of *kathak*, this gesture is usually performed at the beginning and end of a *kathak* class as well as before performances and on important occasions. Many Hindus believe that energy or even knowledge can be passed from the feet of the guru to the fingertips of the bowing disciple, and therefore, at least for some *kathak* dancers, touching the guru's feet is not simply a gesture of humility but more of a ritualistic act with transformative power. While the disciple is bowing or prostrating in front of the guru, the teacher may raise his or her hand in an act of blessing, sometimes touching the disciple's head, shoulder or back. Sometimes the guru may also utter *jīo* or *jīte raho* (lit. 'live' or 'may you stay alive', i.e., 'long life') to the disciple, especially if he or she has done particularly well during a dance class or performance. This is where the boundary between artistic and religious authority gets somewhat blurred: an ideal disciple should worship his guru as a god, and *kathak* gurus bless their disciples in a similar way to how gods are thought to bless their devotees.

Nowadays, it is also quite common to see on *kathak* dancers' websites, as well as social media postings, photos of students touching their guru's feet while the guru is blessing them, perhaps by putting his or her hand on top of the student's head. On throne Munna Shukla's website, too, on top of the Kathak Baithak page (GuruMunnaShukla n.d.e), there is a photo of Munna Shukla sitting cross-legged on a raised platform (which serves as a teacher's seat or throne in the class), palms folded in a gesture of greeting, while a student is kneeling in front of him, touching his feet. Including a photo like this on the website indicates respect toward and adherence to the guru tradition, as well as the continuity of the artistic tradition from guru to disciple.

Bowing in front of one's guru also has another significance. As explained to me by Rajendra Gangani (2015), when a student is bowing in front of his guru, he is not only bowing to one guru but all of them, as if all the gurus in the same lineage were a single guru. In a sense, the heritage is thought to stay alive through the lineage and generations with the blessings of gurus and elders. One often encounters in India that professionals of various fields – be they dancers, musicians or tailors – claim that the profession has been in the family for several generations. It is a matter of great pride to be able to claim to be a 13th generation musician, as it carries much more weightage than to be a second generation musician. But why does an artist become more credible if his ancestors were in the same profession? Is this kind of thinking based on the assumption that knowledge and skill are accumulated over generations? Such assumptions are not usually spelled out, but to a certain extent it seems that authority is perceived to increase with the number of generations spent in the profession, with later generations inheriting some of the proficiency of their legendary ancestors. On Munna Shukla's website, the emphasis on the family lineage is visible on the History page (GuruMunnaShukla n.d.f): it includes a lineage chart where Munna Shukla's ancestors – the lineage of the Lucknow *gharānā* – are traced back seven generations. The page also includes three black-and-white pictures of some of the most legendary gurus of the Lucknow *gharānā*, as well as a photo of Munna Shukla himself. It may be significant that the link to the History page precedes The Guru page on the content banner: the lineage is considered more important than an individual guru in the chain of gurus. The website also includes a page called Legacy (GuruMunnaShukla n.d.g), which introduces Munna Shukla's offspring, thus highlighting the continuity of the lineage: Munna Shukla's daughter Shruti Shukla is a *kathak* dancer and his son Aniruddh Shukla is a *tabla* player. It is also worth noting that even though Munna Shukla has had scores of students during his long career, some of whom have pursued a successful career in *kathak*, only his son and daughter are mentioned by name on the website.

Related to the importance of lineage is also the earlier mentioned *gurukula* or residential way of learning. It is preferred partly for practical reasons: spending time with the guru in a household of musicians and dancers around the clock gives obvious practical advantages when learning the profession, but it is also partly because of the constant blessing presence of the guru. On Munna Shukla's website, this kind of traditional musician and dancer household is also referred to and the importance of the family heritage and lineage is highlighted, for example, on The Guru page (GuruMunnaShukla n.d.c): "Surrounded by the atmosphere of music and dance in Kanpur, Munna Shukla began his training in kathak with his father, Sunder Lal Shukla, disciple of Acchan Maharaj".

Non-hereditary *kathak* artists: Aditi Mangaldas' website

Even though Munna Shukla's website is a typical website of a traditional hereditary male *kathak* guru in many ways, it cannot, of course, represent the websites of all contemporary *kathak* artists. For example, Aditi Mangaldas is a female *kathak* artist who does not come from a family of hereditary dancers and who a modern, Westernized, secular upbringing and English medium university level schooling (unlike many dancers from hereditary backgrounds who, especially in the past, focused entirely on dance and music from childhood onward and received limited schooling). She even mentions this on her website (Aditi Mangaldas Dance Company n.d.b): "Unlike most classical Indian performers, I don't belong to a family of dancers. My family has business people on one side, and intellectuals of philosophy and the sciences on the other". Strictly speaking it is no longer true that "most" Indian performers have a hereditary musician or dancer background, but the most famous ones often have. There is a dichotomy between hereditary and non-hereditary dancers in today's *kathak* community, which is a rather complex issue and beyond the scope of this article. However, with the sentence quoted above Mangaldas participates in the ongoing debate on the issue on her website, and it makes clear where she stands in terms of her background. It also serves as an explanation for why there are no family lineage charts on her website. Because Mangaldas cannot rely on the authority of a family lineage of gurus when constructing her authority as a *kathak* artist, she instead constructs it on the basis of her own creative achievements and, to some extent, radical innovations. She sometimes includes Western contemporary dance vocabulary and concepts in her productions and she uses costumes which do not follow the traditional designs and rules (for example, wearing a scarf). Furthermore, she does not present herself as a guru at all – the website belongs to the Aditi Mangaldas Dance Company and the Drishtikon Dance Foundation (Aditi Mangaldas Dance Company n.d.a), as stated in the top banner. Next to the company name, it is also clearly stated that the company's dance is "classical kathak and contemporary dance based on kathak". The content banner has six titles: Aditi Mangaldas, Production, Tours, Reviews, Gallery and The Dance Co / Get Involved. She is introduced on the Aditi Mangaldas page (Aditi Mangaldas Dance Company n.d.b) as follows:

> Aditi Mangaldas is a leading dancer and choreographer in the classical Indian dance form Kathak. With extensive training under the leading gurus of Kathak, Shrimati Kumudini Lakhia and Pandit Birju Maharaj. Aditi is today recognized for her artistry, technique, eloquence and characteristic energy that mark every performance. Besides dancing and choreographing classical productions, both solo and group, she has broken new ground by using her knowledge and experience of kathak as a springboard to evolve a contemporary dance vocabulary, infused with the spirit of the classical.

As is customary within the *kathak* community, the names of Mangaldas' immediate gurus are mentioned early on in the text, as a sign of respect.

Not mentioning one's gurus would be considered arrogant or inconsiderate, or it can indicate a falling out with the guru. However, there is no lineage chart of her gurus anywhere on this website, as is found on Munna Shukla's website. There are also no photos of Aditi Mangaldas' students bowing down in front of her or touching her feet. The lack of such photos on a *kathak* website may communicate her values and beliefs. Mangaldas told me in an interview (2016) that she went through a phase when she refused to touch anyone's feet, even the feet of her own gurus, because she found the act of touching someone's feet strange. It was not something she was brought up with at home. Nowadays, however, she may touch her gurus' feet and lets her students or company dancers touch hers, according to her, out of habit.

While for some dancers the touching of the guru's feet is a deeply meaningful ritualistic gesture, which is partially related to religious beliefs, for others it is something that is simply part of the cultural code of *kathak*, a tradition which must be adhered to, even if one does not believe in it as such. The changes and diversity in the religious landscape in India are reflected in the diversity of thought related to traditional Hindu authority, including the guru, as well as the adherence to related traditional customs, such as recognizing the authority of the guru by touching his or her feet. The presence or lack of images and texts representing such customs on *kathak* dancers' websites may be indicative of the underlying differences in the notions of religious and/or artistic authority among *kathak* dancers.

Conclusion

As we can see from the case studies, guru websites are increasingly popular sites for constructing and presenting one's identity and authority by means of references to personal beliefs, values and inclinations. That is, the information on the websites is selected, designed and displayed only with the approval of the guru. Thus, such websites are not only means of self-promoting but of explicit self-fashioning. These self-produced constructions – meant to reach, attract and touch a large audience – are embedded in cultural codes familiar to that target group. In the case of the Hindu guru Radhe Maa, they refer in particular to the element of *sevā*, as well as the widespread belief that Hindu gurus may have a calling since childhood; in the case of the *kathak* community and the hereditary *kathak* gurus, it is the lineage and the preservation of its heritage that holds special importance.

Radhe Maa's website has a very clear focus: it emphasizes the (spiritually induced) *sevā* activities and initiatives of the guru as both her main authorizing and identifying characteristics. It refers to the established Hindu practice as her main accomplishment, but additionally it gives *sevā* a specific contemporary twist, by highlighting certain aspects which have not necessarily been part of more traditional understandings of *sevā*, such as donations and handing out gifts to aid in empowerment, and by explicitly calling *sevā* activities *charity*. Through this strategy, the website succeeds in portraying and advertising a modern guru who has adapted a well-accepted Hindu religious practice to a contemporary context.

In the exemplary case of Munna Shukla, the authority construction of a hereditary *kathak* dance guru relies heavily on traditional notions of what a dance guru is or should be: the use of honorific titles, emphasis on the hereditary lineage, presentation as an ideal guru – humble but skilled, innovative but respectful of tradition, showing devotion to his own guru and receiving his blessings in the spirit of *gurubhakti*. Both verbal and visual strategies are used consistently for a uniform effect: the overall depiction is that of a respectable, convincingly traditional guru of *kathak* dance, which aims to appeal to an audience who respects tradition and the related ideology (and possibly religion). In the case of Aditi Mangaldas, the format of the website is very similar, but the text and images paint a different picture, which may appeal to a different audience: that of a modern female *kathak* artist, who in terms of skill and knowledge could present herself as a guru but who chooses not to do so.

In the cases which we have examined, the websites act as a platform for agency: the gurus can decide for themselves what kind of image they present of themselves and how they construct their authority, rather than relying on the traditional media to do it for them in the form of articles, books and reviews (of course, they can quote these on their website if they so choose, but they have the authority to decide which quotes they find that best describe them).

As the personal homepages of individuals (and, to some degree institutions), websites have an explicit goal and follow similar structures. A website can function as an extended multimodal online curriculum vitae, with the individual actors – in this case the gurus – harnessing the chosen media for their own purposes. The website becomes a construct employing elements from cultural contexts of Indian dance, Hindu culture and the guru tradition, as well as the actor's individual beliefs, values and inclinations, that is, the specific characteristics which the individual guru decides to highlight. On a website, the gurus (or someone acting on their behalf) need to present themselves verbally and visually in a way that they did not necessarily have to do in the past. For example, descriptions and expressions of thought, values and beliefs used to be mainly confined to *kathak* classrooms and the stage, apart from an occasional interview in the traditional media. But a website is public and open to view for anyone with access to the Internet, at any time. Therefore, gurus seem to have to create an image and brand of themselves - willingly or not, knowingly or not - and authority construction plays an important role in this.

References

Aditi Mangaldas Dance Company, n.d.a. *Aditi Mangaldas Dance Company*. Available at www.aditimangaldasdance.com/index.php, accessed 15 April 2019.

Aditi Mangaldas Dance Company, n.d.b. *Aditi Mangaldas*. Available at www.aditimangaldasdance.com/about.php, accessed 15 April 2019.

Bakardjieva, M., 2005. *Internet Society: The Internet in Everday Life*. London and Thousand Oaks: Sage Publications.

Bhide, S., 2017. An Artiste Must Relate with the World Around. *The Indian Express*, [online] 30 October. Available at https://indianexpress.com/article/cities/pune/an-artiste-must-relate-with-the-world-around-4913014/, accessed 13 May 2019.

Chakraborty, P., 2008. *Bells of Change: Kathak Dance, Women and Modernity in India*. Calcutta, London and New York: Seagull Books.

Couldry, N. and Hepp, A., 2016. *The Mediated Construction of Reality*. Cambridge: Polity Press.

Ghosh, D., ed., 2015. *10 Facts about Radhe Maa, 'Godwoman' of Controversies*. NDTV.com. Available at www.ndtv.com/cheat-sheet/10-facts-about-radhe-maa-godwoman-of-controversies-1206131, accessed 1 May 2019.

Gonda, J., 1969. *Eye and Gaze in the Veda*. Amsterdam: North Holland Publishing Company.

Grimmer, S., 2011. Continuity and Change: The Guru-Shishya Relationship in Karnatic Classical Music Training. In: Green, L., ed. *Learning, Teaching, and Musical Identity: Voices across Cultures*. Bloomington: Indiana University Press, 91–108.

GuruMunnaShukla, n.d.a. *Guru Munna Shukla*. Available at http:// gurumunnashukla.net, accessed 23 May 2019.

GuruMunnaShukla, n.d.b. *Home*. Available at http://gurumunnashukla.net/home, accessed 23 May 2019.

GuruMunnaShukla, n.d.c. *The Guru*. Available at http://gurumunnashukla.net/guru, accessed 23 May 2019.

GuruMunnaShukla, n.d.d. *Reviews*. Available at http://gurumunnashukla.net/reviews, accessed 23 May 2019.

GuruMunnaShukla, n.d.e. *Kathak Baithak*. Available at http://gurumunnashukla.net/kathak-baithak, accessed 23 May 2019.

GuruMunnaShukla, n.d.f. *History*. Available at www.gurumunnashukla.com/history.html, accessed 23 May 2019.

GuruMunnaShukla, n.d.g. *Legacy*. Available at www.gurumunnashukla.com/legacy.html, accessed 23 May 2019.

Hjarvard, S., 2013. *The Mediatization of Culture and Society*. London: Routledge.

Jacobsen, K. A., 2012. Gurus and ācāryas. In: Jacobsen, K. A., Basu, H., Malinar, A. and Narayanan, V., eds. *Brill's Encyclopedia of Hinduism Online*. Brill.com. Available at https://referenceworks.brillonline.com/entries/brill-s-encyclopedia-of-hinduism/guru-s-and-acarya-s-COM_9000000033?s.num=0&s.f.s2_parent=s.f.book.brill-s-encyclopedia-of-hinduism&s.q=gurus+and+acaryas, accessed 16 August 2018.

Kothari, S., 1989. *Kathak: Indian Classical Dance Art*. New Delhi: Abhinav Publications.

Krotz, F., 2008. Media Connectivity: Concepts, Conditions, and Consequences. In: Hepp, A., Krotz, F., Moores, S. and Winter, C., eds. *Network, Connectivity and Flow: Key Concepts for Media and Cultural Studies*. New York: Hampton Press, 13–33.

Lundby, K., ed., 2009. *Mediatization: Concept, Changes, Consequences.* New York: Peter Lang.

Neuman, D. M., 1990. *The Life of Music in North India: The Organization of an Artistic Tradition.* Chicago and London: University of Chicago Press.

Prickett, S., 2007. Guru or Teacher? Shishya or Student? Pedagogic Shifts in South Asian Dance Training in Indian and Britain. *South Asia Research* 27(1), 25–41.

Radde-Antweiler, K. and Zeiler, X., eds., 2019. *Mediatized Religion in Asia.* London and New York: Routledge.

RadheMaa, n.d.a. *RadheMaa.* Available at http://radhemaa.com/, accessed 1 May 2019.

RadheMaa, n.d.b. *Seva Initiatives.* Available at http://radhemaa.com/seva-initiatives, accessed 1 May 2019.

RadheMaa, n.d.c. *Live Streaming.* Available at http://radhemaa.com/live, accessed 1 May 2019.

RadheMaa, 2019a. *Sewing Machine Donation/Charity Drive By Shri Radhe Maa – Ocean of Kindness.* Available at http://radhemaa.com/seva-initiative-detail/sewing-machine-donation-charity-drive-by-shri-radhe-maa-ocean-of-kindness, accessed 1 May 2019.

RadheMaa, 2019b. *Shri Radhe Maa Charitable Society Sets Up A Mega Blood Donation Camp In Delhi.* Available at http://radhemaa.com/seva-initiative-detail/shri-radhe-maa-charitable-society-sets-up-a-mega-blood-donation-camp-in-delhi, accessed 1 May 2019.

Radhe Maa Ji Anomal Vachan & Bhajan, 2017. [YouTube video] 17 August. Available at www.youtube.com/watch?v=ngC0J7QgBw0&feature=youtu.be, accessed 1 May 2019.

Ratnam, A., 2000. Observations about Diaspora. *Narthaki,* [online] June. Available at www.narthaki.com/info/articles/article2.html, accessed 14 November 2018.

Smith, D., 2003. *Hinduism and Modernity.* Malden: Blackwell.

Thumim, N., 2012. *Self-Representation and Digital Culture.* Basingstoke: Palgrave Macmillan.

Valpey, K., 2012. Pujā and Darśana. In: Jacobsen, K. A., Basu, H., Malinar, A. and Narayanan, V., eds. *Brill's Encyclopedia of Hinduism Online.* Brill.com. Available at https://referenceworks.brillonline.com/entries/brill-s-encyclopedia-of-hinduism/puja-and-darsana-COM_2030050?s.num=0&s.f.s2_parent=s.f.book.brill-s-encyclopedia-of-hinduism&s.q=puja+, accessed 20 August 2018.

Walker, M. E., 2014. *India's Kathak Dance in Historical Perspective.* Farnham: Ashgate.

Weber, M., 1958. The Three types of legitimate rule. *Berkeley Publications in Society and Institutions* 4(1), 1–11.

Zeiler, X., 2019. Mediatized Religion in Asia. Interrelations of Media, Culture and Society beyond the "West". In: Radde-Antweiler, K. and Zeiler, X., eds. *Mediatized Religion in Asia.* London and New York: Routledge, 3–15.

Part 3

Who debates? Contest and negotiation

9 The Internet

A new marketplace for transacting *pūjā items*

Vineeta Sinha

Opening frames

Intersections of religious domains within the realms of popular culture, material culture and visual culture are complicated with the influx of new technologies, such as digital media and increasingly the Internet, into religious and spiritual fields (Lim 2009). The ubiquity of computers – the modes of technological possibilities they enable and their impact on multiple facets of everyday lives – is a well-narrated tale. Rather than awe and overwhelm, the reach of technological innovations – especially digital media and its impact on sociocultural dimensions of daily life – has now been normalized. The intriguing presence of religions and religion-related phenomenon on the Internet has been documented (Campbell 2017; Cobb 1998; Marcotte 2010; Zaleski 1997) and continues to inspire scholarly inquiries. Cyberspace has been approached as a medium for disseminating information, advertising and publicity for religious products and indeed for *marketing* religions themselves. Inevitably, this expansive critical space has now also been appropriated and honed creatively by manufacturers, distributors and sellers of religious products and services. It is a domain that practitioners of different religions too routinely trawl for a variety of reasons – including securing religious goods and commodities for utilization in religious rituals. This embrace of the Internet has been documented across practitioners from a range of religious traditions – Islam, Christianity, Catholicism, Buddhism, Sikhism and Hinduism, as well as adherents of new religious movements.

The enactment of Hindu religious practice requires a range of physical objects, implements and paraphernalia, which have been secured as mass-produced commodities, as made to order, customized goods and sometimes as self-made objects (Sinha 2017). The dependence on ritual objects has meant the unavoidable commodification of *pūjā items* and draws Hindus as devotees/consumers into the dynamics of capitalism, and presently, situating *pūjā objects* in spaces where they are marketed and transacted leads one to multiple marketplaces – real and virtual. A rich body of scholarship on the intricate and intriguing entanglement of digital media (including the

Internet) with Hindu religion and spirituality (Jacobs 2012; Karapanagiotis 2013; Mallapragada 2010; Scheifinger 2009, 2015; Zeiler 2014) is now available and proliferating.

Focusing on Hindu domains, this chapter argues that the Internet can be viewed as yet another marketplace where *pūjā* things are advertised, available for purchase by consumers/devotees and indeed bought and sold. The data for this chapter come primarily from surfing the various search engines on the Internet (specifically Google, Yahoo, MSN) and the coterie of websites, web portals and online stores which offer merchandise for enacting Hindu religious practice and enabling actual commercial transactions. Analyzing the substance of these online portals (claiming to cater to *spiritual needs* of Hindus) is the method I have turned to for wading through the catalogues of products, services and experiences offered online. Even as the Internet is a marketplace for trading in spiritual goods, the architecture of the sites is assembled through a set of components. One of the questions to be asked is if the religious and/or spiritual content of these online portals makes a difference to their structural edifice. The ultimate aim of this research is to analyze the techniques and rationale through which these online businesses and service providers present, package and market their wares to/for online consumers. However, here the chapter can only map the range of spiritual merchandise that exists online.

Alongside merchandise displays with the obvious desire to achieve online sales, a set of messages (explicit and implicit) is simultaneously conveyed – intentionally or otherwise. How these messages are received and the responses consumers make to them is the subject of another paper that would be based on a dramatically different methodology. As an anthropologist trying to understand how individuals engage with and interpret digital messages and signs, and make meanings, I would need to turn to ethnographic methods. This chapter only focuses on the *supply* end of a virtual marketplace for *pūjā items*, and the analysis offers glimpses into the production and distribution dimensions of online shopping. To learn of the complex consumption practices, consumer choices and behaviors and interpretations of digital commerce would require ethnographic engagement with people making concrete choices to buy online or not – through in-depth interviews and fieldwork. Some data about patterns and consumption trends of online religious shopping are included here, available indirectly from the performance of online businesses and the volume of transactions. However, more research is needed to establish how effective campaigns and advertisements are in persuading consumers that acquiring merchandise and services online is more appealing than traditional transaction options. Online portals routinely display customer reviews and ratings about product satisfaction. These inspire skepticism about how genuine these testimonials are, with the lingering suspicion that these might be staged. In general, research on the Internet with a focus on the content (while valuable and informative in some ways) is, of course, limited in addressing the utilization and consumption aspects of digital practices. With these caveats, this chapter also aims at contributing to theorizing the current practices of religious e-commerce, using examples from Hindu domains.

Online shopping and e-commerce

Markets and marketplaces certainly precede modernity and capitalism. Historicizing bazaars and marketplaces in different sociocultural contexts has produced a rich body of scholarship (Limayem, Mohamed, and Frini 2000; Lee and Lin 2005; Roy 1999, 2013). The scale, scope and shape of markets have changed radically over time. The dramatic growth of online shopping and the dominance of the Internet as a marketplace in the last decade have been registered powerfully by economists, sociologists, service providers and online businesses (e.g., Ward 2001; Wolfinbarger and Gilly 2001). Strader and Shaw (2000, 77) noted astutely:

> Commercial transactions have taken place for centuries, but currently there is a revolution taking place that is transforming the marketplace. This transformation is occurring because the relationship between organizations and consumers is increasingly being facilitated through electronic information technology (IT). This is generally referred to as electronic commerce (e-commerce), with a major component of e-commerce being electronic markets (e-markets)...A question that arises from the current growth of electronic markets is whether there are economic incentives for buyers and sellers to participate in them, or whether they are a passing fad.

In 1999, Strader and Shaw identified a comparatively short list of products being traded in electronic markets: flowers, clothing, automobiles, music, books, electronic magazines (e-zines), airline tickets, stocks and securities. They concluded that "Electronic markets are a new institution of capitalism and they are useful" (Strader and Shaw 2000, 77) and that there are economic incentives for buyers and sellers to engage and participate in e-markets. Also speaking somewhat prophetically, in 2002, John McMillan (2002, 5) observed:

> The bazaars of today's global village are on the Internet. Quickly and cheaply connecting people anywhere in the world, the Internet has transformed markets by allowing exchanges between buyers and sellers who might not otherwise find each other. By logging onto the global electronic shopping mall, you can purchase almost anything you want.

Even as the anticipated growth of electronic markets was seen as nothing short of revolutionary, observers and experts were asking if their impact would be sustainable or if this was just a "passing fad" (Strader and Shaw 1999, 77). Leslie Kaufman (1999) notes:

> Amazon.com announced yesterday that it would transform itself into an Internet shopping bazaar, opening its popular Web site to merchants large and small for a minimal fee. In return, the selling powerhouse, which started as an on-line bookstore, will gather huge amounts of information on the buying habits of consumers.

Fast forward to 2016, and the following piece of information, while astonishing was nonetheless also anticipated. Madeline Farber writes (2016):

> For the first time ever, shoppers are going to the web for most of their purchases. An annual survey by analytics firm comScrore and UPS found that consumers are now buying more things online than in stores. The survey, now in its fifth year, polled more than 5,000 consumers who make at least two online purchases in a three-month period. According to results, shoppers now make 51% of their purchases online, compared to 48% in 2015 and 47% in 2014.
>
> One of retail's biggest game changers is Amazon, which is killing its brick-and-mortar rivals. According to data released by eMarketer… Amazon's e-commerce revenue rose 15.8% in the last 12 months, which is roughly the same clip as Wal-Mart. But Amazon posted $82.7 billion in sales, compared with $12.5 billion for Walmart, and that chasm in dollars keeps getting wider.

Clearly the rise of digital commerce is a global phenomenon. Aligned with European and North American trends, Asian consumers are avid online shoppers with the anticipation that it is here that the largest market for e-commerce of the future will be found. A recent Bloomberg report notes:

> Thailand has seen an explosion of internet shopping in recent years as consumers become more tech savvy. And if that's anything to go by, e-commerce in Southeast Asia is taking off as well… Online retail sales in Thailand of everything from washing machines and televisions to fish sauce are growing more than 100 percent, far outpacing purchases made at traditional stores, where sales are rising about 10 percent. (Cheok 2017)

However, the report qualifies that despite the growing enthusiasm for online shopping, this is still a very small percentage of overall retail purchases in Southeast Asia (4%) as compared to China (16%) and South Korea (18%) (Cheok 2017). The KPMG International 2017 Global Online Consumer Report notes this trend globally as well, imploring businesses to be more innovative in attracting and retaining online customers:

> However, despite the rise of online shopping, ecommerce still makes up a relatively small percentage of total retail spending. Retailers' brick and mortar strategies also need to evolve to continue to draw customers into their stores, and to compete with the online retailers opening their own physical outlets. Increasingly, we are seeing innovative marketing strategies, as well as new technologies such as smart shelves, robots, self-checkout, and interactive and virtual reality, being deployed in stores as retailers strive to compete on all fronts. (KPMG International 2017)

Online merchants globally are seizing opportunities to capture markets in Asia for online shopping. The Chinese market, with a population of 1.4 billion potential consumers, is leading the way in fueling online economies. The Indian market is also read as having great potential with a large youthful population and burgeoning middle class – with a huge appetite for online shopping. The market sentiment remains positive about the potential for a much bigger online market in Asia and indeed counsels that companies should attend to the needs of the Asian consumer and deliver what is expected:

> The new Asian consumer expects *seamless shopping experiences that save time and make life easier.* These expectations are evolving in a dynamic new marketplace that creates huge opportunities for consumer packaged goods (CPG) companies. But they must move now to capture them – or risk ceding control to the digital commerce players that have enabled the region-wide upsurge in digital commerce. (emphasis added) (Business Times 2016)

Consumers today are not only familiar with online marketplaces but also active participants. It is another matter that consumers seldom know anything about the invisible intricate back-end operations of e-commerce, nor is this information necessary for consumption. As an almost infinite portal, the Internet can amass a huge range of products for consumers to browse, with tools for comparing prices, buying the product and having it delivered with convenience and ease. Strikingly the array of products now available online is so comprehensive as to be almost universal in catering to consumer needs. The Internet is now a powerful platform for buying and selling a staggering range of goods and services. This extraordinary development has created a new marketplace for commercial online transactions, problematizing boundaries of *local* and *global* and their relevance for differentiating commodities and markets. What explains the appeal of commercial transactions, ask Häubl and Trifts (2000)? For consumers, accessibility to a global marketplace and information, convenience of shopping at the click of a button, less time invested in looking for the right product, getting the best price[1] and a positive, empowering user experience – have all been cited as motivating factors. The online consumer favors a method of transaction that offers convenient low-cost search for commodities and provides a great deal of information, not to mention endless choice and the possibility for customizing a product to suit one's individual taste. As McMillan (2002, 19) notes, "The Internet has spurred the quest for new methods of transacting. Drawing on the internet's speedy two-way communication, a myriad of mechanisms have been concocted to make buying and selling easier".

The advantages of Internet shopping have been stated thus: convenience, ease of shopping, availability of seemingly infinite choices, objective price comparisons, consumer-driven shopping experiences, accessing vast information about goods and services at the click of a button, cashless payments and doorstep delivery (Miyazaki and Fernandez 2001; Overby and Lee 2006; Rohm and Swaminathan 2004; Teo 2002). Online consumer transactions are handled by the marketplace operator who connects consumers and sellers for a fee, the orders are fulfilled by retailers or wholesalers and online or cash payment and delivery to consumers' doorsteps is handled by yet another category of specialists.

For vendors – retailers and wholesalers alike – the appeal of the Internet lies in connectivity to other vendors and service providers, and especially to a vast body of consumers and clients located anywhere. The ease of making connections and assembly – allowing buyers and sellers to congregate in one space – facilitates new forms of communication and enhances the scale of commercial transactions. Consumer businesses are well aware of the potential for further growth in online shopping with a new generation of consumers who are tech-savvy and who are far more at ease in mediated reality than ever before. This new generation spends far more time online – on WhatsApp, Facebook, Twitter, Instagram, YouTube and email – and is virtually connected during all waking hours. Given this realization, the particular method of organizing an online shopping experience is designed to keep consumers online and interested – browsing and window shopping – even if not necessarily buying something during every visit. *Visits* to online sites and portals may not necessarily translate into an online commercial transaction in that particular digital encounter. But the *openness* of online consumers to the visual-aural properties of the digital medium carries enormous potential for keeping this constituency engaged – even in momentarily encountering products, services, experiences, sentiments and affects – despite moving on. Passing and temporary encounters with the catalogue of online products is anticipated as normal browsing behavior. But online merchants invest much energy in creating impressions and effects that will ensure that browsers will transition to being consumers. Much expert knowledge has now been produced about how to market virtual reality effectively, and these are customized to suit specific needs of vendors. The KPMG International 2017 Global Online Consumer Report, "The Truth about Online Consumers", offers advice to companies seeking to grow their online businesses. The message is clear: understand online consumers and online consumer behavior. Their expertise posits that local/global boundaries are now more or less irrelevant for digital commerce – this applies to markets, products and shoppers alike:

> Competition is no longer limited to local shops during business hours. Consumers today are shopping all the time and everywhere; and in a truly global online marketplace, products can easily be purchased from retailers and manufacturers located anywhere in the world—or from those with no physical retail locations at all.
>
> Consumer demand for *richer experiences and greater convenience* means that retailers need to rethink their strategy, both online and in stores. Having the right product mix is no longer sufficient to attract the new wave of consumers including Millennials, who are entirely focused on one transaction—theirs. *Creating an online shopping experience enhanced by technology* such as augmented and virtual reality or 3D is becoming at least as important as providing convenient and personalized ordering, payment and delivery options (emphasis added). (KPMG International 2017)

The interface of religion and commerce and the predictable entanglement of religion with consumerist and commodification processes have engaged scholars across a range of social science disciplines. The emergent scholarship has highlighted the rise of an industry for religious paraphernalia (material objects), religious personnel and expertise, religious practices (rituals, festivals, processions), religious spaces (pilgrimage sites and holy places) and marginally to more symbolic religious notions (blessing, charisma, spirituality, efficacy, piety and devotion) – all of which can be treated as commodities and subject to branding, packaging and merchandising techniques. In the context of reflections about religion and electronic markets, the following broad initial thoughts were helpful in writing this chapter. Does online shopping work effectively for all categories of products and services? Is the appeal of digital commerce universal? Or is religion the last frontier? Increasingly, evidence suggests that religion-related products and services are abundantly found in cyberspace – accessible to consumers/religious practitioners through e-commercial transactions. It would seem that the trade in religious goods and services travels well to the digital medium of the Internet. Of course, this virtual marketplace has not displaced buying and selling of ritual objects as commodities in brick-and-mortar stores in local bazaars and marketplaces. However, the emergence of cyberspace as a competing marketplace has indeed reconfigured the nature of these earlier transacting arenas and demands thinking about how they should relate to the newest kid on the block. The end result is a landscape of overlapping, intersecting and coexisting *real* and *virtual* marketplaces with complex interconnections.

Trawling the Internet for *pūjā items*

In mapping the sites where *pūjā items* are bought and sold, a move beyond physical spaces is inevitable, focusing the lens on the Internet as another marketplace. As a twenty-first century phenomenon, the Internet is a space that has been colonized by manufacturers and distributors of religious objects and religious services. In the course of writing this chapter and surfing the Internet between 2016 and 2017, I noticed a veritable explosion in the number and range of online merchants dealing with Hindu paraphernalia, as compared to my earlier research in 2009. These businesses may be physically based and operating out of Bangalore, Chennai, Mumbai, New Delhi, Singapore, Kuala Lumpur, New York or London, but in terms of their reach they are clearly not limited by these given boundaries. The form that spiritual portals take on the Internet replicates and mimics the template of profane online portals, but infuses them with religion-related content. There is tremendous counsel now about how to construct religion- or spirituality-related portals. Regnant knowledge about why consumers turn to e-commerce in general has been incorporated into the templates for religious e-commerce: offering customized care, professionalized expertise and quality products, ease and convenience for consumers, prioritizing consumer experience, offering choices, not to mention, competitive prices and best value for money.

Pūjā items featured in electronic catalogues and available for purchase include the following: statues of Hindu deities (in a variety of sizes and materials), *pūjā* vessels, prayer altars, recorded devotional music (in video and audio forms), *ghī* (clarified butter), cowdung, *gangājal* (water from the river Ganges, considered sacred by Hindus), even transient objects such as fresh fruits (lime, coconut, sugarcane), dry fruits (raisins, almond, cashew), flowers and leaves for making garlands and decorations, and religious literature [such as pamphlets, brochures, *bhajan* (devotional hymns) books and larger Hindu scriptures such as the *Bhagavadgītā, Mahābhārata, Rāmāyaṇa*]. See, for example, the following advertisement of *pūjā* items at indiamart.com:

> We have broad variety of pooja items made from high quality brass. Please send us your specifications and we will be glad to source the right product for all your prayer and puja needs. If you have any questions please do not hesitate to contact Hapra Exports via email or phone. (indiamart n.d.)

All these websites offer online facilities for making inquiries about available products, purchasing them and having them delivered to one's doorstep. The sites also claim to provide information about the mythology and symbolism of spiritual accessories: it is not just *things* that are being traded online. As is well known by now, the spiritual and material are entangled in complicated ways and the assumption of their unambiguous separation is untenable. It is inevitable that messages, ideas and meanings about the manner and method of proper/appropriate usage of objects in ritual are transmitted together with the objects that are being offered for sale. The actual methods of religious e-commercial transactions are identical to the templates used for trading in secular products. E-commerce merchants seem to assume that like themselves, consumers too do not distinguish between online dealings of *sacred* and *profane*[2] product categories. Their conclusion is that customers will 'add' a statue of the deity Ganesha or Ganges water to the shopping cart for checkout as easily as they would grocery items or a pair of jeans.

Attesting to the dramatic intensification of e-commerce, Rani Nugraha, a WorldFirst author, named seven Asian online marketplaces to watch out for in February 2017: Tmall Global (China), Lazada (Southeast Asia), Flipkart (India; founded in 2007, with 100 million registered users in 2016, with 43% of India's e-commerce market), Rakuten (Japan; founded in 1997, one of the largest e-commerce platforms in the world), Coupang (South Korea), Snapdeal (India; founded in 2010, delivers to over 5,000 towns and cities in India, anticipates 20 million daily visitors by 2020) and Zalora (with a reach across 11 countries in the Asia-Pacific region) (Nugragha 2017).This maps onto the growing base of online consumers in Asia in all product categories. Not surprisingly, both Snapdeal and Flipkart have product categories for religion and spirituality and religion and devotion, as does Amazon.in, currently India's second largest e-commerce site. According to a 2014 *Economic Times* and *The Times of India* survey, "India's spiritual and religious market is estimated to be over $30 billion", an opportunity and potential seized enthusiastically by investors and start-up companies led by seasoned entrepreneurs from the corporate private sector (Nugragha 2017).

Omkarmic E-Commerce Pvt Ltd (originating and operating out of Mumbai, India) is one such venture. The company blurb asserts that it has "successfully created an e-commerce Marketplace to promote spiritual and religious products and services" and aspires to "provide a unique vehicle for the manufacturers, traders, vendors, institutions to tap in to the online revolution and the huge Market for spiritual and religious products and services" (OMKARMIC n.d.). The company's decision to turn its business energies toward "spirituality and religion" and "spiritual and religious products" (OMKARMIC n.d.) has to do with its reading of India as predominantly Hindu (80% of the 1.3 billion population);[3] this segment of a religious populace is grounded in devotional Hinduism, which is practiced in homes and temples by individuals and communities who have to secure things for use during rituals and ceremonies. The company's vision is "... to tap in to the online revolution and the huge Market for spiritual and religious products and services" (OMKARMIC n.d.).

Another company, OnlinePrasad.com, founded in 2012 by Goonjan Mall, formerly a senior analyst in the consulting firm Bain & Co, "launched a first-of-its-kind private label brand, Zevotion" (Phadnis 2014). According to Mall, "Our research showed that about 80% of religious products sold in the country is counterfeit. Zevotion offers certified products assuring customers true value for their money" (Phadnis 2014). Religious personalities in India from the likes of Baba Ramdev and Sri Sri Ravi Shankar (Art of Living) have proven to be adept entrepreneurs as well. The former's business was billed in 2011 to be worth about USD 157,481,500 (PTI 2011) and the company's house brand Patanjali now sells everything – from mustard oil to incense sticks to Ayurvedic health products to jeans. Evidence from multiple sources converges to register firmly that devotion *sells* in the Indian and Hindu context, and that there is a ripe religious and spirituality market ready for profit and that it makes good business sense to invest in this domain. Given the growing popularity of online shopping and the highly technologically mediated reality of everyday individuals' lives, it would be astonishing if these commercial ventures did not seek a visible online presence and claim the religious e-commerce market. In the words of Rajiv K. Sanghvi, the founder of Vistaas Digital Media Private Limited which owns DivineIndia.com, "The devotional market is the next big thing after Bollywood" (NextBigWhat 2012). There is good reason to find in this a precise prediction.

While a majority of religion-related online merchants and shopping malls carry an extensive and almost exhaustive catalogue of religious products (sometimes across religious traditions), there are specialist traders who deal with particular items, promising quality and expertise – as in the following instance of an *altar specialist*:

> Divine Homes- By Big Bazaar is a company which offers you the highest quality of religious altars and religious arts and crafts. we (sic) believe you deserve best... Divine Home Collections brings you the biggest range of prayer altars, murtis and puja items. Our altars are especially designed and crafted by skilled craftsmen and high quality material is always used. At divine home collections we endeavour on bringing joy to the soul of anyone who might be seeking the love of god. (Divine Homes-By Big Bazaar 2018)

In many instances, Hindus abroad are targeted overtly (but not exclusively) as a potential customer base. Some of the websites are directed specifically at Hindu communities in the diaspora who are living at a distance from Indian shores. The websites seek to bridge this physical distance by transporting genuine religious paraphernalia (from India together with counsel from Hindu religious specialists) to diasporic doorsteps – fulfilling their stated mission of keeping communities connected to Hindu religious traditions and to India as the *sacred* center for all things Hindu:

> Rudra Centre has been supplying quality Puja items since 1997 which are selected for their *authentic ingredients as per scriptures*. For Puja

> services, a team of well-versed, karmakandi priests from Shivkashi Temple perform Pujas as per Vedic rituals in a 5,000 sq feet self-owned premise. For more than a decade, Rudra Centre has been conducting Pujas like Ati Rudra, Mahamrityunjaya Yagna, Baglamukhi Homa and many more for the benefit of mankind. (emphasis added) (Rudra Centre 1997)

Additionally, these traditional offerings are sprinkled with a touch of modernity presumed to be appealing to Hindus settled in Europe, North America and Australia. As with retail stores in Little Indias situated in diasporic sites, the online stores too freely mingle profane wares with spiritual offerings, such that basmati rice, *dāl* (lentils) and wheat flour share the same online catalogues and portals as icons of Hindu deities, *pūjā thālīs* (prayer trays) and *pūjā* kits, as seen in this publicity advertisement from an Australian-based online grocery store:

> Pooja Items: Divinity with a touch of Modernity!
>
> Being far away from your homeland doesn't mean you have to stay deprived of your tradition, culture and religious beliefs and practices. 'India At Home' is a leading online grocery store in Australia helping you with things that connects you with your country. *Other than the vast range of grocery and ready to eat products, our online store also provides a distinct collection of pooja items.* We have Pooja packs for different type of poojas, mandir etc. We also provide the statues of various Gods & Goddesses. You can buy Laxmi Vishnu shank, pooja thali, dhoop, havan samagri, loban powder and many other things that can help you with your pooja needs. All these products can be purchased from our online stores and if you want, you can even visit our in-house stores. We deliver excellent quality and timely delivery of all orders made. Also, you are entitled to a great customer support that will make the shopping a wonderful experience for you. (emphasis added) (India At Home 2019)

Historically, the need for objects and other paraphernalia has been a challenge for overseas Hindu communities.[4] The role of the Internet and the digital media in contributing to constructions of diasporic identities (Chopra 2006; Gajjala 2010) has received scholarly attention, but the market for Hindu-related objects and services is very much within India itself. In addition to real marketplaces in the diaspora and in India, the Internet is looking to become the preferred alternative for accessing *pūjā items*. Aspirationally, online businesses see a global market for their products, albeit with a concentrated audience – a community of Hindu devotees in India and beyond – who are potential customers. As a virtual marketplace, the Internet has properties that do render it a transnational global marketplace, where retailers and businesses are not only interconnected but also brought close to a global database of consumers.

Notably in publicity and marketing strategies, the narratives on *pūjā items* are emplaced within commentaries, instructions and often normative directives on various forms of *pūjā* as well:

> This section of **GaramChai** features Puja, *Puja vidhi or the method of worship*, Puja items, samagri, altar, rudraksha, punchang, Indian festival, slokas and related links for Indian Americans and those interested in Hindu mode of worship. For a comprehensive listing of temples in all the states and provinces in North America, visit our temple listing page. (emphasis added) (GaramChai 1999)

The pattern of a conjoined discourse on ritual objects *and* the ritual procedure/method is replicated in multiple examples.

The dominant method for spiritual portals like these is for retailers and suppliers of *pūjā items* to register their existence to consumers by setting up websites and *displaying* their wares, capitalizing on the *visual-aural* properties of this digital medium, using state-of-the-art technology, 3D animation and interactive features of virtual, augmented reality. This is a fairly conventional usage which serves to supplement and consolidate a business that might also exist in the real world. By now, being online is a survival strategy, such that a virtual presence is now required to reach a global customer base – using the Internet to disseminate information, advertise goods and to communicate with potential customers. However, by default, online businesses today have gone beyond this and have actualized the concept of online shopping, which, in my earlier 2009 research on religion and commodification processes, was still an ambition. As a medium, the Internet now is a platform where *pūjā items* can not only be advertised but also bought and sold. This new marketplace, enhanced by the circulation and dissemination of different kinds of knowledge about ritual objects and Hindu rituals themselves, has transformed the secular layperson/religious specialist dichotomy deeply embedded in Hindu frames. New categories of profane experts have emerged in cyberspace – with no claim to religious knowledge or specialization. However, many of these online entrepreneurs draw legitimacy from being connected to a variety of religious experts (sculptors, priests, religious teachers) – to sustain claims not just of *quality* of the product but also its authenticity and purity to 'pass' what practitioners deem to be a sacred register. Both of these assertions rest on trust and confidence that consumers have and which can make the difference between a successful commercial transaction or not. Having to negotiate these terrains has led to the forging of new and different ties and the creation of new alliances for business-making.

The critical role played in many of these online e-commerce start-ups by individuals with corporate, finance credentials and experiences as well as technological acumen is perhaps unsurprising. A good example is shubhpuja.com, the recent player in this market, launched in December 2013 by Saumya Vardhan and her father Harsh Vardhan, who is listed on the website as the its Founder and CEO. S. Vardhan's entrepreneurial dossier includes her work with KPMG London and Ernst & Young London as a management consultant, corporate experiences which she says moved her from "finance to religious industry" (Sen 2015). Driven by the articulated desire to make a difference and improve society, Vardhan's religious e-commerce venture consciously invokes the language of modernity and has implemented new technologies and marketing frameworks as well as utilized print and digital media effectively to create graphic and impactful messaging. The company describes its aims brief thus – all designed to reach as large an online customer base as possible globally:

> Shubhpuja.com is a science and technology based platform for authentic Vedic pujas, astrology, Vastu and spiritual products through educated and qualified professionals. Shubhpuja is an international brand offering exclusive, highly specialized and customized services to *our worldwide audience.*
>
> Our highly customized diagnosis and solutions *differentiates us from all.* We are a team of *highly specialized and educated professionals* who are researching on combining ancient wisdom with modern times! We recommend accurate, practical and appropriate remedial measures to resolve the issue from root.
>
> We believe in upholding our Vedas by catering to the *customized needs* of our clients. We are scientifically revolutionizing the ancient spiritual practices by preserving our customs and traditions.
>
> The *quality of our services and uniqueness in the market* has been well featured by leading Indian and International media houses. The worldwide media coverage in such a short span defines your exceptional faith and support which has facilitated the growth of our venture. (Shubhpuja.com n.d.)

It is clear that these start-up ventures spend considerable energy on advertisement and marketing of their products and the online companies in an increasingly highly crowded and competitive religious e-commerce market. The strategies used are the tried and tested ones adopted by successful online ventures, focusing on branding, expertise, qualifications, professionalization and relevant experiences in order to stand out from the pack. Another excellent example comes from KalyanPuja.com whose presentation of the self deliberately replicates the tone and logic of the world of marketing and finance:

> **ABOUT US**
> **Kalyan Puja** is founded by a seasoned team of professionals having diverse experience across sectors. This experience helps to provide you with a wholesome solution to your spiritual requirements in all

> forms. The quality, use of technology and competitive rates ensure that you would have a complete peace of mind and no running around will be necessary for arranging your rituals. The team of Purohits is a well-qualified one and you can be rest assured of about proper recitation of the mantras and puja procedures.
>
> **Founders:**
> **Harsh Agarwal:** Harsh looks at the overall operations including technology at KalyanPuja. He has earlier worked as the CEO at Ascertiva Group, India reporting to UK headquarters with complete P&L and compliance responsibilities. Harsh has an international consulting experience in several sectors ranging from financial, Information Technology to industrial/manufacturing with projects in many countries like advising clients on international expansion and Product development for multiple finance and IT products across the globe.
>
> **Megha Goel:** Formerly, a professor of education at a degree college in Gurgaon, she is the lynchpin of all spiritual and religious engagements at KalyanPuja. (KalyanPuja 2019)

These readily available products in cyberspace, accompanied by a logic and narrative about why these are necessary and how they are to be utilized in prayer and worship, further reconstruct Hindu religiosity and potentially produce particular kinds of ritual behavior. The market is packed with portals that offer for purchase a range of products for use in Hindu ceremonial life. At the same time, these online merchants provide further service of packaging and promote a variety of *pūjā kits* – which are essentially a select set of objects brought together for use in specific rituals and festivals – examples include *Ganapathy Homam kit*, *Navagraha Homam Puja kit* and *Sampoorna Puja kit*. At the most obvious level, this strategy can be interpreted as a marketing strategy to just sell more products, but other readings are possible too: the very *naming* of specific rituals and bringing this to consciousness of devotees, the *message* that these are important rituals for enacting Hindu religiosity and finally also communicating the *method* of proper *pūjās*. Judging by the select sample of online Hindu e-businesses featured in this chapter, the Internet not only trades effectively in *pūjā items* but embedded in these commercial ventures are critical teaching and learning platforms about Hindu rituals and festivals themselves. Here both *pūjā items* as ritual objects and knowledge/instructions about their correct performance have been commodified. Marketing and advertising of merchandise is entangled with explicit and implicit messaging about not only the *essential products* required for conducting different types of *pūjā*(s) but also the *proper methods* of performing them. Like all markets then, the Internet does not passively respond by simply fulfilling given consumer needs. It creates new needs through the introduction of novel products and services using innovative technologies, not only sustaining the businesses but also feeding back into and impacting in practice the domain of worship.

Conclusion and outlook: Does the medium matter in religious e-commerce?

The empirical material presented here and the comparative lens from my earlier research (Sinha 2010, 2014, 2017) on trading in materials to be used in Hindu ceremonial life nudge toward the obvious conclusion that commercial transactions of *pūjā items* – offline and online – are multidimensional and multilayered phenomena, with overlaps and intersections but *also* distinctions across these two sites. My fieldwork (in Singapore and Malaysia between 2003 and 2009) in retail stores which trade in religious objects offers a useful comparative lens. Face-to-face verbal interactions which are facilitated in real stores between buyers and sellers are clearly not possible in online encounters despite the interactive digital medium and the possibility of live chats with religious experts and the invitation to call in to customer service officers. The verbal exchanges and animated discussions about the object to be purchased, with questions, answers and counter-questions are not facilitated in cyberspace, perhaps not even expected by consumers. Online transactions are, by definition, *disembodied*, and the seller remains invisible; the latter need not have a personal presence here. Observing buyer–seller interactions in retail stores in Singapore's Little India, it was impossible to miss that the business transaction was accompanied by other kinds of exchanges as well. Several traders reported that customers came to them because of their spiritual expertise and knowledge about Hindu rituals, and were thus consulted about the spiritual aspects of *pūjā items* they were selling. During a commercial transaction where money and commodity changed hands, details about proper methods of conducting rituals were also being communicated. This is something that can and does transfer well to cyberspace. Interestingly, the websites dealing with *pūjā items* enhance the transaction by offering instructions to consumers about the *how* and *why* of rituals under consideration, drawing on religious expertise to legitimate their claims. These ethnographic vignettes nudge toward the conclusion that these transactions, while clearly *commercial* in nature, also carry other connotations; priced commodities are sold for money, but, additionally, there are also knowledge flows, of both a practical and a religious nature – what direction a prayer altar should face in a home, what it means to pray with devotion, how statues of deities are to be treated during worship or about which specific *rudraksha* bead (literally eyes of Rudra/Shiva; commonly known as prayer beads) is relevant for a particular problem faced by the devotee/customer. These exchanges suggest that there are other more subtle and implicit dimensions to the otherwise overt and explicit business transaction, which are inevitably reconfigured.

But in my prior ethnographic work, even the Hindu owners of these businesses saw their chosen occupation first and foremost as a way of making a living and were not uncomfortable with the idea of trading in *prayer items* (Sinha 2010). While being concerned about breaking even and making money, they denied that they were driven merely by profiteering motives. Neither did they see a problem with the fact that *pūjā items* were bought and sold, even as they were critical of unethical business practices (Sinha 2010). Not only are commodities priced for sale with a reasonable profit margin but with the anticipation that customers would bargain and negotiate to secure the best price. But are these just marketing strategies to enhance sales? Pricing a product immediately brings into sharp focus its identity as a commodity. Do online and offline merchants take into account any special considerations in deciding on the price of a *pūjā item*? More than any other discussion, the exchanges I had with traders of Hindu ritual objects confirmed that *pūjā items* are treated like other commodities and the ones that I encountered talked about rental, wages, cost price, profit and so forth (Sinha 2010, 2017). Sellers noted that they are in this business to make money, even if they are dealing with *pūjā items*, and so have to be concerned about generating profits. This attitude is even more sharply discernible in online ventures that deal with religion and spirituality. Indeed, my ethnography from Singaporean Hindu domains confirms that the turn to the latter has been stated by entrepreneurs precisely because of the calculation that *religion is good for business* (Sinha 2010, 2014). What about options for bargaining and negotiations over prices? This certainly defines transactions of *pūjā items*, as with all commodities. During my earlier fieldwork, I observed customers negotiating the *right* price for ritual objects, especially if they perceived the price to be inflated – in making comparisons with the Indian prices. Such bargaining is not possible, and is not a feature of online transactions. However, online merchants do offer discount coupons and sale items at slashed prices to attract customers. The possibility of online price comparisons for specific products to some extent satisfies the customer that one is getting good value for money.

Interestingly, I encountered retailers who declined to sell specific *pūjā items* to customers, and met entrepreneurs who interrogated customers about what they intended to do with a specific item before agreeing to sell it (Sinha 2010). In another instance, another retailer declined to sell the *rudrākṣa* seed to a person he felt was not fit to own it, with the full awareness that he thus risked alienating customers and affecting his business negatively. In another example, a retailer admitted that he would feel uncomfortable selling a statue of a Hindu god or goddess to someone who was going to display it in his bathroom, signaling that he as the retailer can sometimes by choosy about customers, something that does not make sense within the logic of capitalist relations, where the ability to pay for a commodity is a primary feature (Sinha 2010). This *refusal* to sell to an inappropriate customer or to one who might use the item in an illegitimate mode is intriguing. Here a religious consciousness mediates market behavior with less than perfect outcome from the perspective of instrumental rationality but nonetheless seems to create a space for Weber's substantive rationality. In contrast, the anonymity of online transactions means that these ethical-moral considerations are not even on the radar. In a virtual marketplace, the maxim that the *customer is king* holds sway and the ability to make a payment is the only factor at work. The intentionality, ethics or politics of consumers are not considerations in achieving online transactions in religious e-commerce.

That a variety of objects required in the practice of Hinduism, and the fact of their incorporation into the global capitalist system of markets and commodities have meant their necessary commercialization (Sinha 2010, 2014, 2017) is well recognized. But invoking the case of *pūjā items*, their availability on the Internet and the fact that consumers/devotees are indeed transacting these online, the following broader questions about relations between Hinduism and e-commerce surface – not all of which have been adequately addressed here. I reiterate these to keep the discussion open rather than offer simplistic responses. Students of religion and commodification will see a family resemblance in these queries in existing deliberations about trading of ritual objects in *non-virtual* capitalist marketplaces. Thus, future research should keep the following questions in mind. What is the nature of entrepreneurship and online shopping in religious spheres? Are these substantively different from commercial transactions of profane commodities? Are these business deals with profit maximization as a goal the same as other dealings? Does the phenomenon of online shopping (rather than a face-to-face, interactive shopping encounter) make a difference to the *experience* of securing and using these products as ritual objects? What can be the nature of interaction between retailers and consumers in a virtual marketplace? Does the fact that the medium of cyberspace is the site for commercial transactions or does the religious content of the online portals make a difference (and to whom?) to the responses that would be made to these queries? Clearly much more research from media studies scholars, religious studies researchers, sociologists and anthropologists in the world of religious e-commerce is needed to nudge toward ethnographically grounded and theoretically informed responses to these questions. I too look forward to participating in this collective endeavor as an ethnographer.

Notes

1 According to Brynjolfsson and Smith (2000, 563) "...prices on the Internet are 9–16% lower than prices in conventional outlets, depending on whether taxes, shipping, and shopping costs are included in the price".

2 The scared/profane binary has long been problematized in scholarship of religious studies scholars (e.g., Bacon et al. 2015) as well as anthropologists and sociologists of religion (e.g., Cova and Rinallo 2017; Kurakin 2013).

3 Online start-ups from India catering to the religious needs of non-Hindu communities also abound. Examples include VedicVaani.com which offers items related to Hinduism, Buddhism, Jainism and Sikhism on a single platform, and ProudUmmah.com, launched by a Hyderabad-based mechanical engineer Abid Khan (formerly with Google), provides customized kits (which include prayer beads, prayer mats, maps of pilgrimage sites) related to Islamic pilgrimages.

4 But this reliance on the *homeland* is not absolute, as Hindus in the diaspora have fashioned new products and services locally to cater to religious needs.

References

amazon.in, 1996. *Puja Articles.* Available at www.amazon.in/Puja-Articles/b?ie=UTF8&node=3591807031, accessed 15 March 2018.

Bacon, H., Dossett, W. and Knowles, S., eds., 2015. *Alternative Salvations: Engaging the Sacred and the Secular.* New York: Bloombury Academic Publishers.

Business Times, 2016. The Future of Commerce has arrived: Understanding the New Asian Consumer. *The Business Times*, [online] 15 April. Available at www.businesstimes.com.sg/hub/accenture/the-future-of-commerce-has-arrived-understanding-the-new-asian-consumer, accessed 15 October 2017.

Brynjolfsson, E. and Smith, M. D., 2000. Frictionless Commerce? A Comparison or Internet and Conventional Retailers. *Management Science* 46(4), 563–585.

Campbell, H., ed., 2017. *Religion and the Internet.* London: Routledge.

Cheok, M., 2017. Online Shopping in Taking off in Southeast Asia. *Bloomberg*, [online] 28 August. Available at www.bloomberg.com/news/articles/2017-08-28/thai-online-shopping-binge-is-sign-of-southeast-asia-market-size, accessed 15 October 2017.

Chopra, R., 2006. Global Primordialities: Virtual Identity Politics in Online Hindutva and Online Dalit Discourse. *New Media & Society* 8(2), 187–206.

Cobb, J., 1998. *CyberGrace: The Search for God in the Digital World.* New York: Crown.

Cova, V. and Rinallo, D., 2017. *Revisiting the Separation between Sacred and Profane: Boundary-work in Pilgrimage Experiences.* Edimbourg: 8th Workshop on Interpretive Consumer Research. Available at https://hal-amu.archives-ouvertes.fr/hal-01492432/document, accessed 26 September 2018.

Divine Homes-By Big Bazaar, 2018. *Divine Homes-By Big Bazaar| Accessories Store| New Zealand|epagenz.com.* Available at www.epagenz.com/biz/divinehomesbybigbazaar, accessed 15 August 2018.

Farber, M., 2016. Consumers are Now Doing Most of Their Shopping Online. *Fortune*, [online] 8 June. Available at http://fortune.com/2016/06/08/online-shopping-increases/, accessed 16 October 2017.

Gajjala, R., 2010. 3D (Digital) Indian Diasporas. In: Andoni, A. and Oiarzabal, P. J., eds. *Diasporas in the New Media Age: Identity, Politics, and Community.* Reno: University of Nevada Press, 209–224.

GaramChai, 1999. *Puja, Pooja and Hindu Worship from GaramChai.com.* Available at www.garamchai.com/puja.htm, accessed 17 August 2018.

Häubl, G. and Valerie, T., 2000. Consumer Decision Making in Online Shopping Environments: The Effects of Interactive Decision Aids. *Marketing science* 19(1), 4–21.

India At Home, 2019. *India Grocery Store in Melbourne, Australia.* Available at www.indiaathome.com.au/prayer-items/pooja-items.html, accessed 15 October 2018.

Indiamart, n.d. *Pooja-articles.* Available at https://dir.indiamart.com/impcat/pooja-articles.html, accessed 25 April 2019.

Jacobs, S., 2012. Communicating Hinduism in a Changing Media Context. *Religion Compass* 6(2), 136–151.

KalyanPuja, 2019. Puja services & wide range of Rudraksha, Yantra, Mala, Saligram, Parad-KalyanPuja. *About us*. Available at http://kalyanpuja.com, accessed 15 October 2018.

Karapanagiotis, N., 2013. Cyber Forms, Worshipable Forms: Hindu Devotional Viewpoints on the Ontology of Cyber-Gods and-Goddesses. *International Journal of Hindu Studies* 17(1), 57–82.

Kaufman, L., 1999. Amazon.com Plans a Transformation to Internet Bazaar. *The New York Times*, [online] 30 September. Available at www.nytimes.com/1999/09/30/business/amazoncom-plans-a-transformation-to-internet-bazaar.html, accessed 16 October 2017.

KPMG International, 2017. *The Truth about Online Consumers: 2017 Global Online Consumer Report*. Available at https://assets.kpmg/content/dam/kpmg/pe/pdf/Publicaciones/The-truth-about-online-consumers.pdf, accessed 15 October 2018.

Kurakin, D., 2013. Reassembling the Ambiguity of the Sacred: A Neglected Inconsistency in Readings of Durkheim. *Journal of Classical Sociology* 15(4), 377–395.

Lee, G. and Hsiu-Fen, L., 2005. Customer Perceptions of E-service Quality in Online Shopping. *International Journal of Retail & Distribution Management* 33(2), 161–176.

Lim, F., 2009. *Mediating Piety: Technology and Religion in Asia*. Leiden: Brill.

Limayem, M., Mohamed, K. and Frini, A., 2000. What Makes Consumers Buy from Internet? A Longitudinal Study of Online Shopping. *IEEE Transactions on Systems, Man, and Cybernetics-Part A: Systems and Humans* 30(4), 421–432.

Mallapragada, M., 2010. Desktop Deities: Hindu Temples, Online Cultures and the Politics of Remediation. *South Asian Popular Culture* 8(2), 109–121.

Marcotte, R., 2010. New Virtual Frontiers: Religion and Spirituality in Cyberspace. *Australian Religion Studies Review* 23(3), 247–254.

McMillan, J., 2002. *Reinventing the Bazaar: A Natural History of the Markets*. New York: W.W Norton & Company Inc.

Miyazaki, A. D. and Fernandez, A., 2001. Consumer Perceptions of Privacy and Security Risks for Online Shopping. *Journal of Consumer Affairs* 35(1), 27–44.

NextBigWhat, 2012. From the New Testament: Wise Men Build Their Businesses on Devotion [Religious Ecommerce Market in India]. *NextBigWhat*, [online] 12 September. Available at www.nextbigwhat.com/religious-ecommerce-market-in-india-297/, accessed 15 October 2018.

Nugragha, R., 2017. 7 Online Marketplaces in Asia You Should Get to Know. *WORLDFIRST Blog*, [blog] 06 February. Available at www.worldfirst.com/au/blog/selling-online/7-online-marketplaces-asia-get-know/, accessed 15 October 2017.

OMKARMIC, n.d. *About*. Available at www.f6s.com/omkarmicthespiritualstore/about, accessed 15 October 2018.

OnlinePrasad, 2019. *Poojas*. Available at OnlinePrasad.com, accessed 15 October 2018.

Overby, J. W. and Lee, E., 2006. The Effects of Utilitarian and Hedonic Online Shopping Value on Consumer Preference and Intentions. *Journal of Business Research* 59(10), 1160–1166.

Phadnis, S., 2014. India's Spiritual and Religious Market Estimated to be over 30 Billion. *The Times of India*, [online] 23 February. Available at https://timesofindia.indiatimes.com/india/Indias-spiritual-and-religious-market-is-estimated-to-be-over-30-billion/articleshow/30881651.cms, accessed 16 October 2017.

PTI, 2011. *Baba Ramdev's Business Empire Worth over Rs 1,100 Crore.* Available at https://economictimes.indiatimes.com/news/politics-and-nation/baba-ramdevs-business-empire-worth-over-rs-1100-crore/articleshow/8790573.cms, accessed 25 April 2018.

Rohm, A. J. and Swaminathan, V., 2004. A typology of online shoppers based on shopping motivations. *Journal of Business Research* 57(7), 748–757.

Roy, T., 1999. *Traditional Industry in the Economy of Colonial India.* Cambridge: Cambridge University Press.

Roy, T., 2013. *An Economic History of Early Modern India.* New York: Routledge.

Rudra Centre, 1997. *Puja Items, Hindu Puja Samagri Online From India to USA, UK, Canada-Rudraksha Ratna.* Available at www.rudraksha-ratna.com/p/puja-items-pooja-samagri, accessed 15 October 2018.

Scheifinger, H., 2009. Om-line Hinduism: World Wide Gods on the Web. *Journal for the Academic Study of Religion* 23(3), 325–345.

Scheifinger, H., 2015. New Technology and Change in the Hindu Tradition. In: Keul, I., ed. *Asian Religions, Technology and Science.* New York: Routledge, 153–168.

Sen, P, 2015. How did India's only Religious E-commerce Platform Come about? Saumya Vardhan, Founder of Shubhpuja Tells us Today. *SHEROES*, [online] 18 December. Available at https://sheroes.com/articles/how-did-india-s-only-religious-e-commerce-platform-come-about-saumya-vardhan-founder-of-shubhpuja-tells-us-today/MTI5NA==, accessed 25 April 2019.

Shubhpuja.com, n.d. *About us.* Available at http://shubhpuja.com/shubhpuja/about-us/, accessed 15 October 2018.

Sinha, V., 2010. *Religion and Commodification: Merchandising Diasporic Hinduism.* London: Routledge.

Sinha, V. 2014. Religion, Commodification and Consumerism. In: Hedges, P., ed. *Controversies in Contemporary Religion.* Santa Barbara: Praeger, 113–136.

Sinha, V., 2017. Made in Singapore: Conceiving, Making and Using Ritual Objects in Hindu Domains. In Koning, J., Njoto-Feillard, G., eds. *New Religiosities, Modern Capitalism, and Moral Complexities in Southeast Asia.* Basingstoke: Palgrave Macmillan, 247–263.

Strader, T. J. and Shaw, M. J., 1999. Consumer Cost Differences for Traditional and Internet Markets. *Internet Research* 9(2), 82–92.

Strader, T. J. and Shaw, M. J., 2000. Electronic Markets: Impact and Implications. In: Shaw, M., Blanning, R., Strader, T., Whinston, A., eds. *Handbook on Electronic Commerce.* Berlin: Springer, 77–98.

Teo, T. S. H., 2002. Attitudes Toward Online Shopping and the Internet. *Behaviour & Information Technology* 21(4), 259–271.

Ward, M. R., 2001. Will Online Shopping Compete More with Traditional Retailing or Catalog Shopping? *Netnomics* 3(2), 103–117.

Wolfinbarger, M. and Gilly, M. C., 2001. Shopping Online for Freedom, Control, and Fun. *California Management Review* 43(2), 34–55.

Zaleski, J., 1997. *The Soul of Cyberspace: How New Technology is Changing Our Spiritual Lives*. San Fransciso: HarperEdge.

Zeiler, X., 2014. The Global Mediatization of Hinduism through Digital Games. Representation versus Simulation in *Hanuman: Boy Warrior*. In: Campbell, H. and Grieve, G. P., eds. *Playing with Religion in Digital Games*. Bloomington: Indiana University Press, 66–87.

10 Taming Hindu *Śakta* Tantra on the Internet

Online *pūjās* for the goddess Tripurasundarī

Sravana Borkataky-Varma

Introduction

Terms such as Hinduism, Tantra, *Śakta* Tantra, goddess and online *pūjā*, used in this chapter, are highly complex and historically entrenched. Each by themselves and/or in combination brings forth materials that are not only rich in content but also provide a challenging landscape for scholars to navigate through.

The meta-objective of this chapter is to explore whether online *pūjās* (rituals) perpetuate normative understandings of Hindu *Śakta* Tantra, or is there room for the esoteric aspects of the *Śakta* tradition to shine through, as well? This question will be examined by a comparative study of the (visual and textual) representations and *pūjās* of the goddess Tripurasundarī in one exemplary temple, Kāmākhyā, and on four websites which offer online *pūjās*. How is the goddess overall (visually and textually) represented, which type of *pūjās* are offered and what information is given on the possible benefits of these *pūjās*? Are there changes when the ritual of Tripurasundarī moves online, and if so, which? Does the Internet depict a representation of Tripurasundarī and her ritual in a sweetened, mainstreamed and overall pacified version of Tantric *pūjā*, or do we find (elements of) more esoteric ritual forms? In doing so, three facets of online religion will also be briefly alluded to: (1) How does online *pūjā* establish authority of the *devī* (goddess) as well as the *pūjārīs*? (2) What is the perceived authenticity of online *pūjās*? (3) What is the perceived efficacy of online *pūjās*?

In order to answer these questions, the depictions of the goddess (description of looks and/or images), the available *pūjā* options and the stated and perceived benefits of performing the *pūjās* have been studied. As a result of this comparative study, I conclude that both in Kāmākhyā and the online *pūjā* space, it is the exoteric and normative understandings of Hindu *Śakta* Tantra that are being popularized. While the esoteric is occasionally alluded to, no details are provided. Thereby, the esoteric is getting pushed deeper into a veiled existence.

The chapter's first section titled "Contextual backdrop" offers a broad overview of the three key terms used here: Tantra, *Śaktā* and *pūjā*. Second, the goddess Tripurasundarī and her ritual will be discussed in the context of the Kāmākhyā temple in the section "Stones and mortar". The third section, "Coded goddess", discusses the representation and ritual of the goddess Tripurasundarī on the following four websites: onlinepuja.org, onlinetemple.com, divine-rudraksha.com and divyayogashop.com. It compares the findings with the representation and ritual of the goddess in her Kāmākhyā temple. Finally, we launch into the "Conclusion".

Contextual backdrop

The modern-day imagining and understanding of Tantra is complex. The term Tantra stands for many different elements of Indian religions and Indian religiosity. *Śākta* (goddess worship) Tantra, historically, has been highly impacted by religious, postcolonial and political dimensions that continue to influence contemporary representations. Historically, forces within the Hindu religious traditions, especially the *smārta*, put a negative connotation to the rituals and practices of *Śakta* Tantra. *Smārta* Hinduism is the religious tradition defined by adherence to the precepts of the Vedic ritual codes and the *Dharmaśāstras* (genre of Hindu theological texts written in Sanskrit which mainly discuss dharma, the prescribed right way of living and/or duties), which drove standard codes rooted in the Vedic and priestly traditions. Commenting on the South Indian Hindu traditions, Douglas Renfrew Brooks states: "They do not wish to be called 'Tantric' or to associate with things 'Tantric.' In contemporary south Indian vernaculars, 'Tantra' and related terms suggest shady connections with illicit sex, forbidden intoxicants, or effective black magic" (Brooks 1992, 405). Caution must be borne to not split the *smārta* ideological views and traditions of rituals from social thought. Social practices and textual traditions are not isomorphic.

In addition to the *smārta* bowdlerization of Tantra, the shifting tides of modern India and the British colonial moral sensibility contributed to push the fierce forms of Tantric rituals and practices into a cloaked existence. Stephen Hay, while commenting on the Hindu reformist leaders that revived Hinduism as understood in the modern period, states: "Just as the Muslim conquest injected a fresh stream of religious thought into the veins of Hindu society, so the British conquest brought with it new views of the world, man, and God" (Hay 1988, 36). The new class of Anglicized Indians felt the need to defend Hinduism in the light of burgeoning British criticisms, many of which were focused on the alleged excesses and superstitions of the Tantric traditions. These ideas of a reformed Hinduism were intended to urge practitioners of Tantra to abandon any aspect of the tradition that was considered, by the British and the reformers, to be illicit or immoral. A systematic demonization of (especially *Vāmācāra*, lit. left-handed) Tantra over many years has influenced the mainstream public view about Tantra and its meanings. Some rituals in the *Vāmācāra* require the use of *pañcamakāra*, lit. the five substances, beginning with the syllable *ma*: *madya* (wine), *māṃsa* (meat), *matsya* (fish), *mudrā* (parched grain) and *maithuna* (sexual intercourse). These substances and practices are regarded impure in mainstream Hinduism. But Tantra continues to evolve, though more often than not the esoteric practices remain hidden from the public eye, including on the Internet.

The so-called "dot com" movement that started in the mid to late 1990s has also initiated a shift in the way cultural technologies are transmitted, stored, cataloged and disseminated. One such avenue is religion. Christopher Helland (2007) has proposed a distinction between "religion online" and "online religion".

> Religion online was lauded for empowering its members to re-form rituals and bypass traditional systems of legitimation or recognized gatekeepers, and the opportunities it provided to transcend normal limits of time, space, and geography. Online religion represented how the fluid and flexible nature of the Internet allowed new forms of religiosity and lived religious practice online. (Campbell 2013, 3–4)

Within this larger space of online religion, the question of tradition, authority, authenticity and efficacy becomes a focal point, which takes on an even deeper investigative lens when we consider the actual influence the digital is making on the religious. This is called digital religion.

In the larger Hindu religious space, websites like onlinepuja.com, shubhpuja.com, mclean.co.in (McLean 2017, specializes in cleaning *pūjā* rooms) are extremely popular. *Pūjās* are also offered through Facebook Live, Messenger and WhatsApp. The popularity of such *pūjās* is not just curtailed to Hindus. For example, in 2017, the widely publicized teen music icon Miley Cyrus performed Lakṣmī *pūjā* over Super Bowl (NDTV 2017). In order for us to get a sense of the scope of *pūjās* on the Internet, let us look at one particular website, shubhpuja.com.

Shubhpuja.com, for example, was founded by Saumyaa Vardhan, a graduate from Imperial College of London. According to Vardhan's background provided on shubhpuja.com under *Our Team*:

> She has previously worked in London for over 7 years as a Mergers & Acquisition executive with KPMG London, EY London and Rolls-Royce UK. Vardhan picked up not just a valuable education and top corporate experience along her journey; but also collected a maze of life experiences whilst retaining her belief in ancient Hindu philosophy. Honing her focus toward this philosophy, Vardhan founded Shubhpuja.com in 2013. (Shubhpuja n.d.)

Among a list of degrees, the website also mentions "Advanced degree in Vedic Astrology, Numerology (Western & Vedic) & Vaastu Shastra / Feng

Shui" (Shubhpuja n.d.). Merely five years since inception, shubhpuja.com in 2018 had become the top acclaimed Vedic spirituality-based online venture and has more than 500 Indian Vedic Brahmins and other professionals as part of their team. Tapping into a 30 billion dollar Indian spiritual market, it has extensive coverage in leading media channels and newspapers. *The New York Times* named subhpuja.com the "Uber for God" (Shubhpuja n.d.).

What is Tantra?

The term Tantra is present in Hinduism, Jainism and Buddhism. Over the long history, the three religions have enriched each other's understanding of the term, yet there are distinct discontinuities in understanding between these religious traditions. There are many variants with regard to Tantra's lexical meaning, and different scholars use different definitions to explain the term. Most agree that Tantra comes from the verbal root *tan*, lit. "to spread", to "stretch" or to "expand". For example, Banerjee (1988, 1) demonstrates that the word Tantra can have the following meanings: "*siddhānta* (conclusion), *śrutiśākhā* (a branch of *śruti*, i.e. Vedas), *itikartavyatā* (set of duties), *prabandha* (composition), and *śāstraviśeṣa* (a particular *śāstra*)". In the scriptural text of the *Ṛgveda*, counted among the four canonical sacred texts, for example, Tantra is used to represent a loom. In short, the term Tantra is complex and possesses a history that is not identical to its contemporary uses and meanings.

Over this fairly complicated historical development, scholars developed the term Tantrism, which was representative of a distinctive category of the Hindu religion. As Douglas Renfrew Brooks explains: "[...] Tantra—and Tantrism, the abstract noun created by scholars to refer to Tantric texts and traditions—is defined most accurately by developing an understanding of oppositional social, political, and religious relations and structures" (Brooks 1990, 6). The French scholar of Tantrism and Hinduism André Padoux reminds us again that the category is largely a construction of Western scholarship and its own questions and interests:

> Tantrism is a protean phenomenon, so complex and elusive that is practically impossible to define it or, at least, to agree on its definition. [...] Tantrism is, to a large extent, a "category of discourse in the West," and not, strictly speaking, an Indian one. As a category, Tantrism is not—or at any rate was not until our days—an entity in the minds of those inside. It is a category in the minds of observers from outside. [...] The term Tantrism was coined by Western Indologists of the latter part of the nineteenth century whose knowledge of India was limited and who could not realize the real nature, let alone the extent, of the Tantric phenomenon. (Padoux 2002, 17)

A majority of scholars concur with Padoux. While there is merit to the interpretive frameworks offered by other scholars in addition to the ones noted earlier – notably David Kinsley (1997), Hillary Peter Rodrigues (2003), David Gordan White (2000), Prem Saran (2008), Hugh B. Urban (2010) and others – that Tantra is partially a product of a continuing legacy of *smārta* politics, colonial influences and integrations, it is not that simple. Tantric traditions are also products of a mutual encounter of Western thought and South Asian intellectual and ritual cultures. As such, Tantra is an extremely complex social and historical phenomenon that continues to evolve, and it seems too simplistic to impugn one side or another for the result.

To give just one minor example for this cross-cultural back-and-forth, taken from my fieldwork: in 2014, while documenting rituals that take place in Hinduism between *Navaratri* (nine nights, ten days festival) and Diwali (Festival of Lights), on Diwali day, a family who was part of the fieldwork offered Ferrero Rocher chocolates as the *prasād* (a material religious substance offering). Chocolates can be found as an offering in some temples, but rarely in family settings. When asked why the host family offered chocolates as the *prasād* and not the traditional Indian sweets, which were easily accessible and available in abundance, the hostess (Chandra 2014) said "My kids hate Indian sweets. I think it is outmoded to offer Indian sweets and then for it to get tossed in the trash". A small incident, for sure, but a great example of the extremely complex social and historical interactions between Europe and South Asia: changing narratives, complex cultural and social fusing and so forth.

Tantric traditions including their ritual practices, unlike those on Diwali, are not entirely public or easily accessible. Many, if not most, Tantric rituals are either hidden or camouflaged from the public space. Tantra is a living tradition, and most Tantric adepts and practitioners continue to vigilantly guard the secrets of the tradition. Many of the practices can only be accessed through the Tantric adepts.

Drawing from the different aspects offered by scholars, the definition of Hindu *Śākta* Tantra as used in this chapter is thus: Tantra is a distinctive alternate ritual and philosophical category within the Hindu religion whose main characteristics might be listed as: (1) mantra-*yantra* (*yantras* are mystical diagrams) or other ritualistic practices of a magical or occult nature; (2) subtle esoteric anatomies or yogic bodies, that is, the presence of the *cakras* (energy centers within the human body often referred to as the *yogic* body or subtle body) and *kuṇḍalinī* (the primordial divine energy that is believed to be present at the base of the human spine, according to Kripal (2011, 496) "It is this mystical energy, 'when aroused,' that activates the various energy centers of the body and so stimulates the psychic powers of the Yogi"); (3) sexual rituals in the form of *maithuna*; and, finally, (4) all the above features may be put into the service of spiritual liberation.

What is *Śakta*?

Historically Śākta and Tantra are closely aligned. Brooks refers to Teun Goudriaan's definition of Śāktism, which is well accepted by most scholars, as it encompasses many elements that constitute the term Śāktism:

> It can be shortly characterized as the worship of Śakti ... i.e., the universal and all-embracing dynamics which manifest itself in human experience as a female divinity. To this should be added that inseparably connected with her is an inactive male partner as whose power of action and movement the Śakti functions .... It is therefore not enough to say that a Śākta worships the female as ultimate principle; nor is it correct categorically to state that Śāktism is characterized by the use of the five ["prohibited substance" known as] makāras .... Although Śāktism is often defined also by means of typical ritual practices, it is advisable to restrict the use of this term for a world view oriented towards Śakti. (Brooks 1990, 47–48)

While Goudriaan's definition is simple and encompasses almost all aspects of Śāktism, it is important to note what Goudriaan makes amply clear – not all Śāktas are Tantrics. Similarly, there is no one understanding of the goddess. Visual representations, texts and attributes such as gentle or fierce, benevolent or malevolent are subject to geography and religious-historical developments in the regions.

What is *pūjā*?

Pūjā is practiced by Hindus and most groups of Jains. It has also traveled beyond India – as a part of Hindus settling in other countries. For example, *pūjā* is found in the Hinduism of Bali, and the Buddhism of Tibet, Japan, Korea and other Asian countries. Texts like the *Āgamas* and the *Purāṇas* are often primary source materials to get instructions on how a devotee should approach the divine, including performing rituals. *Pūjās* are "the core ritual of popular theistic Hinduism" (Fuller 1992, 57).

Ritual study is a well-established interdisciplinary field focusing on the individual, culture, society and the multitude of ways in which rituals intersect with religious symbols and ideologies. One of the pioneer scholars that discussed ritual was Emile Durkheim (1995). According to Durkheim, ritual was a powerful tool that enabled harmony in the society. For Bronislaw Malinowski (1954), rituals were a mechanism for coping with anxiety and uncertainty, especially around activities that entailed danger or fear of the unknown. Victor Turner (1969) further enhanced the theories on ritual by stating that rituals were dynamic and transformative forms of social interactions, enabled through the exchange of religious symbols.

Ritual studies in modern times have taken on far more inclusive approaches. According to Ann Carolyn Klein, rituals operate and affect both body and mind. Klein states that "ritual's operative premise is that physical and imaginative gesture, including the movement of energy in and beyond the body, will reshape our lived experience" (Klein 2016, 69). Hence, ritual practices engage the whole person. "The power of ritual does not lie with facticity. It thrives on keen phenomenological awareness, on a relaxation of the structures of ordinary sensibility. A vital key to ritual power is to remain present to our embodied experience" (Klein 2016, 73). By bringing imagination, body and mind into the conversation on rituals, Klein allows for rituals to be both spontaneous or structured and elaborate or simple. On similar lines, Christopher Helland defines rituals as "purposeful engagement with the sacred (whatever the sacred may be for those involved)" (Helland 2013, 27).

Pūjās fall in the broader category of rituals. They may be an expression of a celebration, mourning, penance, thanksgiving, meditation and so forth. *Pūjās* are performed in both highly ritualized and controlled environments by people called *pūjārīs* or ritual specialists, by individuals at their homes and, currently, we see a growing trend of offering and performing *pūjās* through the Internet. "*Pūjā* has the basic meaning of 'worship' as it is understood in the West, but it is not by any means confined to such a translation: it can also be used in the senses of respect, veneration, honour, adoration, and the like, so that one can honour and respect parents with this same word, *pūjā*" (Fowler 2014, 177–178).

Pūjās in the context of Hinduism is best described by Diana Eck's expression "playing house" with the divine (Eck 1996, 46). In other words, the image of the deity goes through an entire daily cycle. The alarm goes off by using gongs and bells and then the image is bathed with milk, water, honey and so forth. Next, he or she is dressed and adorned with flowers, sandalwood and/or vermillion. This is followed by feeding different meals in sync with the time of the day. And finally, the deity is tucked in for the night occasionally accompanied by lullabies, which are often part of a rich song repertoire called *bhajans*. These actions may be done in the grandest and the most ritualistic of ways, mostly in the temples, in simple ways at private homes and by watching it on the screen, that is, with the assistance of digital media. Gudrun Bühnemann accurately notes that "in spite of its importance the *pūjā* has so far attracted comparatively little attention of scholars, and special studies are few" (Bühnemann 1988, 2).

Stones and mortar: Representation and ritual of the goddess Tripurasundarī in Kāmākhyā

In reference to antiquity, the temple of Kāmākhyā surpasses most of the shrines in India and definitely in eastern India. While it is difficult to date the historical origins, based on numerous sculptures and the oldest stratum, it appears that there must have been an existence of temples in the seventh century, with a larger temple complex from the Pāla dynasty (Bernier 1997, 23). At present, the temple complex epitomizes the retention of many ancient practices.

My data from Kāmākhyā were collected in two phases: first, in 2013, as part of my dissertation fieldwork that focused on *kuṇḍalinī* yoga; second, in 2018, with the goddess Tripurasundarī as the primary focus of the research. In Kāmākhyā, the following questions were asked (though not necessarily in the same order) in each of the interviews: (1) Have you heard of the goddess Tripurasundarī? (2) What are her other names? (3) How does she look or show me a picture of the goddess? (4) What blessings or boons does she shower on her devotees? What are the different types of *pūjās* offered to the goddess here?

A large majority of the devotees as well as the priests referred to the goddess as Ṣoḍaśī (a secondary name for Tripurasundarī). But if and when the name Rājarājeśvarī (another name for Tripurasundarī) appeared in the conversation, then further questions were asked: (1) When do you perform Rājarājeśvarī *pūjā*? (2) Who all are part of this *pūjā*? (3) Have you hosted or sponsored or have you been part of the *pūjā* ritual?

In both classical and folk *Śakta* spaces, we find the presence of Tripurasundarī. She also appears under the names of Ṣoḍaśī, Lalitā, Kāmeśvarī, Śrividyā, Rājarājeśvarī and many more. Tripurasundarī is conceptualized as the supreme deity in text focusing on her, a beautiful and auspicious manifestation of the Great Goddess.

A harmonial blend of the classical and folk *Śakta* is characteristic of the Kāmākhyā temple. The confluence of the two can be best experienced in the temple especially during Ambuvācī Melā, the Deodhānī festival and the long everyday tradition of *kumārī pūjā*. The Ambuvācī Melā is a three-day festival celebrated annually in Kāmākhyā during the monsoon season (mid to end of June). This festival is a "celebration of the yearly menstruation of the goddess Kamakhya" (Borkataky-Varma 2018, 481). Deodhānī is a three-day religious festival that is held sometime in August. Deodhānī is derived from the Sanskrit word *devadhvani*, lit. sound of the deity. "This annual festival pivots around the worship of Manasā, the serpentine goddess. The central feature of this festival is the possession of nine to fifteen people (all men) called the *deodhā*. The finale is held in the *nāṭamandira* portion of the Kāmākhyā temple" (Borkataky-Varma 2017, 12). And finally, *kumārī pūjā* is a ritual where *pūjā* is mostly performed on pre-pubscent girls.

In the temple of Kāmākhyā, Tripurasundarī is popularly known as Ṣoḍaśī and/or Tripurabālā. She is also recognized by the name Rājarājeśvarī, although Rājarājeśvarī mostly comes in a very specific ritual context. The name Lalitā is very rarely heard of. Ṣoḍaśī is the main deity of Kāmākhyā and is understood to be a beautiful young girl of 16. Her four arms hold a noose, goad, bow and arrows.

The central ritual in Kāmākhyā for Ṣoḍaśī is the *kumārī pūjā*. Textual references to the worship of *kumārī devī* is found, for example, in the *Devībhāgavatapurāṇa*. The *Devībhāgavatapurāṇa* also gives different names to girls of different age: 2 year old is Kumārī, 3 year old is Trimūrti, 4 year old Kalyāṇī, 5 year old is Rohiṇi and so forth. Girls above the age of ten are "not allowed in all ceremonies" (Mukherjee 2016, 152). In Kāmākhyā, however, the names are different, and the *kumārī pūjā* can be performed until the age of 16, as long as the girl is pre-pubscent. The names used from one to 16-year-old are: (1) Sandhyā, (2) Sarasvatī, (3) Tridhāmūrtī, (4) Kālīkā, (5) Subhagā, (6) Umā, (7) Mālinī, (8) Kubjikā, (9) Kālasaundarbhā, (10) Aparājitā, (11) Rudrāṇī, (12) Bhairavī, (13) Mahālakṣmī, (14) Pīṭhanāyikā, (15) Kṣetrajñā and (16) Ambikā.

In Kāmākhyā after performing the *pūjā* in the sanctum sanctorum of the temple and completing the *parikramā* lit. circumbulation of sacred places, such as temple, tree, occassionally a guru, the majority of the devotees offer *kumārī pūjā* (ideally to a Brahmin girl between five and ten years old). Questioning during fieldwork revealed perceived benefits of *kumārī pūjā* that corresponded to the *Devībhāgavatapurāṇa*. For example, it is believed that the worship of a two-year-old girl leads to extinction of misery and poverty, of a five-year-old girl provides cure to diseases, of a six-year-old girl destroyes enemies and so forthetc. (Mukherjee 2016, 153).

The *Śakta* Tantra devotees and the *Śakta* Tantra priests perform the Rājarājeśvarī *pūjā* during *Chaitra Navarātri* (March-April). While Ṣoḍaśī in Kāmākhyā is kept in the exoteric, Rājarājeśvarī is understood as in the realm of *Kamakalā-vilāsa* where the meaning of Tripurasundarī is explained within the context of sexual fluids: "red being the female sexual fluid; white, semen, [and] the union of the two" (Kinsley 1997, 121). Also, "offerings of the *pañcamakāra* or the *pañca tattva* ritual is central and essential" (Sarma 2018). In the Rājarājeśvarī *pūjā* ritual, the tantric *sādhaka* views intercourse as a sacred ritual in which or by which one realizes one's cosmic identity. A wide range of textual references and interpretations broadly elucidate the *pañca tattva* as suggested in the *Guptasādhanātantra*.

The way in which *Tripurasundarī* inhabits the exoteric and the esoteric under two different names in Kāmākhyā is a magnificent exemplar of the multilayered world of *Śakta* Tantra. It is the *kumārī pūjā* and Ṣoḍaśī that captures the popular socio-cultural-religious narrative. Most lay devotees are unaware of the Rājarājeśvarī *pūjā*.

A website called kamakhya.com (2002) lets devotees request online prayers. In addition, priests in Kāmākhyā accept prayer requests and/or specific *pūjā* requests via WhatsApp. In such cases, the devotee makes an online payment and the ritual is either recorded and sent via WhatsApp or the devotee personally takes part in the *pūjā* by watching a live feed at the time the *pūjā* is being performed.

Coded goddess: Representation and ritual of the goddess Tripurasundarī online

In this subsection, we will analyze the description of Tripurasundarī in four websites: onlinepuja.org, onlinetemple.com, divine-rudraksha.com and divyayogashop.com. There are several other websites that either mention Tripurasundarī and/or offer online *pūjās* to the goddess. These four websites were selected because they overall contain the most information on the theme of this chapter's discussion.

Onlinepuja.org

Tripurasundarī on onlinepuja.org is described as the third *Mahāvidyā* off the list of ten *Mahāvidyās*. Onlinepuja.org begins the webpage on Tripurasundarī by stating three other main names for the goddess: "Tripura Sundari, also called Shodashi, Lalita and Rajarajeshvari. The goddess Tripura Sundari in her aspect as Shodasi is represented as a sixteen-year-old girl, and is believed to embody sixteen types of desire" (Onlinepuja 2016). The web page further goes on to describe her as someone with a dusky complexion and in an "intimate position with an aspect of Shiva" (Onlinepuja 2016). The intimate position of Śivā and Tripurasundarī is described as "on a bed, a throne, or a pedestal resting on the significant male gods of Hinduism like Brahma, Visnu, Rudra, and Indra" and in bold red letters, the website highlights and comments: "Tripura Sundari is described in great detail as extremely attractive, beautiful and erotically inclined" (Onlinepuja 2016). These descriptions are further elucidated by referring to a text *Lalitāsahasranāma*, which is part of a larger treatise, *Brahmāṇḍapurāṇa*:

> The Lalitha Sahasranama details her charms from head to foot, and the most part of the Saundaryalahari is similarly occupied with her attractive appearance. She is often said to give desire and to suffuse the creation with desire. The Saundaryalahari also states that a worn-out old man, ugly and sluggish in the arts of love, can be restored to sexual attractiveness and vigor by her glance. (Onlinepuja 2016)

As seen earlier, the sexual overtones as an aspect of goddess Tripurasundarī are fairly explicit on this website. But it does not provide any details; for example, no information is provided on the mentioned 16 types of desire. On similar lines, the website mentions that the goddess is in an intimate position with an aspect of Shiva – but which aspect? Silence is also maintained on the roles of the gods Brahmā, Viṣṇu, Rudra and Indra as the supporters of the bed. And finally, by referring to selected verses from the *Lalitāsahasranāma*, the sexual prowess of the goddess is further heightened by stating that the sexuality of an old man can be restored by merely the sight of Tripurasundarī's beauty.

Onlinepuja.org continues to describe Tripurasundarī and the blessings that she bestows on her devotees within the Tantra lineage by also making references to the *Prapañcasāratantra*:

> Her worship has such an amorous effect that celestial females such as gandharvas, yakshis, and siddhas come to the sadhaka (devotee) "with gazelle-like eyes, breathing heavily, their bodies quivering ... and moist with the pearly sweat of passion; and throwing away their ornaments and letting their clothes fall from about them, [they] bow themselves before him and offer to do his will. (Onlinepuja 2016)

And finally, the erotic qualities of the goddess on the website is qualified by a text *Vāmakeśvarīmata*, composed by Adi Shankaracharya, in which he describes her as a "Mother, her nourishing breasts akin to mountain peaks that give birth to rivers. She is described wearing a blue dress with red spots, holding a pot of honey, her eyes quivering with intoxication" (Onlinepuja 2016). Prominence of texts from a sweetened Tantric tradition, like *Vāmakeśvarīmata*, *Lalitāsahasranāma* and *Saundaryalaharī*, is well visible on the website, and that the offered *pūjās* are under the larger umbrella tradition of *Śrīvidyā*. Śrīvidyā is a relatively recent name for a sweetened Tantric tradition centered on the worship of the goddess Tripurasundarī which is especially popular in South India. This tradition has been popularized by the *śaṅkarācāryas*, "the spiritual authority of the broader community of the orthodox Śaiva Brahmans known as Smārtas" (Golovkova 2012, 816).

Moving on to the *pūjās*, the website simply states that the *pūjās* can be performed using either the Tantra techniques or the non-Tantra methods, which, according to them, appear to be the Vedic way. No explanations of what these two entails and how they are different are provided. It is left to the user to interpret, understand the differences and make the choice. The user can simply order the *pūjā* and expect the following potential benefits:

> 1 If you do online puja of goddess Triura Sundari, you may get better spouse.
> 2 If you are having problem of not getting married, then Tripura Sundari online *pūjā* would be extremely helpful for you to get married.
> 3 Tripurabhairavi as Tapas is especially worshipped by those seeking knowledge or by those seeking control of their sexual energy. Tripurabhairavi gives control of the senses, the emotions and wandering thoughts. [...] Whatever obstructions arise to our practice of Tapas we can call on Tripurabhairavi to help eliminate it. (Onlinepuja 2016)

No information is shared on where these *pūjās* will be performed, the qualifications of the people performing the *pūjā* and what specifically the *pūjā* will entail. Ambiguity is maintained, for example, on the definition of a *better spouse*. The only information available to the individual ordering the *pūjā* is a phone number and a P.O. Box address.

Far more enthralling is the introduction of Tripura-bhairavī. Tripura-bhairavī appears particularly in an approximately sixth-century CE text, *Devīmāhātmya*. In this text, the goddess Durgā is the primary figure, and the ten Mahāvidyās appear when there is a battle between Durgā and two demons, Śumbha and Niśumbha. Within this meta narrative, the Mahāvidyās are primarily responsible for protecting the cosmic order. In the course of this great and fierce battle, the goddess Durgā produces several goddesses, off which a group of seven goddesses are known as Mātṛkās. The Mātṛkās are fierce and wild. Tripura-bhairavī is an epithet given to the Mātṛkās (Brahmāṇī, Maheśvarī, Kaumarī, Vaiṣṇavī, Vārāhī, Cāmuṇḍā and Indrānī) (*Śāktapramoda* 1992, 268). Hence, it is rather surprising that the fierce and wild aspect of the goddess is referred to in the larger spectrum of sexual energy and emotions.

Onlinetemple.com

Onlinetemple.com provides the user with access to 150 temples. Number 112 on the list is a Tripurasundarī temple, popularly known as the Mātābārī Temple in Udaipur, Tripura. The webpage on this temple establishes its authority by referring to the popular mythological story of Śivā, his dead wife and the creation of the goddess pilgrimage centers the *Śakti Pīṭha*. The principal deity of the temple is Tripurasundarī, popularly known as Tripureśwarī and also Ṣoḍaśī, believed to be a "divine manifestation of Goddess Parvati, Lord Shiva's consort, the deity symbolizes a potent feminine power. The temple is the holy abode of two identical idols of the same deity. Apart from Tripurasundari, there is Chhotima" (Onlinetemple 2017).

In the context of *pūjās*, the website states that "worshipping the goddess are strictly the responsibilities of the red-robed priests, popular as the ministers to the goddess. Moreover, the worship procedure at the Tripura Sundari mandir is a unique amalgamation of the Mantra, Tantra and Yantra forms of worship" (Onlinetemple 2017). The website further states that by visiting the temple, the devotees will "experience a complete revelation of a tantrik sadhana" (Onlinetemple 2017). No information is provided on what and how the Tantra *sādhanā* is performed. *Sādhanā* lit. is a means of accomplishing something. But it is largely used for a dedicated spiritual exercise undertaken for several years in order to accomplish a set of ritual objective/s. Similarly, there are no explanations provided on what *pūjās* are performed, and what the unique amalgamation of the Mantra, Tantra and Yantra forms of worship stands for. A link to matabaritemple.in then takes the devotee to the temple's website. On this website, the user can place an offering for online bhog (*bhog* is another term for *prasād*).

There is a separate link for *Anna Bhog*, which is priced at INR 40 (about 60 US cents). The name *Anna Bhog* suggests an offering of grains. But ambiguity is maintained in the *online bhog* link, and the fact that what is meant is animal sacrifice is only revealed when actually opening the link. As the *online bhog* web page on the Mātābārī Temple website (Matabari Temple 2016) states, animal sacrifice is central to the *pūjā* offerings: "Religious practices of the tribals of the region largely influence the rituals of the temple". Animal sacrifice is a noted feature here, with separate rate charts for goats and buffaloes available online: He-goat: INR. 10 (about 14 US cents), pigeon: INR. 10 (about 14 US cents), duck: INR. 10 (about 14 US cents) and buffalo: INR 30 (about 50 US cents). It is now clear that ordering online *bhog* here includes the option to order *bhog* from an animal sacrifice (*balī*). It appears that authority and authenticity of the website and/or the temple simply requires the stamp of Śakta Tantra, but information on non-vegetarian elements of the online *pūjās* is kept vague, on purpose, so as not to reveal the temple too openly as a place where animal sacrifice takes place.

In conclusion, while onlinetemple.com associates and markets the Tripurasundarī temple as a *Śakti Pīṭha* where Tantra *sādhanā* is performed and animals' sacrifices are offered to the goddess, no further details are provided to the devotee. A deep level of ambiguity is kept on the website.

Divine-rudraksha.com

Divine-rudraksha.com describes the goddess Tripurasundarī similar to onlinepuja.org. But before we focus on the goddess, there are two questions answered on the website that are worth looking into, since they directly speak to the question of authority and effectiveness: (1) What are online *pūjās*? (2) Can the online *pūjās* be deemed effective without the presence of the person who has ordered the *pūjā*?

Answering the first question, the website begins by stating the importance of how a group of trained priests (brahmins) are necessary for the efficacy of the *pūjā*, since they have the necessary acumen to follow the guidelines. This is followed by the relevance of the venue, because not all *pūjās* can be performed at home. Once these two requirements are addressed, the challenge of mobility is addressed:

> NRI people performing a Puja in a proper way either becomes impossible or otherwise exorbitantly expensive. It is due to these situations that a concept of Online Pujas has been invented wherein a client residing abroad can book a Puja through our Online Puja service providers. Once the puja is booked, the client can get the Puja performed on their behalf that too in a perfect way and at affordable cost. Any Puja that is ordered Online is performed by a team of Brahmins (usually at least 3–5 Brahmins). Out of them, one of the Brahmins takes a "Sankalp"

> in client's name who has booked the Puja and then he performs all the recitals and rituals that were supposed to have been done by the person if he was himself physically present in the Puja. This means that the Brahmin who has taken the sankalp virtually represents the client who has booked the puja during the entire puja procedure. (Divine Rudraksha 2016)

Target marketing toward the Hindu diaspora is particularly interesting. This may be indicative of the customer base, which may be taken up as a separate research project. In reference to the effectiveness of the online *pūjās*, the website states: "We are pleased to declare that the online *Pūjās* have already benefited a large number of people which is confirmed by the very fact that the same people have given repeated bookings for other *Pūjā* after their initial order [...] beneficial and effective is further ascertained by large number of feedbacks and testimonials sent by our grateful and esteemed clients" (Divine Rudraksha 2016).

Returning to the goddess, the web page (Divine Rudraksha 2016) opens with the different names for Tripurasundarī and depicts her as a 16-year-old extremely beautiful goddess who has the powers of "arousing the senses, possessing 16 type of desires, enhancing the intellectual and emotional aspects in the three worlds of Aakash, Paatal and Dharti. The name Shodashi is associated to her since she is sixteen years old and remains the same as well as she also possesses Sixteen Supernatural Powers". Yet again, no information is shared on the 16 types of desires. In reference to its online *pūjā* offerings, this website is far more descriptive:

- This *pūjā* bestows Beauty, Good Fortune, Wealth and all the worldly pleasures
- An all-round Financial Prosperity and Stability
- An increased Business as well as Name & Fame
- This *pūjā* is highly beneficial in instances of Delay in Marriage
- For getting a right Life Partner
- A Blissful Marital Life
- The adverse results of planet Mercury are nullified by this *pūjā* as per Ancient Vedic Texts
- Infertility (problem in conceiving child) and for good sexual life
- Disharmony between couple and Divorce (Divine Rudraksha 2016)

The list of these nine benefits can be clubbed into three broad categories: (1) wealth and prosperity, (2) getting married and (3) blissful married life including solutions for infertility and divorce. It almost appears that the representation of the goddess Tripurasundarī here is that of an *all-inclusive one-stop shop*. The web page then moves on to establishing authenticity of the priests that are part of their team who will perform the *pūjā* on behalf of the online devotee, by stating the following:

> We are very religious minded people and are deeply bothered regarding the problems of our clients who place their precious trust on us for performing the pujas on their behalf so that they can get a desired result as per their expectations. These Pujas are performed by our learned and well experienced Brahmins/Pundits who have expertise in this line since they have been practicing it since a span of at least last two generations. All the pujas are performed exactly according to the guidelines prescribed by our ancient sages and our Vedic literature so that our clients can derive the maximum benefit of them. (Divine Rudraksha 2016)

There are no profiles shared on these self-claimed "learned and well experienced" priests. Therefore, the user has no information on the lineage and the methods used by the priests who perform the *pūjā*. However, unlike the matabaritemple.in webpage, divine-rudraksha.com publishes the mantra to be chanted and thus does provide certain details of the *pūjā* procedures for the benefit of the end user. A VCD and the *prasād*, which also includes a *yantra*, are sent by mail to people who order a *pūjā* online. There are over 100 published testimonials from across the globe that further substantiate the authenticity and effectiveness of divine-rudraksha.com.

Divyayogashop.com

This website gives the same narrative of Tripurasundarī as being part of the ten Mahāvidyās and lists similar benefits as those in divine-rudraksha.com and onlinepuja.org. But, divyayogashop.com introduces a new element into the conceivable blessings that are bestowed by the goddess Tripurasundarī, magic. According to this website, one of the most important benefits of performing the *pūjā* is to acquire "success in varied types of shatkarma [ṣaṭkarman]" (divyayogashop 2018).

Gourdiaan's understanding of the six acts called *ṣaṭkarman* maps well to the topography of indigenous understanding of magic in Kāmākhyā. Textual evidence agrees that most rites that call upon magic are performed for one or a combination of the following results: *Ākarṣaṇa* "attraction", *vaśikaraṇa* "subjugation", *stambhana* "immobilization", *uccāṭana* "eradication", *maraṇa* "liquidation" and/or *vidveṣa* (*ṇa*) "creating dissention" (e.g., Gourdiaan 1992). Divyayogashop.com in particular lists *vaśikaraṇa*, *stambhana*, *uccāṭana* and adds "many others" (divyayogashop 2018), indicating that the list is long.

Introduction of magic by divyayogashop.com brings us right back to the classic and folk elements of Tantra as well as to the split between the esoteric and the exoteric. In Kāmākhyā and in the larger realm of *pūjās* dedicated to her, Tripurasundarī is invoked in the space of magic, for example, for breaking black magic spells, attracting a desired partner, divination, snake bites, overcoming the grip of *bhūtas* (supernatural creature, ghost, spirit of a deceased person), *piśācas* (flesh-eating demons in Hindu theology) and so forth. The aspect of magic and goddess worship, in Kāmākhyā, is best highlighted during the annual Deōdhanī festival. Possession, magic, oracles and blood are the highpoints of this festival. The sacrificial agent may be a buffalo, goat, pigeon and so forth (Borkataky-Varma 2017).

While the website claims to operate in the space of both casting a spell and breaking of a spell, of course subject to the desires of the devotee paying for the service, it absolutely does not share any information of how will it be done. What rituals will be followed? What kind of liabilities are associated with partaking in such rituals, which often are perceived to may have a very dangerous outcome, including sometimes fatality? We are yet again left with the finding that these websites are very selective with regards to sharing of information, especially around rituals.

Conclusion

There have been numerous studies on the Internet and religious traditions, especially in the past three decades. In the 1990s and 2000s, scholarship on religion and the Internet focused on the basic questions, for example, "How is religion represented in new media environments? How do religious groups use new media to serve their causes and needs? What challenges do new media technologies pose to traditional religious communities and institutions?" (Lövheim and Campbell 2017, 6). This phase of research was followed by more nuanced questions on particular topics, for example, questions on identity were explored by Turkle (1995), Chandler (1998), Cowan (2005), Bayam (2006) and so forth. Similarly, the topic of virtual community has been studied, notably by Rheingold (2000), Helland (2007) and Hutchings (2013). Finally, Campbell (2005), Scheifinger (2010), Cheong (2013) and Wellman (2011) have deliberated on the topic of authority.

Turning to studies on Hinduism and the Internet, the scholarship addresses a wide range of topics, a large majority of which have started to appear mostly in the last decade or so. For example, Bachrach (2014), Lal (2014), Warrier (2012), Mohan (2015), Udupa (2015) and Zeiler (2018) are some of the frequently quoted authors.

Let us now circle back to the meta question asked at the beginning of the chapter: Does the Internet perpetuate a normative understanding of Hindu *Śakta* Tantra? Also, we return to the three sub-questions: (1) How does online *pūjā* establish authority of the *devī* (goddess) as well as the *pūjārīs*? (2) What is the perceived authenticity of online *pūjās*? (3) What is the perceived efficacy of online *pūjās*?

In reference to Tripurasundarī, the websites frequently refer to her in the context of the *Mahāvidyās*. The authority of the *devī* entirely rests on her being one of the ten *Mahāvidyās* who are frequently linked to terms like Tantra, Tantra *sādhanā* and, *Śakta pīṭha*. In other words, by contextualizing

Tripurasundarī in the larger space of Hindu *Śakta* Tantra, the websites authorize her with immense perceived power, for example, to impact financial prosperity, matrimony, having offspring and also bestow the ability to cast spells or break an incantation. However, no detailed information is shared on the *Mahāvidyās* and the *Mātṛkās*.

The same assumed authority is woven into establishing the authority of the ritual specialists. Either specific qualifications are listed, as seen in the case of Saumyaa Vardhan, or the website simply states that the *pūjā*s are performed by experienced Brahmins/*pundits*. Reference to the caste of the *pūjārīs* and stating that their expertise comes from a long lineage of *pūjārīs* are expected to resonate with the person ordering the online *pūjā*. It is almost like a rubber stamp, embossed to create a sense of authority.

The question of authenticity and efficacy in the context of online *pūjā* can be answered together. Authenticity and efficacy, on the websites studied here, build on the assumed authority of the *devī* (goddess) and *pūjārīs*. Often the online space of rituals, in our case more specifically *pūjās*, are "doubted as being a mere simulation or a reproduction of something 'real,' rather than being authentic as such" (RaddeAntweiler 2013, 88). Questions are raised as to whether they are serious or flawed simulations, authentic or forged, fantasy or reality, and if they have the same level of efficacy as non-online rituals.

Heinz Scheifinger succinctly investigates online *pūjā*: "[T]hreats to the sacrality of the online *pūjā* environment can be overcome, that the ability to partake in the core practice of *darśan* remains in online worship [...] Hindu *pūjā* rituals that are performed online are not fundamentally different from traditional forms of the ritual and hence possess efficacy" (Scheifinger 2013, 126). Customer testimonials are a great resource to find the answer to these two questions. The following are just a few sample testimonials from our analysis:

> Hello, first of all I am extremely thankful to you for performing the Lawsuit Winning Puja on very short notice. The judge will give his judgement next month but by this hearing, I am very much confident that the case will be in my favour. I am so confident that this puja will definitely going to help me. You have supported me and given your valuable guidance for which I am highly thankful to you... Harry, New Zealand. (Divine Rudraksha 2016)
>
> The Sindhurmani Puja that was recommended last July upon thorough scrutiny of my Chart was truly potent in addressing the problems that were present at the time. Babita L. Garg. (Shubhpuja n.d.)
>
> Hello Neeta Ma, I wanted to say Thank you a million times for the great service that you provided me. I am really very happy for all the things I received and day by day I see the changes in me. I have lots of faith in you and have no words to explain. Bhargavi Patel, USA. (Rudra Centre 1997)

The online *pūjā* websites are filled with positive testimonials, which bolster Scheifinger's theory that fundamentally from the lens of the devotee, online *pūjā* is believed to be effective and not too different from being physically present in a temple setting. Authenticity is further woven into these websites by frequent mentions to Sanskrit texts: *Lalitāsahsranāma*, *Prapañcasāratantra*, *Vāmakeśvarīmata*, *Saundaryalaharī* and so forth. Accolades by external bodies in addition to the devotees are also very helpful, as seen in the rapid rise of subhpuja.com. Summing up, efficacy is supposedly established via testimonials and accolades. Authority and authenticity are presumably proven by making references to the larger world of Hindu Śakta Tantra.

With regards to Hindu *Śakta* Tantra, the Kāmākhyā temple and online *pūjās*, a veil exists at the social, cultural and subconscious levels. As seen in the case of Kāmākhyā, while Ṣoḍaśī and Rājarājeśvarī are two names for the same goddess Tripurasundarī, Ṣoḍaśī and the *kumārī pūjā* are in the public view while Rājarājeśvarī *pūjā* is done in a closely guarded private space. Further, while Kāmākhyā is well known as a *Śakta* Tantra temple, devotees (although accustomed to the term Tantra) do not necessarily have deeper knowledge of the term, the historical developments and present-day implications and connotations of the Tantric *pūjā* rituals. In general, Tantra generates a sense of fear, often associated negatively with magic and spells. This more often than not translates into ensuring that the *pūjā* is done according to the directions given by the priests, who are seen as the religious authority. Devotees want neither the priest nor the goddess to be upset.

With regards to the online *pūjās* and the world of Tantra, the Internet operates as an effective New Age veil. As seen here, websites use the term Tantra and make references to Sanskrit texts and rituals. But again, there is no specificity provided. The world of esoteric Tantra is further hidden behind the web of algorithms and codes. It is the exoteric, cleansed Tantra that remains in the public eye.

References

Bachrach, E., 2014. Is Guruji Online? Internet Advice Forums and Transantional Encounters in a Vaishnav Sectarian Community. In: Sahoo, A. K. and de Kruijf, J. G. eds. *Indian Transnationalism Online: New Perspectives on the Diaspora*. New York: Routledge, 163–175.

Banerjee, S. C., 1988. *A brief History of Tantra Literature*. Calcutta: Naya Prokash.

Bayam, N. K., 2006. Interpersonal Life Online. In: Lievrouw, L. and Livingstone, S. eds. *The Handbook of New Media*. London: Sage, 35–54.

Brooks, D. R., 1990. *The Secret of the Three Cities: An Introduction to Hindu Śākta Tantrism*. Chicago: University of Chicago Press.

Brooks, D. R., 1992. *Auspicious Wisdom: The Texts and Traditions of Śrīvidyā Śākta Tantrism in South India*. Albany: SUNY.

Bernier, R., 1997. *Himalayan Architecture*. Madison: Farleigh Dickinson University Press.

Borkataky-Varma, S., 2017. The Dead Speak: A Case Study from the Tiwa Tribe Highlighting the Hybrid World of Śakta Tantra in Assam. *Religions* 8(10), 221.

Borkataky-Varma, S., 2018. Menstruation: Pollutant to Potent. In: Jain, P., Sherma, R. D. and Khanna, M., eds. *Hinduism and Tribal Religions Encyclopedia of Indian Religions*. Dordrecht: Springer. doi:10.1007/978-94-024-1036-5_481-1.

Bühnemann, G., 1988. *Pūjā: A Study in Smārta Ritual*. Publications of the Be Nobili Research Library, Institute for Indology University of Vienna, 2–155.

Campbell, H., 2005. *Exploring Religious community Online: We Are One in the Network*. New York: Peter Lang.

Campbell, H., 2013. Ritual. In: Campbell, H. A., ed. *Digital Religion: Understanding Religious Practice in New Media Worlds*. New York: Routledge, 57–71.

Chandler, D., 1998. *Personal Home Pages and the Construction of Identities on the Web*. Available at http://visual-memory.co.uk/daniel/Documents/short/webident.html, accessed 28 April 2019.

Chandra, N., 2014. *Interview on Diwali*. Interviewed by Sravana Borkataky-Varma. 24 October 2014, 20, 30.

Cheong, P. H., 2013. Authority. In: Campbell H. A., ed. *Digital Religion: Understanding Religious Practice in New Media Worlds*. New York: Routledge, 24–40.

Cowan, D. E., 2005. *Cyberhenge: Modern Pagans of the Internet*. New York: Routledge.

Divine Rudraksha, 2016. *Tripura Sundari Yantra, Maa Tripura Sundri Yantra for Beauty & Marriage*. Available at www.divine-rudraksha.com/products/tripura-sundari-yantra#desc-bookmark, accessed 2 February 2019.

divyayogashop, 2018. *Divyayogashop Spiritual and Tantra Products*. Available at www.divyayogashop.com/, accessed 2 February 2019.

Durkheim, E., 1995. *The Elementary Forms of Religious Life*. New York: The Free Press.

Eck, D. L., 1996. *Darśan: Seeing the Divine Image in India*, 2nd ed. New York: Columbia University Press.

Fowler, J., 2014. *Hinduism Beliefs and Practices: Major Deities and Social Structures Volume I*. Chicago: Sussex Academic Press.

Fuller, C., 1992. *The Camphor Flame*. Princeton: Princeton University Press.

Golovkova, A., 2012. Śrividyā. In: Jacobsen, K. A., Basu, H. and Malinar, A., eds. *Brill's Encyclopedia of Hinduism*, Vol. 4. Leiden [etc.]: Brill, 815–822.

Goudriaan, T., ed., 1992. *Ritual and Speculation in Early Tantrism*. New York: State University of New York.

Hay, S., ed., 1988. *Sources of Indian Tradition. Vol. 2*. New York: Columbia University Press.

Helland, C., 2007. Diaspora on the Electronic Frontier: Developing Virtual Connections with Sacred Homelands. *Journal of Computer-Mediated Communication* 12(3), 956–976.

Helland, C., 2013. Ritual. In: Campbell, H. A., ed. *Digital Religion: Understanding Religious Practice in New Media Worlds*. New York: Routledge, 24–40.

Hutchings, T., 2013. Considering Religious Community through Online Churches. In: Campbell, H. A., ed. *Digital Religion: Understanding Religious Practice in New Media Worlds*. New York: Routledge, 164–172.

kamakhya.com, 2002. *www.kamakhya.com: ॐ Maa Kamakhya Devi*. Available at http://kamakhya.com/, accessed 2 February 2019, p. 194.

Kinsley, D., 1997. *Tantric Visions of the Divine Feminine.* Berkley: University of California Press.
Klein, A. C., 2016. Revisiting Ritual. *Tricycle,* [online] Fall. Available at https://tricycle.org/magazine/revisiting-ritual/, accessed 10 May 2019.
Kripal, J. J., 2011. The Evolving Siddhis: Yoga and Tantra in the Psychical Research Tradition and Beyond. In: Jacobsen, K. A., ed. *Yoga Powers: Extraordinary Capacities Attained through Meditation and Concentration.* Leiden: Brill, 478–508.
Lal, V., 2014. Cyberspace, the Globalisation of Hinduism, and the Protocols of Citizenship in the Digital Age. In: Sahoo, A. K., de Kruijf, J. G., eds. *Indian Transnationalism Online: New Perspectives on the Diaspora.* New York: Routledge, 121–145.
Lövheim, M. and Campbell, H. A., 2017. Considering Critical Methods and Theoretical Lenses in Digital Religion Studies. *New Media & Society* 19(1), 5–14.
Malinowski, B., 1954. *Magic, Science and Religion and Other Essays.* New York: Doubleday.
Matabari Temple, 2016. *Mata Tripurasundari Temple.* Available at http://matabaritemple.in/, accessed 2 January 2019.
McLean, 2017. Pooja Room Cleaning Archives-McLean Max. Available at https://mclean.co.in/homeservices/keywords/pooja-room-cleaning/, accessed 21 October 2018.
Mohan, S., 2015. Locating the "Internet Hindu": Political Speech and Performance in Indian Cyberspace. *Television & New Media* 16(4), 339–345.
Mukherjee, C. B., 2016. *Kūmarī Pūjā: A Religious Custom.* Kolkata: Jadavpur University, 151–156.
NDTV, 2017. Miley Cyrus Chooses Lakshmi Puja Over Super Bowl. *NDTV.Com,* [online] 6 February. Available at www.ndtv.com/offbeat/miley-cyrus-chooses-lakshmi-puja-over-super-bowl-1656521, accessed April 29, 2019.
Onlinepuja, 2016. *We Offer Online Puja of Mahavidya Devi Tripura Sundari or Sodashi.* Available at www.onlinepuja.org/p/devi_tripurasundari.php, accessed 28 November 2018.
Onlinetemple, 2017. *Tripura Sundari Temple.* Available at www.onlinetemple.com/pages/tripura-sundari-temple, accessed 27 October 2018.
Padoux, A., 2002. What Do We Mean By Tantrism? In: Harper, K. A. and Brown, R. L., eds. *The Roots of Tantra.* Albany: State University of New York Press.
Radde-Antweiler, K., 2013. Authenticity. In: Campbell, H. A., ed. *Digital Religion: Understanding Religious Practice in New Media Worlds.* New York: Routledge, 88–104.
Rheingold, H., 2000. *The Virtual Community.* Cambridge: The MIT Press.
Rodrigues, H. P., 2003. *Rituals Worship of the Great Goddess: The Liturgy of the Durgā Pūjā with Interpretations.* Albany: SUNY.
Rudra Centre, 1997. *Rudraksha, Buy Rudraksha, Yantra, Gemstones, Puja. Rudraksha Ratna.* Available at www.rudraksha-ratna.com/testimonials, accessed 2 April 2019.
Śaktapramoda, 1992. Bombay: Khemrāja Śrikṛṣṇadāsa Prakāśān.
Saran, P., 2008. *Yoga, Bhoga and Ardanariswara: Individuality, Wellbeing and Gender in Tantra.* Delhi: Routledge.
Sarma, 2018. *Interview on Kuṇḍalinī Yoga.* Interviewed by Sravana Borkataky-Varma, 25 November 2018, 20, 30.

Scheifinger, H., 2010. Internet Threats to Hindu Authority: Puja Ordering Websites and the Kalighat Temple. *Asian Journal of Social Science* 38(4), 636–656.

Scheifinger, H., 2013. Ritual. In: Campbell, H. A., ed. *Digital Religion: Understanding Religious Practice in New Media Worlds.* New York: Routledge, 121–127.

Shubhpuja, n.d. *Our Team-shubhpuja.com.* Available at http://shubhpuja.com/our-team/, accessed 2 December 2018.

Turkle, S., 1995. *Life on the Screen: Identity in the Age of the Internet.* New York: Touchstone.

Turner, V., 1969. *Structure and Anti-Structure.* London: Routledge.

Udupa, S., 2015. Internet Hindus: New India's Ideological Warriors. In: Van der Veer, P., ed. *Handbook of Religion and the Asian City: Aspirtaion and Urbanization in the Twenty-first Century.* Berkley: University of California Press, 432–450.

Urban, H. B., 2010. *The Power of Tantra: Religion, Sexuality and the Politics of South Asian Studies.* New York: I. B. Tauris.

Warrier, M., 2014. Online Bhakti in a Modern Guru Organisation. In: Singleton, M. and Goldberg, E., eds. *Gurus of Modern Yoga.* New York: OUP, 308–321.

Wellman, B., 2011. Studying the Internet through the Ages. In: Consalvo, M. and Ess, C., eds. *The Blackwell Handbook of Internet Studies.* Oxford: Blackwell, 17–23.

White, D. G., 2000. *Tantra in Practice.* New Jersey: Princeton University Press.

Zeiler, X., 2018. Durgā Pūjā Committees. Community Origin and Transformed Mediatized Practices Employing Social Media. In: Simmons, C., Sen, M. and Rodrigues, H., eds. *Nine Nights of the Goddess: The Navaratri Festival in South Asia.* Albany: SUNY, 121–138.

11 New media and spiritualism in India

Understanding online spiritualism in convergence cultures

Jesna Jayachandran

Introduction

The interrelation of religion and media has visibly transformed contemporary life in India. Media proliferation, heightened religiosity and consumerism since liberalization have brought spiritualism into the public domain, entrenching diverse spiritual and religious cultures into India's media networks, business, governance and consumer modernity (Gooptu 2013; Lewis 2016; Nanda 2009; Rajagopal 2001). Noting the prolific popularity of spiritualism in India, these scholars observe that unlike institutional religion with ritually bound practices, recent spiritualism is mass-oriented, with flexible affiliations to the broad institutional structures of Hinduism. This recent spiritualism is corporatized by organizations and religious leaders and permeates notions of nationalism, consumption, identity, politics and welfare. Gooptu (2013, 74) argues that this "new spiritualism" is distinct from traditional religion, although it emerges from and relies upon extant religious traditions, spiritualism emphasizes introspective, self-enterprising expressions that are non-dogmatic, personalized geared to, psychological well-being, health, personal agency and self-making.

Both media and religion are entangled in articulating the politics of spiritualism. Recent works have drawn attention to the global cultural scale, politicization and mediatization of Hindu identities, practices and traditions with the expansion of new media technologies (Mallapragada 2010; Scheifinger 2012; Zeiler 2014). These and other scholarly works are part of broader attempts to understand new realities of digital religion, that is, the interconnection between digital technology (interactivity, convergence and networking) and religion on one hand and, the integration of offline and online religious practices and the recasting of religious experiences and meanings on the other (Campbell 2013, 3–4; Grieve 2013; Helland 2016; Hoover 2013; Hoover and Echchaibi 2014; Lundby 2013). Extending this notion to spiritualism offers an opportunity to understand the online dimensions of emerging spiritualties which often look beyond traditional religions, and of individuals to prioritize *the self* in unique ways, combining notions of *quest* with *various religious elements and media resources* to create meaningful practices and experiences (Hoover 2008, 6). New media, in particular, facilitate individualized expressions of faith, religious belief and experimentation – aspects which are key elements of recent spiritualism. As Lundby (2013, 233) notes: "much contemporary expression of spirituality and religiosity" takes place through the "religious uses of new media that are outside the tight control of religious organizations".

In my study here, I explore online spiritualism with a focus on www.speakingtree.in,[1] a digital venture of India's most circulated English newspaper, *The Times of India*. In this chapter, I use spiritualism to refer to multiple forms of beliefs and practices related to the spiritual and religious which are shaped through creatively prioritizing the inner-self, individuality and choice that evolve through introspective constructions and blending of self-hood modalities in relation to the market, media, faith and religion. In simple terms, online spiritualism refers to the interconnection of spiritualism and new media. Www.speakingtree.in claims to be the number one spiritual networking site in India (Times Internet Limited 2010). This newspaper-connected platform is an example that displays convergence and prosumer culture where digital technology facilitates different forms of participatory cultures (see Jenkins 2006). With hundred thousands of (ever expanding) users, virtually interconnected to each other, and over a hundred strong social networks of the so-called spiritual masters, it is a 24/7 spiritual site available for spiritual consumption, sharing, creation and reflection.

This chapter examines complex interactions, online participatory practices and meaning-making to understand articulations of online spiritualism, that is, how digital technology and spaces facilitate the convergence of spirituality and new media. It traces how people relate to, construct, practice and experience online spiritualism.

The first section reviews three interrelated dimensions: transformations of Indian media markets, spiritual/religious publics and contemporary spiritualism. The second section elaborates the methodology and contextualizes www.speakingtree.in and its broad premises. The third section analyzes this digital environment from two perspectives.

I rely upon Hoover and Echchaibi's (2014, 8) theory of "third spaces of digital religion", a fluid, conceptual and imagined understanding of "third places" or spaces of constructive action that emerge as people engage with religion and spirituality in digital spaces. They emphasize the significance of reflexive engagements and subjectivities in reimagining religious practice, especially "when individuals use technical capacities of the digital to imagine social and cultural configurations beyond binaries of the physical versus the virtual and the real versus the proximal religious experience" (Hoover and Echchaibi 2014, 18). I also examine how key elements of spiritualism such as *quest* (inner search) and *choice* create meanings and practices, often in relation to Hinduism. The fourth section demonstrates that commodified production for the market and online structures shape the way people create, practice, engage and experience online spiritualism. In the process, people's articulation of bottom-up notions of spiritualism support spiritual-consumerist cultures and media organizations as well. In conclusion I argue that www.speakingtree.in's users may actively pursue *individualized*, personal experiences of spiritualism, but it is often in relation to *traditional* religious elements and the participatory aspects of digital cultures which shapes these experiences within the online imagined community.

Newspapers, digitalization and spiritualism

A brief look at India's print industry is important to understand such participatory initiatives by newspapers. India's newspaper industry is the world's largest newspaper circulation market and is growing, unlike its Western counterparts (KPMG-FICCI Media and Entertainment Report 2017, 2). Yet, while the core business of traditional print propels growth, much of it is by regional language papers that cater to 90% of India's readership. English language papers, with readerships largely concentrated in urban centers, face immense pressures as readers increasingly move online (KPMG-FICCI Media and Entertainment Report 2017, 103). The Internet and Mobile Association of India (IAMAI) and the market research firm IMRB estimated that there were 432 million Internet users in India in December 2016, with 269 million urban users (that means a 60% Internet penetration in urban areas, given the estimated population of 444 million urban Indians) and 163 million rural area users (Anon., 2017a). English newspapers have to cater to this evolving readership and face immense competition from electronic and digital media.

Certainly digital analytics and traditional grassroots market research in urban cities influence media organizational strategies that combine religion, secular-spiritualism and neo-lifestyle/consumerism in their competition to meet changing class aspirations and demands. The Indian census (2001), for instance, reports that Hindus formed the largest religious community, followed by Muslims, Christians and other minorities. A slew of surveys by news organizations observe the centrality of religion and its implication for media markets. For example, the *hindustantimes*-MaRS Youth Survey 2014 found that a relationship with God was important for the youth, the majority praying regularly and practicing power yoga for spiritual and physical well-being (Banerjee 2015). Other surveys document the popularity of religious TV shows, singing religious songs (*bhajans/satsangs*) and visiting religious place of worship frequently (CSDS-KAS Report 2017). Reports about how urban middle classes (who drive consumer growth) look beyond quantitative indicators to qualitative values, like "secular-rational", "self-expression, individuality" and "traditional values" based upon Hindu faith and lifestyle habits as influencing consumption behaviors (Isozaki, Sasaki, and Pandit 2017, 1). These reports show that while secular-spiritual lifestyle cultures are rising, people also affirm to traditional religions. Therefore, newspapers too have expanded spiritual contents, secular-religious branding, advertisement markets and readerships. *The Indian Express Digital*, for instance, recently launched www.lifealth.com, a health and lifestyle portal on spiritual, physical and mental well-being.

The background to such accelerated transmission of spirituality can be located in post-1990s globalization, media expansion and subsequent visibility of Hindu identity. Much before liberalization, state television Doordarshan's broadcast of the television series of Hindu epics, the *Mahabharata* and *Ramayana*, infused politics and nationalism with Hindu high culture (Rajagopal 2001). Post 1990s, the rapid rise of privately owned devotional channels expanded tele-visual popular cultures with Hindu religious sensibilities, boosting religious commoditization and consumerism, making Hinduism more visible in public spheres. Visual constructions of the nation added layers to cultural symbolism and circulation of identities, crafting religious nationalism and publics (Rajagopal 2001) as enterprise cultures furthered a growing entanglement of business, spiritualities and self-making (Gooptu 2013, 75–76). Projections of India's spiritual antiquity with global aspirations and enterprise cultures further supported a growing entanglement of business, human resource management, spiritualities and "enterprising" selfhood (Gooptu 2013, 75–76). Nanda (2009, 3) argues that this resurgence of contemporary Hindu religiosity and its commercialization can be attributed to the "state-temple-corporate complex" of a "god market". These studies thus indicate the steady mediatization of religion and spirituality through recreations of religious and nationalist symbolism, consumerism, enterprise cultures and the crafting of self-hood and identities (Gooptu 2013; Nanda 2009; Rajagopal 2001).

Spiritualism, as term and concept, has been varyingly defined *in relation to* religion in academic research. Most understandings of spiritualism emphasize *the prioritization of self*, *choice* and *personalization of religious beliefs* such as connecting to a supreme power based on one's mind, actions and experience. There are perceptible common elements like the focus on the self, exercising choice and the use of different wellness techniques (reiki, yoga, meditation). Hybrid philosophies, plural practices and their commodification have meant that understandings vary widely (Einstein 2008). In the 1980s, spiritualism in North Atlantic contexts began to be increasingly described in academia as New Age Spiritualism to refer to very heterogeneous approaches that blended pre-Christian and Eastern religious philosophies, types of holistic healing and positive-thinking techniques, mind-body-spirit healing practices like yoga, divination, alternative / natural living and varied holistic and humanism philosophies (Sutcliffe and Gilhus 2013, 2–3). The concept has also evolved with changing notions of self-empowerment, inner-subjectivities and personal spiritual quest in New Age Spiritualism and how they related to capitalism, enterprising consumptive cultures and alternatives to consumer modernity (Heelas 2008, 3–10).

Scholars also attribute the rise in spirituality and spiritual quest cultures to personal autonomy in matters of faith, the decline in the authority of institutionalized religious doctrines and institutions and changing dynamics of secularization (Hoover 2008). However, these trajectories vary according to varying histories and religious contexts.

If New Age spiritualism emerged as marginal and even as an alternative to the mainstream institutionalized religions of Christianity in North Atlantic contexts, the story was different in postcolonial India. Here, contemporary spiritualisms have elements of continuity with established mainstream religion, guru-led reformist and revivalist traditions, and very plural traditions of self-introspection, mind and body. Emphasizing the shaping of contemporary spiritualism within the context of consumerism and enterprise cultures in India, Gooptu (2013, 74) writes that new spiritualism, although premised on traditional philosophies and practices of Hinduism and Buddhism, primarily emphasizes the centrality of the inner-self along with lifestyle-well-being and aspirational components like self-development, self-help, self-empowerment and self-realization. Some variations draw elements from New Age Spiritualism of the West, while others articulate indigeneity and reject Western aspects. There is tremendous diversity in contemporary spirituality, given India's sociocultural diversity and the prominence of family, religion, caste and class in matters of faith.

Heelas (2008, 222) writes that in developing countries where "religion and poverty" are rampant, ideologies of "inner-life spiritualities" may aid social upliftment as the consuming "individualism of the wealthy". However, in India, where class and caste exclusions exist, contemporary forms of spiritualisms, while entangled in religious traditions, are largely elitist, consumerist and individualized with personalized orientations. The increasing demand to deal with modernity is, among other things, interconnected, with spiritual *gurus* and organizations successfully marketing self-help, self-paced personalized capsules of wellness, spiritual and self-development techniques nurturing guru-based spiritual lifestyles, publics and self-help cultures. Most Indian spiritual leaders have their own distinct *brand* and use the media and religious teachings to distinguish themselves from others, especially through their public and political engagements.

Media scholars note that the "converging" of media and religion has gained significant attention as religion has increasingly become a "public, commodified, therapeutic and personalized set of practices", while the media collectively constitute a realm where "important projects of "the self"' (spiritual, transcendent and deeply meaningful "work")" take place (Hoover 2006, 2). New media have given a new agency to people to participate and construct a wide spectrum of religious and spiritual discourses and practices in more personal and accessible ways, an agency that also perhaps differs from established top-down articulations by media and spiritual *gurus*. Given this broader context of media competitiveness and religious consumerism, the chapter now explores how niche social networking platforms run by newspapers give rise to spaces for mediatized practices of spiritualism. Spiritualism as used here emphasizes evolving personal orientations and subjectivities of forms of spiritual reflexivity, selfhood-expressions, individuality and choice in evolving negotiations of religious faith.

The Times of India's Speaking Tree

The Times of India is the only English newspaper among the top ten paid-for circulating newspapers in India, and its news website tops the list based on the number of unique visitors (KPMG-FICCI Media and Entertainment Report 2017, 98, 106). In the 1990s, the newspaper introduced a daily spiritual column in its editorial section, called *The Speaking Tree*. The most popular columns were later published as books on personal growth. In March 2010, the spirituality column was expanded into an independent weekly, 8-page newspaper, *The Speaking Tree*. With this venture, it became one of the first newspapers to offer exclusive content on spirituality, inner-life and inner-freedom, giving voice and space to various gurus or spiritual leaders.

Based on the success of the print version, the newspaper launched www.speakingtree.in in December 2010. The expansion from column and weekly newspaper to a digital portal suggests astute marketing, demand and popularity among readers. A digital app followed in 2013. In 2014, https://hindi.speakingtree.in was launched. Www.speakingtree.in claims to be "India's first spiritual networking website", with "spiritual blogs and articles written by over 500,000 members, comprising the most well-known spiritual Masters and avid seekers", "a platform where people who like spirituality could network" globally, participate in live spiritual events and instantly connect with one's "otherwise remote but favorite Master" (Speaking Tree n.d.a). E-notifications, tweets and alerts continuously impart a sense of connect. For instance, subscribers can receive *Daily positive life tips*, which is a blend of motivational cosmopolitanism with spirituality, just like the spiritual "pep-talk" morning shows on televisions (see Lewis 2016, 291). Evidently, the premises of digitality, interactivity and connectivity are important to the promise of personalized religious experiences and direct personal relationships with gurus.

Given that social networking sites have seen exponential growth, it is not surprising that *Speaking Tree's* Facebook page, which had 2,502,698 followers at the time of writing this chapter, in July 2018, declares itself as "India's number 1 spiritual website as per Comscore" (Times Internet Limited 2010). *Speaking Tree* also has a YouTube channel and a Twitter page. Analysis from www.alexa.com shows that the majority of users of www.speakingtree.in are from India (83.6%), with the rest coming from regions with significant Indian diaspora population (USA, UK, Qatar, UAE and Australia).

This chapter is based on multiple methods. Www.speakingtree.in, as a complex website, poses methodological difficulties. Given the theoretical orientations and objectives, a broad data set was required to understand online practices and culture and to identify broad themes. Basic website analytics were gathered from Alexa.com. Quantitative methods were used to analyze the *Discussions* section, a section where users can post impromptu queries, discuss and exchange views. A cumulated total of 420 discussions were collected for a six-month period (April 2017–September 2017). Roughly one-third, that is, a sample of 145 discussions with 914 comments (only user-to-text), was analyzed using content analysis to identify broad themes. The analysis also relied upon a survey of the profile pages of all 141 so-called Masters and some Seekers in www.speakingtree.in to understand their online activities.

In detail, the chapter is based on non-participant observation which was done for more than eight months (called *lurking* in virtual circles), after an even longer period of having initially followed speakingtree.in. Specifically themed user-generated posts were identified and collected using the search engine: self, meditation, motivation, spirituality, happiness, speaking tree, blogs, Masters, Seekers, points, badges and followers, all of which are self-reflexive creations of users. Of these, 20 each were randomly saved, summing up to 260 posts altogether. As they span over wide time periods, sorting these year-wise generated an archive that captured developments over time. Just like conversations, hyperlinks spun off into other spiritual themes providing insights into the community, practices, expectations and motivations. This helped explore online spiritualism and the intersection of media, religion and culture.

Findings related to the multi-spiritual site

Www.speakingtree.in's homepage epitomizes the ethos of contemporary spiritualisms: cultural discourses and commodity marketing steeped in self-transformation, personal health and inner-self transformation. There are editorials, user-generated blogs and slideshows about the mind, soul, ego, divinity, astrology, mantras, mysticism, natural healing, herbs, affirmations and other themes. Users can navigate these and archives using the site's tags like *most popular, most followed, latest* and so forth. As a networking site, www.speakingtree.in incorporates the blurred boundaries between public and private spheres associated with YouTube and social media sites (like privacy, individualization, flexibility in sharing contents like *spiritual diaries* etc.). Personal profile pages document users' activities indicting their online *spiritual journeys* and personal growth. The *Times Loyalty Program* allows registered users to accumulate points and badges for different activities and levels attained. The badges represent beings, guides and themes related to fields of spiritualism and symbolize mind-soul transcendence or spiritual attainments. Given that growth is a central dimension of spirituality, these levels allude to offline levels achieved by practitioners through body-mind spiritual-lifestyle trainings. Thus, flexibility in choosing activities, freedom to adhere to religious discourses and combining interests on the site reinforce two key notions: *self-choice* and *self-motivation* – elements that are integral to meaningful prosumption and contemporary spiritualism.

Www.speakingtree.in's participants are categorized into two – Masters (spiritual leaders as invited by *Times*' management) and Seekers (users). Masters include gurus with large offline followers, like Sri Sri Ravi Shankar, Jaggi Vasudev, Deepak Chopra, Osho, Maulana Wahiduddin Khan and Andre Cohen. Masters also include organizations like Bahai Faith, Scientology India, youth directors of spiritual organizations apart from tarot readers, holistic healers and five so-called anti-aging pundits (all of them doctors, including a famous bariatric surgeon, running successful hospitals). Sri Sri Ravishankar (*Art of Living*) is the most followed Master (88,406 followers). Meena Om with about 1,800 blogs is most active.

The two categories of *Masters* and *Seekers* exemplify the manner in which both spiritualism and media commonly organize their followers and reader-users. As expressions associated with spiritualism, *Master* and *Seeker* also embody a certain interconnected market fragment oriented to neo-spiritual and lifestyle-secular cultures. This strategically marks virtual interactions, embodying online spiritual practices and actions. Besides, the complex, socially networked, layered interconnections within the site and with Twitter and Facebook allow both to constantly evolve as heterogeneous, dynamic, interconnected digital publics. This uneven but global connection can be captured using Hepp's (2015, 5–6) interpretation of Immanuel Castells network and flows: as disparate, structurally connected nodes that link content, cultures and flows. These networks show both diversity and interconnectedness, with the potential to be involved in complex religious and spiritual activities, identity formations and online communities.

Besides, while www.speakingtree.in hosts a wide range of bottom-up contents, there are no markers to clearly distinguish professional creations by the editorial team (who also post as Seekers) and those by the user-Seeker. This can be gauged only through immersion in the site. Editorials (also written by prominent gurus) and spiritual articles in the section *Spiritual Writer* are clearly controlled by the management and therefore top-down. Besides, professionally created user-generated contents, for instance, feature a mix of spiritual topics and trending news stories like popular social media videos, magical beliefs, shocking news, stranger-than-fiction stories, positive community initiatives and inspirational stories. This blurring of professional and user-generated contents capitalizes the participatory orientation and also epitomizes *blending* which is a characteristic feature of contemporary spiritualisms. To give one example: coverage from TV is repackaged into slideshow and blog formats. For instance, Lal's blog (Lal

2016) on funny videos and memes about a yoga promotion, jointly presented by Bollywood film actress Shilpa Shetty and yoga guru Baba Ramdev, is also embedded with a YouTube video of an ABP Television news report about the session. Such circulation of spiritual discourses and audiovisuals through the digital medium indicates modes of content creation under media convergences and competition, the complex links between new and old media and evolving mediatization of spiritualism.

Emerging beliefs and spiritual community

The aforementioned background about this digital space is important in order to understand the dynamic nature of online spiritualism in spiritual-prosumer cultures, including the enabling aspects of the digital and the spiritual. As discussed further, participatory aspects like user-generated contents (prosumption) along with creativity, motivation, user agency and the intimate privacy of going online (digital engagement) with complex ways of spiritual relating, awareness, negotiation and experimentation are central to the construction of a range of complex spiritual identities, beliefs and the community.

As is common to networking sites, www.speakingtree.in's users (Seekers) mobilize around sharing intimacies, freedom to post / comment, non-judgmental learning, collective meaning-making and seeking advice, correction, guidance and so forth. The user-generated, networked aspects support the creation of affective bonds, love, friendship and relationships. These include ways of relating to Hinduism, nurturing personal notions of spirituality, creating meanings and connecting online-offline spiritual practices. Most importantly, these interconnections nurture and sustain a virtual, dynamic and evolving *Speaking Tree community*. For instance, a Seeker who had returned after a long time blogged how he missed his old friends, "beautiful educative blogs" and wonderful inspiring personalities" (Sharma 2016). The attribution of spiritual ideologies and sensorial experiences to digital interactions, as evidenced in the manner in which diverse self-hood practices and experiences of realizing the divine and selfhood are constructed and shared among the online community, is also important. Observations show that for many users the anonymity of users and interactions is even socially desirable, enhancing the interactive experience for the spiritually inclined. This blurring of digital and spiritual apparently accentuates the perception of the divine or, as a Seeker explained, a state of being "unknown while completely known as soul" (Sud 2014). Thus, identity formations, spiritual aesthetics and the interconnection of digital and spiritual are central to notions of participation, community and online spiritualism.

Users (Seekers) usually contribute slideshows and blogs about science and spiritualism, personal narratives, evidence of auras, meditation, ayurveda, self-help, neo-motivational / life-management, lifestyle, food, health, beauty, traditional religious philosophies, mythological stories, rituals and mantras.

Other spiritual topics include existentialism, god, gurus and experiences on www.speakingtree.in. Reflections that negotiate religion and spirituality are common. Seekers thus personally construct their spirituality and some actively consider online pursuits as an extension of their offline spiritual membership of guru-based practices. Sociocultural familiarity and affinity, for instance, the fact the site's contents are of an "Indian standard", appear to attract and motivate participants (Sahoo 2016a)[2]. Personalization (self-narratives), raw, unedited rhetoric in conversational style and using a mix of Hindi and English are common. Users also post personal contents about family which illustrates aspects of interpreting and integrating Hindu traditions in online constructions. Such posts are sometimes criticized as being irrelevant, for instance, "Husband & Wife, Children, Nature etc. as a sort of advertising of their loved ones" (Iyer 2012). Usually, comments and discussions around such posts encourage reflexive, personal spiritual meaning-making and meaningful consumption (like motivations, sharing and gaining), particularly the use of spiritual and media resources to meet broader humanist goals (e.g., to benefit mankind) and to enhance the individual quest for the *deepest knowledge* or *inner light*.

The multi-spiritual, virtual diversity is itself aspirational for users, given *the hybrid blending* of broad rhetorics of religion, faith and choice, cosmopolitan self-awakening and plural beliefs. As a seeker has put it, "all good thoughts come to us from any part of the world. We know Lord is infinite, so is the tales of that infinite and it told and listened by different enlightened masters and seekers in many different ways" (Sahoo 2016b). Being able to *pick-and-choose* online is described as a blessing and is eulogized as:

> I like st dialogs,
> direct, indirect
> twisting, stretching, bending
> alluding, elluding,
> digressing, diverting,
> evading avoiding,
> yet one wanting to give what one wants to give
> yet one wanting to receive what one wants to receive
> none matching up,
> all patching up. (Dlg 2012)

Negotiating online spiritualism: Masters, Seekers and seeking

Online spiritualism, here, is shaped by media, capital, digital technology, new and old beliefs and users in interconnected ways. As Jenkins (2006, 2–3) notes, active participation by consumers is central to "convergence cultures", "where grassroots and corporate media intersect" and "the power of the media producer and media consumer interact in unpredictable ways". The context of prosumer spiritual ethos and digital interaction in www.speakingtree.in increases avenues for fluid, personal self-selected forms of spiritual production and consumption in the context of community participation. Studies posit that digital religion is articulated through the increasing "prominence of digital mediation" and the "persistence and re-imagining" of "'the religious' in contemporary life" (Hoover and Echchaibi; 2014, 4). As Grieve (2013, 105) writes, complex digital religious practices are important expressions of being religious in contemporary culture (given technology's integration with economics, politics and culture) and facilitate "a workaround or an innovative temporary solution" as a means of overcoming the problems of "a liquid modern life".

To consider these dimensions, a brief initial analysis of www.speakingtree.in's discussions section, where users pose queries, statements, confessions or even vent frustrations, was undertaken to illustrate the diverse everyday ways in which spiritual meaning-making is experimented within new media contexts. As discussed earlier, the sample was collected during a six-month period (April 2017–September 2017) and roughly 145 discussions (out of a total of 420) with 914 comments were analyzed (Table 11.1).

The table shows that dominant themes of *Discussions* are personal circumstances (23.4%) and existential / philosophical issues (18.6%), with a greater number of responses (23% and 30% respectively). These personal concerns are often related to worries about house ownership, burden of work, family politics, horoscope anxieties, money issues and superstitions. Incidentally, queries addressed to Masters or gurus are always unanswered. Instead, seekers answer them, sometimes with multiple responses to a single query.

Table 11.1 Themes, queries and replies from the sample

Discussion Themes	*Percentage of Queries (%)*	*Answers/ replies (%)*
General chat	1.3	0.3
Speakingtree.in	4.1	2.1
Current affairs and spirituality	2.8	2.5
Hindu philosophy/myth	5.5	4.4
Hindu religious objects/practices	1.8	9.8
Everyday personal circumstances	23.4	23
Existential/ultimate reality/god	18.6	30
Secular	2.1	2.8
Inter-religious	2.8	3.1
Emotions	4.1	6
Tradition/culture	2.8	2.5
Astrology/numerology/superstitions	13.1	6.7
Gender	2.8	4.3
Miscellaneous	2.8	1.5
Advertisements	2.1	1.1
Total	100 (145)	100 (914)

One consequence of such interactivity, 24/7 connectivity and hyper-textual links to spiritual resources is that it gives flexibility and autonomy to the querying Seeker to choose any of the many user-responses that resonate with his/her beliefs. However, these workarounds or temporary solutions (Grieve 2013), such as suggestions like de-stressing online, changing oneself, following motivational online discourses and so forth, reinforce *self-making* as a *choice* without providing any concrete solution to problems. Self-development, self-empowerment discourses and practices of spiritualism are promoted, and shape and strengthen notions of online spiritualism. Also, while spiritual feel-good discourses and specialist advice from TV gurus might be prominent (e.g., Lewis 2016, 287), avenues like www.speakingtree.in are intimate spaces to engage with religion, spiritualism and life stresses without resorting to spiritual experts.

To query further: How do online interactions construct forms of faith expressions and digital spiritual cultures? First, spiritual meaning-making and imaginations of self, collectivity and practices create an emerging social space, which renegotiates the contours of religion (Hinduism) and contemporary spiritualism. An example can be illustrated in the negotiation of authority; that is, among the 141 spiritual Masters and 12,1000 registered so-called Seekers of speakingtree.in. Masters are considered revered teachers and, as one Seeker has put it, their online contributions are the "LINES, DOTS, ZIG ZAGS, WAVES, SQUIGGLES", which all lead to salvation (Velishala 2016). However, a survey of their profile pages showed that almost all of these Masters never replied to the hundreds of questions posed to them by Seekers. Instead seekers answer queries. Complaints and requests to the Masters to interact are very common (e.g., Gurjar 2013). This lack of response to discussions and questions directly posed to them seemingly contradicts the promise of interactivity and connections with gurus, which is one of the premises of this website.

However, this encourages a form of online practice with implications for online engagements, that is, continuous self-seeking online in *the quest for answers*. This practice fits the quest-culture ethos of spiritualisms in which the Seeker is a channel that continuously aspires for mind-body-spirit well-being, self-improvement by choice and is *perpetual seeking*. Fellow Seekers use spiritually rooted interpretations to answer queries posed by Seekers. Advice blogs and comments quote self-help discourses and ultimate goals like inner consciousness to encourage Seekers to believe in themselves. Often interspersed with the verses of seeking and instances from mythology, seeking is encouraged as a spiritually endless fulfilling *self-endeavor* experienced during the quest for knowledge. In this process, Seekers negotiate knowledge, traditions, authenticity and practices as they integrate *online seeking* with the *seeking of spiritualism*. For instance, to an unanswered query posed by a Seeker to a Master about his relentless quest for a spiritual *guru*, other Seekers posted suggestions to wait, follow the self or inner light or seek knowledge since the *real guru is within*, while one Seeker even suggested to "reject gurus" completely since they are given to "self-aggrandizement" and "contemporizing the knowledge of the past" (Vishwakarma 2017). Besides, the lack of interaction with Masters has consolidated Seekers into groups that advocate various self-making modalities, like those who encourage independence from guru-Seeker traditions.

The *user-seeker*, therefore, is crucial to the structural dynamics of wwwspeakingtree.in and its community. The distance of the Masters might appear to reinforce traditional power structures of both media and religion. However, social networking and interactions among fellow Seekers have led to the emergence of new positions of spiritual masterships online. Many of these Seekers have gained a following in thousands because of their online spiritual discourses, persona and engagements (including their rankings in www.speakingtree.in). Such Seekers can be located using the site's search engine. As one Seeker commented, "I have found masters… among seekers…& I never miss a word of them. They talk only spiritual &I nothing but spiritual. May be not popular in the normal sense. But admired and appreciated & respected" (Sonti 2016). These Seekers are addressed with the traditional language marker that conveys respect in Indian tradition, namely, with the suffix *ji*. Other Seekers seek their blessings, exude words of admiration, give them the right of response and express a feeling of honor to be able to comment and interact with them.

Second, interactivity and multiple representations provide both the context and rationality to relate spiritualism with Hindu traditions. The site's homepage maintains sublime-secular images such as representations of idealness, purity, mindful activities and nature. However, the user-generated aspect facilitates the use of images of Hindu religious figures and calendar art images of gods and goddesses in Seekers' contributions. Such user-generated religious themes increase during festivals, although their visibility is carefully managed. Besides, blogs, slideshows, discussions and situational responses generally intersperse a neo-spiritual vocabulary of self-growth and self-motivation mixed with terminology and concepts taken from Hindu philosophy as stated in established Hindu texts, such as the *Bhagavadgita*, *Vedas*, *Puranas*, *Mahabharata*, *Ramayana* and the teachings of Swami Vivekanada. Also, the use of Sanskrit mantras and translated verses in Hinglish as well as Hindu prayers (sometimes with links to spiritual resources) gives a distinct Hindu orientation to this interactive space despite the sublime-secular representations and professed ethos of www.speakingtree.in. Such scriptural references, while actively promoting the central idea of "enterprising self", are not unusual to contemporary spiritualism (Gooptu 2013, 76). Besides, for many Seekers, religious identities are part of their self-development as a Seeker. They also believe that "90% users are Hindu" (Sahoo 2016b).

Third, ritualized online activities construct a social space where the spiritual sensorial experiences of offline practices can be experienced with a focus on the inner self. Virtual aspects on the website like sublime visuals (symbolism of gods, goddesses, gurus and spiritual motifs), spiritual discourses and continuous alerts about spiritual ongoing interactions heavily frame spiritual immersion. Navigating the site's homepage and archives invokes the aesthetics of an expanding spiritual vortex where users can travel and experience the stillness of timeless-time beyond barriers of world, space and time facilitated by digital technology. Offensive comments are removed, unlike those on www.indiatimes.com (see Jayachandran 2015). Www.speakingtree.in's *Good Karma* editorial team calls this *purification*. Vigilant Seekers moderate comments and collect badges, while propagating discourses on positivity.

One would therefore go with Hoover and Echchaibi's (2014) argument that essentially individuals use digital technologies to assert a sense of autonomy, express their subjectivities and create shared spaces. The sacredness attributed to *divine* technology and experiences thereof seems to cultivate a reverential sacredness to the site. Profound spiritual experiences are attributed to mindful presumption in the course of interactions with other Seekers, as users encourage sensorial experiences of *divine love* and raising self-consciousness, although such posts are often framed within the multiple experientiality of Hindu religious beliefs. As this seeker's blog reveals:

> The site is a place of Satang at my doorsteps. It provides me—peace, solace, divinity, ecstasy, a total satisfaction, a mental food, a food for my soul and it always soothes me as my Guru, a friend, philosopher and the guide... My Lord Krishna resides in the recital of the seekers and the site of the Speaking Tree...So I feel the presence...As He resides—where His devotees recite his names and remember Him—so I feel Him... (Sud 2014)

Such beliefs are reconstructed around the incorporation of an important feature of Hindu traditions and worship: *darśan*, consisting of simultaneously seeing the divine while being seen by the divine. Recent studies show that digital technologies and virtual spaces articulate sacrality through digital *darśans*, thus constituting new practices and religious symbolism (Mallapragada 2010; Scheifinger 2012).Similarly, as a Seeker's (Rishi 2011) post illustrates, speakingtree.in is imagined as a "new temple", a "manifestation of IT age, "blessed with knowledge" by "gods from heaven to get deliverance in the most modern style", as "knowledge of the God" leads one to "the inner temple, and the ultimate god, one's self". For users, it is a platform empowered with *spirit*. Here, sharing spiritual experiences collectively, the affinity and imagination of *what is perceived as divine* is important for consumption and inspirational realization of spiritual consciousness through online activities. In this context, Birgit Meyer's (2009) "aesthetic formations" of communities bound through sensorial experiences of religion are instructive.

Finally, examining practices throws light on the "religious uses of new media" (Lundby 2013, 233) and how people use "technologies to live out the spiritual" (Hoover 2013, 268). In all forms of contemporary spiritualisms (including yoga and meditation), self-motivated daily bodily practice is important to realize a mind-body-soul consciousness. Similarly, seekers see the act of daily, continuous online participation and dedication as important for their mindful awakening, transformation and larger spiritual journey. It is physically experienced, and claimed to provide tangible benefits like those of daily meditation practices. These forms are many, and similar to other methods of mobilizing selves to reach divinity in spiritualism (Gooptu 2013, 80). For instance, practicing online mindfulness or meditating over online words, actions and interactions are considered as important as the other mindful activities of blogging and reading. Seekers suggest ways such as maintaining a dialogue between *the self* and *verse*, or by translating Hindu mantras:

> ... first of all read it (material pertaining to spirituality) two to three times with the help of your intellect, if no special results are visible even then, pray and talk to yourself....Let my intellect be pure, may the subtle negative energies not be able to create any obstacles while I am reading the spiritual articles... able to implement it in my day-to-day life. (Sahoo 2016b)

Thus, the idea of digital spiritual practice and space is constantly expanded. Various forms of religious and spiritual positioning are apparent, such as attributing their online activity and drive or *inner-quest* to the power and belief in personal deities. As one Seeker noted, the energy kept "the creative sap flowing", and he experienced satisfaction in practicing "knowledge based" blogging and "seeking answers from seekers" as being more comfortable than "intuition-based spiritual living" and "meditation" (Kumar 2013). Debates that compare blogging or worldly self-realization practices are common. Posting his 5,000th blog, another Seeker offered salutations to gods, goddesses, the *Bhagavadgītā* and his spiritual guru:

> Blogs are medium to worship almighty god...since they remind us about very pious, holy, sacred names of almighty god again and again...it is like chanting the holy names...it is like meditation...it is like worship. (Agrawal 2015)

Others articulate experiences like positive vibrations, tears, gratitude and happiness while reading, sharing and reflecting upon spiritual thoughts online. This spiritual meaning-making is recreated in the *everyday sacredness attributed to digital practices*, which are not at all perceived as mere practices to pass time. To summarize, the constant articulation of participatory elements like sharing, non-judgmental reactions and the so-called knowing (while simultaneously experiencing each other remotely) as connected souls, thus adds a collective dimension to *experiencing* the individual, online quest for self-transformation. Thus, the allusions to the common linkages of virtual-spiritual duality, the possibility of experiencing the simultaneously distant as nevertheless known/intimate is central here.

Online spiritualism: The political economy of faith

Having traced that, this last section focuses on the mediatization of multi-spiritualism in convergence contexts. As documented later, the user-generated, prosumer dimensions constantly shape new modes of online spiritualism practices which dynamically emerge through varying practices of relating to spiritual ethos and changing commercial or promotional negotiations by the site. When speakingtree.in introduced a points / reward system in 2013, there were debates whether such commercial orientations contradicted its professed spiritual philosophy, since the previous online activities of Seekers were not counted under the new system. Some Seekers argued that this contradicted the ethos of spiritual evolution which considers past actions of mankind. For spiritual Seekers who focused on personal spiritual gains, the points were illusionary criteria that made no difference to their quest for *self-realization and enlightenment*. Others welcomed it as innovation necessary for motivation (see Speaking Tree 2013[3]). In mid-2015, the site changed its format again, supposedly to update, but also to tweak the amassing of points, prompting furious responses from users. The technical disruption supposedly made it less user-friendly and difficult to locate posts. Connections to Facebook were allegedly strengthened and provisions to copy-paste, hyperlinks and personal messaging were removed. Users claimed that it was intended to promote the blogs of Masters who paid to put their contents online. Some Seekers even made an attempt to form a separate site, a speaking tree club, which did not take off (see comments in Savjani 2015).

One consequence of the points system was that pressures to confirm user-generated contents more rigorously to "media logic" (Altheide and Snow 1979) intensified, since tweets, comments and tags became important for interactivity and visibility. Prosumer practices vary, for example, in motivations, use of technology and understandings of spiritualism. For instance, users differ over what they perceive as participation for the sake of *real* spiritualism (meaningful spiritual engagement, experiences and personal transformations without coveting points) and participation motivated by *worldly rewards* (such as prioritizing visibility, points and badges). The multidimensions to spiritual prosumption and the intertwining of spiritual meanings to their user-generated prosumption foreclose any possibilities of strict distinctions.

As users share, revise and construct new spiritual imaginaries, spiritual knowledge, authenticity and community, they also negotiate and discuss desirable forms of online–offline spiritual behavior and actions like commenting, points and controversies over topics (e.g., differing explanations of positivity, encouragement, dignity, perseverance), while amassing points for every action. For many Seekers, their actions are a spiritual, emotional, relational and enterprising online investment, visible through embodying an online *spiritual self* which distinguishes his/her identity. Ritualized actions like *thanking* people, *appreciating*, *creating* spiritual content, *responding* to discussions, *positive* motivations and spiritual vocabulary are construed as ways to spread positivity and to encourage offline self-transformation while garnering points and levels. *Learning* to tackle the *negativity* of adverse comments from co-Seekers, *ignoring* so-perceived negative Seekers who are accused to block divinity and *forgiving* others for their online behavior are other actions that are perceived as helping to deal with online criticism and aid self-growth while collecting points, advancing levels and gaining visibility. This is understood as *spiritual advancement*, which demonstrates offline–online transcendence and serves as an example for others. For instance, a Seeker claimed to have created his "best blogs" by "encashing on the frivolous emotions", "online fights and abuses" and frustrations "experienced by poor souls on their path to being enlightened" (Ananth 2012). Thus, a dynamic system of practices promotes notions of transcendence and self-growth while relying upon the *ethos of choice* to legitimize online strategies which establish credibility and authenticity in online constructions.

This further propels spiritual prosumption in the expansive new media contexts. The hundreds of Seeker blogs on *how to* publish, write, attract and promote spiritual topics demonstrate that motivations range from engaging in spiritual activity, for personal gains including the accumulation of points, to providing *seva* (social service) and to networking to assist others in their spiritual journey. The ritual of visiting www.speakingtree.in and posting there is itself considered as self-disciplining, and testimonies of this discipline's positive impact on daily life are posted online. For the enterprising Seeker, for instance, speakingtree.in is a morally creative digital avenue to self-help and learn about the digital as well. For instance, a prolific Seeker (Agrawal 2015), narrating his journey since 2011 (which he describes as addiction), wrote that his interest in spirituality and "motivation & inspiration" (badges, views, shares) helped him in the physical world to overcome his "lack of internet knowledge" (not knowing how to type).[4] Such networking in the community and associated practices encourages online engagements, being spiritual and connects users to a global spiritual network.

Interestingly, online spirituality ranges widely: from what Seekers would consider as meaningful pursuits driven by *authentic* faith motivations to pursuits that combine *faith and publicity* (spiritual but attached to collecting points, for instance) and only *publicity*. Seekers purposefully use personal messaging, commenting, hyperlinks and social network connections to promote their views and contents in creative ways such as creatively advertising various religious services. Spiritual *flame* topics (that enflame discussions) are common. Since there are different commitments to one's inherited or chosen traditions, interpretations and meanings differ and are even lost in the translations of Sanskrit or Hindi verses. The differences among spiritual publics thus come to the fore as contending groups (followers) discuss, try to garner support and views and influence rankings. An irate Seeker once posted what he identified as "most abused 85 words" to show his angst at the way "the context and real meaning is subjected to mundane interpretation" and poor understanding that supposedly spawned "communal hatred" and "spiritual danger" online (Orthodox 2014). Among the many examples he listed were *nirguna*, god realization, religion, guru, atomic *atma* (soul), *param-atma* (cosmic super-soul), *satvik* food, self-realization, *dharma*, *karma*, meditation, yoga and happiness. Discussions and posts evidence differences as users usually evoke recurrent, idealistic religious themes and spiritual binaries like light and darkness, and righteous conduct and righteous duty (*dharma*), supported by contending interpretations of established Hindu traditions and texts interspersed with comments about positivity and self-growth. These are supported by references, hyperlinks and freshly researched posts. This appears to encourage debate and dialogue in a democratizing process of active bottom-up, very diverse interpretations of spiritualisms.

An active imagination of a space existing between real and virtual, that is very close to an actual religious experience, sustains it as well (Hoover and Echchaibi 2014). Observations show that Seekers express gratitude to the platform owners for their great service to humanity in providing a site for personal spiritual quests, often hailing it as *divine* technology. Seekers often rationalize that as a digital venture www.speakingtree.in requires profits and advertisements to survive, while advocating positive, self-focused subjectivized practices and forms of relating to community, the site and spiritualism. This supports Gooptu's (2013) observation about the links between enterprise cultures, business and spiritualism. Still, as this study shows, public imagination and ideas of enterprising selves of spirituality are evolving, with the Internet being integral to self-making and new notions such as challenging the guru-to-practitioner models advocated by some spiritual leaders. Meanwhile the formations of such complex spiritual publics and prosumer culture proactively aid media companies to remain competitive in the marketplace.

Conclusion

Www.speakingtree.in, created by *The Times of India*, is an important instance of how news media-connected social networking content platforms facilitate and disseminate expressions and modes of individualized spiritual subjectivities and formations of online community. Taking Hoover and Echchaibi (2014) as a starting point, this chapter briefly captured the third space which emerges at the intersections of lived spiritual practices and emerging digital cultures. The analysis indicated, among other things, the substantive shifts that may happen with the mediatization of spiritualism, the forging of self-enterprise cultures and commodification of spiritual practices and beliefs.

Additionally, the dynamic interplay between practice and media shows the manner in which spiritualism (and Hinduism) in relation to new media is currently changing in India. While new media, spiritual faith and culture are imbricated in spiritual prosumption, online spiritualism is shaped by contexts and structures created by media companies. User-generated aspects of www.speakintree.in importantly galvanize users to use forms of enterprising Hindu versions of spiritual engagements, although online interactions such as with spiritual Masters are usually one-sided. Since spiritualism advocates different experiences and paths, the rhetoric and foregrounding of online participation as a choice and prioritization of individuality further reinforces spiritual prosumerism and identity constructions of *the spiritual-user*, for instance, through participating and relating to experiences, religion and spiritual interpretations even as the act of visiting, going online, posting, attaining milestones is highly ritualistic, structured and deterministic in certain ways.

Online spiritualism in India, with its multiple, hybrid notions of faith, largely Hindu practices and mix of consumerist self-discourses, is constituted through experiences of faith, varied online practices, networked interactions and participation within the online community. Participatory cultures, as Jenkins (2006) argued, significantly bring new modes of literacies, learning and collective meaning-making. Many users believe that they are simultaneously participants and witnesses of the spiritual awakening of others online, making digital participation cathartic and pedagogical.

To conclude, sites like www.speakingtree.in provide private gateways for individuals to actively create personalized collages of hybrid knowledge and lifestyle, blending Hindu traditions and spiritualism, at grassroots levels, evidently with potentials to reinforce forms of market-friendly contemporary spiritualisms. In contextualizing the political economy of Indian media, this chapter indicates the interconnectedness of commerce, new media and spiritualism, as well as the construction of new modes of expressions of spirituality in a demand-driven context modulated by enterprise cultures, markets, media convergences, spiritual-consumerism and audiences interested in spiritualism. User-generated constructions of online spiritualism cannot merely be attributed to anxieties of social life or to pressures of capital and individualized subjectivities alone. The online thus has the potential to build new meanings of being religious and spiritual, with implications for understanding emerging religiosity and spiritualism in Indian society.

Notes

1 Www.speakingtree.in is freely accessible in India, but not in all countries – in some countries, access to the website will be denied.
2 This comment is no longer online. Last accessed 1 September 2017.
3 This link is no longer online. Last accessed 19 February 2017.
4 For instance, Pravin Agrawal has posted thousands of blogs and initiated more than 500 discussions since 2011, earning about 2,500 followers (see Agrawal n.d.).

References

Agrawal, P. n.d. *www.speakingtree.in seeker* [profile page]. Available at www.speakingtree.in/pravin-agrawal, accessed 25 April 2019.

Agrawal, P., 2015. Blogs are medium to worship the Almighty God. *www.speakingtree.in Slideshow*, [slideshow] 23 August. Available at www.speakingtree.in/allslides/blogs-are-medium-to-worship-the-almighty-god, accessed 29 August 2018.

Alexa, 1996. *Find, Reach, and Convert Your Audience with Marketing That Works*. Available at www.alexa.com, accessed 25 August 2017.

Altheide, D. and Snow, R. P., 1979. *Media Logic*. Beverly Hills: Sage.

Ananth, A., 2012. Some of My Best Blogs Were as a Result of My Encashing On t. *www.speakingtree.in Blog*, [blog] 5 August. Available at www.speakingtree.in/blog/some-of-my-best-blogs-were-as-a-result-of-my-encashing-on-t, accessed 12 September 2017.

Anon., 2017a. *Internet in India-2016: An IAMAI and Kantar IMRB Report*. Available at http://bestmediainfo.com/wp-content/uploads/2017/03/Internet-in-India-2016.pdf, accessed 29 August 2018.

Banerjee, P., 2015. India's Youth Reinterpreting God in a Whole New Way. *hindustantimes*, [online] 3 September. Available at www.hindustantimes.com/india/india-s-youth-reinterpreting-god-in-a-whole-new-way/story-aA5djox7Z3GeWh44htaBzI.html, accessed 29 August 2018.

Campbell, H. A., 2013. Introduction: The Rise of the Study of Digital Religion. In H. A. Campbell, ed. *Digital Religion: Understanding Religious Practice in New Media Worlds*. London: Routledge, 1–22.

Census of India, 2001. *Religious Composition*. Available at http://censusindia.gov.in/Census_Data_2001/India_at_glance/religion.aspx, accessed 29 August 2018.

CSDS-KAS Report, 2017. *Key Highlights from CSDS-KAS Report 'Attitudes, Anxieties and Aspirations of India's Youth'*, 3 April. Available at www.kas.de/wf/doc/kas_48472-1522-1-30.pdf?170508130757, accessed 18 March 2019.

Dlg, D. R., 2012. I Like ST Dialogs. *www.speakingtree.in Blog*, [blog] 19 November. Available at www.speakingtree.in/blog/i-like-st-dialogs, accessed 29 August 2018.

Einstein, M., 2008. *Brands of Faith: Marketing Religion in a Commercial Age*. London: Routledge.

Gooptu, N., 2013. New Spiritualism and the Micro-politics of Self-making in India's Enterprise Cultures. In Gooptu, N., ed. *Enterprise Culture in Neoliberal India: Studies in Youth, Class, Work and Media*. London: Routledge, 73–90.

Grieve, G. P., 2013. Religion. In Campbell, H. A., ed. *Digital Religion: Understanding Religious Practice in New Media Worlds*. London: Routledge, 104–118.

Gurjar, N., 2013. To ST Manager!!!!. *www.speakingtree.in Blog*, [blog] 8 January. Available at www.speakingtree.in/blog/to-st-manager, accessed 29 August 2018.

Heelas, P., 2008. *Spiritualities of Life: New Age Romanticism and Consumptive Capitalism*. Malden and Oxford: Blackwell.

Helland, C., 2016. Digital Religion. In DeLamater, J., ed. *Handbook of Sociology and Social Research*. New York: Springer, 177–196.

Hepp, A., 2015. *Transcultural Communication*. Malden and Oxford: Wiley-Blackwell.

Hoover, S., 2006. *Religion in the Media Age*. Abingdon: Routledge.

Hoover, S., 2008. *Media and Religion*. A White Paper from The Center for Media, Religion, and Culture. Colorado: University of Colorado at Boulder. Available at https://rolandoperez.files.wordpress.com/2009/10/media-and-religion.pdf, accessed 29 August 2017.

Hoover, S., 2013. Concluding Thoughts: Imagining the Religious in and Through the Digital. In Campbell, H., ed. *Digital Religion: Understanding Religious Practice in New Media worlds*. New York: Routledge, 266–268.

Hoover, S. and Echchaibi, N., 2014. *Media Theory and the "Third Spaces of Digital Religion"*. Colorado: University of Colorado at Boulder. Available at https://thirdspacesblog.files.wordpress.com/2014/05/third-spaces-and-media-theory-essay-2-0.pdf, accessed 17 August 2017.

Isozaki, H., Sasaki, D. and Pandit, I., 2017. *India's Changing Middle Class*. Tokyo: Nomura Research Institute. Available at http://india.nri.com/pdf/Reports-English-1.pdf, accessed 15 August 2017.

Iyer, S., 2012. So many blogs.... *www.speakingtree.in Blog*. [blog] 20 May. Available at www.speakingtree.in/blog/so-many-blogs, accessed 29 August 2018.

Jayachandran, J., 2015. Outrage, Debate or Silence: An Analysis of Reader Comments and Online Rape News. In Schneider, N. and Titzmann, F., eds. *Studying Youth, Media and Gender in Post-Liberalisation India*. Berlin: Frank & Timme, 47–79.

Jenkins, H., 2006. *Convergence Culture: Where Old and New Media Collide*. New York: NYU Press.

KPMG-FICCI Media and Entertainment Report, 2017. *Media for the Masses: The Promise Unfolds*. Available at https://assets.kpmg.com/content/dam/kpmg/in/pdf/2017/04/FICCI-Frames-2017.pdf, accessed 5 August 2017.

Kumar, S. M., 2013. Satisfaction in Posting. *www.speakingtree.in Blog*, [blog] 18 November. Available at www.speakingtree.in/blog/satisfaction-in-posting-blogs-consistently-on-the-subject-that-i-contemplate, accessed 14 July 2017.

Lal, P., 2016. This Shilpa Shetty and Baba Ramdev's Joint Yoga Session is the Funniest You Will See Today. *www.speakingtree.in Blog*, [blog] 21 January. Available at www.speakingtree.in/blog/this-shilpa-shetty-and-baba-ramdevs-joint-yoga-session-is-the-funniest-thing-you-will-see-today, accessed 18 August 2017.

Lewis, T., 2016. Spirited Public? Post-secularism, Enchantment and Enterprise on Indian Television. In Marshall, P. D., D'Cruz, G., MacDonald, S. and Lee, K., eds. *Contemporary Publics: Shifting Boundaries in New Media, Technology and Cultures*. London: Springer, 283–298.

Lundby, K., 2013. Theoretical Frameworks for Approaching Religion and New Media. In: Campbell, H. A., ed. *Digital Religion: Understanding Religious Practice in New Media Worlds*. London: Routledge, 225–237.

Mallapragada, M., 2010. Desktop Deities: Hindu Temples, Online Cultures and the Politics of Remediation. *South Asian Popular Culture* 8(2), 109–121.

Meyer, B. 2009. *Aesthetic Formations: Media, Religion and the Senses*. New York: Palgrave Macmillan.

Nanda, M., 2009. *The God Market: How Globalization is Making India More Hindu*. New York: Monthly Review Press.

Orthodox, S. B., 2014. 85 Most Abused Spiritual Words That is Leading to Spiritual Danger on Speaking Tree. *www.speakingtree.in Blog*, [blog] 7 December. Available at www.speakingtree.in/blog/10-most-abused-spiritual-words-which-is-leaidng-to-spiritual-danger-on-speaking-tree, accessed 3 July 2017.

Rajagopal, A., 2001. *Politics after Television: Religious Nationalism and the Reshaping of the Indian Public*. Cambridge: Cambridge University Press.

Sahoo, A., 2016a. Comment in Reply to Dhara Kothari.In Sahoo, A., *Speaking Tree*. [slideshow] 29 February. Available at www.speakingtree.in/allslides/speaking-tree-effectiveness/be-a-valuable-to-listed-here, accessed 1 September 2017.

Sahoo, A., 2016b. Speaking Tree. *www.speakingtree.in Slideshow*, [slideshow] 29 February. Available at www.speakingtree.in/allslides/speaking-tree-effectiveness/be-a-valuable-to-listed-here, accessed 1 September 2017.

Savjani, V., 2015. New ST Format. *www.speakingtree.in Blog*, [blog] 27 August. Available at www.speakingtree.in/blog/new-st-format, accessed 1 September 2017.

Scheifinger, H., 2012. Hindu Worship Online and Offline. In Campbell, H., ed. *Digital Religion: Understanding Religious Practice in New Media Worlds*. New York: Routledge, 121–127.

Sharma, A., 2016. Where Have the Old Friends Gone? *www.speakingtree.in Blog*, [blog] 13 February. Available at www.speakingtree.in/blog/where-have-the-old-friends-gone, accessed 29 August 2018.

Sonti, K., 2016. Comment on *Speaking Tree*. *www.speakingtree.in Slideshow*, [slideshow] 26 February. Available at www.speakingtree.in/allslides/speaking-tree-effectiveness/be-a-valuable-to-listed-here, accessed 1 September2017.

Speaking Tree, n.d.a. Speaking Tree [Linked in]. Available at www.linkedin.com/company/speaking-tree, accessed 22 September 2017.

Speaking Tree, n.d.b. Speaking Tree [YouTube]. Available at www.youtube.com/user/myspeakingtree, accessed 20 September 2017.

Speaking Tree, 2010. *Speaking Tree* [Twitter]. Available at https://twitter.com/speakingtree, accessed 20 July 2018.

Speaking Tree, 2013. Speaking Tree Times Point Program [Spiritual Discussion]. *www.speakingtree.in*, 4 February. Available at www.speakingtree.in/discussion/speaking-tree-times-points-program, accessed 19 February 2017.

Sud, P. M., 2014. The Seekers and the Site of ST. *www.speakingtree.in Blog*, [blog] 17 July. Available at www.speakingtree.in/blog/the-seekers-and-the-site-of-st, accessed 29 August 2018.

Sutcliffe, J. S. and Gilhus, S. I., 2013. *New Age Spirituality: Rethinking Religion*. London: Routledge.

Times Internet Limited, 2010. Speaking Tree [Facebook]. Available at: www.facebook.com/pg/speakingtree/about/?ref=page_internal, accessed 30 July 2018.

Velishala, M., 2016. Master's Blogs! *www.speakingtree.in Blog*. [blog] 28 March. Available at www.speakingtree.in/blog/masters-blogs, accessed 1 September 2017.

Vishwakarma, P., 2017. Sir, without Real Guru.... *www.speakingtree.in Spritual Discussions* [Spiritual Discussion], 17 May. Available at www.speakingtree.in/discussion/sir-without-real-guru-l-feel-there-is-a-void-in-my-life-and-there-are-many-which-come-across-in-my-as-guru-but-they-did-not-quench-my-thirst-for-knowledge-and-true-essence-of-life-please-guide-me-how-, accessed 29 August 2018.

Zeiler, X., 2014. The Global Mediatization of Hinduism through Digital Games: Representation versus Simulation in *Hanuman: Boy Warrior*. In: Campbell, H. A. and Grieve, G. P., eds. *Playing with Religion in Digital Games*. Bloomington: Indiana University Press, 66–87.

12 Streaming the divine

Hindu temples' digital journeys

Yael Lazar

Introduction

Situated in their local communities and devoted to a particular deity, Hindu temples also exist on the wide space of the Internet. Many Hindu temples have their own website, where they provide information about the respective temple's history, mythology, services and current affairs. Beyond their informative elements, many of these websites also provide an array of online services. Some services facilitate visits to the temple, including advanced payments for temple amenities, online booking of customized rituals and so on. Other online services provide alternative ways to do things usually done at the temple, such as donating to the temple, booking a worship to be performed on the devotee's behalf, purchasing religious artifacts and even watching a livestream of the idol. These websites attempt to answer the religious needs of devotees who are too busy to visit the temple, those who are remote due to domestic or international migration as well as the elderly and the physically disabled individuals. In one way or another, online services function as alternative and additional ways to visit the temple. The websites of Hindu temples enable religious practice to cross oceans while deities and devotees stay in their locale, revealing undercurrents of *bhakti* (Hindu devotional movements) literature which will surface throughout this chapter.

This digital presence indicates that temples participate in Hindu adoption of digital media, that is digital Hinduism. Since implementation requires resources, temples that are larger, wealthier and more popular tend to adopt digital media before others. In what follows, I refer to such temples as mega-temples. The wealth and popularity of mega-temples lead not only to grandiose physical structures, but also to a parallel digital presence, strong connections with the state and the private sector, overall organization and operations like that of a large corporation and a vast influence on the larger landscapes of Hindu devotion. Through an examination of two different case studies — a mega-temple and a local, smaller one — this chapter depicts the different digital journeys temples navigate and the manner in which external forces shape these paths. I argue that mega-temples play a major role in the utilization of digital media to devotional needs. These temples set an example for other Hindu temples and communities.

First, I explore the role of mega-temples in the emerging landscape of digital Hinduism through a case study of the Shree Siddhivinayak temple in Mumbai. This wealthy and very popular temple is a pioneer in all aspects of Indian Internet. The temple's official website offers various digital products and services, including online donations, online booking of rituals and online streaming of the idol called *Live Darshan* (Shree Siddhivinayak Ganapati Temple Trust 2014–2018b). Then, I look at the case of the Sri Naga Sai temple in Coimbatore, Tamil Nadu, which presents the very different challenges local temples face in the attempt to establish their websites and online services. Sri Naga Sai is a smaller and less wealthy temple. Although it maintains a wide-ranging online presence, the temple faces different struggles and a bumpier road toward technological progression.

Taken together, these case studies provide a fuller picture of Hindu temples' online services. They also shed light on an influential player in the field: both temples have a different relationship to a large Indian communications company, and the different nature of these relations dramatically affects their digital presence and reach. This corporate–religious interaction is only one example of the myriad ways in which powerful yet external entities refashion religion. This chapter suggests that, by influencing the digital lives of temples, the communications company plays a major role in shaping digital Hinduism specifically, and future landscapes of Hindu devotion more broadly.

This is not novel. What becomes the known landscape of any religious tradition is almost always determined by financial, corporate, political and other power-rooted factors. An example of this interplay can be found in what is scholarly known as the orientalist creation of Hinduism as a world religion. Max Müller and the Oxford University Press' publication of *The Sacred Books of the East* established the known landscape of Hindu texts (Masuzawa 2005). The East India Company and the Brahmanic elite had their own interests in commissioning specific texts for translations, establishing Hinduism as unified, mystical and philosophical (King 1999, 101–108). To this day, these texts are widely recognized as the building blocks of Hinduism, but they are not necessarily the most popular. This example strengthens my argument that the digital visibility of temples has the potential to shape what will be known as Hinduism to its outsiders in a few years or decades, as external interests tend to determine which Hindu locales will get exposure on the dominant media of the time.

Through observing digital initiatives in general, and the *Live Darshan* specifically, this chapter unveils the route religious institutions take in the implementation of a new medium. Through conversations with temple IT consultants, trustees and administrators, as well as through vast online research, I investigate the motives of temples in adopting this new technology, the various players involved and the role the private sector plays in these efforts. In what ways do temples' online services exhibit traces of *bhakti* literature? How do the digital initiatives of mega-temples affect other temples' digitization? How do these attempts influence the role of external players in this process? And among the many forces involved, who is acting as the agent of the divine in reaching its publics?

To answer these questions, I first introduce my theoretical framework. Contextualizing temples' utilization of digital media within contemporary media culture, I use Henry Jenkins' (2006) convergence culture theory. Through Walter Benjamin's (1968) discussion of sound cinema, I explore the powerful role of infrastructure and distribution in Hinduism's digital transition. Next, I provide a brief review of *bhakti* literature, arguing that temples' digitization reveals traces of *bhakti*'s configurations of networks and publics, its emphasis on democratization and its inherent tension between the universal and the particular.

As the *Live Darshan* feature is central to this discussion, I briefly review the traditional practice of *darśan* and the ways it is understood by existing scholarship, and suggest my own working definition. Next, I present the case of the Shree Siddhivinayak temple and its extensive digital presence. I then focus on the *Live Darshan*'s meaning and history, introducing the communications company's involvement and impact on the digitization of Hindu temples. Afterward, I briefly present the case of Sri Naga Sai temple and its different location in this intricate web. In conclusion, I discuss the many forces involved in Hindu temples' adoption of digital media, revealing how they serve as agents of the divine in reaching out to their devotional publics.

Theoretical framework

Convergence culture

Hindu temples operate similarly to media companies in the ways they situate themselves as part of contemporary media culture. Especially helpful to this discussion is Henry Jenkins' description of media culture as convergence culture. Although Jenkins (2006) mainly deals with American popular culture and does not aim his theory at the religious sphere or non-American locales, I claim that his approach contextualizes Hindu temples' embrace of digital media.

Jenkins (2006, 2) describes convergence as "the flow of content across multiple media platforms, the cooperation between multiple media industries, and the migratory behavior of media audiences who will go almost anywhere in search of the kinds of entertainment experiences they want". Convergence is a cultural shift taking place both in the production and consumption of media, forcing media institutions to reinvent themselves for an era of media convergence. In this sense, the mediated lives of temples and their idols described later, answer the need of devotees to get devotional content delivered in various forms. Jenkins (2006, 19) demonstrates that one of the strategies to embrace convergence is "to expand the potential markets by moving content across different delivery systems". While I do not claim that devotees are markets in the same way, it is easy to identify this logic in temple utilization of different delivery technologies. Temples share images and videos of the deity on their websites and smartphone apps, through WhatsApp groups and via live-streaming, thus expanding their reach.

A central element of convergence culture is its participatory nature. This idea contrasts the notion of passive media consumption. Producers and consumers do not occupy separate roles anymore; they do not share equal responsibility, but the user's role in the production of culture is constantly growing. Jenkins wrote this in the nascent years of social media. More than ten years later, the participatory element is stronger and more evident than ever. Today, in order to be a media producer, one only needs a digital device of some sort and an Internet connection; people record their own videos and upload them to YouTube, share the news of current events from their smartphone cameras and social media accounts and so on.

The participatory element of today's media culture is particularly important to the digital paths of small Hindu temples. Now, digital technologies are affordable and accessible. This is also true of India, especially to its new middle classes. For this population, computers and digital devices are ordinary belongings and IT professions are widespread. This participatory potential explains how local and not-so-wealthy temples can also have an online presence and services. Creating a website and installing a camera is not necessarily out of reach to many local institutions. Technical support and maintenance might be more cumbersome but are still possible if temples have knowledgeable people on board. However, technological skills are not necessarily sufficient to build the infrastructure and distribute the content. These capacities are still restricted to the big communications companies like those discussed here.

The power of infrastructure

Ownership over digital infrastructure that allows religious innovation and distribution has the potential to shape not only digital Hinduism, but Hindu devotional landscapes at large. In a footnote to his famous essay, "The Work of Art in the Age of Mechanical Reproduction", Walter Benjamin (1968, 244) briefly discusses the relationship between the introduction of sound to film and the electrical companies that were involved in the process:

> In 1927 it was calculated that a major film, in order to pay its way, had to reach an audience of nine million... The introduction of the sound film brought about a temporary relief, not only because it again

brought the masses into the theaters but also because it merged new capital from the electrical industry with that of the film industry.

The capital and technology of the electrical companies allowed films to achieve the reach they needed in order to be profitable. The electrical companies thus had an important function in the massification of films, increasing its audiences. Laura Mulvey (2003, 21–22) states the capital of the electrical companies made it possible for films to keep up with other entertainment industries: "[T]he transition was achieved by the research, manufacturing and marketing of the huge corporations represented by AT&T and General Electric". Mulvey explains that the electrical companies' institutional power was essential to both developing the recording technology and financing the conversion of cinema halls.

In discussing the effects of digitization, Richard Paterson (2012, 183) explains how the infrastructure of telecommunications companies has the potential to shape other spheres: "Rather than simply acting as utilities, and with the control of distribution, they could gain the power to define content.... Culture is about content and its production and dissemination, whether it is music, film or any other form". Paterson argues that control over distribution may lead to a redefinition of the content itself. The content Paterson is discussing is cultural, that is, produced by media and art creators. The question is how this logic translates to the religious sphere, which is also cultural but in a different way. What does it mean for Hindu institutions to give external forces control of infrastructure and distribution? If this interaction follows the same logic, how does it create the potential for companies to control the Hindu content that they distribute?

Bhakti's digital publics

In its common understanding, *bhakti* stands for a devotional movement originated in Tamil regional communities that flourished between the fifth and the ninth centuries and is "characterized by the singing of devotional songs composed in vernacular languages by poets who have attained the status of saints" (Hawley 2015, 6). These communities prioritized emotional and direct devotion to a personal god who is open to all castes and sexes, challenging the hegemony of Brahmanical, Vedic religion. By singing poems in languages lay people can actually understand, *bhakti* poets democratized Hindu religiosity. However, A. K. Ramanujan (1973, 36) argues that they also developed a new kind of religious establishment: "They become, in retrospect, founders of a new caste and are defied in turn by new egalitarian movements". Does the digitization of Hindu temples follow a similar dynamic in democratizing devotion by making them more accessible for those who cannot reach them physically, while also restricting this access to a limited tech-savvy caste?

Albeit *bhakti* began with regional communities, its ideas and practices now permeate almost all aspects of Hindu traditions. There is a strong connection between *bhakti* and temple worship. This is evident in *bhakti* poet's emphasis on particular shrines and idols and in their insistence on the divine presence as literally embodied in these idols and places, reflecting an understanding inherent to temple worship (Cutler 1987, 112–113). Nonetheless, *bhakti* poets also highlighted universal and omnipresent qualities of the divine (Novetzke 2007, 268). *Bhakti* devotion is the expression of a mutual relationship of love and grace between the deity and his or her devotee. This relationship is bound to be very intimate as it "connotes sharing in, partaking of, and participating in the deity as Other" (Holdrege 2015, 21). One way of achieving this union with the deity is by disinterested service (*seva*). Interestingly, several scholars have pointed on a triangle of communication embedded in *bhakti* poems, linking the poet both with the deity and an audience (Cutler 1987, 19). Following that, Christian Novetzke (2007, 256) argues that *bhakti* needs audience as it seeks to form publics of reception and participation, through the agency of both the poet and the deity. This model of communication becomes interesting when considering temples' websites and especially the *Live Darshan* feature. Who are these devotional publics in this case and who carries the responsibility of reaching out to them?

What is *darśan*?

This chapter takes the *Live Darshan* feature of temple websites as its main case study, exhibiting both the aforementioned power of infrastructure and distribution mechanisms, as well as undercurrents of *bhakti*. To enable this examination, it is important to first understand what *darśan* is. *Darśan* is commonly understood by scholarship as a central element of Hindu worship, in which the devotee stands in front of the divine in order to see it and be seen by it. In fact, the believer's gaze creates and affirms the god's image as god itself. The god in return bestows blessings and powers on the devotee. In her elaborated work on *darśan*, Diana Eck (1998) established the canon for understanding this element as an auspicious exchange of sights. Almost every scholar who has dealt with *darśan* since has relied on her definition. However, by exploring the various ways people refer to and experience *darśan*, it becomes evident that there is much more to the practice. John E. Cort (2012, 2) points to scholarship's need to "revisit this central category and to begin to see it as a highly variable rather than singular super-category". *Darśan* is a widespread practice in many South Asian traditions, and as such, it has different applications and understandings; there is no one traditional and fixed *darśan*. We need a wider definition, which can encompass the complexities of the practice in its various settings.[1]

Can we say it is a visual intermingling when blind people take *darśan*, when one imagines *darśan* or when devotees practice it without entering the temple? Thinking about the Hindu temple, how can we isolate the visual element of the practice as its basic component when it is always accompanied by multisensorial input? *Darśan* at a temple is never only seeing. It is smelling, singing, hearing, giving offerings or a combination of these elements depending on the specific community, temple and event. No one can stand at the temple and only see; it is not an isolated activity. Sight is not what the temple experience is all about; rather, as was described to me, "it is the vibration; it is the ambience that actually charges you and empowers you".[2] I do not wish to eliminate the visual element from the understanding of *darśan,* as it is certainly a significant part of it, but I also do not think it can be considered the first and foremost aspect of *darśan.*

Various thinkers refer to the multidimensional nature of *darśan,* understanding vision itself as mutual and tactile (Pinney 2002) or claiming the gaze is a means of making contact with the deity (Babb 1981; Gonda 1969). Although these scholars add a tactile and embodied dimension to the understanding of *darśan,* they uphold vision as the main element. Situating *darśan* in specific contexts of practice, other scholars have shown it is also an emotional and aesthetic experience (Bennet 1990, 187; Packert 2010, 13), an interior one (Cort 2012, 31) and a physical circulation of energy (Lucia 2014, 42–47). The common thread throughout the varied ways *darśan* is thought of and performed is its essence as a devotional encounter with the divine that results in an intimate and emotional experience. This encounter charges the devotees; it rewards them with divine blessings. I suggest understanding *darśan* as an experience of *being in the presence of the divine.*[3] I argue this categorization encompasses the different manifestations of the practice, while maintaining a core that is common to them all. As an intimate encounter between the divine and the devotee, both should be present. The devotees' presence can be actualized in different ways but must include pure mind and heart toward their devotion. The divine and its presence emerge from this devotion, as well as from the multisensory ecology that creates it as sacred in the practice's specific setting.[4]

@SiddhivinayakOnline

Siddhivinayak is a form of Ganesh that is known to give *siddhi* — prosperity, success, skills and good luck — to his worshippers (Dwyer 2015, 263). The Shree Siddhivinayak temple began its life in 1801. In general, the temple's idol follows the popular iconography of Ganesh, except for its trunk, which is tilted to the right side and not to the left as usual. Through the years, the number of visitors grew, leading to such long queues that most visitors were unable to reach the deity (Valenta 2013, 101). Eventually, the temple was rebuilt in 1990, "restored into a magnificent, multistoried and palace like temple" (Shree Siddhivinayak Ganapati Temple Trust 2014–2018c). The temple has around 300 staff members and 500 volunteers. Its annual income, almost entirely from donations, is about 11 million dollars,[5] which makes the temple one of the ten wealthiest temples in India (Surendran 2016). Half of the temple's funds go to charitable activities such as an on-campus dialysis center, financial aid and textbook bank. The temple is one of Mumbai's most popular temples, with 100,000 visitors daily and twice as many on Tuesdays, which is the most auspicious day to visit the temple (Valenta 2013, 100). The temple is known to attract politicians, Bollywood actors and cricket players, who come to get blessings from Siddhivinayak.

The temple's utilization of media did not start with the digital era. A kind of a remote *darśan* is built into the temple's architecture; the temple's golden roof serves as a representation of the deity, enabling devotees to take *darśan* of the dome from the main road. Film and television also take part in the mobilization of the temple and its deity. In 2009, the temple trust produced a devotional film, and some of the morning rituals are broadcasted live on religious television channels (Valenta 2013, 106). These examples show the resourcefulness of the Siddhivinayak temple in finding creative ways to circulate the deity, as well as their acculturation to the current convergence culture. One of the most prominent sites of this creativity is the Internet. The temple's website offers multiple services, including information about the temple and its deity, announcements, a photo gallery and an online donations portal. The website (Shree Siddhivinayak Ganapati Temple Trust) facilitates the practice of *darśan* both at the temple — by a paid service that allows devotees to book *darśan* for an appointed time — and remotely through the *Live Darshan* feature. Furthermore, devotees can book a ritual to be performed at the temple in their presence or in their absence. The temple is very active on Facebook (Shree Siddhivinayak Ganapati Temple Trust 2013), Instagram (Shree Siddhivinayak Ganapati) and WhatsApp (Nadkarni 2015). Its Instagram handle shows images of the idol and temple events, as well as videos of devotees at the temple. The temple has dedicated staff who upload photos and live footage to their social media profiles.[6] These platforms help people to be in touch both with the temple and with each other, building a global and networked public of devotees.

In February 1998, the outset of Indian Internet, Shree Siddhivinayak temple launched its website and became one of the first Indian religious institutions to go online. Ashok Nadkarni, an independent IT consultant, created the temple's website and has been maintaining and updating it since. He also offers temple management solutions to other temples, assisting in establishing e-services and developing their online presence. Nadkarni is an ardent devotee of Shree Siddhivinayak and considers the work he does for the temple his service to the lord. He embodies the idea of *seva* by facilitating the deity's quest to reach his devotees, and vice versa. His involvement has a significant impact on the temple's digital initiatives.

In its first month, the website recorded over 650,000 hits.[7] In a newspaper article, the chair of the temple's trust at the time, Vasudha Wagh, explains that the decision to create a website came from the feeling that "all believers of Lord Siddhivinayak, who are not able to visit the temple, need to be given a better opportunity to feel close to the god" (Bhagnari 1998, 68). But not everyone at the temple board shared this sentiment. Nadkarni says when the chair first brought the idea, there was a conflict among the board of trustees. The trustees on the opposing side thought the website might harm the temple, causing people to stop coming physically. But the chair was a woman with a vision. Along with few other trustees, she was resolute that the Internet is here to stay and the temple must adopt it to reach as many devotees as possible. This motivation, that all believers should have direct access to the divine, resonates with *bhakti*'s mission of democratizing Hindu devotion. Post factum, everybody celebrated the decision; the website serves as a publicity avenue for the temple as it increases visitors, popularity and contributes to the temple's reputation as innovative. Now, the website gets around 80,000–200,000 visitors a day. On Tuesdays, the auspicious day, the number goes up to 300,000 hits. During festivals, this number can reach half a million. Nadkarni even says the temple's footfalls have increased since they launched the website, especially with the younger generation. Previously, mainly the elderly visited the temple. But now, more than 50% of the visitors are 20–35 years old.[8]

According to Nadkarni, the divine is the driving force of the entire project; the temple executed it, but it was god's wish.[9] The fact that the deity is portrayed as supportive — and even more than that, as the driving force of the adoption of digital media as a way to achieve the deity's goal to be close to devotees — is illuminating. It indicates that, in the mind of devotees, the deity validates and encourages the performance of such practices. Moreover, by depicting these digital initiatives as the wish of the divine, the temple can be seen to be issuing a divine stamp of approval on the medium, leading other players to offer digital Hindu services. Additionally, Nadkarni attributes the temple's technological novelty to the nature of its lord: "Hindus believe that everything starts with Ganesha. Anything new people want to do, they first worship Lord Ganesha, Lord Shree Siddhivinayak".[10] The temple was the first to employ several technologies, thanks to its deity's characteristics. Temple officials also justify their use of technology by referencing the Hindu epics. One of the temple's trustees, Nitin Vishnu Kadam, explained to me that technology already existed in the epic period; it is merely being rediscovered now. For example, Sita's protective circle, in which Rama secured her in the famous scene from the Ramayana, was what we now call a sensor. Sanjay's narration of the Mahabharata battle to the king was possible, thanks to a sort of a closed-circuit television camera. If not the technology per se, at least the concept was there "that a person could sit in his house and watch what is happening around the world".[11] The temple's digital initiatives are not seen as bringing something new but as drawing from the past. From this point of view, the rationale behind the *Live Darshan*, for example, is based on the Hindu tradition, and does not at all present a deviation from it. Following the trust's wish, Nadkarni always explores new technologies to implement at the temple.[12]

Live Darshan: The entanglement of religion, media and commerce

The *Live Darshan* feature (Shree Siddhivinayak Ganapati Temple Trust 2014–2018b) is especially revealing in regard to the temple's influence on the larger realm of digital Hinduism. Before I delve into its history and impact, I situate it in my proposed understanding of the practice, exploring its possibility of producing an intimate devotional experience of the divine, albeit the meaning of *being present* undoubtedly shifts.

Devotees and temple officials state that *Live Darshan* from the temple is not supposed to replace the one performed at the temple:

> Whenever they go to the website the live *darshan* is there but there is a desire to also take the real *darshan*...Live *Darshan* is real also but the satisfaction that we get from actually visiting the center sanctum of the temple is different. [The same as] listening to any audio on CD and seeing the live orchestra is different.[13]

Like the difference between listening to a CD and a live concert, the listener is present and experiences the music, but not in the same way. Summit Singh describes it as different from being in the temple the same way a Skype call is different from sitting with a friend in the same room, but, for him, it provides the closest *darśan* experience that one can get without physically being there: "*Live Darshan* allows us to feel that we are in the temple. ... or we are really there, in that place".[14] Summit, who is actively involved in distributing temple broadcasts on the Internet,[15] sees *Live Darshan* as creating new ways to visit the temple. A sense of presence remains in these understandings. It is a different kind of presence, but the potential to establish an emotional connection and an intimate encounter with the deity persists.

Scholarship strengthens the assertion that *Live Darshan* does not replace the temple experience. Jenkins argues that new media forms do not annihilate older ones; rather, "[e]ach old medium [is] forced to coexist with the emerging media" (2006, 14). *Live Darshan* is not supposed to replace the temple; they coexist, interacting and supporting each other in complex ways. Srinivas Aravamudan (2006, 227) argues that "media should never be understood as functioning only at the level of mimetic reproduction". We should not address mediated versions of traditional practices as attempting to imitate the practice as is, but as reconfiguring it. Albeit a modification, I contend that *Live Darshan* enables a sense of intimate encounter with the deity at times when a temple visit is out of reach.

Indeed, people are emotionally attached to the *Live Darshan* feature. Sanjay Bhagwat, the executive officer of Shree Siddhivinayak at the time they launched this feature, says they received many emails from people saying "they have put it as permanent icon on their desktop. Whenever they have time they click the icon".[16] I was also told a story about a man who experienced technical problems with *Live Darshan* and was furious:

> My mom is like 70–80 years old, and every morning at 4:30 she wants to see *darshan*, for the early morning *arati*.... she is so crazy that she climbs up and she changes the angles of the antenna — 'why it's not coming, why it's not coming.'[17]

Temple officials say this kind of response happens a lot when people face technical issues with the streaming.

Marketing deities

The Siddhivinayak *Live Darshan* was launched in 2004. The idea came from an unexpected source — cameras for traffic surveillance that were positioned outside the temple. Bhagwat explains that the traffic camera infrastructure made him realize the possibility of providing *darśan* 24/7 to people around the world.[18] To execute his idea, he joined forces with a big Indian communications company (as I was asked to call it by their project manager). Since then, this company has played a significant role in the temple's digital initiatives, and Hindu digital landscapes at large. The communications company did the complete installation necessary for the *Live Darshan*. They also made the service available to their subscribers, and — in order to avoid being seen as making a profit — they agreed to pay royalties to the temple.[19] Now, they power and monitor the temple's website and the *Live Darshan* mobile app. After the successful collaboration with Siddhivinayak, they offered the same service to Shirdi Sai Baba Temple. Nadkarni worked closely with the communications company and the Shirdi temple to execute it.[20] Having the biggest temples in Maharashtra on board, the company continued to partner with temples, supplying the infrastructure and technical support to 18 temples across India to date. Their project manager explains their interest in this project as a way to give back to society,[21] but it also serves their own objectives.

The communications company has the exclusive DTH (direct-to-home TV) rights for the temples' live feed in India, enabling their sister company — a direct broadcast satellite television provider — to offer 18 different *darśan* channels to their subscribers for free. As the main sponsor of this project, the DTH company decides which temples to support. The project manager approaches temples in which the company is interested. In fact, *Live Darshan* serves as a marketing tool for the DTH company; according to company records, over 41% of their 7.5 million subscribers watch these channels, which "build a high emotional cost to switch and [are a] key differentiator in the already crowded DTH market".[22] As Paterson (2012, 176) explains it: "The telecommunications companies ... derive their revenues through carrying services provided by other companies ... The key to future profitability for the telecommunications companies will then become ownership or participation in value-added services". Temple broadcasts serve as a value-added service, building an emotional connection to the company. Therefore, the company wants to have the most popular temples available on their channels. Moreover, if they want to add subscribers from a specific region, they try to provide them with local content, that is, live feeds of local temples. For example, the company's project manager tirelessly attempts to get South Indian temples to join the project. These temples are reluctant due to religious reasons; the belief in South India is that nothing should touch the idol, including the camera's focus: "For the last 1–2 years, we had been visiting South temples to get something in South ... if we'll [be] able to get that, we'll also be able to get consumers from those regions".[23]

Nadkarni states that, currently, the *Live Darshan* page receives 10,000–12,000 unique views daily. This number actually presents a decrease in viewership on the temple website itself, as the temple's live feed is offered through many other platforms.[24] In 2014, the temple launched a mobile app for *Live Darshan* in collaboration with the communications company. In addition, the communications company not only provides this service on their website and through their DTH sister company, but also joins forces with various mobile content providers, such as Videocon's Connect Broadband, Viacom's Colors and HP's Dream Screen.[25] The fact that the Siddhivinayak live stream is available to users of various mobile platforms significantly boosts the temple's reach.

In conclusion, the communications company and its sister company offer these services for free to both expand their viewership and prevent existing subscribers from switching to a different provider. The emotional connection generated by the practice of *darśan* serves the companies' interests. By providing this possibility, they situate themselves as an agent of the divine, bringing devotees their favorite deities to their living room. In this way, they also preserve and expand the deity's devotional public. Mulvey (2003) and Benjamin (1968) elucidate the meaning and impact of the Indian communications companies' involvement in the digitization of temples. I suggest that this company has a similar role in the Hindu devotional landscapes, transitioning and adapting temples to the digital culture in which they now operate. Like the electrical companies in the case of the sound film, the communications company both provides the necessary technology and is able to wire the temples for this digital transition. The company significantly extends the reach of temples beyond their local, or even national, community. This kind of expansion is not available to temples that are not supported by the company. The technological wiring and the distribution mechanisms open up temples to the contemporary global and digital world in which they feel obliged to participate. In an effort to bring the deities closer to their devotees, Hindu temples hand over ownership of the one thing that will determine their positioning in a future and global world: infrastructure. The communication company's control of supporting infrastructure explains the influential role it plays in the digitization of Hindu practices.

Sri Naga Sai's pursuit of the digital

The *Live Darshan* feature demonstrates that the growth of temples' digital presence is partly dependent on corporate marketing needs. When one corporation monopolizes the resources and infrastructure, the small temples that the company does not want to pursue are left aside. The small Naga Sai temple in Coimbatore serves as a perfect example of this distorted interplay. Sri Naga Sai temple was established in 1939, and was the first Shirdi Sai Baba temple in Tamil Nadu. In 1943, the shrine got its unique name and meaning after a cobra had appeared during an evening worship and stayed immobile next to a Sai Baba picture for 48 hours. This event is considered as "the day baba gave *darśan* to his devotees in the form of a snake".[26] Indicating the size differences between the two temples, Sri Naga Sai temple gets 1,000–2,000 visitors daily and around 14,000 on Thursdays, when they hold the golden chariot procession.[27] Similar to the Shree Siddhivinayak temple, though on a smaller scale, the Naga Sai trust operates several philanthropic programs, including a middle school, medical financial assistance and a homoeopathic clinic. "Our shrine is not a big massive trust. We don't get that much funding, but we make sure that what we get from the people will reach back to the people".[28]

Sri Naga Sai trust has a well-designed website (Sri Naga Sai Trust, Coimbatore) with various online services, such us online donations, online booking of *darśan* at the temple and *Live Darshan*. The temple also has an Android app (Sri Naga Sai Trust, Coimbatore 2018), which provides the same information and services as the website. Vadivel Kumar is the person in charge of all Naga Sai Temple's IT and communications, from developing and designing the website to handling the temple's email communication, live broadcast and technology more broadly. Similarly to Nadkarni, he does it free of charge as his service (*seva*) to the lord, and many of the temple's technological initiatives can be attributed to his vision and execution. An IT professional working in Bangalore, Kumar is exactly the knowledgeable person the temple trust needs to execute its participatory potential.

Kumar launched the temple's website in 2010. For the first few months after its launch, the website had very few visitors. Slowly, more people came to know about the website. At some point, he added audio and video archives, which drew more people. Toward the end of 2011, the temple opened a Facebook page (Sri Naga Sai Trust, Coimbatore, 2012), spreading the word of their e-services. The Facebook page has proven to be a good publicity avenue, which draws more people to the website itself. Currently, the website gets around 6,000–7,000 visitors per month.[29] The temple started the *Live Darshan* service in 2012 to allow more people to get Baba's blessings. Kumar's own life experience had led him to seek ways to take *darśan* from his local temple. As he puts it: "I moved from Coimbatore to Bangalore and I thought how to have *darśan* of Baba. So that's how I thought we should fix a camera and broadcast, like Shirdi".[30] Note that Kumar could watch the Shirdi *Live Darshan*, but it is important to him to take his local Baba's *darśan*, his personal god. The temple's secretary, S. Balasubramanian, explains the rationale as the need to keep the tradition alive in a digitized world: "Nowadays, it is very much necessary. We have to go according to technology"[31]. He explains their ability to put cameras in the temple, even as part of a south Indian tradition, given that Sai Baba was a human being and thus different from other Hindu deities.

During our conversations, Kumar repeatedly mentioned the challenges they are facing, because they do not have sponsorship. They started *Live Darshan* with the only camera they could afford, and the quality of their broadcast was poor. Luckily, in 2013, they received new equipment from an American video company that allowed for better quality. However, in July 2016, this camera did not work for a few days, and the *Live Darshan* feature streamed only audio: "The camera was gone so it was fully miserable. People started to call the temple asking what happened".[32] Even before it went down, the temple was looking to raise money to buy a new camera that would allow for higher-quality streaming. In an effort to get support, Kumar has been chasing the aforementioned communications company for help, with no success. When I asked the company's project manager about Kumar's attempts, he said they already have Shirdi, which is the main Sai Baba shrine, "so it doesn't make sense to us to go and tie up to another [Sai Baba] shrine".[33] Or, in other words, they do not need the Naga Sai temple.

In August 2016, Kumar switched the *Live Darshan* servers to YouTube (Sri Naga Sai Temple, Coimbatore, 2017) to have greater exposure and let more people know of this service. In addition to being easier to maintain, he explains that the rationale for the switch was that, at YouTube, "everybody who search for Sai Baba will find us".[34] Although this move was indeed helpful — bringing more traffic to the *Live Darshan* — they are still not where they could have been with the distribution mechanism of the communications and DTH companies. The YouTube live stream mentions how many people are watching the broadcast simultaneously. Every time I plugged in to the stream in the last year, there were around three other people watching. Comparing this to the Siddhivinayak temple's numbers is illuminating. Of course, Siddhivinayak is also much more popular and well known on a national level, but the impacts of their collaboration with the private sector are undeniable.

Conclusion: Who is the agent of the divine in creating digital publics?

Exploring two very different Hindu temples' digital journeys, and the birth and growth of the *Live Darshan* feature, this chapter discussed the various players entangled in Hindu temples' online services: the temples' administration, the individuals that drive their IT operations and corporations that use the mediated practices to their own ends. Through an examination of the practice of *darśan*, I argued that understanding *darśan* as being in the presence of the divine – resulting in an intimate and emotional experience – does more justice to its various manifestations and affirms *Live Darshan* as a part of the canon. This digitally mediated *darśan* does not aim to generate the same devotional affect. Nonetheless, it serves as a devotional encounter with the divine and, therefore, is included under the umbrella of digital Hinduism.

I also contextualized the temples' digital creativity and efforts in contemporary convergence culture, showing how Hindu temples imitate the work of media companies, providing devotees with content in various mediated forms. Following the scholarship of Jenkins, Benjamin, Mulvey and Paterson, this chapter demonstrated the impacts of the communications companies on the temples' digital transition, providing the capital, technology, infrastructure and distribution mechanism. The companies' involvement undoubtedly adds to the massification of these temples, in the sense of getting their name and content to the masses through various media platforms on which they distribute the live stream. In what ways the communication companies' control over the infrastructure will allow them to shape its content, if at all, is still unknown.

An interesting element in this process is the diverse ways divine agency is being utilized and reappropriated. First, we saw how both temples explain and justify their use of technology in general, and *Live Darshan* in specific, with the deities' desire to be made available to their devotees. I argue that, as a mega-temple and the first temple to employ this technology, the Shree Siddhivinayak temple provided a stamp of approval for such use. This temple is also the one which added the external communications companies as significant players, deciding who will be part of the digital transition they are leading. The result of this religious–corporate interaction is that the digital services and exposure of temples are not necessarily determined by religious reasons (although sometimes they are, as in the case of South Indian temples), or lack of motivation or even the temple resources, but rather by marketing considerations of external yet very influential forces. The implications of this interaction are not only restricted to the realm of the digital; temples' online presence affects which temples will be perceived as sophisticated and relevant to modern lifestyle, will become more famous with time and will get more footfalls as a result.

This role of the company, and of technology more broadly, raises the question how does the *bhakti* devotional triangle of communication manifests in this contemporary expression. This chapter argued that in the absence of the traditional poet, the role of reaching out and forming devotional publics is now split up between the temples' administration and IT visionaries, the technology itself as a new kind of vernacular, and the external companies. All of these players take part in the attempt to allow devotees to participate in the devotion and presence of their particular deities, thus serving as the divine's agents in creating and expanding its publics. Echoing Ramanujan's depiction of *bhakti*, in this process Hindu devotional practices become both more accessible and more limited to a specific kind of public. In this way, temples' digitization continues the *bhakti* egalitarian tradition by making devotion available to devotees who could not have accessed it otherwise — due to disability, busy lifestyle, migration, among others — while also creating a new kind of class as these practices mandate Internet connection and the appropriate devices which are available only to upper-middle-class Hindus. However, this public will expand as Internet connection and mobile devices continue to spread around the subcontinent. Moreover, the involvement of the communications companies adds to this potential growth, as their DTH service is more affordable and accessible to a larger fragment of India's population.

Notes

1 For more notable attempts to re-theorize the concept of *darśan*, revisiting it through various indigenous theories, see Hawkins (1999), Rotman (2009), Packert (2010), McHugh (2011) and Lucia (2014).
2 Nadkarni, Ashok. Interviewed by author, 22 July 2016.
3 By this definition, I wish to rephrase Eck's (1998) book title, which refers to *darśan* as "seeing the divine".
4 For more on the construction of the sacred through the specific ecology of human and non-human actors, see Morgan (2014).
5 Shinde, Mangesh. Interviewed by author, 15 December 2016.
6 Nadkarni, Ashok. WhatsApp conversation with author, 6 April 2018.
7 Nadkarni, Ashok. Interviewed by author, 15 December 2016.
8 Nadkarni, Ashok. Interviewed by author, 15 December 2016.
9 Nadkarni, Ashok. Interviewed by author, 22 July 2016.
10 Nadkarni, Ashok. Interviewed by author, 22 July 2016.
11 Kadam, Nitin Vishnu. Interviewed by author, 14 December 2016.
12 Nadkarni, Ashok. Interviewed by author, 14 December 2016.
13 Shinde, Mangesh. Interviewed by author, 15 December 2016.
14 Singh, Summit. Interviewed by author, 1 December 2013.
15 Summit Singh Thakur is currently a computer science student at Drexel University. Originally from Jabalpur, Madhya Pradesh, he moved to Philadelphia, Pennsylvania. to pursue undergraduate studies. Summit developed the website livedarshan.net by himself in 2009, when he was only 13 years old. Livedarshan.net serves as a portal providing free live broadcasts from 12 different temples.
16 Bhagwat, Sanjay. Interviewed by author, 19 December 2016.

17 Communication Company Project Manager. Interviewed by author, 15 December 2016.
18 Bhagwat, Sanjay. Interviewed by author, 19 December 2016.
19 Communication Company Project Manager. Interviewed by author, 15 December 2016.
20 Nadkarni, Ashok. Interviewed by author, 15 December 2016.
21 Communication Company Project Manager. Interviewed by author, 15 December 2016.
22 Communication Company Project Manager. Email to author, 26 December 2016.
23 Communication Company Project Manager. Interviewed by author, 15 December 2016.
24 Nadkarni, Ashok. Interviewed by author, 15 December 2016.
25 Communication Company Project Manager. Email to author, 26 December 2016.
26 Balasubramanian, S. Interviewed by author, 29 December 2016.
27 Kumar, Vadivel. Interviewed by author, 8 August 2016.
28 Kumar, Vadivel. Interviewed by author, 8 August 2016.
29 Kumar, Vadivel. Interviewed by author, 8 August 2016.
30 Kumar, Vadivel. Interviewed by author, 8 August 2016.
31 Balasubramanian, S. Interviewed by author, 29 December 2016.
32 Kumar, Vadivel. Interviewed by author, 8 August 2016.
33 Communication Company Project Manager. Interviewed by author, 5 December 2016.
34 Kumar, Vadivel. Interviewed by author, 29 December 2016.

References

Aravamudan, S., 2006. *Guru English: South Asian Religion in a Cosmopolitan Language*. Princeton: Princeton University Press.

Babb, L. A., 1981. Glancing: Visual Interaction in Hinduism. *Journal of Anthropological Research* 37, 387–401.

Benjamin, W., 1968. The Work of Art in the Age of Mechanical Reproduction. In: Arendt, H., ed. *Illuminations*. Translated from German by H. Zohn. New York: Harcourt, Brace & World, 217–251.

Bennet, P., 1990. Nanda Baba's House: The Devotional Experience in Pushti Marg Temples. In: Lynch, O. M., ed. *Divine Passions: The Social Construction of Emotion in India*. Berkeley: University of California Press, 182–211.

Bhagnari, S., 1998. Listen to Lord Siddhivinayak's aarti, Shlokas on the Net. *Computerworld* 16–30 April, 68–71.

Cort, J. E., 2012. Situating Darśan: Seeing the Digambar Jina Icon in Eighteenth- and Nineteenth-century North India. *International Journal of Hindu Studies* 16(1), 1–56.

Cutler, N., 1987. *Songs of Experience: The Poetics of Tamil Devotion*. Bloomington: Indiana University Press.

Dwyer, R., 2015. Vighnaharta Shree Siddhivinayak Ganesh, Remover of Obstacles, Lord of Beginnings in Mumbai. *Comparative Study of South Asia, Africa and the Middle East* 35(2), 263–276.

Eck, D. L, 1998. *Darśan, Seeing the Divine Image in India*. New York: Columbia University Press.

Gonda, J., 1969. *Eye and Gaze in the Veda*. Amsterdam: North-Holland Publishing Company.
Hawkins, S., 1999. Bordering Realism: The Aesthetics of Sai Baba's Mediated Universe. In: Brosius, C. and Butcher, M., eds. *Image Journeys: Audio-visual Media and Cultural Change in India*. New Delhi: Sage Publications, 139–162.
Hawley, J. S., 2015. *A Storm of Songs*. Cambridge: Harvard University Press.
Holdrege, B. A., 2015. *Bhakti and Embodiment: Fashioning Divine Bodies and Devotional Bodies in Krsna Bhakti*. London: Routledge.
Jenkins, H., 2006. *Convergence Culture: Where Old and New Media Collide*. New York: New York University Press.
King, R., 1999. *Orientalism and Religion: Postcolonial Theory, India and 'The Mystic East*. London: Routledge.
Lucia, A. J., 2014. *Reflections of Amma: Devotees in a Global Embrace*. Berkeley: University of California Press.
Masuzawa, T., 2005. *The Invention of World Religions, or, How European Universalism was Preserved in the Language of Pluralism*. Chicago: University of Chicago Press.
McHugh, J., 2011. Seeing Scents: Methodological Reflections on the Intersensory Perception of Aromatics in South Asian Religions. *History of Religions* 51(2), 156–177.
Morgan, D., 2014. The Ecology of Images: Seeing and the Study of Religion. *Religion and Society: Advances in Research* 5, 83–105.
Mulvey, L., 2003. Cinema, Sync Sound and Europe 1929: Reflections on Coincidence. In: Sider, L., Sider, J. and Freeman, D., eds. *Soundscape: The School of Sound Lectures, 1998–2001*. London: Wallflower Press, 15–27.
Nadkarni, A., 2015. *Siddhivinayak Bhakt Parivar* (Siddhivinayak Devotees' Family), [WhatsApp group] 4 April 2015.
Novetzke, C. L., 2007. Bhakti and Its Public. *International Journal of Hindu Studies* 11(3), 255–227.
Packert, C., 2010. *The Art of Loving Krishna: Ornamentation and Devotion*. Bloomington: Indiana University Press.
Paterson, R., 2012. Policy Implications of Economic and Cultural Value Chains. In: *Exploring the Limits: Europe's Changing Communication Environment*. European Communication Council (ECC). Berlin: Springer, 169–186.
Pinney, C., 2002. The Indian Work of Art in the Age of Mechanical Reproduction. In: Ginsburg, F. D., Abu-Lughod, L. and Larkin, B., eds. *Media Worlds: Anthropology on New Terrain*. Berkeley: University of California Press, 355–369.
Ramanujan, A. K., 1973. *Speaking of Siva*. Translated from Kannada by A. K. Ramanujan. Harmondsworth: Penguin Books Inc.
Rotman, A., 2009. *Thus Have I Seen: Visualizing Faith in Early Indian Buddhism*. Oxford: Oxford University Press.
Shree Siddhivinayak Ganapati Temple Trust, 2014–2018a. *Home Page*. Available at www.siddhivinayak.org/index.asp, accessed 30 July 2018.
Shree Siddhivinayak Ganapati Temple Trust, n.d. *Official Website of Shree Siddhivinayak Ganapati Temple Trust, Prabhadevi, Mumbai, INDIA*. Available at www.siddhivinayak.org, accessed 25 July 2018.
Shree Siddhivinayak Ganapati Temple Trust, 2014–2018b. *On-Line Live Darshan*. Available at www.siddhivinayak.org/virtual_darshan.asp, accessed 31 July 2017.

Shree Siddhivinayak Ganapati Temple Trust, 2014–2018c. *Temple Architecture.* Available at www.siddhivinayak.org/temple_architecture.asp, accessed 17 October 2017.

Shree Siddhivinayak Ganapati Temple Trust, 2013. *Shree Siddhivinayak Ganapati Temple Trust*, [Facebook] 16 March 2013. Available at www.facebook.com/SiddhivinayakOnline, accessed 31 July 2018.

siddhivinayakonline, n.d. *Shree Siddhivinayak Ganapati*, [Instagram]. Available at www.instagram.com/siddhivinayakonline, accessed 31 July 2018.

Sri Naga Sai Temple, Coimbatore, 2017. *Live From Sri Naga Sai Temple, Coimbatore*, [YouTube] 14 August 2017. Available at www.youtube.com/watch?v=jq8VQIVA7Lg, accessed 31 July 2018.

Sri Naga Sai Trust, Coimbatore, 2018. *Home.* Available at www.srinagasai.com, accessed 31 July 2018.

Sri Naga Sai Trust, Coimbatore, 2018. *Sri Naga Sai Mandir,* [mobile app]. Available at http://play.google.com/store/apps/details?id=com.snstcb.srinagasai, accessed 31 July 2018.

Sri Naga Sai Trust, Coimbatore, 2012. *Sri Naga Sai Temple Coimbatore*, [Facebook] 21 April 2012. Available at www.facebook.com/srinagasai/, accessed 31 July 2018.

Surendran, V., 2016. If These Temples Give Away Their Wealth, India's Poverty Will be Solved. *India Today*, [online] 16 November. Available at http://indiatoday.intoday.in/story/siddhivinayak-hundi-rich-temple-india-demonetisation/1/812163.html, accessed 5 December 2017.

Valenta, M., 2013. Divining Siddhivinayak: The Temple and the City. In: Verkaaik, O., ed. *Religious Architecture: Anthropological Perspectives*, Amsterdam: Amsterdam University Press, 99–116.

Part 4

Critical reflection

13 Reflections on digital Hinduism

Sacred images, dominant Hindu narratives and the generational digital divide

Heinz Scheifinger

Introduction

There are a great many topics that can form the focus of a study which aims to explore the convergence of Hinduism and digital media. This is something amply demonstrated in the preceding chapters which range, for example, from analyses of the online Hindu marriage market (Titzmann) and the online marketplace for *pūjā* items (Sinha), to a consideration of the online presence of Hindu spiritual and classical dance gurus (Mannila and Zeiler) and a contemporary Hindu monastic institution (Jacobsen). Taking into consideration the fact that there are many different areas within the field of digital Hinduism, it is particularly conspicuous that more than half of the chapters that make up this current volume, at the very least mention online *darśan*, with some of these chapters also offering further comment and analysis to varying degrees. Indeed, this continues a recognized trend because, as Zeiler remarks in her Introduction to the volume, if we trace the history of the literature on Hinduism and the Internet, we can see that a fair amount of attention has been paid to this topic.

This interest is unsurprising because *darśan* – the act of devotion and worship that involves seeing and being seen by a deity or holy person (see, e.g., Eck 1985) – is a central feature of many of the strands that make up the multifaceted socioreligious tradition commonly referred to as Hinduism. Furthermore, the World Wide Web (WWW) is clearly visual in nature which, alone, already affords it some level of suitability as a medium for *darśan*. The WWW was, in effect, the catalyst for online *darśan* and still provides a popular venue for it today. More recently, newer forms of digital media such as apps commonly accessed via a smartphone (including social media apps such as Facebook, Instagram, Twitter and WhatsApp) also offer the opportunity to partake of online *darśan* (see, e.g., Kulkarni 2018, 47; Lazar this volume).[1] Moreover, in addition to the presence of the facility to practice online *darśan* via the WWW and the more recent forms of digital media, there is also clear evidence that Hindus are availing this opportunity (see, e.g. Gittinger this volume). This continued relevance and importance of online *darśan* is further magnified by the fact that although the younger informants in a recent study by Kulkani (2018, 48) did still utilize computers for online *darśan*, it was more common that their smartphones were used for this purpose.

While it is unsurprising, then, that a number of studies have focused upon online *darśan* or have taken it into account when focusing upon other aspects of digital Hinduism, one aspect regarding this scholarship *is* perhaps surprising. This is that, as yet, there is an absence of a coherent statement regarding the status and efficacy of online *darśan* which draws upon the findings from the various scattered journal articles and chapters in edited volumes which explore this issue (see, e.g., Herman 2010; Karapanagiotis 2013; Kulkarni 2018; Scheifinger 2009). Moreover, a consideration of the literature in this area might give the impression that there is a lack of consensus amongst scholars as to the status of online *darśan*. Indeed, the current volume alone could elicit such an impression. For example, in her chapter concerning ISKCON in which the views of devotees regarding online *darśan* are garnered, Karapanagiotis concludes that there is no qualitative difference between online *darśan* and *darśan* of a physical *mūrti*.[2] In contrast, in Lazar's chapter which features an investigation of the online presence of Mumbai's *Shree Siddhivinayak* temple, the conclusion drawn is that there *is* a qualitative difference.

However, despite this, I hold that by drawing upon and bringing together the various scattered findings within the digital Hinduism literature, a coherent and succinct general statement can be formulated regarding the status of online *darśan*. In addition to the fact that such a synthesis is long overdue, this volume, which constitutes both a coherent and authoritative volume on digital Hinduism, provides a fitting venue for this undertaking. Following the presentation of the general statement regarding online *darśan*, I will comment upon two aspects of digital Hinduism that also feature in the current volume – dominant Hindu narratives (Nayar, Sundaram) and the generational digital divide (Gittinger, Titzmann).

A typology of online images

Prior to this, it is helpful to offer a typology of the images of deities online for which *darśan* can be taken. This is because, while the differences between the various forms may seem fairly obvious, these differences are typically not made explicit in studies which make claims regarding the implications of online *darśan*. However, it is important to explicate their differences because the implications of online *darśan* vary, depending upon which type of image is used. A brief explanation of this will follow the presentation of the typology which, for reasons of clarity, is far from exhaustive and instead broadly differentiates between the main types of images of deities online for which *darśan* can be taken. The four main types are:

i still images of generic deities not associated with specific sites
ii still images of particular deities or *mūrtis* associated with specific sites

iii recorded (or live) images of particular *mūrtis*
iv live images (via webcam) of particular *mūrtis* residing in temples

Although it is the case that the presence online of still images of generic deities not associated with specific sites does constitute a new form of presentation, these images are not markedly different from representations that became available as a result of earlier forms of new technology such as that which enabled color printing on a mass scale. The same can be said regarding still images of particular deities that, as a result of this technology, are also available for purchase at their respective sacred sites and elsewhere. Therefore, the major significance of the first two categories of images in the typology is predominately associated with the vastly increased level of dissemination and subsequent far wider availability that their presence online gives rise to. Instead of bringing about new effects, then, the presence of these images online has the potential to exacerbate the various processes that printed images of deities gave rise to that scholars have already identified. For example, regarding the first type of image, both Inglis (1995, 67) and Beckerlegge (2001, 79, 90) note their role in the increased standardization of images of Hindu deities. Applicable to both generic and particular images of deities, Smith (1995, 37) identifies the rise of a "democratic devotionalism" which dispenses with the need for a *pujari* and features idiosyncratic, abbreviated rituals. As regards solely particular images of deities, Smith (1995) reveals that the increased dissemination that color printing technology allowed for was a significant factor in the spread of devotional cults.

As for the third type of image that I have categorized, there is no fundamental difference between such images and corresponding images that are transmitted on television during important festivals at major temples. As in the case of the previous two categories, the significance of this category lies in the fact that the images of the *mūrtis* have become far more widely available. This is especially the case because such images are sometimes produced with the sole intention of transmitting them online. In addition, when not watched live, footage which offers the opportunity for *darśan* may still be available on-demand. In the light of this wider availability but lack of any new effects, the implications of the presence online of recorded or live images of particular *mūrtis* are again predominantly limited to the exacerbation of the aforementioned already identified processes associated with pre-Internet forms of technology.

So, for example, in this volume, Karapanagiotis's chapter shows how images of Krishna are able to be disseminated far more widely through the medium of Facebook than was previously the case. This is especially so because the way that Facebook works means that some users will be exposed to images of Krishna even if they do not seek out these images. As Karapanagiotis (this volume) explains, in the view of many ISKCON devotees, even the accidental viewing of Krishna's image constitutes *darśan* and is henceforth beneficial to the viewer. Moreover, the posting and sharing of images through Facebook is explicitly recognized by ISKCON as an important proselytizing opportunity as it is believed that the viewing of images of Krishna by non-devotees has the potential to arouse interest in the god and in ISKCON's tradition. Although these findings are clearly valuable, the nature of the online images of Krishna has not changed vis-à-vis printed pictures or video footage, and henceforth in this case, online *darśan* does not bring about any unique implications. For example, accidentally seeing an image of Krishna through Facebook is not fundamentally different from seeing his image by chance in an offline context such as via the cover of a distributed book, flyer, poster or a sticker. This is an experience that many people would have had prior to the introduction of the Internet and continue to have today (coincidentally, I saw the latter on a car on the same day that I wrote this!). The absence of any fundamentally new implications is something emphasized by Karapanagiotis (this volume) who compares the accidental viewing of images of Krishna on Facebook to someone hearing by chance the chanting of Krishna's name while "sipping their afternoon tea at a roadside tea stall" – an experience which is similarly understood to bring about a beneficial spiritual experience.

In contrast to the first three types of images in the typology, it is the fourth type – live images (via webcam) of particular *mūrtis* residing in temples – that constitutes a new development in the long process of the mediatization (Livingstone and Lunt 2014) of Hinduism. Viewing such webcasts allows a devotee to gaze at the deity within the temple without actually being there – something that was previously not possible. This therefore has the potential to engender genuinely new transformations within Hinduism. These include the process of universalization (see Scheifinger 2010, 340) and, as Lazar (this volume) asserts, democratization – although, importantly, a large Indian telecommunications company that is involved in the provision of live online *darśan* also has a negative impact upon this as a result of its capitalistic commercial interests.

Conceptions of the *mūrti*

In addition to differentiating between the distinct forms of images online that *darśan* can be taken from, it is also important for studies to take into account that there are multiple conceptions as to the nature of *mūrtis*. This is the case even if we restrict our use of the term *mūrti* to how it is most commonly understood that has already been set out earlier – to refer to a physical form of a deity which is usually three-dimensional and has some kind of history of veneration.

Firstly, it is worth noting that, as scholars of religion, it is naturally prudent to distance ourselves from the idea that *mūrtis* can possess an ontological reality that can somehow be measured against when considering the status of online *darśan*. Moreover, even the faithful have different conceptions of the nature of *mūrtis*. That the perception of *mūrtis* held by devotees is subjective is something that is well known in the literature on Hinduism, and an investigation into the status of online *darśan* needs to appreciate the various subjective viewpoints and avoid making universal claims based upon a particular case study. The different viewpoints are helpfully set out by Beckerlegge (2001, 108) who reminds us that, within Hinduism, there are those who regard the *mūrti*:

i as the embodied deity
ii as the location of the deity's *shakti* or power
iii as merely representative of the deity but nevertheless valuable for worship and meditation
iv as a valuable religious aid for those who need it but personally unimportant
v as something that leads away from true religious insight

Relating this to online *darśan*, it is the case that for those Hindus who hold the belief that a *mūrti* possesses divine power, there is a qualitative difference between online *darśan* and *darśan* of a specific physical *mūrti* because the online representation does not contain this power. However, online *darśan* is still of value in the same way that *darśan* taken from, for example, a color poster of the *mūrti* has value, but is less preferable to *darśan* from the physical *mūrti*. As one of Lazar's (this volume) informants states, it is analogous to listening to a CD compared to attending a live concert (see also, e.g., Kulkarni 2018, 46; Scheifinger 2009).

One view given by informants (see, e.g., Karapanagiotis 2013; Scheifinger 2012, 314) is that, because "god is everywhere", there is thus no philosophical difference between online *darśan* and *darśan* from a physical *mūrti*. Although this may well be indicative of a genuine view held by many devotees belonging to certain traditions, it is worth noting some important points regarding this. Firstly, according to the scholar of Hinduism, Waghorne, the belief that *mūrtis* can actually be an embodiment of god is often seen as "an embarrassment" to educated Hindus (and, interestingly, even scholars) (Waghorne 2001, 286). As a result of this, it is common for educated Hindus not to express the view that god can be literally embodied in a *mūrti*. Instead, regardless of the tradition that they may belong to, and as Waghorne intimates, their possible personal unarticulated viewpoint, they tend to assert something along the lines of god being everywhere and hence there is a heavy emphasis on the notion of oneness. It is this that has resulted in Waghorne having to listen to what she refers to as the "all is one cliché" (Waghorne 2004, 5) on numerous occasions during interviews with educated Hindus. It is not my argument that the notion of oneness is not the genuine view held by some Hindu informants, but, as Waghorne's point warns us, scholars do need to be careful when they encounter such a view. In the context of online Hinduism, they need to be wary of making universal claims regarding the status of online *darśan* based solely upon the articulated views of informants that considerably downplay the idea that *mūrtis* can literally be embodied deities.

An additional important point to note regarding the caution that needs be exercised regarding the view of divinity which subsequently gives rise to the idea that there is no philosophical difference between the two forms of *darśan*, is that even those who do articulate this view still tend to privilege *darśan* of a physical *mūrti* over that of an online image (see, e.g., Karapanagiotis 2013, 74). Moreover, one of the reasons given for this preference is the additional belief commonly held by these informants that certain *mūrtis* do somehow possess special power and that "therefore, cyber-forms of these powerful deities are more likely than other cyber-forms to be considered [for *darśan*]" (Karapanagiotis 2013, 77). It is true that such online images are more likely to be preferred than generic images of deities that are not associated with particular famous temples. But I would further add that it is equally the case that it is the very belief in the power of certain *mūrtis* (regardless of the perceived source of this power) that explains why, for most Hindus, it is preferable to worship physical *mūrtis* rather than their online replications. The additional finding that while many middle-class Hindus espouse notions of oneness, on a practical level this plays little or no role in their lives and *darśan* remains a central practice for them (Jacobs 2010, 54–55), is further illuminating. This is because it suggests another reason as to why even those who say that there is no theoretical difference between different forms of god are highly likely to be less attracted to online *darśan* compared to *darśan* of a physical *mūrti*.

Online *darśan*: General statement

Taking all of the aforementioned into account, a succinct general statement regarding the status of online *darśan* can now be put forward which brings together the previous findings scattered throughout the literature. Because the level of generality of this statement does not seek to comment upon the implications of online *darśan*, the types of images set out in the typology do not need to be differentiated between. Additionally, the statement does not refer to the myriad philosophical views within Hinduism. To do so would detract from the essence of the statement and impinge upon its succinctness, and hence its heuristic value would be severely diminished. The fact, though, that I deliberately do not go into details regarding philosophical views within Hinduism is in no way reductively problematic. This is because complex differences in philosophical conceptions of divinity in Hinduism are able to be encapsulated within the broad parameters of the views of divinity that are referred to. The general statement regarding online *darśan* is as follows:

> *Mūrtis* do not possess an ontological reality. In addition, as a result of the diversity of Hinduism, devotees have various subjective conceptions

> of the nature of *mūrtis* and this affects their views as to the status and efficacy of online *darśan*. For devotees who believe that god is literally embodied in a *mūrti* or that the *mūrti* has intrinsic supernatural power in some other way, online *darśan* is qualitatively inferior to *darśan* of a *mūrti*. However, although not as desirable, it is still considered to be beneficial. On the other hand, for those devotees who hold philosophical views associated with one-ness, there is no real difference between online *darśan* and *darśan* of a *mūrti*. However, despite this, such devotees are still highly likely to favour *darśan* of a *mūrti* rather than partake of online *darśan*.[3]

In short, it is fair to say that the views of devotees concerning online *darśan* are largely idiosyncratic and that its practice is commonly regarded as being less desirable than *darśan* of physical *mūrtis*. Despite this, the practice is still popular, and this is largely due to the convenience that it affords or because it is availed out of necessity when it is difficult or impossible to visit deities for one reason or another (see, e.g., Gittinger this volume; De and Nandi this volume).

Final comments: The generational digital divide and dominant Hindu narratives online

In Kulkarni's (2018) study of online *darśan* in the BAPS *Swaminarayan* tradition, a distinct generational digital divide is observed: "younger devotees were more likely [than older devotees] to reference the use of their phones and sometimes computers to access the 'Daily Darshan' app or view YouTube videos in their daily praxis" (Kulkarni 2018, 48). When it comes to Hindus' engagement with online media for religious purposes, several other scholars have also pointed out a similar generational divide (see, e.g., Bachrach 2014, 166–170; Balaji 2018, 162; Gittinger this volume; Titzmann this volume). Bachrach (2014) reveals that it is common for young diasporic followers of the Hindu *Vallabh* tradition to go online to find about religious matters. This provides an interesting contrast to Gittinger's (this volume) study concerning "how Hindus living in the US are encountering Hinduism online" in which it is surprisingly revealed that a huge 93% of second-generation US Hindus preferred to ask family members questions about religion rather than seek out their answers online.

This difference to Bachrach's (2014) study is likely to be due to several reasons. Firstly, the young Hindus in Bachrach's study are already members of a distinct tradition and tend to ask specific questions regarding aspects of it. Furthermore, they are in the diaspora living away from their family members, and they often consider the religious lifestyles of elderly *Vallabh* devotees to be too strict – something which seems to dissuade them from approaching members of this demographic group for religious advice (Bachrach 2014, 168). These characteristics are not shared by Gittinger's informants – many of whom appear to have gone online in the past to seek answers to general questions about Hinduism as opposed to seeking answers to specific questions pertaining to a particular tradition. It is this quest to find out more about Hinduism that has led to them eschewing such a practice in favor of consultation with family members about religious matters. Some of the reasons given by these young Hindus as to why they were dissatisfied when they went online to find out more about their faith tallies with what some scholars have discerned about a key characteristic of online Hinduism.

Several scholars have pointed out that, intertwined with offline developments, there has been an emergence of dominant Hindu narratives online and that this is at odds with the multiplicity of Hinduism. Moreover, such narratives are often associated with the ideology of Hindutva[4] (see, e.g., Lal 2014, esp. 122; Mohan 2015; Scheifinger 2018). Such a view is disputed by Balaji (2018) who believes that the Internet can give voice to traditionally marginalized Hindu populations and that this henceforth promotes diversity within Hinduism. He also adds that at the same time, these distinct groups can utilize online media to define their particular identity as a part of a larger Hindu identity online. However, that the Internet promotes diversity within Hinduism is contested by Sundaram (this volume) who makes the point that, although "unlike in material sacred spaces such as temples, ... virtual spaces devoted to Hindu[ism] ... do not bar participation from any group", for a number of reasons it is difficult in practice for marginalized Hindu groups to be able to have a voice online. In other words, "individuals are granted access rather than true accessibility to market their ideas" and, related to this, Sundaram (this volume) finds evidence of "dominant Hindu narrative[s]" online associated with Hindutva. In summation, the identification of the development and prevalence online of dominant Hindu narratives has been flagged by various scholars as constituting a threat to the multiplicity and diversity of Hinduism.

However, as Gittinger's (this volume) chapter suggests, this threat is perhaps not as great as it might appear. This is because her study shows that, in some cases, it is exactly such representations of Hinduism online that young Hindus are actively rejecting, which consequently leads them to favor obtaining knowledge about Hinduism from family members. The highlighting of this finding which uncovers agency amongst the young in relation to an aspect of online Hinduism that many believe is a negative development that has the potential to influence, or is influencing already, the way that Hindus understand their faith (see, e.g., Kurien 2007, esp. 238) is surely an encouraging way to conclude this volume on digital Hinduism.

Notes

1 There are some apps that do not require an Internet connection once they have been installed. Nevertheless, because such apps initially require a user to be

online in order to install them on a device, the term *online darśan* can be comfortably retained to refer to the practice of receiving *darśan* via any type of app.

2 Throughout this chapter, although the term can also encompass a broader range of representations of the divine (see, e.g., Kulkarni 2018), the use of the term *mūrti* refers to a physical form of a deity which is usually three-dimensional and has some kind of history of veneration. This is congruent with common usage and facilitates clarity within the discussion. On occasion, in order to provide further clarity when contrasting *mūrtis* with online images, I prefix the term with "physical".

3 The last sentence of this general statement is drawn from Karapanagiotis (2013). A key assertion in that article which does not feature voices that affirm a belief in *mūrtis* as embodied gods, is that the predominant Hindu devotional perspective is that "God is everywhere and everything" (Karapanagiotis 2013, 63). In my general statement regarding online *darśan*, this belief in oneness articulated by some devotees is combined with other findings, and this overcomes the possibility of arriving at an incomplete general understanding of online *darśan*. In this current volume, Karapanagiotis does not report the belief in the idea of oneness and instead draws our attention to the ISKCON belief that Krishna dwells in physical *mūrtis*. However, she reiterates her (2013) finding that for most ISKCON devotees, there is no qualitative difference between online *darśan* and *darśan* from physical *mūrtis*.

4 See Sundaram (this volume) for an explanation of Hindutva.

References

Bachrach, E., 2014. Is Guruji Online? Internet Advice Forums and Transnational Encounters in a Vaishnav Sectarian Community. In: Sahoo, A. K. and de Kruijf, J. G., eds. *Indian Transnationalism Online – New Perspectives on Diaspora*. Farnham: Ashgate, 163–176.

Balaji, M., 2018. Digitalizing the Diasporic Subaltern: How Caribbean Hinduism Is Preserved through the Web. In: Balaji, M., ed. *Digital Hinduism – Dharma and Discourse in the Age of New Media*. Lanham: Lexington, 3–23.

Beckerlegge, G., 2001. Hindu Sacred Images for the Mass Market. In: Beckerlegge, G., ed. *From Sacred Text to Internet*. Milton Keynes: Open University Press, 57–116.

De, A. and Nandi, R., 2020. Whats(up) with Hinduism? Digital Culture and Religion among Bengali Hindus. In: Zeiler, X., ed. *Digital Hinduism*. London and New York: Routledge.

Eck, D. L., 1985. *Darśan – Seeing the Divine Image in India*. Chambersburg: Anima Books.

Gittinger, J. L., 2020. Cultural Regrouping in the Diaspora: Mediating Hindu Identity Online. In: Zeiler, X., ed. *Digital Hinduism*. London and New York: Routledge.

Herman, Phyllis K., 2010. Seeing the Divine through Windows. Online Darshan and Virtual Religious Experience. *Online – Heidelberg Journal of Religions on the Internet* 4(1), 151–178.

Inglis, S. R., 1995. Suitable for Framing: The Work of a Modern Master. In: Babb, L. A. and Wadley, S. S., eds. *Media and the Transformation of Religion in South Asia*. Philadelphia: University of Pennsylvania Press, 51–75.

Jacobs, S., 2010. *Hinduism Today*. London: Continuum.

Karapanagiotis, N., 2013. Cyber Forms, Worshipable Forms. Hindu Devotional Viewpoints on the Ontology of Cyber-Gods and -Goddesses. *International Journal of Hindu Studies* 17(1), 57–82.

Karapanagiotis, N., 2020. Automatic Rituals and Inadvertent Audiences: ISKCON, Krishna and the Ritual Mechanics of Facebook. In: Zeiler, X., ed. *Digital Hinduism*, London and New York: Routledge.

Kulkarni, D. D., 2018. Digital Mūrtis, Virtual Darśan and a Hindu Religioscope. *Nidān* 3(2), 40–54.

Kurien, P. A., 2007. *A Place at the Multicultural Table: The Development of an American Hinduism*. New Brunswick: Rutgers University Press.

Lal, V., 2014. Cyberspace, the Globalisation of Hinduism, and the Protocols of Citizenship in the Digital Age. In: Sahoo, A. K. and de Kruijf, J. G., eds. *Indian Transnationalism Online – New Perspectives on Diaspora*. Farnham: Ashgate, 121–143.

Lazar, Y., 2020. Streaming the Divine: Hindu Temples' Digital Journeys. In: Zeiler, X., ed. *Digital Hinduism*. London and New York: Routledge.

Livingstone, S. and Lunt, P., 2014. Mediatization: An Emerging Paradigm for Media and Communication Research? In: Lundby, K., ed. *Mediatization of Communication. Handbooks of Communication Science* (21). Berlin: De Gruyter Mouton, 703–724.

Mohan, S., 2015. Locating the "Internet Hindu": Political Speech and Performance in Indian Cyberspace. *Television and New Media* 16(4), 339–345.

Scheifinger, H., 2009. The Jagannath Temple and Online Darshan. *Journal of Contemporary Religion* 24(3), 277–290.

Scheifinger, H., 2010. *Om*-line Hinduism: World Wide Gods on the Web. *Australian Religion Studies Review* 23(3), 325–345.

Scheifinger, H., 2012. Hinduism and Hyper-Reality. In: Possamai, A., ed., *Handbook of Hyper-Real Religions*. Leiden: Brill, 299–318.

Scheifinger, H., 2018. The Significance of Non-Participatory Digital Religion: The Saiva Siddhanta Church and the Development of a Global Hinduism. In: Murali, B. ed., *Digital Hinduism – Dharma and Discourse in the Age of New Media*. Lanham: Lexington, 3–23.

Smith, H. D., 1995. Impact of "God Posters" on Hindus and Their Devotional Traditions. In: Babb, L. A. and Wadley, S. S., eds. *Media and the Transformation of Religion in South Asia*. Philadelphia: University of Pennsylvania Press, 24–50.

Sundaram, D., 2020. Instagram your Durga Puja! Social Media, Hashtags and State-Sponsored Cultural Marketing. In: Zeiler, X., ed. *Digital Hinduism*. London and New York: Routledge.

Titzmann, F.-M., 2020. Hindu Religious Identification in India's Online Matrimonial Market. In: Zeiler, X., ed. *Digital Hinduism*. London and New York: Routledge.

Waghorne, J. P., 2001. The Embodiment of Divinity in India. In: Beckerlegge, G., ed. *From Sacred Text to Internet*. Milton Keynes: Open University Press, 281–287.

Waghorne, J. P., 2004. *Diaspora of the Gods: Modern Hindu Temples in an Urban Middle-Class World*. New York: Oxford University Press.

Zeiler, X., 2020 Digital Hinduism: Studying Hinduism at the Intersection of Digital Media and Culture. In: Zeiler, X., ed. *Digital Hinduism*. London and New York: Routledge.

Index

Note: **Bold** page numbers refer to tables; *italic* page numbers refer to figures and page numbers followed by "n" denote endnotes.

Printed in the United States
by Baker & Taylor Publisher Services